Business Information Systems and Technology

Business information systems and business information technology are integral aspects of modern business, and managers in these areas are now expected to have knowledge of human and managerial issues, as well as technical ones.

This concise and readable book is a level-by-level primer that addresses the core subjects in business information systems and business information technology to enhance students' understanding of the key areas. Each chapter begins with a case study and features at the end: a summary of major points, a glossary of terms, suggested further reading and student activities. Some areas covered include:

- Different functional areas of business, including accounting, HRM and marketing
- Development and implementation of information systems
- Methods to support the analysis and design of policy and practice
- Strategic management to align information technology with organizational needs.

Covering the subject matter in a highly accessible manner, this is an ideal text for both undergraduate and masters students on business information systems, business information technology and business information management courses.

Brian Lehaney is Director of Postgraduate Research at the University of Wollongong in Dubai. He has many years of experience in managing and teaching in higher education, as well as in applied research. He focuses on operational and strategic organizational process improvement, especially in regard to knowledge management theory and practice. He is the author of numerous books and journal papers.

Phil Lovett is Senior Lecturer in Information Systems at Coventry University. He has extensive teaching experience with a specialization in database management. His research centres on information modelling, knowledge elicitation and knowledge-based engineering.

Mahmood Shah is Regional Director of the Institute of International Business (IIB) and a Senior Lecturer at the Lancashire Business School. His research interests include mobile government, identity theft prevention methods and technology alignment. He has published papers in several high-quality journals, including the *European Journal of Information Systems*.

Routledge series in information systems
Edited by Steve Clarke
Hull University Business School, UK

M. Adam Mahmood
University of Texas at El Paso, USA
and

Morten Thanning Vendelø
Copenhagen Business School, Denmark

The overall aim of the series is to provide a range of textbooks for advanced undergraduate and postgraduate study and to satisfy the advanced undergraduate and postgraduate markets, with a focus on key areas of those curricula.

The key to success lies in delivering the correct balance between organizational, managerial, technological, theoretical and practical aspects. In particular, the interaction between, and interdependence of, these often different perspectives is an important theme. All texts demonstrate a 'theory into practice' perspective, whereby the relevant theory is discussed only in so far as it contributes to the applied nature of the domain. The objective here is to offer a balanced approach to theory and practice.

Information Systems is a rapidly developing and changing domain, and any book series needs to reflect current developments. It is also a global domain, and a specific aim of this series, as reflected in the international composition of the editorial team, is to reflect its global nature. The purpose is to combine state-of-the-art topics with global perspectives.

Information Systems Strategic Management
An integrated approach, 2nd edition
Steve Clarke

Managing Information and Knowledge in Organizations
A literacy approach
Alistair Mutch

Knowledge Management Primer
Rajeev K. Bali, Nilmini Wickramasinghe and Brian Lehaney

Healthcare Knowledge Management Primer
Nilmini Wickramasinghe, Rajeev K. Bali, Brian Lehaney, Jonathan L. Schaffer and M. Chris Gibbons

Systems Practice in the Information Society
José-Rodrigo Córdoba-Pachón

Business Information Systems and Technology
A primer
Brian Lehaney, Phil Lovett and Mahmood Shah

Business Information Systems and Technology

A primer

Brian Lehaney, Phil Lovett and
Mahmood Shah

Routledge
Taylor & Francis Group

LONDON AND NEW YORK

First published 2011
by Routledge
2 Park Square, Milton Park, Abingdon, Oxon OX14 4RN

Simultaneously published in the USA and Canada
by Routledge
711 Third Avenue, New York, NY 10017

Routledge is an imprint of the Taylor & Francis Group, an informa business

British Library Cataloguing in Publication Data
A catalogue record for this book is available from the British Library

Library of Congress Cataloging in Publication Data
Lehaney, Brian, 1953–
  Business information systems and technology: a primer / Brian Lehaney, Phil
  Lovett and Mahmood Shah.
    p. cm. – (Routledge series in information systems)
  Includes bibliographical references and index.
  1. Management information systems. 2. Information technology–Management.
  I. Lovett, Phil. II. Shah, Mahmood, 1971– III. Title.
  HD30.213.L44 2011
  658.4'038011–dc22

                                                      2010043773

ISBN: 978-0-415-55918-8 (hbk)
ISBN: 978-0-415-55919-5 (pbk)
ISBN: 978-0-203-81846-6 (ebk)

Typeset in Garamond
by Wearset Ltd, Boldon, Tyne and Wear

Printed and bound in Great Britain by
TJ International Ltd, Padstow, Cornwall

To our families, friends and loved ones.

Contents

15 Digital society   222

16 E-commerce 3   239

17 Knowledge management   257

Case studies

Figures

Tables

Preface

> Practical men, who believe themselves to be quite exempt from any intellectual influences, are usually the slaves of some defunct economist.
>
> (John Maynard Keynes[1])

Why read this book?

Starting a degree in business information systems (BIS) or business information technology (BIT) or starting an MBA can be a daunting task. What should you study first? What is most important? How can you grasp the basics of subjects quickly? And so on. This book is not intended as a substitute for reading prescribed module material or for reading around subjects. It has not been written as a 'five week MBA' type of text. It does, however, cover the most common subjects in the domain that are covered in undergraduate and postgraduate study programmes. It covers the subject matter in a highly accessible style. Each chapter commences with a case study, followed by the main text. At the end of each chapter a summary of the major points, a glossary, references, further reading and suggested activities are provided. If you use this material wisely, participation, practice, preparation, reflection and sheer hard work are the key components of your success.

BIS and BIT are integral aspects of modern organizations, and managers in these areas are now expected to have knowledge of human and managerial issues, as well as technical ones. This concise and readable book is a level-by-level primer that addresses the core subjects in BIS and BIT to enhance students' understanding of the core material. Some of the areas covered include:

- models for the development and implementation of information systems;
- approaches in accounting, e-commerce and human resource management;
- methods to support the analysis and design of policy and practice; and
- strategic management to align information technology with organizational needs.

Reasons for this book

BIS are at the heart of every successful organization in today's world. There is still confusion about what BIS do and how they may be used to best effect. There have been many notable failures in information systems and some of these are discussed in the case studies. Most failures have tended not to be due to technology, but more to do with process. Without understanding related issues, good technology may be misunderstood and mishandled by managers and can lead to poor outcomes.

There is no other single book that covers the full range of undergraduate and postgraduate material in this area. Programmes of study tend to treat each subject as separate, with no taught integration. Students are supposed to take all these individual subject areas and somehow integrate them by doing an independent piece of work (the dissertation or project). Typically, they have no prior experience of anything like it, and there is a risk of poor performance in a module that may be worth as much as half of their final year's marks.

The penultimate chapter discusses how to do a dissertation or project, what your markers will expect and how to undertake relevant research that links academic concepts with applied contexts. The case studies in this text show how many different concepts, methodologies, principles, theories and techniques are needed when addressing real-world issues. Being a great technician is not enough. Being good at business is not enough. Most businesses today could not compete without appropriate technology, and might not survive without it. A business run by people who do not understand their information systems will be blown out of the water by a business run by people who do.

The motivation for this book was to produce a primer that introduces the multifarious nature of BIS and BIT for undergraduate and postgraduate students. There are numerous texts that deal with information systems or information technology, but they tend to be geared towards practitioners, either at a very low or very high level. They are normally very specific, so they might be suitable for a single information system or information technology module, but they do not cover the business side of the material. In addition, many texts are simply out of the price range of most students.

This book deals with the essence of BIS and BIT, and covers the material in a simple and easy to understand manner. The authors' extensive experience in both the academic and business worlds has resulted in the presentation of concepts that are academically grounded and credible while remaining vocationally relevant and applicable. By considering carefully the content of every BIS and BIT programme run in the United Kingdom, and combining that with substantial knowledge of MBAs, the content of this book has been devised to provide the vital core material that students in the domain will need.

Who should use this book?

The book is targeted at students new to BIS and BIT. The domain comprises a mix of disciplines such as information system development, project management, organizational behaviour and systems analysis. A good understanding of the core elements of the areas covered in this book is essential for anyone wishing to do well in any related study. The main intended audiences are undergraduate BIS/BIT and MBA students, but new practitioners may also find it helpful, especially if they come from a technical background but lack related business knowledge.

The book would be very helpful to students studying business administration, business studies or management. It would be equally valuable for anyone undertaking a national vocational qualification, diploma in management studies or other masters courses where business and information management form important parts of the study. Managers and practitioners may find they benefit from revision and may learn that the domain has developed since they last studied.

Structure and distinctive features of the book

The layout followed is along the lines found in most texts in the Routledge Information Systems series. The book aims to provide a basis for courses of study appropriate to its target audience.

- The chapters may be used sequentially as subject primers, ranging from initial degree level to MBA.
- As each chapter is 'standalone', chapters may be read in any order to suit the reader. Clearly, a chapter such as 'E-Commerce 3' builds on previous chapters, but a reader with basic knowledge may wish to skip these.
- Each chapter begins with a case study.
- Intended learning outcomes are given at the outset of each chapter.
- Each chapter concludes with a summary that states clearly the main points that have been covered.
- Each chapter has a glossary of terms.
- Further reading is suggested at the end of each chapter.
- Suggested activities are given at the end of each chapter.
- Suggested answers are available to lecturers.

Note

1 John Maynard Keynes, *The General Theory of Employment, Interest and Money*, reprinted 2007, Basingstoke: Palgrave Macmillan; main text originally published 1936, London: Macmillan, reproduced with permission of Palgrave Macmillan.

Acknowledgements

The authors thank Professor Steve Clarke (Series Editor) for encouraging and supporting this development from the beginning. We are especially grateful to Terry Clague (Senior Commissioning Editor) and Alexander Krause (Editorial Assistant) at Routledge for their enthusiasm and help in getting the book to publication.

We thank Deborah Matthews for contributing to discussions on the concept of the book and for drafting Chapter 4. We also thank Nick Wright for the material that formed the basis of Case 8.

We thank Dr Thomas Jackson for writing an extremely interesting and positive Foreword.

We thank Peter Donaldson for his constructive comments and proofreading.

We acknowledge our respective employers for allowing us time to work on this project, as well as colleagues, family, friends and partners for their conversation, feedback and patience.

Foreword

In a truly integrated organization the distinction between business processes and information technology systems should be almost indiscernible. Information technology is one of the most diverse and hybrid disciplines, and one that affects each one of us in our everyday life. As the digital information revolution progresses, so the role of the business IT professional continually changes.

This calls for a new skill set, including knowledge about information systems, project management, strategy and information systems, database management, accounting and finance, management and organizations, and a broader range of business issues. The business IT professional needs to be technology- and business-specialized at the same time. For example, how are organizations to innovate if the technologists do not explain the potential benefits to their non-technical colleagues in terms they can understand and act upon? Information management professionals must embrace the business application, be prepared to stand on the bridge between disciplines and get involved in the strategic business decisions. Much of innovation, on which businesses increasingly rely for success and survival, comes from the intermediate spaces between departments and disciplines.

Gaining this knowledge can take time. I can clearly remember my first few weeks as an undergraduate at university, excited at the thought of learning new topics, but also filled with trepidation, wondering if I would be able to cope with the complexities of the new topics I would have to learn to gain my degree. Back then textbooks contained lots of theories but failed to provide case studies to help the reader understand how they could be applied and their value to organizations. Only in recent years has a new breed of author started to emerge and write books that contain both academic theory and its relevance to the world.

The business information systems domain can be complex and difficult to navigate, but this book provides much-needed guidance for both undergraduate and postgraduate students. Covering the core topics and how to gain the maximum from your studies, you will be well equipped for your exciting business information systems journey.

Thomas William Jackson, BSc (Hons), PhD

1 Introduction

Case study 1.1 K-Mart and Wal-Mart

This case study has been included by the authors to facilitate class discussion rather than to illustrate effective or ineffective management practices. Only publicly available material has been used to write this case study, and it does not reflect any opinions of employees or management at the organizations mentioned.

In 2010 the three largest discount stores in the USA were K-Mart, Target and Wal-Mart. Target has tried to differentiate from the other two by offering what it considers to be more stylish, upmarket goods. This case study therefore focuses on K-Mart and Wal-Mart.

Both K-Mart and Wal-Mart developed from other-named 'five and dime' stores and both first opened in 1962. During the 1970s K-Mart put a number of competing retailers out of business and was highly successful. By 1987 K-Mart had 2,223 stores and Wal-Mart had 1,198 stores. K-Mart's sales were $25.63 billion, while Wal-Mart's were $15.96 billion. With around half the number of K-Mart's stores, Wal-Mart was achieving more than half of K-Mart's sales.

By 1991 Wal-Mart's sales exceeded those of K-Mart, but K-Mart still had more stores. In the year ending January 1996, Wal-Mart's sales were $93.6 billion and K-Mart's were $34.6 billion. From 1987 to 1995 K-Mart's market share declined from 34.5 per cent to 22.7 per cent, while Wal-Mart's market share increased from 20.1 per cent to 41.6 per cent. By 2002 K-Mart wanted to sell 250 unprofitable stores and install a new information technology (IT) system, but it was too late. Before these things could happen, K-Mart was declared bankrupt.

During this time, Wal-Mart had been investing millions of dollars in its operations to lower cost. It developed a sophisticated system that integrated its IT with its distribution management. K-Mart's employees lacked the skills needed to plan and control inventory, but Wal-Mart had invested in the staff development needed to implement the new systems.

Poor supply-chain management appears to have contributed significantly to the downturn in K-Mart's market share and profitability. Wal-Mart had almost no supply storage areas because it had developed a vendor-managed inventory system, with suppliers responsible for delivering products. By contrast, it was reported that at K-Mart it was not uncommon for suppliers' representatives to find shelves empty of their company's goods, but their products piled up in stockrooms. Although K-Mart had invested in IT, it happened too late.

Over the 2001 Christmas period Wal-Mart saw a substantial increase in sales over the same period in the previous year. K-Mart's Christmas sales were less than they had been for the same period in 2000.

IT systems are very much connected to the success and failure of the supply-chain management of the two companies. During the 1970s–1980s K-Mart lagged behind Wal-Mart on the adoption of several new aspects of retail technology, including back-end computers for individual stores, electronic cash registers and scanners that could read barcodes. In 1973 Wal-Mart had computers in 22 of its 64 stores and went on to ensure every store was IT-equipped.

K-Mart had computers in every store by 1982, but sales data was not current as the company did not have scanning cash registers. Wal-Mart's scanning cash registers fed updates to store computers, which enabled sales and inventory figures to be adjusted in real time. This was of major importance to supply-chain management, as Wal-Mart's store managers could place replenishment orders virtually as sales were occurring. Wal-Mart was replacing items in 2–3 days, while K-Mart was taking 21 days for replenishment. Wal-Mart positioned itself as a modern low-cost discount store, offering good service and efficient supply-chain management (which helped to keep prices down).

Many K-Mart stores were older than Wal-Mart's and were located in less attractive areas. This made K-Mart's stores less appealing to shoppers and also made deliveries to stores more difficult. K-Mart was still competing on price, but with higher costs than those of Wal-Mart. K-Mart did not achieve the marketing appeal or the economies of scale achieved by Wal-Mart. Even if K-Mart had caught up and achieved these things before bankruptcy, Wal-Mart, as the first mover, would have been likely to retain many of its customers. In other words, K-Mart had the huge task of trying to catch up with Wal-Mart, and would also have had to offer something extra (such as price reduction or increased quality) to entice customers away from Wal-Mart.

Prior to bankruptcy there had already been concerns about K-Mart's cash flow, with a reported $400 million in cash and $3.8 billion in debt. Following its poor 2001 Christmas sales, K-Mart's fourth-quarter earnings were projected to drop to 20¢ per share, down from an original estimate of 43¢ per share. This was particularly worrying, as winter is traditionally a retailer's best season. A major knock-on effect was that K-Mart had to offer its fourth-quarter excess stock at deeply discounted prices. Normally, retailers use credit to buy stock for the fourth quarter and they use the proceeds from sales to pay for those purchases in January. In K-Mart's case, this simply was not possible for 2001–2002.

K-Mart did not compete with Wal-Mart in producing clear strategy and operational management to implement that strategy. On 22 January 2002, K-Mart filed for bankruptcy. It had failed to manage properly its supply chain, IT, marketing and cash flow. It also retained too many stores in unprofitable locations. Understanding its business, its management and the IT needed to make it succeed were key factors in Wal-Mart's success.

1.1 Intended learning outcomes

On completion of this book the reader should be able to:

1   evaluate the operational and strategic roles of information systems and information technologies in organizations;
2   analyse cases of information systems and information technology implementation;
3   using business, organizational and technological bases, present critical arguments for the use of information systems and information technology in organizations;
4   evaluate different approaches to learning and choose appropriate actions.

1.2 Don't panic!

If you are reading this as a first-year undergraduate or someone who is just starting an MBA, you may be rather concerned that you would be asked to act as a consultant for such a huge project. Don't panic! That is very unlikely to happen – yet. Hopefully, something like this will happen during your career and this book aims to provide relevant subject material in all the appropriate background areas. Each chapter is accompanied by a case study, a glossary, some exercises, references and suggested further reading. You will find that the case studies help to put the material in an understandable applied context. Read the case study before reading the chapter, then read it again afterwards and you should find that you view it differently the second time around. Look at the case study and the chapter material in light of the intended learning outcomes. Also look at the intended learning outcomes of the modules you are studying. It is against these you will be assessed.

The book is not a quick-guide to becoming a consultant, as that comes with experience and training. It covers a range of subject areas that are to be found in many programmes of study that focus on business information systems. It also covers much of the material found on most MBA programmes and masters degrees in management. It is not a substitute for specialist texts, but it does provide a one-stop guide to most subjects you will come across in these areas. Your particular programme of study may not cover everything in this book, and you may cover topics in a slightly different order from that presented here. You should still find the contents of this text to be invaluable to your study.

1.3 Chapters

The chapters are split into three main groups that coincide with typical subject splits on business information systems degrees. MBA students will find they can dip in and out of these to suit their purposes. You will find that chapters overlap. This is because the issues are not isolated, as they may be considered from different perspectives. This is very important when the time comes for you to produce a dissertation or project. At that stage you will find that academic staff are very keen on integration, and first-class dissertations pull together subject material from more than one subject area.

'Management and organizations' is concerned with what managers do, management decisions and organizational functions and structures. 'Introduction to information systems' covers the nature and scope of information systems, business information technology and business information systems, types of information system, procurement and development. 'Applied information technology' includes the importance of IT, hardware and software. 'E-commerce 1' covers the Internet, electronic commerce and barriers to electronic commerce. 'Quantitative methods' provides a review of some of the basics, descriptive statistics, charts and graphs and simple inference, including trends, moving averages and seasonal adjustments. 'Accounting and finance' covers organizational types, sources of funds, financial accounting and management accounting.

'Database management' introduces relational databases and fundamental concepts such as normalization, data manipulation and database administration. 'E-commerce 2' covers some of the common e-commerce systems and technologies and gives an introduction to data warehousing and knowledge management. 'Organizational behaviour' covers organizational culture and development, change management, teams and human resource management. 'Systems analysis and design' covers information systems development, systems lifecycles and information systems methodologies. 'Data warehousing and business intelligence' discusses the main features of data warehousing, some benefits and drawbacks associated with its implementation, business intelligence, some common terms used, and why business intelligence is considered to be important in competitive environments.

'Strategy and information systems' provides an overview of strategy, some well-known approaches such as the five-forces model, and specific information system strategies. 'Project management' offers an overview of planning, criteria, methodologies, tools and risk. 'The digital society' is concerned with how individuals and groups relate to technology, and includes computer crime, credit card fraud, ethics, IT law and employment. 'E-commerce 3' covers strategy development, customer service, security, trust, e-marketing, channel integration, media, technological infrastructure, change, ethics and human resource management. Knowledge management is about how to facilitate explicitly and specifically the creation, retention, sharing, identification, acquisition, utilization and measurement of information and new ideas. 'The project' covers selecting a topic, you and your supervisor, research methods, academic writing and referencing, and ethical, legal and professional issues. The chapter on final thoughts includes some important topics that have not been covered elsewhere in the book.

1.4 Your study

Typically, programmes of study in the business information systems and technology domain are divided into modules. At your place of study 'programmes of study' (programmes) might be called 'courses'. 'Modules' might be called 'courses' or 'units'. These are just examples, and other terms may be used. Essentially, the programme of study is the complete set of everything that comprises your degree. A module is an individual component within that. Typical modules are 'Introduction to Information Systems' and 'Database Management'. Normally, an honours degree in the United Kingdom comprises 360 credits. This usually works out to 120 credits per year, and equates to six 20-credit modules per year. Programmes may vary.

A standard working week in many jobs is 35–40 hours. Full-time degree study typically involves around 12 contact hours (scheduled teaching sessions) per week. It is not accidental that those students who do just the contact time do not perform particularly well. Those who put in 12 hours per week of their own time, in addition to scheduled sessions, do a lot better. Those who do the equivalent of a full working week (say 36 hours) tend to do best. In other words, the best students do two hours of preparation and reflection for each taught hour. They participate and practice. A really good way of helping to do this is by using a diary and scheduling your non-contact study time. For this to work you have to treat that schedule very seriously. One day you will want a reference from a lecturer – get a good reputation and make it easy for them to write positive things about you. Turn up on time, participate properly and show that you are a serious student.

Teaching is usually by a mix of lectures, seminars (tutorials) and workshops (labs). The best way to get the most from your studies is by participation, practice, preparation and reflection. To participate properly you have to prepare. To get the most from any taught session you have to reflect on what went on and try to understand the concepts. Going to sessions unprepared will not help you to gain a good degree. In other words, you need to work hard. Knowledge is not imparted via osmosis by standing next to someone in the student bar that has been to the lecture you did not attend!

A lecture would normally be delivered to everyone taking the module, unless there are too many students to fit into one session. In such a case the lecture would be repeated in the same week the first one was delivered. Most lecturers now use Microsoft PowerPoint slides. Each lecture is normally for a nominal one hour, but time has to be allowed for lecturers and students to move from one place to another, so each lecture may be 50 minutes in practice. Lectures tend not to be interactive and usually involve the lecturer providing the main 'skeleton' of the subject. Questions tend to be limited to clarification. To put the 'flesh' on this skeleton requires you to read and take notes. Even if you have copies of the PowerPoint slides, make your own notes to aid understanding. Read before the lecture. Read after the lecture. Make notes before, during and after the lecture.

Your module should have a reading list. Use that as a start, but do not be afraid to 'read around the subject' by looking at other material. In your first year you will probably find that textbooks give you almost all you need. These may be supplemented by case studies, simple journal papers, articles from newspapers, and so on. In your final year you should read journal papers – these should be the main source of references for your dissertation. A dissertation is sometimes called a project. This is a piece of final-year independent work, sometimes based on a job placement, which is usually just before the final year. The dissertation is normally at least a double module, but may be as large as four modules. Chapter 18 offers more information on this subject. It is a good idea to read that chapter after you have read this one. Read it again and again. Students who get a first-class dissertation grade (70 per cent or more) often get a first-class degree. Students who get a poor dissertation grade never get a first-class degree. What grade of degree would you like to get?

Seminars are sometimes called tutorials or workshops. The number of students in a seminar varies. It could be six; it could be 40. Commonly, it is around 20 students. A seminar is usually much more interactive than a lecture. In a lecture, you try to gain knowledge of the subject from the material delivered by the lecturer. You use the generic learning skills you have. In a seminar, you also use your learning skills. In addition, you need to demonstrate your subject knowledge and skills. It often requires prior reading and other preparation. It also often involves students discussing the outcomes of investigations. Sometimes lecturers will ask students to work in a small group for a particular exercise. In advance of attending a seminar, think: what do you want from it? How should you prepare? After a seminar, think about what you have gained from it and any additional work you could do to enhance your knowledge and skills.

The term 'workshop' is used here to mean a scheduled contact session that involves using a computer. Workshops are sometimes called 'labs'. As an example, you may use a spreadsheet for forecasting or budgeting in your contact sessions. Again, participation, practice, preparation and reflection are key elements to success. For example, make sure you can perform basic spreadsheet functions as second nature and make sure you understand the input and the output.

Lecturers often use office hours for student contact outside of the normal scheduled teaching hours. To get the best of your lecturer's time, go prepared. Office hours are not a substitute for attending taught sessions. Do not expect your lecturer to repeat the material that was delivered in the lecture you missed. An example of good use of office hours is a student who goes along with work that has been seriously attempted:

> I have attended all the lectures, seminars and workshops. I have reached this point. I have done all of this written work on the exercises. I have read the chapter. I understand most of what we are doing. I am struggling with this one part. Would you mind helping me with this please?

This attitude tends to generate a positive response. Not reading the relevant chapter, not attending the lecture and seminar and not attempting any work are all things that are likely to generate negative responses. Remember, you are the only one who can complete your degree. Lecturers are there to help you do it, but they are not there to do it for you. You have to work hard. If your lecturer has marked your coursework and indicates office hours that are available to collect it and get feedback, do just that. The feedback may be invaluable in improving what you do.

Your module will have a list of objectives (often called 'learning outcomes'). Look at these carefully. Your assessments will be based on them, and these are the things you need to demonstrate you have achieved in order to pass the module. Assessment is normally by means of a mix of instruments. These tend to be divided into coursework and examinations, but the split can be more complicated than it first appears. Examinations tend to be at the end of a semester, term or year, and often take place in large groups in halls or rooms.

Examinations are normally 1–3 hours in length. Their format varies considerably. Some examinations may require you to answer all the questions asked; some may require you to answer one or two compulsory questions, with a choice of options from the remainder. Some may be in essay format; some will be multiple choice; some will require calculations. Some examinations are known as 'closed book', meaning the student is not allowed to take written material into the examination. Some are 'open book', and in some cases any written material may be taken to the examination by the student, while in other cases this material is limited or prescribed. Some examinations are 'seen'. This means the questions are known in advance, but the student still has to come and sit the examination. A typical seen examination for quantitative methods will involve the student seeing the examination paper in advance but with no numbers given. This means the student can practice similar questions but cannot practice the actual question in advance. A major key to examination success is practice. Find out as far in advance as possible the examination format. If you can, obtain past papers. Practise doing them. This involves not just content, but timing. Do not waste 30 minutes on a 5-mark question when you can gain 20 marks by answering another one. Organizations that have a high success rate in tutoring students for professional examinations often have a simple formula. From day one they practice answering examination questions.

Coursework can be a confusing term as it covers a myriad of assessment types. Traditional coursework is done by an individual over a period of days or weeks, at the end of which the work is handed in. An example of this might be a report on trends in a particular sector of the economy. Such coursework may be 1,000–5,000 words long, depending on how much weighting it is given in the overall assessment for the module. If it is worth just 10 per cent of the overall assessment, it tends to be shorter; if it is worth 100 per cent, it tends to be longer. A variation on this is a group assessment that involves something like 3–6 students doing a piece of work together. The requirement for this kind of coursework, whether group or individual, may be an academic report, a management report, a poster presentation, a PowerPoint presentation or something else. You must ensure you know what is required and that you meet those requirements. Coursework can also cover in-class tests and workshop tests. These tend to be sat under examination conditions.

Personal development portfolios (PDPs) are now an integral part of many degrees, often with a PDP module (or half-module) for each stage of study. Students are normally introduced to opportunities for personal development at the start of a degree. Students are expected to reflect on their own learning and achievements and to plan for their own personal, educational and career development. A PDP module is intended to help students become confident and independent learners who can plan and reflect on achievements. Using a diary effectively, as mentioned previously, will be an enormous help. Of course, diaries are only really useful if accompanied by appropriate actions.

A first-level PDP module would typically introduce students to programme learning outcomes, which are not the same as the module learning outcomes. If a student is successful in achieving all of the module learning outcomes in all of their modules, it would be reasonable to expect success in achieving the programme learning outcomes. The first-level PDP module would normally include discussion of any relevant benchmarks. In the United Kingdom these are normally related to the Quality Assurance Agency, and sometimes to professional bodies. There would usually be opportunities to explore personal strengths and weaknesses and to develop approaches to using strengths to the best advantage and to address weaknesses. In particular, oral and written communication skills are normally covered.

Work placements (sometimes called sandwich placements) are often available on degrees. These may vary from a few weeks to almost a full year. Often they involve placement in commerce or industry during the third year of a full-time degree. Some are paid and some are unpaid. Placement is normally managed by a supervisor in the placement organization and an academic supervisor. A programme of professional development will be worked out in advance and you will be expected to reflect on your experience with your academic advisor, who will visit you at regular intervals. This is not simply a period of work experience, but is an integral part of your learning to become an effective professional. Many placement students get jobs at the placement organization when they graduate. A graduate with a degree and a year's relevant work experience may be more attractive to many employers than an equally qualified graduate who does not have relevant work experience. Most students who undertake work experience find they have ready sources of material for their dissertations, and by the start of the final year have much of their dissertation completed. Many students who do not do a work placement struggle to find a suitable topic.

Academic writing uses referencing as a cornerstone of strength. It is vital that you learn how to reference properly as soon as possible, and that you use this skill in your written work. Your written work must be distinguishable from the kind of debate you might have with your friends. You must distinguish between fact, inference and opinion. Facts must be supported by references. If you state that the population of a country is X, then you must indicate the source of your data. If you state that there is currently a shortage of trained nurses in the United Kingdom, you must indicate the source of this information. If you state that the elderly population of the United

Kingdom is growing, you must indicate the source of your information. These things can be stated as facts only if you provide legitimate sources.

Learning which sources are legitimate and which are not is vital. Examples of legitimate sources include government statistics, company reports and refereed journals. Sources that would not be considered credible include Wikipedia and tabloid newspapers. You will learn more about this on your programme of study.

Inference is about reasoned argument. If you have established, with legitimate sources, that the shortage of trained nurses in the United Kingdom has been increasing over the past five years, and that the UK elderly population has been growing over the past five years, you could go further. You could argue the case that the elderly tend to need more health care than the rest of the population. You would need references to support this. You could then argue that, other things being equal, the elderly population is likely to continue to grow and that the shortage of trained nurses will continue to grow. You can do this by a mix of evidence and reasoning. Evidence comes from citations (references). You could find demographic reports that give the information you need. You could also argue that these trends would continue unless something happens to change them. This is 'reasoning'. Finally, you could make the point that, with an increased shortage of trained nurses and an increased elderly population that require relatively more health care, in five years there would be a bigger gap between provision of health care and demand for health care than there is now.

Notice that the preceding paragraph gives no opinion about health care provision for the elderly or the shortage of trained nurses. There is no room for unsubstantiated opinion in academic work. If it is reasoned argument, then it is inference. Your academic writing needs to contain facts and inference. Your conclusions should be based on what you have written, using facts and inference, and nothing else. Notice also that the preceding paragraph shows how to craft an academic argument. This is a key skill; one you should develop quickly.

The following is a small example of academic writing. You will see that the main text is supported by citations. At the end of the piece the citations are given in full, in the reference list.

Prior to the establishment of the National Health Service (NHS), health care was provided to some extent by the state, but much was also provided by charities, or on a private basis (Walker, 1995). The National Health Service Act of 1946 created a provision of clinical care for all, with six fundamental principles (NHS, 1995).

1   A distinction between primary and secondary care was made. General practitioners (GPs) were to provide first-contact treatment and diagnosis, while hospitals and local health authorities were to provide a more comprehensive range of medical facilities.
2   All health care was to be provided free at the point of service.
3   Financing of health care was to come from general taxes.
4   A full service was to be provided, from accident and surgery to geriatric and mental care.
5   Health care was to be available to all.
6   The government was to own the organization and to employ its staff.

The management and coordination of the 2,800 hospitals in existence in 1991 accounted for £23.3 billion (the second largest government expenditure element), and the NHS was the third largest organization in the world, with 1.25 million employees (Anonymous, 1994). During the 1960s, 1970s and early 1980s, a number of reports were commissioned regarding the running of the NHS, but although these may have influenced later thinking, little action arose from them (Webster, 1992). From 1989 to 1991 various influential White Papers were produced, including the 1991 'Patients' Charter' (Moorbath, 1994). The reforms proposed by these papers attempted to deregulate the internal market, reduce bureaucracy, increase accountability, and encourage efficiency, with audits proposed as a major means to assess performance.

References

Anonymous (1994) Documents on the NHS reforms. *Nursing Standard* 9(33): 33.
Moorbath, P. (1994) A guide to documents on the NHS reforms. *Nursing Standard* 9(3): 33.
NHS (1995) *The NHS Performance Guide*. NHS.
Walker, M. (1995) Health care provision before the NHS. *Nursing Times* 91(27): 15.
Webster, C. (1992) Beveridge after fifty years. *British Medical Journal* 305: 901–902.

1.5 Summary

This book covers the major subject material you would find on many degree programmes in business information systems or business information technology. It also covers much that would be found in a typical MBA. It gives an overview of the main topics, but it is not a substitute for further specialist reading. It does, however, provide a thorough grounding in the main concepts, methodologies, principles and theories within the domain. The book is laid out for ease of access, with case studies to help develop useful insights into practice. The suggested further reading and activities given at the end of each chapter will help to provide depth and richness.

Your success in studying depends on your knowledge, skills and hard work. Gain the best from your learning by improving your study skills, and by participation, practice, preparation and reflection. Having the chance to study for a degree qualification is something that most of us only get once in our lives. Make the most of it.

Further reading

Bali, R. and Dwivedi, A. (2006) *The Small Book of Big Presentation Skills*. Colchester: Lexden Publishing.
Clarke, S.A. (2007) *Information Systems Strategic Management: An Integrated Approach*. London: Routledge.
Cottrell, S. (2008) *The Study Skills Handbook*. Basingstoke: Palgrave Macmillan.
Cottrell, S. (2010) *Skills for Success: The Personal Development Planning Handbook*. Basingstoke: Palgrave Macmillan.

Suggested activities

1   Discuss the quotation from Keynes given at the start of the Preface.
2   Find out (provide sources):

   a   the names of all the modules on your programme of study;

   b   the means of assessment for all modules you take this term or semester;

   c   any prerequisites for all the modules you will take on your programme of study, including the dissertation or project;

   d   job titles that relate to areas of work for which your programme of study may qualify you.

3   Find out (provide sources) for K-Mart, Target and Wal-Mart:

   a   sales figures for last year;

   b   number of people employed;

   c   market share.

It does not matter if you use figures for the USA or for the world, as long as you are consistent.

2 Management and organizations

Case study 2.1 London Ambulance Service

This case study is drawn from Finkelstein, A. (1995) Report of the Inquiry into the London Ambulance Service. *Available online at www.cs.ucl.ac.uk/staff/A.Finkelstein/las/lascase0.9.pdf.*

This case study has been included by the authors to facilitate class discussion rather than to illustrate effective or ineffective management practices. Only publicly available material has been used to write this case study, and it does not reflect any opinions of employees or management at the organizations mentioned.

The London Ambulance Service (LAS) computer-aided despatch (CAD) system failed on 26 October 1992, shortly after it was introduced. The system was not able to cope with normal use, and emergency call responses took hours in many cases. Communications between ambulances and their bases broke down and ambulances disappeared from the CAD system. At the time the LAS was the largest ambulance service in the world and was managed by the South West Thames Regional Health Authority.

The LAS covered a residential population of 6.8 million people, but because London has many employees and visitors who reside elsewhere, the actual population of the city is higher, especially during daytime, and especially in the city centre. The LAS transported over 5,000 patients per day across an area of over 600 square miles. Around 1,500 emergency calls were received daily out of a total of around 2,300 calls.

It was clear at the time that success of the new system would be crucially dependent on almost total reliability of the technology and the 'buy-in' of all stakeholders, especially the Central Ambulance Control (CAC) staff.

During the procurement stage the contract had to be put out to open tender, with the regulations emphasizing best price. Most of the 35 organizations that showed interest indicated that it was not realistic to have a fully implemented system within one year. The chief executive had commissioned Arthur Andersen (management consultants) to advise on the best way forward. Amongst other things, Arthur Andersen reported that 19 months would be an appropriate timeframe from specification to implementation. They also reported that if a packaged solution could not be found, then the project would take significantly longer. The LAS management did not take this advice, and the report was never shown to the new director of support services, who would be responsible for the new system.

The successful bidder's only previous experience of development related to emergency services was for administrative systems, not for emergency dispatch. LAS staff did not have experience of computer-aided systems. Concerns were raised at project meetings but were not followed up. The contractor was regularly late in delivering software and there were concerns about quality. There was no formal independent quality assurance process at any stage of development. There was a large time lag between when ambulance crews and CAC staff were trained and the system implementation.

The CAC staff and ambulance staff faced some challenges in appreciating each other's roles, and this was worsened by separate training sessions for each. A climate of poor industrial relations and a management fear of failure exacerbated all of this. It appeared that senior management was using the CAD system to address what they considered to be outdated working practices.

In the end the new CAD system was implemented. Its failure is well documented. While there were technical issues, the technical system did what it was supposed to do (though it did fail three weeks later due to a program error). In fact, the failure in this case was one of managing an organization and organizational change. The case helps demonstrate that successful development and implementation of information systems are just as much about understanding and managing organizations as they are about the technology that is used.

2.1 Intended learning outcomes

On completion of this chapter the reader should be able to:

1   explain the functional approach to organizations, the value chain approach, chain of command, span of control, centralization, decentralization and formalization;
2   argue why successful development and implementation of information systems involves organizational understanding and management;
3   explain the classical and behavioural views of management;
4   summarize the differences between tactical, operational and strategic levels, and compare rationality, bounded rationality and intuitive thinking;
5   describe structured problems, unstructured problems, programmed decisions, non-programmed decisions, certainty, risk and uncertainty.

2.2 What do managers do?

Chapter 1 provided an overview of the book and its context. This chapter gives an outline of management and organizations. Think how effective a manager can be in today's world if they are not involved in the information systems (IS) or information technology (IT) decisions of their organizations. Should managers rely on experts to make these decisions? If they do, do they then expose the organization to risks that stem from critical IS/IT decisions being taken by IS/IT experts who are not experts in the industry in which that organization operates?

Organizational managers need to be involved in important IS/IT decisions, because information facilitates communication and people working as a team. Information is now part of almost any organization in the world, and is often integrated with the various processes within organizations. It is a critical resource that can help develop opportunities and strategies. Managers must therefore understand their organizations in order to make the best use of information resources.

There are four key activities in the classic view of management:

* planning
* organizing
* leading
* controlling.

Planning is a process that involves deliberating on systems, activities and resources, and the interactions between these that would be needed to achieve something. Generally speaking, the goal would be something desirable. Planning is about considering this and whether the goal is also feasible. Plans are not developed in isolation from other plans, and planning thus requires consideration of various scenarios. One common approach to planning is to consider pessimistic, realistic and optimistic projections. Planning is also about the formal paperwork and procedures that are required within an organization. If plans are too rigid there is no room for contingencies and flexibility. If plans are too loose they do not help provide direction, policies and procedures.

Organizing tends to take place after planning, though planning can be ongoing and should not be seen as a one-off event. Managers have to start somewhere, however, and it would be difficult to organize without some plans regarding what is intended. Organizing can mean many things to a manager. It is often about the allocation of resources. Which person should do which job? When should the jobs be done? What equipment should be used? Which people should be in which team? In general, it is about assigning tasks to individuals and teams and allocating resources to achieve goals.

Leading is about developing and sharing vision. Leading helps establish values and is about influencing the behaviour of others. It involves helping create a climate in which visions can be achieved. A leader tends to influence individuals or groups in a certain direction, but a leader might not have a formal line-management role. In fact, a shop steward of a trade union may be a leader, but that person's goals may conflict with those of management. Leaders are only leaders if others follow willingly, regardless of the formal post of the person. In other words, a manager may get people to do tasks because of their formal position, but people may resent doing those tasks. The term 'willingly' is important in regard to leadership. Leadership may be strongly affected by organizational culture and structures, which will be discussed later.

Controlling is about checking for quality and reducing errors. It involves taking actions so plans and standards are achieved in appropriate ways. These need to be in a timely fashion, within financial, legal and other constraints. Such actions may be predictive and may control actions taken to avoid problems occurring. Control may also be reactive and may be to address errors that have arisen. The two can work in conjunction, so if errors are spotted they are not only addressed, but actions are also taken to help prevent them re-occurring. Control is also about performance of individuals and groups, and covers setting standards, measuring performance, and taking action.

Managers can work at different levels. A common approach to considering levels is to divide them into tactical, operational and strategic (be wary about this, as some sources use tactical to mean operational and vice versa). What do these terms mean? Consider a manager at work. He or she finds that an employee is absent that day. The manager's options are limited. It would not be feasible to employ someone new on a permanent contract. It may be possible to employ someone for that day. It may be possible to put off some work until another day. It may be possible to ask the employees who are there to try and cover the work as best they can. These are tactical considerations. Later that day the same manager sets the roster for the following week. In doing this, the kinds of things considered are: different employees' skills; what tasks need to be done; holiday bookings; and the satisfaction of staff and customers. These things are at the operational level. The same manager (busy person!) is asked to provide a report for the following week outlining the major achievements and issues in the department over the past year, and giving a reasoned case about likely demand over the next year, its impact on the department, and any possible staff needs. The report also requires a five-year projection on staffing and training needs. These things exist at a strategic level.

Some commentators perceive the classical view of management to be at a tactical level only. Minzberg (1973) provides an alternative to the classical view, describing management in the following behavioural terms:

- interpersonal
- informational
- decisional.

Interpersonal roles involve being a figurehead, leader and liaison. As a figurehead the manager represents the organization, department or team to the outside world. In this role the manager may be representing the organization to external viewers or may be, for example, representing a department within the organization to people outside of that department. The figurehead is a symbolic role. As a leader, the manager seeks to motivate team members, help create and foster a team, and unify effort. The leader attempts to create a good work atmosphere and will help to develop members of staff. The role of liaison is about fostering and maintaining contacts and trying to keep communication open and effective.

Informational roles are about monitoring, disseminating and being a spokesperson. As a monitor the manager oversees information flows and gathers internal and external information relevant to the organization or team. As a disseminator the manager provides factual and value-based information to employees. As a spokesperson the manager relays information to outsiders and represents the team or organization in regard to things such as performance and policies.

Decisional roles involve being an entrepreneur, dealing with disturbances, allocating resources and negotiating. As an entrepreneur a manager is involved in initiating and designing change. As a disturbance handler a manager is concerned with handling non-routine events such as operational breakdowns. As a resource allocator a manager decides who gets what and who will do what. As a negotiator a manager is involved in arbitration and bargaining with other organizations, teams and individuals.

2.3 Management decisions

How does a manager make decisions? Are managers totally rational? Are they intuitive? What do these words mean? *Rationality* is a view of decision-making that involves consistent choices to maximize some value, with specified constraints. It assumes that managers are fully objective, logical and fully informed. Under this scenario managers would carefully define a problem and identify all viable alternatives within the framework of a clear, specific goal. Managers would select options that maximize outcomes for the organization rather than for their personal interests. *Bounded rationality* recognizes that not all the conditions for rational decision-making will hold. In particular, managers do not have time to evaluate every option for every decision. Under this scenario managers make decisions rationally, but are limited (bounded) by their ability to process information. Managers will not seek out or have knowledge of all alternatives, and as such they will satisfice; that is, they will choose the first alternative available that works satisfactorily. For example, a manager may be involved in deciding on new desks and cabinets for staff. The criteria may include limitations on price and space and so on. Given these limitations, under rationality the manager would seek out all alternatives and choose the best. Under bounded rationality a manager would seek the first set of desks and cabinets that met the criteria, even though this may not be the best deal available.

Intuitive decision-making involves making decisions on the basis of things such as experience, feelings and accumulated judgement. But what really goes into intuition? It is a mix of many things. Past actions and outcomes accumulate to form experience. Emotions at the time of making a decision can impinge. Cultural and ethical issues also affect what a manager may think. Existing knowledge and skills and previous training can help with conscious cognitive processes. The subconscious may also play a role, which the manager would not be aware of. All of these things together can be considered as intuition.

What types of problem does a manager face? *Structured problems* involve clear goals and are usually familiar because they have occurred before. They are defined and easily addressed, as information about these types of problems is available and complete. A programmed decision is one that is repetitive and can be handled by a routine approach and would normally be used for a structured problem.

Unstructured problems are new or unusual and information tends to be ambiguous or incomplete. Typically, these problems require non-programmed decisions; that is, decisions that are unique. Strategic decisions tend to be in this category. Tactical decisions tend to involve programmed decisions.

Decision-making may be under a number of conditions. *Certainty* is a situation in which the outcome of every alternative choice is known. *Risk* is a situation in which the manager is able to estimate the likelihood (probability) of outcomes that result from the choice of particular alternatives. *Uncertainty* involves limited information and the estimation of probabilities for alternatives is not known. This kind of decision-making requires much more intuition. The further away we are considering over time, the more strategic the decisions tend to be and the more likely it is that we are facing uncertainty. The closer we are to the outcome in time, the more certain we can be – this is more likely to involve tactical decisions.

2.4 Organizational functions and structures

Typical functional areas of an organization include administration, finance, human resources, information systems, operations, sales and marketing.

The administrative function is sometimes known as facilities management. It involves administrative tasks that are not covered by specialist departments, such as mail handling, enquiries and complaints, catering and building maintenance. It may include the production of documents such as forms and stationery. This function helps the organization work and may be considered as the oil in an engine. Without an administrative department, customer complaints would have to go to other functional areas and orders may not be processed.

The finance department keeps records of money received and paid out by the organization, and produces the reports required to show the organization's financial position (financial accounting). It may also be involved in forecasting, considering interest rate changes, suggesting alternative large equipment purchases and planning of the labour force (management accounting). The finance department may also be responsible for administering employee expenses and salaries (payroll). In order to do this, the department will need expertise in tax codes and their application and various other factors, such as holiday pay entitlement, maternity pay entitlement, etc.

The human resources department (formerly personnel) is involved in the recruitment, selection, training and development of staff, as well as formal processes such as disciplinary hearings. Human resources will usually need to comply with the legislation of the country in which they are based. For example, in the United Kingdom employers are required to maintain accurate personnel records in a manner compliant with the legislation. Human resources may also have a welfare role, which includes duty of care for employees while they are at work. They will also interpret employee welfare legislation and ensure the organization complies with it. This may involve absence policies and procedures, maternity leave, annual leave and so on.

The information systems department is responsible for the systems that use information technology and for the information technology itself. The IS function helps an organization to implement its business strategy. In particular it is concerned with the hardware, software, networks and data that an organization needs and has. Information systems deal with the development, use and management of an organization's information technology infrastructure. In many countries manufacturing has declined and the service sector has increased. This has resulted in information becoming more valuable, so the IS function is more important than ever.

The operations function is concerned with the production of goods and services, and has the responsibility of ensuring that business operations are efficient and effective. It is about the efficient and effective management of resources, the distribution of goods and services to customers and the analysis of queue and stock-holding systems. Operations also refers to the set of value-added activities that transform inputs into outputs. These value-adding creative activities should be aligned with sales and marketing.

The marketing department ascertains customer needs to help develop products and packaging to address that need. The marketing department investigates the market they are aiming at – the type of consumer making up the market (age, background, sex, etc.) and the preferences of the consumer within that market. The marketing department will then need to marry consumer preferences with producing a product that is profitable. Once the product has been designed by the production department, marketing will then need to package, advertise and promote the product. Sales are responsible for persuading the consumer to purchase the end product, based on the marketing department's research.

The term 'organizational structure' refers to the formal arrangement of jobs within an organization. Organizing needs to be done in order to: divide work into specific jobs and departments; assign tasks and responsibilities associated with individual jobs; coordinate diverse organizational tasks; cluster jobs into units; establish relationships among individuals, groups and departments; establish formal lines of authority; and allocate and deploy organizational resources.

Organizational design is a process involving decisions around four key factors:

- work specialization
- departmentalization
- chain of command and span of control
- centralization, decentralization and formalization.

Work specialization is about dividing tasks within an organization into separate jobs, with different bits being done by different people. This is based on what is known as the 'division of labour'. It is the basis of car manufacturing production lines and can be a very efficient way of operating. Over-specialization can, however, result in human boredom, fatigue, stress, poor quality, increased absenteeism and higher turnover of labour. Do not confuse 'division of labour' with 'economies of scale', though they may be connected. Economies of scale are about obtaining cost advantages through things such as bulk purchasing of materials, extensive introduction of plant and machinery, and financial strength in negotiating interest rates with banks. The division of labour tends to increase with increased economies of scale.

Departmentalization may be functional, product-based, geographical, by process or by customer. This view of the firm is sometimes considered as functional or hierarchical. This can be confusing, as within this use of the term 'functional' there is another distinct use of the same term. Figure 2.1 shows a simple example of functional departmentalization. In this situation there are three directors who report to the chief executive officer (CEO). Each director has reporting staff, but for simplicity only the finance function is considered here. The director of finance has two heads reporting. Again, for simplicity just one route is now considered. The head of financial accounting has two clerks reporting – purchasing and sales. Each function (HR, IS, operations, etc.) could be considered in a similar way. This approach gains efficiencies from putting together similar specialities and people with common skills, knowledge and orientations. It enables coordination within the functional area and in-depth specialization. It has the disadvantages that poor communication across functional areas could arise and employees may focus on their own functions, resulting in limited views of organizational goals.

As an alternative to the functional grouping, product type could be used as the differentiating factor. For example, a vehicle manufacturer could have departments grouped by heavy-goods vehicles, cars and agricultural vehicles. Geographical departmentalization groups jobs on the basis of territory or geography. Thus, there could be areas in the north, south, east and west of a country with similar products produced in each. Process departmentalization groups jobs according to the activity within the overall process. This is only useful in certain situations, especially where jobs are done sequentially. Customer departmentalization groups according to the customer type. This could, for example, be government, domestic private and overseas private. A matrix structure is an attempt to get the best of all worlds, with a functional structure mixed with a project-based structure, allowing specialists from each functional area to assist with particular projects. Examples of challenges with this are: who chooses which members of staff to work on which project? Who is the boss?

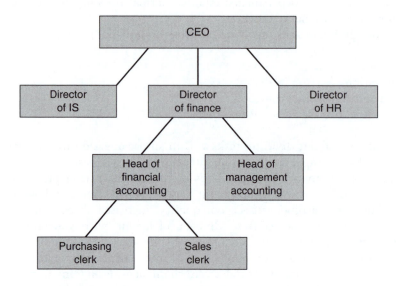

Figure 2.1 A simple example of functional departmentalization.

The process view of the firm uses horizontal flows to achieve value. This was developed by Porter (1985) and is known as the 'value chain' (Figure 2.2).

In this model, business is described in terms of its primary and support activities. Primary activities include inbound and outbound logistics, operations, marketing and sales. Support activities include human resources, technology, procurement and infrastructure. The activities form a sequential process to create the value chain. The amount that buyers are willing to pay for what a firm provides results in the value (total revenue). A firm is profitable to the extent that the value it receives exceeds the total costs involved in creating its product or service.

Inbound logistics are concerned with receiving, storing and distributing inputs to the product. They require: distribution facilities; material and inventory control systems; systems to reduce time to send returns to suppliers; and warehouse layout designs.

Operations are about transforming inputs into the final product. This requires: efficient plant operations; appropriate levels of automation in manufacturing; quality production control systems; and plant layout and workflow designs.

Outbound logistics are associated with collecting, storing and distributing the product or service to buyers. This requires: effective shipping processes; efficient finished goods warehousing processes; shipping of goods in large lot sizes; and quality material handling equipment.

Marketing and sales cover purchases of products and services by end users and the inducements used to get them to make purchases. This involves: having a highly motivated and competent sales force; innovative approaches to promotion and advertising; selection of the most appropriate distribution channels; proper identification of customer segments and needs; and effective pricing strategies.

Service is about enhancing or maintaining the value of the product. It involves: the effective use of procedures to solicit customer feedback and act on information; quick

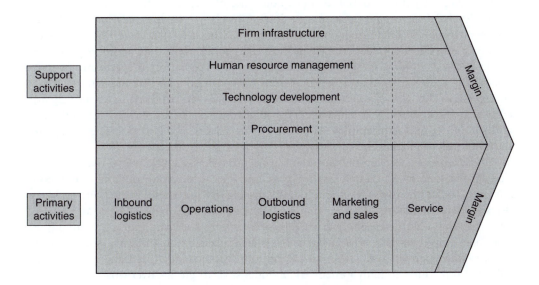

Figure 2.2 The value chain (source: adapted from Porter, 1985).

responses to customer needs and emergencies; ability to furnish replacement parts; effective management of parts and equipment inventory; quality of service personnel and ongoing training; and warranty and guarantee policies.

The firm's infrastructure encompasses its administration. This typically supports the entire value chain rather than individual activities. It involves: effective planning systems; the ability of top management to anticipate and act on key environmental trends and events; the ability to obtain low-cost funds for capital expenditures and working capital; excellent relationships with diverse stakeholder groups; ability to coordinate and integrate activities across the value chain; and high visibility to help develop organizational culture, reputation and values.

Human resource management covers the activities involved in recruitment, hiring, training, development and compensation of all types of personnel. Key elements are: effective recruiting, development and retention mechanisms for employees; quality relations with trade unions; quality work environment to maximize overall employee performance and minimize absenteeism; and reward and incentive programmes to motivate all employees.

Technology development is related to a wide range of activities, including those embodied in processes and equipment and the product itself. It involves: effective research and development (R&D) activities for process and product initiatives; positive collaborative relationships between R&D and other departments; state-of-the-art facilities and equipment; a culture to enhance creativity and innovation; excellent professional qualifications of personnel; and the ability to meet critical deadlines.

Procurement is about purchasing inputs used in the firm's value chain. It includes: procurement of raw material inputs; development of collaborative 'win–win' relationships with suppliers; effective procedures to purchase advertising and media services; analysis and selection of alternate sources of inputs to minimize dependence on one supplier; and the ability to make proper 'lease versus buy' decisions.

The chain of command is the continuous line of authority that extends from the upper levels of an organization to the lowest levels of the organization. It clarifies the reporting lines. There are a number of concepts linked to this. *Authority* is about the right of someone in a managerial position to tell people what to do and to expect them to do it. *Responsibility* is about the obligation or expectation to perform. *Unity of command* is the concept that a person should have one boss and should report only to that person. The *span of control* is the number of employees who can be effectively and efficiently supervised by a manager. This is affected by issues such as the skills and abilities of the manager, employee characteristics, nature of the work being done, similarity of tasks and complexity of tasks.

Centralization is decision-making being concentrated at a single point in an organization. In this kind of structure, centrally based managers and administrators make important decisions, while lower-level employees simply carry out those orders, with very few decision-making powers. *Decentralization* is decision-making by managers at the local level. *Employee empowerment* is about the decision-making authority (power) of employees. The more employees have this power, the less centralized an organization is likely to be. *Formalization* is about jobs within an organization being standardized and controlled by rules and procedures. Highly formalized jobs offer little discretion over what is to be done. Low formalization means fewer constraints on how employees do their work.

2.5 Summary

This chapter has provided a basic introduction to management and organizations. The chapter opened with the London Ambulance Service case study, which helped to demonstrate that successful development and implementation of information systems involves organizational understanding and management.

The classic view of management as planning, organizing, leading and controlling was presented. The difference between tactical, operational and strategic levels was explained. A behavioural view of management was discussed (as an alternative to the classical view), involving interpersonal, informational and decisional roles. Management decisions were outlined in terms of rationality, bounded rationality and intuitive thinking. Structured problems, unstructured problems, programmed decisions and non-programmed decisions were considered. This was followed by an outline of what is meant by decision-making under certainty, risk and uncertainty.

Organizational functional areas were explained and examples of administration, finance, human resources, information systems, operations, sales and marketing were given. Organizational structures were considered as functional departments and as a process (value chain). The chain of command, span of control, centralization, decentralization and formalization concluded the chapter.

The next chapter provides an introduction to information systems.

Glossary

Authority   The right of someone in a managerial position to tell people what to do and to expect them to do it.

Bounded rationality   Recognition that not all the conditions for rationality will hold. Managers will satisfice by choosing the first alternative available that works satisfactorily.

Centralization   Decision-making concentrated at a single point in an organization.

Certainty   A situation in which the outcome of every alternative choice is known.

Chain of command   The continuous line of authority that extends from the upper levels of an organization to the lowest levels of the organization and clarifies the reporting lines.

Controlling   Checking for quality and reducing errors by taking appropriate actions so plans and standards are achieved.

Decentralization   Decision-making by managers at the local level.

Decisional role   Being an entrepreneur, dealing with disturbances, allocating resources and negotiating.

Employee empowerment   The decision-making authority (power) of employees.

Formalization   Standardization of jobs within an organization, having them controlled by rules and procedures.

Functional area   A task-based set of activities in an organization that have a cohesive connection, such as finance, marketing or operations.

Informational role   Monitoring, disseminating and overseeing information flows; acting as a spokesperson.

Interpersonal role   A figurehead, leader and liaison in a symbolic position.

Intuition   A mix of experience, emotions, culture, ethics, knowledge, skills, training and subconscious.

Leading   Developing and sharing vision, establishing values and influencing the behaviour of others.

Operational   Short-term actions with scope to switch resources around but not add to them.

Organizing   Assigning tasks to individuals and teams and allocating resources to achieve goals.

Planning   Deliberating on the systems, activities and resources, and the interactions between these that would be needed to achieve something.

Programmed decision   A repetitive decision that can be handled by a routine approach and would normally be used for a structured problem.

Rationality   A view of decision-making that involves consistent choices to maximize some value, with specified constraints. It assumes that managers are fully objective, logical and fully informed.

Responsibility   The obligation or expectation to perform.

Risk   A situation in which the manager is able to estimate the likelihood (probability) of outcomes that result from the choice of particular alternatives.

Span of control   The number of employees who can be effectively and efficiently supervised by a manager.

Strategic   Long-term planning with scope to extend resources.

Structured problems   Clear problems, usually familiar, defined and easily addressed – information about these types of problems is available and complete.

Tactical   Very short-term actions with very limited scope for options.

Uncertainty   Involves limited information and the estimation of probabilities for alternatives is not known.

Unity of command   The concept that a person should have one boss and should report only to that person.

Unstructured problem   New or unusual problem in which information tends to be ambiguous or incomplete.

Value chain   The process view of the firm that considers the horizontal flows to achieve value via its primary and support activities.

Work specialization   Dividing tasks within an organization into separate jobs, with different tasks being done by different people.

References

Finkelstein, A. (1995) *Report of the Inquiry into the London Ambulance Service.* Available online at www.cs.ucl.ac.uk/staff/A.Finkelstein/las/lascase0.9.pdf (accessed 7 July 2010).

Mintzberg, H. (1973) *The Nature of Managerial Work.* New York: Harper & Row.

Porter, M. (1985) *Competitive Advantage: Creating and Sustaining Superior Performance.* New York: Free Press.

Further reading

Witzel, M. (2009) *Management History.* New York: Routledge.

Suggested activities

1   Find out (provide sources):

   a   how many small or medium enterprises (SMEs) there are in the European Community, United Kingdom and the USA;

   b   what proportion of the total number of firms these comprise in the European Community, United Kingdom and the USA;

   c   at least two definitions of SME.

2   Based on any organization for which you work or have worked, full-time or part-time, use the categories from this chapter to outline what specific tasks you have known managers to do.

3   Think of examples of organizations that are highly formalized and others that are not formalized. Explain why you think they are like this. Could they function properly if this changed?

4   Discuss the London Ambulance Service case study in light of this chapter.

3   Introduction to information systems

Case study 3.1 Usability in an anonymous organization

This case study was prepared by the authors to facilitate class discussion. Any resemblance to existing organizations or people is coincidental.

In the not too distant past there existed a computerized information system for booking passengers and their cars, bicycles, dogs, spouses and children onto ferry services between two European ports. The ports, service operator and booking agents will not be named in order to avoid their embarrassment. Passengers made bookings in person at the premises of the agent, who used a dedicated computer terminal (i.e. a specially designed unit that was used only for this purpose, connected by telephone line to a central computer).

Quite a lot of information had to be input for the booking to be made, so it was split into three sections. The first section was devoted to details of the journey and the passengers, such as the date and time of sailing, the lead passenger's name and address, names of accompanying passengers, the ages of any passengers entitled to age-related discounts, and any other discounts that applied (because of special offers, discount vouchers, etc.).

All of this information was entered into a template displayed on the monitor screen, and the 'Accept' key was pressed. In order to prevent detectable errors causing incorrect information from being accepted, validation checks were carried out at this point. Many types of error were possible: an invalid date (e.g. 13/13/02) could be entered; the time of the sailing could be incorrect; a letter rather than a number could be entered as a passenger's age; required information could be accidentally omitted. The system's response to any of these errors was exactly the same – all of the information that had been entered was deleted from the monitor screen, and the words 'INVALID DATA' were displayed at the bottom in red flashing letters. The agent was left to enter all the information again, with the strong possibility of repeating the mistake as he/she had no indication of what the error had been in the first place.

The second screen was used for entering information about the customer's car – make and model, engine size, number of doors, registration number, etc. This was also subject to a validation check with the same potentially embarrassing outcome should incorrect information be entered.

The third screen was for miscellaneous information concerning 'extras' such as bicycles, special seating (e.g. reclining seats) and optional cabin accommodation. When all of this had been entered, and assuming no further errors were identified, the system calculated a price, and if accepted, printed the tickets.

Very often, at the point where a price was quoted, the customer would remember they had a discount voucher, or that one of the party qualified for a discount because of their age. Pressing the 'Back' button on the keyboard the required number of times would return the agent to the required screen, but as in the case of validation checking, the page would be blank, and all information would have to be re-entered.

This is not a fabrication or an exaggeration. The author was the unfortunate agent, and this experience goes a long way to explain his current interest in interface usability. As will be seen later in this chapter, observational and/or participatory approaches to requirements capture can greatly improve the human–computer interface. Or, to put it another way, if the person who designs an information system has to use it, they are much more likely to get it right.

3.1 Intended learning outcomes

On completion of this chapter the reader should be able to:

1   explain major terms used within the domain;
2   describe what is meant by an information system;
3   outline the main considerations in introducing a new information system;
4   explain the techniques employed in requirements capture, and the types of information and situations for which they are most suitable.

3.2 Introduction

Information systems have existed ever since human beings developed language and began to work together to accomplish shared tasks. They are certainly not a product of the computer age. Before computers were dreamed of, railway companies, libraries, banks, hospitals and multinational companies were managing vast amounts of information relating to timetables, loans, accounts, medical records and payrolls.

Nowadays, paper documents, cardboard files and metal filing cabinets are being replaced by magnetic, optical, solid-state and even more strange and exotic storage media. Much (but by no means all) processing is carried out electronically. This use of advanced technology obliges us to adopt a more scientific and methodical approach to the development and management of information systems.

This begins with our shared understanding of some common terms.

Data is the raw material that is input and output, stored, processed and sometimes created by computers and related technology. Machines can do this quickly and accurately with no need to understand the meaning of the stuff with which they are working. Incidentally, 'data' is the plural of 'datum', and derives from the Latin for 'something given'. So, strictly speaking, one should say 'data are ...' rather than 'data is ...'. However, both forms are now widely accepted, with use of the latter becoming increasingly common.

To be of value to human beings, however, there must be some meaning or relevance attached to or associated with this abstract matter. Laudon and Laudon (2004) describe information as 'data that have been shaped into a form that is meaningful and useful to human beings'. Oz (2006) writes: 'Information ... is facts or conclusions that have meaning within a context.' Many definitions exist, with different shades of meaning (which is regrettable considering that the term is central to the discipline of information systems science). However, most or all practitioners agree that the essential quality of information is that it has meaning and context (i.e. it is clear to what it refers) to human beings.

As we will also see in a later chapter, this hierarchy of intellectual matter can be extended to include knowledge and (with increasing contention) understanding, intelligence and wisdom. The word 'system' is used (and misused) to mean many things. In the area of information systems, it describes a way of looking at things. In essence, a system is regarded as a set of components or elements that work together to achieve a task or purpose.

The human digestive system (Figure 3.1) has a great many components (stomach, pancreas, etc.) that all contribute to one overall task – to extract the nutrients from ingested materials to provide the body with the sustenance it needs to survive (and hopefully thrive).

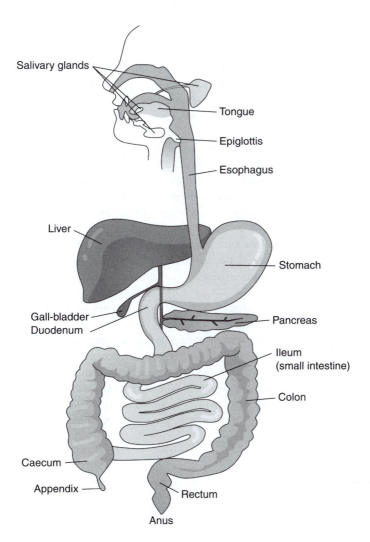

Figure 3.1 The human digestive system.

Some other characteristics of systems follow.

- Systems have a boundary, so it is possible to distinguish between what is part of the system and what is not. In the case of the digestive system, this is a physical boundary – the peritoneum that surrounds the digestive organs.
- Systems may have sub-systems. Organs such as the liver and pancreas can themselves be regarded as systems within a system, and themselves consist of components working together to fulfil a specific purpose.
- One of the most important characteristics of systems is that they have 'emergent properties'. We say that the whole is more than the sum of the component parts. Consider a motor car, for example. This can be regarded as a complex system with components that control fuel flow, generate electricity, cool parts that would otherwise overheat, absorb the energy of sudden shock, and so on. None of these components provide forward motion. This is the result of all the components working together – it is an emergent property of the system as a whole.
- Systems need a controlling or coordinating force, which can be external to the system. In the case of the digestive system this is the brain; in the case of a motor car it is a human being, by way of the controls – brake, accelerator, etc.
- Most systems have inputs, such as fuel, food, water, etc., and outputs such as heat, waste products and movement. Sometimes an output (or part of an output) can be returned to the system as an input. This is known as feedback (Figure 3.2).

An example of feedback is provided by a central heating system: it outputs heat, some of which is input back into the system to operate a thermostat. The thermostat shuts off the heating when the maximum required temperature is reached, and turns it on again when it falls to the minimum required temperature. This type of feedback is known as negative feedback. It maintains the equilibrium of the system.

Positive feedback produces the opposite effect – it tends to create instability by causing any increase in one or more of the outputs of the system to be further intensified. An example of this is the feedback produced in a guitar amplifier or public address system when the sound from speakers enters the pick-up or microphone and is amplified even further.

So we can say that an information system is a set of components or elements that work together to process, store and transmit information.

The terms *information systems* and *information technology* are sometimes used imprecisely and interchangeably. Within this text we will try to be consistent – when we use the term *information technology* we will simply be referring to hardware and software. We will apply a much broader meaning to the term *information systems*, to include in addition the processes that are applied to information, the information itself and (in many cases) the people who play an essential role in maintaining, controlling and using the systems.

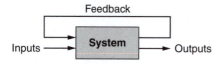

Figure 3.2 Feedback.

3.3 Business information technology and business information systems

A business can be defined as a group of people that form a structure with rules and authority, pursue an objective or set of objectives and operate under financial constraints (Shafto, 1990). This is a pretty wide-ranging description, and as well as organizations whose principal aim is the pursuit of profit, includes charitable, governmental and purely social organizations, where money may not be the prime objective, but cannot be ignored.

So we can say that *business information systems* (BISs) are those information systems used by business organizations, and which are in some way concerned with profitability or the efficient use of resources. *Business information technology* (BIT) refers to the equipment, usually digital (computers, networks, communication devices, etc.) and software that enable the systems to function.

BISs also belong to a special class of information system known as *human activity systems*. One of the special characteristics of such systems is that one or more of the elements (the human ones) can have such a strong influence that they can change the nature of the system itself.

3.4 Types of information system

One useful way to classify information systems is according to the extent to which they simply automate processes which were previously carried out manually.

3.4.1 Systems that automate manual processes

Many of the earlier information systems did no more than replicate the actions of human beings. They were nevertheless valuable as they carried out their tasks more quickly, cheaply and with fewer errors (often, as a result, taking away the jobs of the human beings). Systems of this sort include payroll systems and billing systems.

3.4.2 Systems that add functionality

Over time it has become apparent that the functionality of the previous type of systems could be extended to include tasks that *could* be carried out by human beings, but which would need more time and effort than was available, or reasonable to expend. For example, summary statistics could be extracted from a payroll system (such as the average salary; the number of hours overtime worked in a particular week; or the total amount of tax paid by company employees for the last five years). These could then be presented graphically, in a matter of moments.

3.4.3 Systems that extend human capabilities

More and more information systems nowadays perform tasks, and types of tasks, that humans could never do. Control ('fly-by-wire') systems enable pilots to fly aircraft that would otherwise be completely uncontrollable. Vast communications networks transmit and receive complex data almost instantaneously over enormous distances. High-speed graphical systems enable exciting games and realistic simulations to be created. There's no need to feel inferior, however – there are still many things that human beings do that computers cannot!

3.5 Procurement or development?

As the power and capabilities of information systems increase, and as competitors take advantage of this extra potential, the need (or opportunity – depending on one's point of view) arises for organizations to replace or upgrade their own systems. On such occasions a decision has to be made whether to upgrade the existing information system or install a completely new one. It may be possible and/or desirable to postpone the adoption of a new system for quite some time, but sooner or later it will probably become necessary to opt for a replacement.

This presents us with a new set of decisions:

Do we buy a system 'off-the-shelf', as we might buy clothes from a department store for everyday use? (It might be necessary to make a few adjustments to our purchase to make sure it fits our needs). Of course, a system suitable for our purposes may or may not be available.

Or:

Do we pay someone to build a system for us, as we might pay a bespoke tailor or dressmaker to make a set of clothes for a special occasion?

Or:

Do we design and build the system ourselves? (Not many people make their own clothes nowadays!)

The answers to these questions will depend upon many factors, including:

- the size of the organization – small organizations are unlikely to have the resources to be able to build their own information systems;
- the information development skills within the organization;
- the size of the system to be built;
- the urgency with which the new system is needed;
- the cost of hiring developers versus the cost of the do-it-yourself approach;
- whether we want the new system to interface with existing hardware and software within our organization;
- whether we want the new system to maintain the 'look and feel' of the old system;
- whether we are prepared to become dependent on the developers of the new system (for updates/upgrades, training and support, etc.);
- whether there are security issues that mean we are not prepared to give outsiders access to our business processes and/or information;
- whether our needs are highly specific, and whether we feel they can be met by a generic 'off-the-shelf' package, however much we attempt to tailor it to our particular circumstances.

3.6 Information system development

3.6.1 *Goals of system development*

Let us assume that we have decided to build our own information system (or that we are information system developers and we are going to build a system for a client).

What sort of things should we be aiming for if we want our development project to be successful?

1 *Delivering the system on time.* If we are developing a system for our own organization, then any delay to its introduction is likely to be costly. First, any benefits it was to provide will be deferred. But, more importantly, the complex nature of business operations means that activities across an organization must be tightly coordinated, or efficiency will suffer. Late introduction of a new system could have serious repercussions across the entire firm. On the other hand, if we are developing a system for a client, then we could be liable to financial penalties for delays to the delivery of a new system. Ensuring timely delivery of an information system is one of the central goals of project management, which is discussed later in the book.

2 *Staying within budget.* The importance of keeping development costs within predetermined levels needs little explanation. Meeting financial targets is another vital aspect of project management, and is also discussed later.

3 *Meeting stakeholder requirements.* One of the most common reasons for creating a bespoke system (using the organization's own 'in-house' developers or employing external developers for the purpose) is that such systems can be expected to meet more closely the needs of the organization. But just who are the individuals within the organization whose needs must be met? We call them 'stakeholders', as they have an interest or 'stake' in the new system, what it does and how it does it. There may be many such stakeholders – depending on the type of system and the size and nature of the organization – and sometimes the needs of one set of stakeholders can conflict with those of another.

The needs of the following stakeholders (or groups of stakeholders) need to be considered and satisfied as far as possible (see Figure 3.3). Note that a stakeholder can fall into more than one of these groups:

- Approver – there is likely to be a person (or perhaps a panel, board, committee, etc.) whose authorization is needed before development can be started. The same person or group may also need to approve the work before payment is made.
- Financer – the person or group of people who must find the money for the new system.
- Sponsoring department – there may be a department within the organization who will be the chief beneficiary of the new system, whose support will be vital.
- Users – those people at the 'coal face', who will be interacting with the system, probably on a day-to-day basis.
- Customers of the organization – with the rapid expansion of e-commerce, these may well be users of the system too.
- Legal department – organizations must make certain that their own actions are fully legal and that they are protected from criminal activity. In particular, the legal department will want to be sure that new systems (software, hardware and manual processes) incorporate measures to ensure the security of personal data.
- Developer – finally, the developers (you!) will want to be sure that the new system meets their personal standards.

4 The last goal of system development, the success of which may not be apparent for some time, is that the new system should be used and that it should deliver the benefits to the organization that were promised. This has not always been the case.

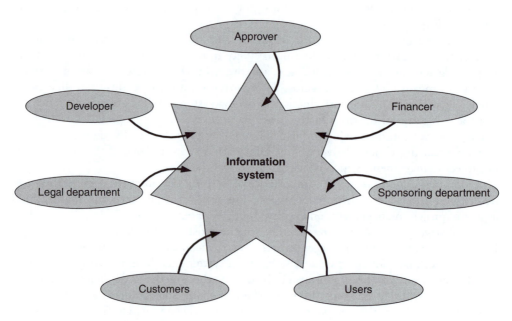

Figure 3.3 Information system stakeholders.

There have been many instances where a new system has been used for some weeks or months, but has then been abandoned because it was not delivering a business advantage, or even because it was doing more harm than good. Many of the case studies in this book demonstrate these points.

3.6.2 *System development activities*

The activities involved in developing a new information system can take many forms. They can be generalized (see Figure 3.4), but depending on the type of system to be built and the type of organization that will use it, they may be modified, sub-divided, re-ordered, repeated and given varying amounts of emphasis. This section discusses those activities that take place around the start of a new system development project. Later chapters will discuss activities that follow, and various ways in which they are carried out (known as methodologies).

1   *Business analysis and project initiation.* There are many activities that take place and many questions that need to be answered before the development of a new information system can begin. Many of these are discussed in greater detail in later chapters of this book.

- For a business to remain competitive, its information systems specialists need to be constantly aware of the latest developments in the field, and the opportunities they may present. A company may appear to be thriving, but if similar concerns in the sector obtain a competitive advantage by adopting new technologies (software and/or hardware), or new ways of using information systems, the business may soon find itself struggling to keep up. One of the most important functions

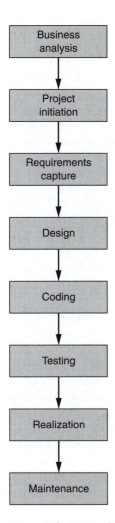

Figure 3.4 System development activities.

of an information systems specialist is to keep abreast of technological advances and new ideas in the field, and to advise higher management on how they might be exploited for commercial gain.

- It may well be the case that there are several or many competing ideas for additions or improvements to the information systems within an organization. But, of course, the resources available for their realization are not infinite. So each idea needs to be considered and weighed up to judge how much each one would cost to bring to fruition, and what benefits it would provide. Then, based on the outcome of this cost–benefit analysis, work can be prioritized. It is quite probable that only those ideas near the top of the list will be approved. Those responsible for making spending decisions may even choose to invest in something completely different, such as manufacturing equipment, a marketing campaign or human resources.

- Finally, before developing and introducing a new information system, or making significant changes to an existing system, the 'human factor' needs to be considered. The technological aspects of information systems cannot be considered in isolation from the human beings that will use them. However good a system may be in technical terms, if those for whom it is intended decide not to use it, or decide to use it to a limited extent, or to use it in the way they want to rather than the way it was intended when designed, then there will be problems. People often don't like change, and are resentful or fearful of it. They may even resist it. Indeed, this may be justified – new information systems can result in the loss of jobs or major changes to working practices. We ignore the human aspects of our actions at our peril.

2   *Requirements capture and analysis.* The goals of requirements capture and analysis (also referred to as requirements investigation or elicitation), are to identify, agree and document in detail the nature of a new information system. If this is not done fully and correctly (and often it is not) then all the subsequent activities can become a waste of time. The task is certainly not as simple as it sounds, and can be subject to all sorts of pitfalls. In particular, it is worth repeating that the requirements should be those of the stakeholders – while the developer may contribute ideas and advice, he/she must avoid thinking that he/she knows best what is needed.

System requirements can be categorized into functional requirements and non-functional requirements. Functional requirements describe what the system will do; non-functional requirements describe certain qualitative and quantitative aspects of the functional requirements. For example, a functional requirement might be that the system should print out payslips, while the corresponding non-functional requirement might specify the speed of printing and print quality. Another type of non-functional requirement is the overall usability of the system. This refers to factors that affect the experience users have when using the system (such as the quality of the interface). Users will be reluctant to use a system that is difficult or irritating to work with, even if it does what it is supposed to do.

There are a wide range of techniques used for capturing system requirements. These include the use of interviews, questionnaires, observation, participation, documentation studies and external research.

Interviews are usually carried out on a one-to-one basis, although the person conducting the interview to establish the requirements (often known as a requirements engineer) may find it useful to deal with more than one interviewee at the same time. This can have the advantage of 'drawing out' a reluctant interviewee by making him/her feel more comfortable in the company of a colleague. Interviews are time-consuming – and therefore costly – so they can only be used to a limited extent. We would normally restrict their use to those individuals with expertise in critical areas – probably managers or supervisors, but this depends very much on individual circumstances. It is worth noting that our interviewees' time is valuable too, as well as our own!

Interviews are particularly suitable when we want to ask open-ended questions – ones that cannot be answered with a 'yes' or a 'no', and that may require follow-on questions that depend on previous responses. Similarly, they are good for dealing with complex topics that call for detailed answers and explanations.

Questionnaires are used when the same questions are to be directed at relatively large numbers of people. In this case it would not make sense to speak to them all individually, so we design and distribute a form for them to complete. We may use email for this purpose, or we may design a form that can be completed online. Alternatively, we may use the more traditional methods of sending forms out by post or delivering them in person. Each of these methods is likely to generate a different response rate (i.e. the number of returned questionnaires compared to the number distributed). Generally speaking, the best way to achieve a high response rate is to deliver forms in person and stand over your victims while they complete them. The worst response rate is obtained with emailed questionnaires, which are so easy to delete.

While questionnaires are suitable for both open-ended and closed questions, question-naire design is not as simple as it might seem. In particular, great care must be taken to ensure the questions do not contain bias – i.e. that they do not lead the respondents to answer in a particular way. An extreme example of such a question might be: 'Do you think that your boss is: (a) a fool; or (b) a liar?' Bias can also be built into a survey by the way it is carried out, where it is carried out or by the people who are selected to particip-ate. If you wanted to find out how much exercise the average person engages in, it would not be a good idea to distribute your questionnaires in a sports centre. Finally, the number of people taking part in a survey must be great enough to ensure statistical sig-nificance. There are various techniques and formulae for determining the minimum numbers that satisfy this requirement. If this is of particular interest you, see the recom-mended reading at the end of this chapter.

A lot can be learned by *observing* potential system users as they go about their day-to-day activities (whether with the use of an existing information system or by performing tasks manually). This can be more cost-effective than the methods previously discussed, because workers do not have to interrupt their normal duties in order to complete ques-tionnaires or take part in interviews. In addition, the requirements engineer is able to see what individuals do, rather than listen to what they say they do. (This is not to say they can't be trusted to explain their jobs, but explaining this sort of thing to the level of detail that may be required can be extremely difficult.) The observational approach to requirements capture helps the requirements engineer to appreciate not only what users do, but the environment in which they work.

The observational approach can be further extended by arranging for the requirements engineer to do more than just observe the activities of potential system users – he/she can also take part in them. This is a good way to get a real insight into the difficulties a poorly designed user interface can present to users, as demonstrated by the case study at the start of this chapter.

Most organizations will possess large quantities of documentation that can be of use in establishing the requirements for a new system. Some of this may have been produced when the last system was built (such as requirements and design documentation, user guides and technical manuals). Some may have been used to prepare input to the old system (such as forms and templates), and some will have been produced by the system itself (such as paper reports and/or files on various electronic/magnetic/optical storage media). There will also probably be documentation relating to working practices – instructions, job descriptions, rules and regulations, etc. One problem with these sources of information is their sheer volume – it can be very difficult to identify just what is of value amongst a mass of unstructured paperwork and/or electronic files (probably old cardboard boxes full of print-outs and floppy disks). One would need to be guided by employees of the organization and users of the existing system.

Useful information can and should be obtained from sources outside of the organization for which the new system is to be built. This might include comparable organizations, academic journals and professional and trade publications. It may be possible to benefit from the experiences (and even mistakes) of similar concerns with similar projects. The requirements engineer will need to ensure that ideas resulting from such research meet with the approval of the stakeholders – he/she must not assume that he/she knows best what the organization needs.

Information system requirements can be difficult to communicate and easy to misunderstand. It is essential to employ methods to ensure they have been correctly understood and are being correctly implemented.

For this reason it is important to document requirements fully and clearly. Many techniques have been devised for this purpose, some of which we will examine later in this book. Most of them are graphical in nature, involving the use of diagrams or models, with accompanying text. Formal 'inspections' or 'reviews' may be used, in which the requirements engineer 'walks through' the documentation that has been produced, while a team of experts and users examine it in detail, asking questions where necessary. A prototype may be built. This is an initial incomplete version of a system or sub-system with very limited functionality, built to demonstrate an aspect of the requirements and to aid communication. (As we will see, prototypes may also serve other purposes.) The documentation resulting from requirements capture is known as the requirements specification, and is often a very formal document that can be used as the basis of a contract between the developer and client.

Nowadays most practitioners place great importance on involving both users of the system and other stakeholders throughout all stages of system development. This reduces the likelihood of errors and misunderstanding, and helps to reveal issues at an early stage.

3.7 Summary

Terms that are employed quite loosely in everyday situations must be employed with much greater precision in the fields of information technology and information systems. We must be clear, for example, what we mean by 'information', 'system' or 'business' if we are to communicate effectively about our discipline.

After discussing characteristics and types of systems, this chapter considered the introduction of new systems into an organization. This included the means by which we acquire or develop new systems (bespoke or 'ready made'), and how we prioritize the introduction of new systems according to their urgency or value to the organization. The goals of systems development include delivering the system on time, staying within the allotted budget and meeting the needs of the stakeholders.

Finally, we looked at the activities that take place around the start of a new system development project. In particular, we examined some of the techniques employed in requirements capture and the types of information and situations for which they are most suitable.

The next chapter will examine the technology (hardware and software) that make today's information systems possible.

Glossary

Business information system   An information system used by a business organization, which is in some way concerned with profitability or the efficient use of resources.

Data   The raw material (facts/figures) used by computers.

Emergent properties   Those properties of a system that are exhibited by the system as a whole rather than its components.

Feedback   A system output that is returned as input to the system.

Functional requirements   System requirements that relate to what a system must do.

Information   Data in context.

Information system   A set of elements that work together to process, store and transmit information.

Information technology   The software and hardware used within information systems.

Non-functional requirements   System requirements that qualify functional requirements or relate to usability.

Prototype   An incomplete version of a system that can be used to demonstrate an aspect of the system requirements.

Stakeholder   An individual or group of individuals having an interest ('stake') in an information system.

System   A set of elements that work together to achieve a task or purpose.

Usability   The sum of factors affecting the experience of users of a system.

References

Laudon, K. and Laudon, J. (2004) *Management Information Systems: Managing the Digital Firm*, 8th edition. Upper Saddle River, NJ: Prentice Hall.

Oz, E. (2006) *Management Information Systems*, 5th edition. Boston, MA: Thomson Course Technology.

Shafto, T. (1990) *The Foundations of Business Organisation.* Cheltenham: Stanley Thornes (Publishers) Ltd.

Further reading

Fink, A. (2003) *How to Manage, Analyze, and Interpret Survey Data.* Thousand Oaks, CA: Sage.

Suggested activities

1   Think of a business information system and identify the following:

   a   its system boundary;
   b   any sub-systems within the system;
   c   its controlling or coordinating force;
   d   its inputs, outputs and internal elements;
   e   its emergent properties.

2   Think of some business information systems and decide to which of the categories in Section 3.3 they belong (systems that automate manual processes; systems that add functionality; or systems that extend human capabilities).

3   Consider the information system described in the case study for this chapter.

   a   What techniques would have been appropriate for determining its requirements?
   b   Who are the stakeholders?

4 Applied information technology

The IT director of the department store chain House of Fraser has retired, and the retailer has confirmed it currently has no plans to appoint anyone to that role. Frank Berridge, the retailer's IT director, has left to begin his retirement and, according to sources close to the company, Berridge's two immediate subordinates – director of systems development Mike Hiscock and head of computer services Duncan Gray – will now report to the CFO, Stefan Cassar. House of Fraser confirmed there are no plans to reappoint an IT director for the company in the foreseeable future but did not comment on the reasons why.

It is understood that House of Fraser has reached a stage in its IT strategy where the major IT implementations have been completed and there are few new projects of any size in the pipeline. House of Fraser's decision not to replace Berridge could be a sign that retail sector CFOs are taking on more responsibility for their company IT strategy. At John Lewis, for example, the department store arm of John Lewis Partnership (JLP), the role of director of computing services, which focuses on systems shared by all JLP divisions, now reports directly to the group CFO, Marisa Cassoni, although divisional IT directors still report to their respective boards.

Cathy Holley, partner at executive headhunting company Boyden UK, said some retailers are no longer willing to spend money on C-level wages for their IT departments. She said

> I think retailers are sitting in two camps. There are companies like Sainsbury's who bring in big heavy-hitters like [director of European strategy] Angela Morrison. They hire top people because they are not just looking at driving out cost but looking at technology to deliver the exciting future of retail. Then you have the boards who simply don't get it and they try to bring in cheap senior IT people or hunt around internally.

Most of the major retail players like M&S and Tesco seem to take IT very seriously and are committed to having the right people, with the right skills to ensure success. It seems rather short-sighted to assume there will be no future innovations within the retail IT sector.

4.1 Intended learning outcomes

On completion of this chapter the reader should be able to:

1   explain what is meant by information technology (IT);
2   describe the roles of IT in an organization;
3   state what is meant by hardware and software;
4   summarize the main features of input devices, output devices, storage and processing;
5   outline what is meant by application software, systems software and networks.

4.2 Introduction

The previous chapter focused on information systems, which are intended to aid in the collection, storage, processing, analysis and dissemination of information for given purposes. A computer-based information system is one that uses computer technology to perform some or all of its tasks. This chapter will look at the technology behind and in front of computerized information systems and what benefits these may bring to organizations.

IT can be defined as the collection of computing systems an organization uses in order to enable or facilitate the activities and processes carried out by the organization while providing the mechanisms for change, improved performance and increased competitiveness. For these reasons, every manager or professional should be aware of how information systems and information technology can be utilized and managed in order to achieve these outcomes, thus enabling them to be more effective in their chosen field.

Within large organizations a computerized information system will usually consist of other smaller information systems or applications (application programs). These applications are computer programs that have been developed by systems programmers and developers to carry out a particular task or support a specific business process – for example, a sales order system.

Within each functional area of an organization there will typically exist numerous different applications, each supporting a different task. For example, within the finance department there may be an application to deal with payroll and a separate application to deal with accounting. All the applications in one department will make up the information system for that department – for example, the finance information system (FIS).

The structure of a computerized information system usually follows a standard format consisting of hardware, software, data, procedures and people; the secret behind a successful computerized information system lies in determining the most appropriate combination of these elements in order to meet the needs of the organization.

4.3 Hardware

4.3.1 Outline

The term *hardware* refers to all the physical parts of a computer such as input devices, output devices and storage mechanisms, as distinguished from the software which provides instructions for the hardware in order for it to accomplish given tasks.

As shown in Figure 4.1, the basic structure of a computerized system consists of data being input into the system, that data being processed into something more useful and then output in the form of information to the user. At any point after the data has been input into the system it may be stored away and retrieved at a later time for further processing or output to the user.

4.3.2 Input devices

Data or instructions are entered into the computer-based system using input devices which convert the input into a format the computer can understand. The most common types of input device are a keyboard and mouse (or other similar pointing device such as a lightpen, trackball or touch screen) which are often used in conjunction with a graphical user interface (GUI) which allows the user to input data and instructions into a computer by selecting options from a set of icons and menus.

A range of other input devices, grouped into the category of *source data automation*, exist which capture and input data in computer-readable format directly into the computer system. The primary benefit for this type of data input is that the data is captured at source, thus removing the potential for errors to arise from humans keying in the data at a later time. An example of such a device can be seen in supermarket point-of-sale system, which use barcode readers to measure the intensity of a light beam reflected from a barcode (a printed set of thick and thin lines) to identify the digits making up a unique identification number; this type of data input is typically used to identify a product for the purposes of price retrieval or stock control, for example.

Optical character recognition (OCR) software also fall into the category of source data automation that enables the recognition of individual hand-written or typeface characters which are then stored in a suitable format in the computer system. Optical mark recognition software detects the presence of simple marks made on a document, but unlike OCR does not require a recognition engine to transcribe the data being captured; a typical application of this type of input is in the marking of multiple choice question examination scripts. Students mark their responses to questions by shading circles marked on a pre-printed sheet. Afterwards the sheet is automatically graded by a scanning machine. Another familiar application of this type of input can be seen in the slip customers use to select numbers for the UK National Lottery.

Data can also be input to a system via a variety of other mechanisms, such as voice recognizers that convert spoken words into digital form. Other, more familiar, forms of input device are things such as digital cameras, which record and store photographic

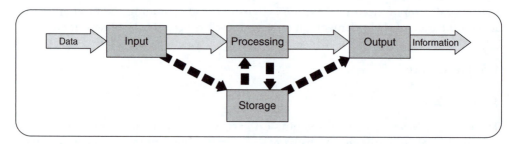

Figure 4.1 The basic structure of a computerized information system.

images in digital form, which can be uploaded to a computer for further processing; and optical scanners which capture graphics and text from printed documents and convert them to digital images which can be stored and manipulated by the computer system.

4.3.3 Processing

The process of converting data into information through arithmetic computation and logical comparison is carried out by the central processing unit (CPU), also known as a microprocessor. The CPU comprises the control unit, arithmetic logic unit (ALU) and primary storage (main memory).

Inputs in the form of data and instructions are sent to the CPU via an input device and stored temporarily in registers until they are needed for the next step in the processing sequence. It is the responsibility of the control unit to direct the flow of data and instructions as and when they are required to the ALU, which carries out the desired computation. When the ALU receives the data and instructions it will be in the form of 0s and 1s (binary code), which is the only format the CPU can process data in. The ALU has the ability to add, subtract, multiply, divide, compare or determine whether a number is positive, negative or zero. As such, all computer applications can be broken down to these six basic operations. Operations within the ALU are performed sequentially, based on instructions and data supplied by the control unit, which moves data and instructions one operation at a time from the primary storage to the arithmetic registers in the ALU. Registers are specialized, high-speed memory areas for storing temporary results of ALU operations, as well as for storing certain control information.

This processing cycle is carried out millions of times per second and is known as a machine instruction cycle. The exact number of times per second the processor can perform an operation is determined by its clock speed (usually measured in gigahertz).

Once data has been processed it will be passed on to another register and ultimately either back to the user via an output device or to secondary storage.

4.3.4 Output devices

The output generated by a computer can be transmitted to the user via several devices and media, the most common of which is undoubtedly a monitor or visual display unit (VDU). A monitor is basically a video screen that displays output from a computer, providing a user-friendly format.

A printer is another common output device which provides a more permanent form of output than a monitor. There are two main categories of printer: impact and non-impact. Impact printers use some form of striking action to press a fabric or carbon ribbon against paper to create a character; the dot matrix printer is a typical example. Non-impact printers are devices such as laser printers and ink-jet printers. Laser printers use laser beams to write an entire page of information onto photosensitive drums before transferring the image to paper using toner. Ink-jet printers reproduce text and graphics by shooting tiny dots of ink onto paper. This type of printer is relatively inexpensive and is especially suited for low-volume graphical applications when different colours of ink are required, in contrast to laser printers which are more expensive but produce high-quality reproductions in a short space of time.

Other common output devices used to present the user with information from the computer are speakers, LCD projectors and plotters, the last of which are often used in computer-aided design (CAD) applications for printing out high-quality, accurate drawings of A3 size or bigger, representing plans for houses or car parts.

4.3.5 Storage

In computer programs, data that is awaiting processing and output by the computer needs to be stored either temporarily or permanently. There are two types of storage that a computer uses; primary storage (or main memory), which stores data and program statements that are required by the CPU; secondary storage which provides the computer with large amounts of space for storing and processing large quantities of software and data.

Primary storage is directly accessible by the CPU and is used to:

- store data that is waiting to be processed by the ALU;
- store intermediate results during processing;
- store data while it is waiting to be transferred to an output device;
- store program statements received from input devices and secondary storage.

The main memory is split into two types; ROM (read only memory) and RAM (random access memory). ROM cannot be changed or erased by a program or user and the contents of this memory are retained even after the computer is turned off. One of the functions of ROM is to store the instructions for the computer to start up when it is turned on again. RAM is a temporary but very fast type of memory in which programs and data are stored while the computer is switched on. This type of memory is considered 'volatile' in that if the computer loses power, data stored in RAM is lost. Application programs such as word processors are loaded into RAM when they are opened by a user; the operating system is loaded from the hard disk and stored in RAM while the machine is being used. The screen contents displayed on the monitor are also held in RAM. Consequently, the larger the RAM capacity, the larger the size and number of programs that can be stored and executed simultaneously.

Secondary storage differs from primary storage in that it is not directly accessible by the CPU; instead, the computer uses its input/output channels to access secondary storage and transfers desired data to be processed to the CPU, where it is held temporarily in storage registers within primary storage.

Secondary storage is non-volatile, which means data is not lost when the device is powered down. It is slower than primary storage, but due to its comparatively low price, secondary storage provides the computer with vast amounts of storage space compared to main memory and is available in a variety of different media such as magnetic disks (hard disk), optical storage devices such as CD-ROMs and DVDs and memory sticks.

4.4 Software

4.4.1 Outline

No matter how sophisticated the hardware of a computer system is, it is virtually rendered useless without the presence of instructions to tell it what to do – these come from software, or programs. It is the software that enables the user to customize a computer to provide business value.

A software package or a computer program is basically a series of detailed instructions developed by a computer programmer to control the operation of a computer system. These detailed instructions are written using programming languages consisting of a set of symbols and rules (syntax) used to write program code. Numerous different programming languages exist. *Object-oriented programming languages* – for example, Java and C++ – are based around the concepts of objects, classes, encapsulation, inheritance and polymorphism, and are used to model objects in the real world, whereby data and procedures are stored together in programming blocks called objects which may then be reused wherever needed, thus providing for more efficient and error-free programming. *Visual programming languages* allow users to create computer programs by manipulating program elements such as icons and controls (buttons, drop-down lists, etc.) graphically rather than by specifying them in text format, thus making programming easier and more intuitive.

Several programming languages exist which are specifically designed to produce applications which run on the Internet. These languages, most notably HTML (hypertext markup language), have enabled programmers to develop dynamic and interactive webpages which increase the usability of the Internet. *Hypertext* means that sections of text in an HTML document are linked to other locations, either in the same page or on a different page; therefore, when a user clicks on a text 'hot spot', they are immediately transferred to the linked location. *Markup* means that specific portions of a document are 'tagged' to indicate how they should be displayed in the browser. The benefit of this is that it enables documents to be presented in a variety of ways to a diverse group of users using different fonts, font size and paragraph spacing, without the need to change the information contained in the original document.

Software can be divided into two major categories: applications software and systems software.

4.4.2 Application software

Application software provides a set of information, data or processing activities to the user to enable them to carry out functional tasks. This type of software covers *general purpose applications*, also referred to as productivity software, such as word processors, databases and spreadsheets, which are not linked to any specific business task, but instead support general types of information processing. It also covers *application specific software*, which is software that has been produced to satisfy a specific need – for example, inventory control software, sales order software and human resource management software.

A spreadsheet program such as Microsoft Excel, Lotus 1–2–3 or Apple Numbers stores data in a grid of rows (usually labelled numerically) and columns (usually labelled alphabetically), as shown in Figure 4.2.

Each individual row/column intersection, such as A1 or J12, is referred to as a cell, into which can be inserted an item of data such as a piece of text, a number or a date to represent some real-world fact. Business scenarios can then be modelled and alternative scenarios can be analysed using functionality provided by the spreadsheet package in the form of graphs, formulae and calculations. Spreadsheet packages are typically used for decision support, with the analysis and sharing of information facilitating more informed decisions to be made.

	A	B	C	D	E	F	G	H	I	J
7	Child	Child ▾	Child	Check	Days of the week					Classroom
8	ID	Surname	First name	List	Mon	Tue	Wed	Thurs	Fri	
9										
10	01	Butler	Molly	☐						seaside
11	02	Brown	Jack	☐		M			M	Rainbow
12	03	Smith	Reese	☐						Jungle
13	04	Harding	Isabella	☐				A	A	Woodland
14	05	Bell	George	☐	A					Rainbow

Figure 4.2 An example spreadsheet.

Database management software provides a mechanism for the efficient storage and retrieval of large amounts of related data by multiple users in different locations. Typical examples of database application software are Microsoft Access, Microsoft SQL Server and Oracle (further information on this can be found in Chapter 8).

A word processor is a software application that provides a user with a variety of tools required to write, edit, format, review and print text, producing professional-looking documents that satisfy a variety of needs within the business world, home and education. Today's word processing packages will usually incorporate grammar-checking functionality, dictionaries, a thesaurus and mail-merge facilities, in addition to providing graphics, charting and drawing capabilities. Typical examples of word processing application software are Microsoft Word, Apple Pages and Lotus Word Pro.

Presentation software typically includes three major functions: an editor to insert and format text, a graphic and image manipulation tool and a slide-show system to enable the content to be packaged and displayed in a presentation format.

Many of the applications described above often come bundled together in the form of software suites such as Microsoft Office, Lotus SmartSuite and Apple iWorks.

Graphics software – also referred to as image editing software – allows a user to create, store and manipulate computerized images on a computer screen. Specialized versions of graphics software exist in fields such as engineering and are used to reduce product development times and increase productivity; the most notable of these are CAD and computer-aided manufacturing (CAM).

Middleware is the term used to describe applications that enable different applications to communicate with one another across different hardware platforms and network environments. This type of software or communications layer allows companies to interact with one another across the Internet despite the fact that their individual software applications may be written in different programming languages. It is the role of middleware to manage the exchange of information between these disparate systems.

Groupware, also known as workgroup software, is designed to help teams of people work together and improve their productivity by providing facilities to enable the sharing of information between the team and controlling the workflow with the group. This software may provide such facilities as project management and scheduling tools, team and individual calendars and workflow (defining the process and procedure in which tasks are completed and progress tracked, such as thorough the use of flow charts). Examples of groupware include Lotus Notes and Microsoft Outlook.

The final category of application software of interest to business professionals is *enterprise software* or *enterprise resource planning* (ERP) software. This type of software provides a set of tools which enable the management, automation and integration of all the data and business processes within an entire organization or enterprise. An ERP package can provide support for such things as supply-chain management (managing the movement of goods or raw materials from supplier to final customer), inventory management, ordering human resources, production planning, manufacturing and accounting. Typical examples of ERP software are SAP ECC and Oracle Enterprise Applications.

4.4.3 Systems software and networks

Systems software consists of a group of programs – rather than just one program – which control the operations of a computer system. Software which falls into the category of systems software includes: *control programs*, which control the hardware, software and data resources used by a computer system during the processing of a user request – operating systems such as Unix, Mac OS X and Windows are typical examples; *utility programs*, which help manage and fine-tune the operations and users of the computer system through a variety of services such as network managers, file managers, security monitors and performance monitors; and *development programs*, which facilitate the programming, testing and debugging of computer programs – these include such things as language compilers, translators and interpreters.

The subject of databases and data management is covered in detail in Chapter 8. However, a brief explanation of the purposes and benefits of a database and database management system will be covered here in the context of computerized information system structure. A database often lies at the heart of a computerized information system, storing, managing and manipulating data and providing information to people and departments as and when they need it. Data is a key strategic asset to an organization; therefore, the data needs to be carefully managed in order to ensure its quality, as inaccurate data can lead to poor decision-making and poor customer service, which could threaten the existence of the organization. Part of the data management process is to make sure that data scattered across the organization can be accessed by authorized people as and when they require it; this task is handled via networking.

It is usually beneficial to the organization for information systems to be connected in some way. This allows data to be shared between different departments, providing: up-to-date access to relevant data; increased information as data from different departments can be combined in new and useful ways; and data to be exchanged between the organization and its external business partners such as suppliers or customers.

Traditionally, data within an organization has been stored and communicated in a variety of different formats such as documents, telephone calls and data files. This can cause numerous problems due to the lack of interoperability between these different systems in terms of how the data or information is transferred and the format the data is stored or sent in.

The way a network is configured is referred to as the *network architecture*, which facilitates the operation, maintenance and growth of the network. The network architecture includes: protocols, which are rules governing the syntax, semantics and synchronization of communication between two computing devices; standards, which allow different manufacturers' devices to communicate with one another; interfaces, which are the points of interconnection between a computer and a network and which act as liaisons for the machine to both send and receive data via the network; and the topologies which define the physical layout and connectivity of a network.

Computers (nodes) connected to a network must access and share the network to transmit and receive data, and as such must adhere to a common set of rules which allow them to communicate effectively with one another. These are known as protocols. Two people cannot talk at the same time across a telephone connection and assume they have conveyed their message clearly – we have unwritten rules about conducting a telephone conversation which usually means that when one person is talking, the other is listening. This is a protocol. A similar set of rules allow for effective communication between devices across a network. These protocols specify things such as how to gain access to the network in order to send information; how data transmission is managed so the data does not collide; and how to perform recovery in the event of an error occurring. The *transmission control protocol/Internet protocol* (TCP/IP) is a typical example of a protocol for sending information across networks which provides efficient and reliable transmission of data between different systems. It is the standard protocol of the Internet and intranets.

As a network will usually have hardware and software from a variety of different vendors, the system needs to ensure that they are able to communicate with one another. Standards organizations such as ISO (International Standards Organization) have developed electronic interfacing standards, such as the Open Systems Interconnection (OSI) Reference Model – covering areas such as networking, transmission and software – which aim at standardizing data communications between devices from different manufacturers.

In order for data to be transmitted from one location to another across a network, a physical connection – referred to as a pathway, communication medium or channel – must be used to link the nodes together. The type of communication medium used to do this could be wire (e.g. twisted-pair wire) or cable (e.g. coaxial cable or fibre-optic cable) in the case of physical channels, or wireless, in which case individual nodes are able to share data and resources (printers, servers, etc.) without the need for wiring; signals will be sent through the air or space using a variety of media including microwave, satellite, radio and infrared.

The configuration used to connect the nodes of a network together using the channels is referred to as the network topology. Several basic network topologies exist, including the bus, star, ring, mesh and hierarchical. In a bus topology (Figure 4.3), the individual nodes are arranged along a single length of twisted-pair wire, coaxial cable or fibre-optic cable. All nodes in a bus topology will receive every packet of information broadcast from the server, although this information will only be acted upon by the node that the information is intended for.

The bus provides one of the simplest arrangements of networked computers and is often the cheapest to set up. Additional nodes can easily and inexpensively be added to the ends of the bus – thus extending the network – and easily removed from this topology without causing the network to fail. This type of topology is most suited to smaller networks as it is prone to disruptions in service due to breaks in the links. The major drawback to this type of topology is that any breaks in the channel will mean that the nodes either side of the break will not be able to communicate, thus causing the network to fail.

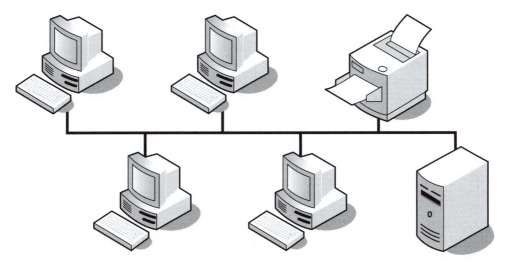

Figure 4.3 A bus network.

A network with a star topology (Figure 4.4) has a central node (usually a hub or server) which is connected to each of the other nodes in the network via a single, point-to-point link. Communication between nodes on a network of this kind must always pass through the central node. This type of configuration tends to be used for larger networks as it is easier to manage than the bus, given that it is not necessary to break the existing cabling in order to add more PCs. A further benefit is that if any of the cabling is damaged, only one node will be affected.

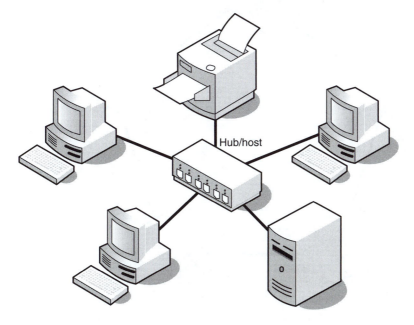

Figure 4.4 A star network.

As its name suggests, in a ring topology (Figure 4.5), nodes are connected to one another in a closed ring such that any data transmitted passes through each node in the ring before ending up at its originating node. With this type of topology, adding nodes to the network is relatively easy and the loss of a node does not automatically mean that the network will fail.

A mesh topology (Figure 4.6) is one in which each device is connected to every other device located on the network. The advantage of this setup is the redundancy of the con-nected devices – if one link fails the others will remain unaffected. This robustness is, however, costly in terms of the additional medium required to connect an extra node to all other nodes. Consequently, this type of network suffers from limited scalability.

Hybrid topologies (Figure 4.7) are ones that combine more than one type of network (such as ring, star or bus). This way, companies can take advantage of the benefits provided from several different topologies.

When selecting an appropriate topology, consideration needs to be given to issues centring around performance, such as delay, speed and reliability, and the network's ability to maintain connectivity or recover after the failure of one or more of its nodes.

Another characteristic of a data communications network is its size. As people com-municate over a variety of distances – some organizations will be based in a single office building in one location, while others will have offices all over the world – the geographic size of a data communications network is important and dictates the network configuration that will be used.

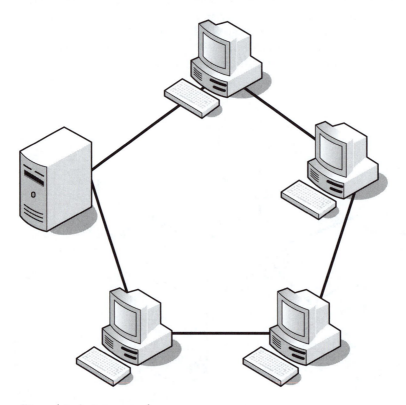

Figure 4.5 A ring network.

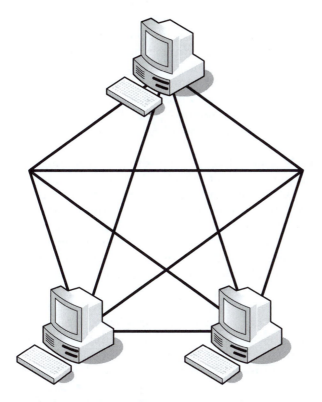

Figure 4.6 A mesh network.

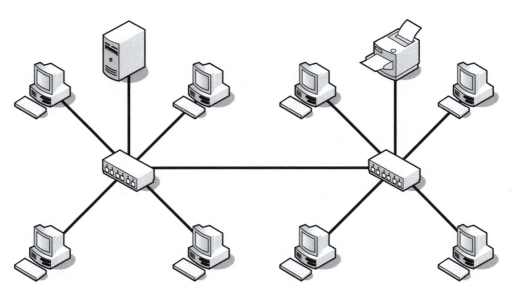

Figure 4.7 A hybrid network.

There are two primary sizes of network: local area networks (LANs) and wide area networks (WANs).

A LAN connects two or more computers/devices in close proximity to each other (e.g. within a single office building), providing each user connected to the LAN with the ability to communicate with other devices connected to the same network. Typically, a LAN will be used to allow the sharing of limited resources such as printers, applications and data files. A LAN will tend to exist within a single organization, although this organization could exist across several separate buildings within an area (e.g. a university), although it is often the case that a LAN may be connected to other LANs, and to the Internet or other WANs.

As the term implies, a WAN spans a large physical distance. The Internet is the largest example of a WAN, spanning the entire globe. A WAN is a geographically dispersed collection of LANs. A network device called a *router* connects LANs to a WAN. In IP networking, the router maintains both a LAN address and a WAN address. Most WANs differ to LANs in that they tend not to be owned by any one organization due to the vast costs that such a system would incur, but rather exist under collective or distributed ownership and management. The Internet is an example of a public WAN and is self-governing in terms of its content, management and access.

An organization may have its own internal version of the Internet accessible only to those granted access to it by the organization – e.g. employees. This is called an *intranet*. An intranet is like an organization's own private website – it exists on a private business network that uses the same underlying structure and network protocols as the Internet but is protected from unauthorized access by a firewall. A company's intranet will generally contain such things as: administrative information (company manuals, procedures, room bookings); corporate information (document templates, mission statements, newsletters); financial information (annual reports, performance statistics); IT information (training, support); and human resources

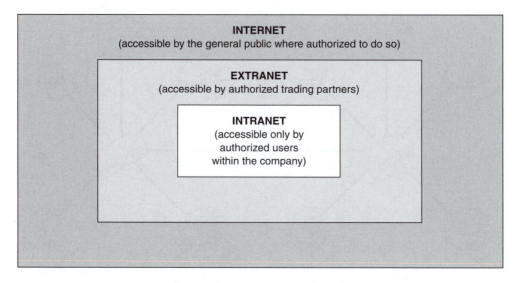

Figure 4.8 An intranet, extranet and Internet.

information (appraisal procedures, vacancies, expenses forms). Intranets provide easy access to a shared and common knowledge base and storage area for those authorized to use it. Because intranets are secure and easily accessible via the Internet, they enable staff to access this data from any location around the globe, simply by using a web browser.

An organization may choose to provide access to their intranet to selected external partners such as business partners, suppliers and key customers over computerized networks called *extranets*. The extranet will be used for exchanging data and applications and sharing information. Extranets offer a cheap and efficient way for businesses to connect with their trading partners, providing access to the information they require 24 hours a day. This facilitates the automation of certain tasks between individual businesses, which may lead to enhanced business relationships and help to integrate a business within the supply chain, such as automatic invoicing into a company's system of any orders they place with particular suppliers connected to their extranet.

Most networks typically found in organizations today are based on the client–server model (Figure 4.9), which comprises three elements: the client; the server; and the network.

The client is a node (typically a workstation or PC) on the network which runs front-end applications that assist an end user in carrying out their day-to-day tasks by accessing data storage and other facilities on a more powerful remote server.

The end user interacts directly with the client machine via a keyboard, mouse or similar device to enter data or request information from the network. The client node then sends the user's request to the server and displays the data returned by the server. As the client is generally only there to send requests to and display information from the server, the client workstation does not require lots of storage space or processor speed and can instead be optimized for its job. All processing and storage facilities are provided by the server; thus many clients can share the resources provided by one server, allowing the server to perform its job more efficiently by moving non-critical data and functions to the desktop workstation.

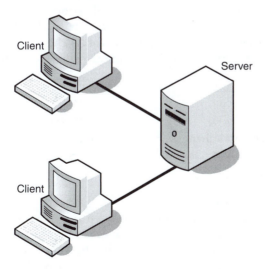

Figure 4.9 A client–server network.

Each client node on a network is connected via a LAN or WAN to one (or more) powerful computer(s) known as a server. The server is often referred to as the back-end of a computer system, with the client being referred to as the front-end. The server receives and processes requests originating from client applications and controls the flow of information to and from the clients around the network, processing requests from one or more clients concurrently over the network. Network security is also the responsibility of the server, preventing unauthorized users from accessing information held in the system, and allowing information, applications and devices connected to the network – such as printers and faxes – to be shared.

The network is the mechanism via which the client and server are able to communicate, and comprises the network media and telecommunications processors which route information being sent across the network to the correct client or server.

The benefit of using a client–server model is that tasks that need to be carried out can be shared between the client(s) and the server(s) rather than being performed on a single computer. This means clients and servers can be configured to carry out their specific tasks more effectively; for example, the client may have better display capabilities in order to present the data to the user, while the server will have a large hard disk for the purposes of storing large amounts of centralized data accessed by numerous different clients.

Processing of data can be shared between the clients and the servers, and in a typical client–server system, when a user chooses to run an application from their client, the application – which is usually stored on the hard disk of the server – will be loaded into client memory and will run on the client's processor. Any documents generated using the application may then be stored on the hard disk of the server, although this is only one type of setup. Many others exist.

Many different types of server may be found on a client–server network, such as a print server which allows the sharing of printer facilities by providing a queuing mechanism for clients' requests to print documents on shared printers; a database server which processes requests for information (queries) from the user and stores data; a network server which manages the actual network in terms of user access control and resource requests; or an application server which stores software applications which are run on the client and thus removes the need to store each application on the client machine. In larger networks the use of several dedicated servers enables the workload to be distributed across several different machines, thus improving the efficiency of the network.

4.5 Summary

IT has provided the catalyst for fundamental changes in organizations. Selecting the correct combination of hardware and software has enabled companies to achieve a variety of business objectives, including:

- reducing costs via the automation of routine tasks;
- enhancing customer relations and service – for example through the provision of an Internet-based system providing customers with worldwide 24-hour access to relevant information such as allowing customers to pay a utility bill, book a hotel room or track the status of a package sent via a courier, without ever needing to contact a member of staff directly;

- improving productivity by providing employees with a set of tools to make their jobs easier and more efficient;
- improving decision-making through the provision of relevant, accurate data and information to those that need it in an instant;
- capturing new markets or expanding markets – for example, by introducing a new line of business that requires IT for delivery to the customer, such as online sales or auctions;
- the development of new strategic applications that enhance business competitiveness and help create a strategic advantage over competitors – for example, streamlining the supply chain through the use of an ERP system.

This chapter has covered hardware, input devices, output devices, storage, processing, application software and systems software. The case study indicated how IT may be used and perceived in a large organization. A definition of IT was provided and discussed.

Glossary

Application software   Software that provides a set of information or data or processing activities to the user to enable them to carry out functional tasks.

Central processing unit (CPU)   Hardware that carries out the process of converting data into information through arithmetic computation and logical comparison.

Graphical user interface   A visual interface that allows the user to input data and instructions into a computer by selecting options from a set of icons and menus.

Hardware   The physical parts of a computer such as input devices, output devices and storage mechanisms.

Hub   A device used to connect PCs to a network in a convenient way.

Information technology   The collection of computing systems an organization uses to enable or facilitate the activities and processes carried out by the organization while providing the mechanisms for change, improved performance and increased competitiveness.

Inter-operability   The ability for systems of different types to work together to exchange information and to use the information that has been exchanged.

Input device   The means to enter data into a computer, such as a keyboard, mouse, lightpen, trackball, touch screen, scanner or barcode reader.

Object oriented programming language   A programming language such as Java and C++ that is based around the concepts of objects, classes, encapsulation, inheritance and polymorphism, with data and procedures stored together in programming blocks called objects.

Output device   The means to extract data from a computer, such as a screen (monitor), printer, loudspeaker or projector.

Primary storage main memory   Memory for storage of data and program statements that are required by the CPU.

Random access memory (RAM)   Temporary memory in which programs and data are stored while the computer is switched on.

Read only memory (ROM)   Memory that cannot be changed or erased by a program or user; the contents of this memory are retained even after the computer is turned off.

Secondary storage   Space for storing and processing software and data.

Software Programs that provide instructions for the hardware in order for it to accomplish given tasks.

Source data automation Automation that enables input of data in computer-readable format directly into the computer system.

Systems software A group of programs – rather than just one program – that controls the operations of a computer system.

Visual programming language A programming language that allows users to create computer programs by manipulating elements such as icons and controls (buttons, drop-down lists) graphically rather than in text format.

Further reading

Snyder, L. (2005) *Fluency with Information Technology: Skills, Concepts, & Capabilities.* Addison Wesley: Boston.

Suggested activities

1 Find out (provide sources):

a what an IT director does;
b what the most common programming languages are;
c what the most common applications are.

2 Discuss how you would establish what the computing needs of end users are in a medium-sized manufacturing company.

3 Write a specification for a laptop to meet your study needs.

4 Establish how much the IT industry is worth in each of: China, India, the European Community, the United Kingdom and the USA.

5   E-commerce 1

Case study 5.1 Dell Inc.

This case study is drawn from: Kraemer, K. and Dedrick, J. (2001) Dell Computer: Using E-commerce to Support the Virtual Company. *Available online at http://crito.uci.edu/ papers/2001/dell_ecom_case_6-13-01.pdf. Reprinted with permission.*

This case study has been included by the authors to facilitate class discussion rather than to illustrate effective or ineffective management practices. Only publicly available material has been used to write this case study, and it does not reflect any opinions of employees or management at the organizations mentioned.

Dell Inc. is a major supplier of computers and peripherals, founded by Michael Dell in 1984. Dell began by selling upgrades of IBM-compatible personal computers (PCs), and in 1985 began to sell its own brand. Dell used a direct sales model, taking orders over the phone and building PCs to individual specifications. Dell entered the retail market by opening its own high-street stores in the early 1990s, but a downturn in business in 1993 led it to return to direct sales.

Dell was one of the earliest entrants to e-commerce in 1994, and moved many of its business processes to the Internet. Its direct business model experience gave it an advantage over suppliers such as Apple, IBM, HP and Compaq in online selling.

Dell used its direct interaction with customers to develop close relationships with organizations that are now its core customers. This helped it to understand its customers and to provide a high-quality service at relatively low cost. This knowledge also enabled it to retain customers, target them for cross-selling and to sell products and services from third parties. The Internet has given Dell a channel for extending the reach and scope of its direct sales model, and it automated business processes such as product configuration, order processing and technical support, enabling the company to grow rapidly with relatively low investment in tangible assets.

Dell used the Internet to develop a strong network of suppliers and partners who carry out many of the tasks involved in building, distributing and supporting customized PCs. Suppliers are selected carefully to ensure high product quality and reliability. Suppliers are well integrated into the order fulfilment process, forming an impressive value chain. The value chain is managed by a sophisticated combination of internal and external information systems.

Despite huge success in many ways, in 2007 Dell lost considerable market share and damaged its stockmarket reputation, in part because its famous technology-enabled processes had a flaw. When a delivery went wrong or a product was found to be faulty, customers were left struggling as the human element in the customer services had been reduced to a minimum.

5.1 Intended learning outcomes

On completion of this chapter the reader should be able to:

1   explain what e-commerce is;
2   outline the factors that have contributed to the current e-commerce environment;
3   describe how e-commerce operates;
4   summarize the potential benefits and drawbacks of e-commerce;
5   explain why e-commerce is about organizations as a whole and not just a technical issue.

5.2 Introduction

This chapter will provide the context in which many subsequent chapters of this book about e-commerce and related topics are set. It will begin with a presentation of meanings of the major terms. The basic concepts of e-commerce are explained and different types of business using e-commerce are discussed.

Major potential benefits and drawbacks are outlined. The organizational context is explained and the nature and role of e-commerce beyond its technical aspects are considered.

5.3 The Internet

The Internet is a massive global network of interconnected packet-switched computer networks. Krol and Hoffman (1993) note that historical definitions of the Internet include: a network of networks based on the TCP/IP protocols; a community of people who use and develop those networks; and a collection of resources that can be reached from those networks. The most exciting commercial developments are occurring on that portion of the Internet known as the World Wide Web (WWW, the Web). The Web is a distributed hypermedia environment within the Internet, which was originally developed by the European Particle Physics Laboratory (CERN). Global hypermedia allows multimedia information to be located on a network of servers around the world, which are interconnected, allowing one to travel through the information by clicking on hyperlinks. Any hyperlink (text, icon or image in a document) can point to any document anywhere on the Internet.

The homepages of the Web utilize the system of hyperlinks to simplify the task of navigating among the offerings available. These attributes enable the Web to be an efficient channel for advertising, marketing and even direct distribution of certain goods and information services. Rapid developments in this area resulted in the introduction of Web 2.0, with ever-increasing interactivity and functionality. The tremendous growth of the Internet has led to a critical mass of consumers and firms participating in a global online marketplace, and has encouraged organizations to experiment with innovative ways of marketing and delivering products to consumers.

The Internet influences future distribution channels in major ways. It is in itself a new distribution channel for a variety of products and services. The costs of using it are different from those of other available distribution channels, and the service output it provides is different from the service output provided by traditional distribution channels. The Internet influences consumers, and older distribution channels gradually give way to newer ones, but do not necessarily become redundant. Consumers have access to greater amounts of information and the interactive nature of the Web and the hypertext environment allow for deep, non-linear searches initiated and controlled by customers. There is also potential for wider availability of products and services, which were previously difficult to find. Increased competition between suppliers is also likely to result in lower prices.

As shown in the Dell Inc. case study, Internet technology can make a significant contribution to a company's value chain. It can improve a company's relationship with vendors and suppliers, its internal operations and its customer relations, and offers the prospect of reaching a rapidly expanding user base. The Internet has also resulted in dramatically lower communications costs by eliminating obstacles created by geography, time zones and locations.

The rise of the Internet has resulted in the formation of virtual organizations that have relatively little physical presence but which enjoy access to national and international markets. One example is Amazon.com, which is a virtual bookstore supplying books, music CDs, DVDs and many other products to customers around the world. Other examples include Smile.co.uk and e-Bay. Many physical organizations have found they can leverage their core competencies in primary activities by a virtual presence.

5.4 Electronic commerce

Electronic commerce (e-commerce) is about buying and selling information, products and services via computer networks such as the Internet and electronic data interchange (EDI). For the purposes of this book, a broad scope definition by Kalakota and Whinston (1997) will be used.

- *Communications*: e-commerce is the delivery of information, products/services or payments over telephone lines, computer networks or any other electronic means.
- *Business process*: e-commerce is the application of technology towards the automation of business transactions and workflow.
- *Service*: e-commerce is a tool that addresses the desire of firms, consumers and management to cut service costs while improving the quality of goods and increasing the speed of service delivery.
- *Online*: e-commerce provides the capability of buying and selling products and information on the Internet and other online services.

The first e-commerce wave pointed to how companies save money by publishing on the Web. The second wave gave enterprises the ability to profit from online sales. The third wave created new places on the Internet to meet and buy and sell goods and services using innovative trading methods. E-commerce allows the new products to be created and/or for existing products to be re-created in innovative ways. E-commerce also allows suppliers to gather personalized data on customers. Building customer profiles, as well as data collection on certain groups of people, is often used as a source of information for customizing existing products or designing new ones.

Mass customization enables manufacturers to create a tailored product for each customer, based on his or her specification. As an example, Motorola gathers customer needs for cellular phones and transmits them electronically to the manufacturing plant, where they are produced – according to the customer's specification – and delivered within 24 hours. Levi Strauss also uses this approach to enable their customers to tailor their order. E-commerce has created major changes in business. Engaging in e-commerce requires rethinking the nature of the buyer/seller interaction. It requires business transformation.

5.5 E-commerce applications

5.5.1 Overview

E-commerce has touched almost all aspects of business and life in general, especially in Western countries. This section covers the most common applications of e-commerce, such as banking, retailing, e-tailing, manufacturing, human resource management, travel and property.

5.5.2 E-banking

Offering extra service delivery channels such as e-banking means wider choice and convenience for customers. E-banking can be available 24 hours a day throughout the year, and the widespread availability of the Internet, even on mobile phones, means that customers can conduct many of their financial tasks virtually anywhere and anytime. E-banking often attracts high-profit customers with higher than average income and education levels, which helps to increase the size of revenue streams (Shah and Siddiqui, 2006). For a retail bank, e-banking customers are therefore of particular interest, and such customers are likely to have a higher demand for banking products. Most of them are using online channels regularly for a variety of purposes, and for some there is no need for regular personal contacts with the bank's branch network (Berger and Gensler, 2007).

Some research suggests that adding the Internet delivery channel to an existing portfolio of service delivery channels results in non-trivial increases in bank profitability (Young *et al.*, 2007). Extra revenues mainly come from increases in non-interest income from service charges on deposit/current accounts. The customers tend to be high-income earners with concomitant profit potential.

E-banking has changed the traditional retail banking business model in many ways. For example, by making it possible for banks to allow the production and delivery of financial services to be separated into different businesses. Now banks can sell and manage services offered by other banks. This is especially attractive to smaller banks with a limited product range. E-banking has also resulted in increased credit card lending as it is a form of transactional loan that is easily deliverable over the Internet. Electronic bill payments have also had important impacts on retail banking practices. E-banking usually results in load reduction on other delivery channels, a trend that is likely to continue with services such as mortgages and asset finance. It is important to note that e-banking does not automatically bring these benefits, as other organizational issues also have to be considered.

5.5.3 Electronic retailing

E-commerce plays a major role in retailing and has changed many organizations from traditional high street outlets to virtual and direct business models. Electronic retailing or e-tailing is the direct sale of products, information and service through the

Internet, usually designed around an electronic catalogue, auction or comparative format. Almost all types of products from CDs to luxury cars are available online, and comparing prices and other features has become very easy. Consumer shopping behaviour has also changed dramatically, given the ease and power of Internet access. The retention of online consumers may be difficult and expensive, as online consumers can easily compare and evaluate services offered by various providers.

Retailers that offer multi-channel retailing such as Argos usually enjoy larger revenue growth. This is mainly because people trust the companies with high-street presence more, but also want the convenience of Internet shopping. This could also be linked to ease of returning items and local customer services offered by the physical stores. Argos enables online purchase and home delivery, as well as online purchase and collection at store.

Generally speaking, a web-based store would have an e-catalogue, which is a database of information about products and prices alongside stock information. Customers browse through the catalogue and if they like an item, they add it to a shopping cart. The total price, including any delivery charges, is presented and the customer proceeds to checkout. Customers make payments using credit or debit cards or through financial intermediaries such as PayPal.

E-retailing requires support services for successful operations. These services include: communication backbone (information systems); payment mechanism; order fulfilment; and logistics to acquire stock and deliver to the customers. Innovations in these support services or innovative combinations of these services are often the main source of competitive advantage (Pirakatheeswari, 2009). E-retailing has many potential benefits, including enabling existing brick-store retailers opportunities to reach new markets while leveraging e-retailing strengths – 24-hours availability and the ability to buy from home. It also offers the potential of considerable savings on operational costs, which can be passed to the customer in prices.

E-retailing also has various drawbacks. For example, it lacks an emotional shopping experience that a customer can get in a shopping store, as virtual display does not provide sensory support (the customer cannot hold, smell, feel or try the product). This results in the ratio of returned items being much higher than in traditional stores. Security is a concern, and retailing sites are one of the biggest sources of identity theft, so customers can be reluctant to use credit or debit cards. Despite these drawbacks, e-retailing is still growing rapidly.

Pirakatheeswari (2009) notes that some of the important factors in the success of e-retailing include: strong branding; a range of attractive products; competitive pricing; good customer service; good marketing and customer relationship management; distribution efficiency; easy to use website; provision of details about the products (including reviews); and secure environment to protect customers' personal details.

5.5.4 *Other areas*

E-commerce is changing manufacturing systems from mass production to demand-driven, and possibly customized, just-in-time manufacturing. Production systems are integrated with finance, marketing and other functional systems. Using Internet-based enterprise approaches such as enterprise resource planning (ERP) systems, orders that are taken from customers can be directed to designers and on to the production floor moments later. Companies such as Boeing and General Electric assemble products from components manufactured in many locations. This all means that manufacturing processes have become much more integrated with the rest of the functions within an organization and its environment.

E-commerce has had a major impact on education, and distance learning online is exploding, providing more and more opportunities to individuals, as well as businesses. Companies are cutting training costs by providing virtual training. They are finding that distance learning may be a key factor in survival and competitiveness because of changing environments and new technologies making it necessary for employees to be trained and re-trained. E-learning enables training to be provided at employees' desks, so there is no need for them to be away from their usual commitments. Universities are also taking advantage of e-learning capabilities offered by information and communication technologies. For example, City University of Hong Kong teaches an interactive MBA programme almost entirely on the Web.

E-commerce is changing the ways people are recruited, evaluated, promoted and developed, and the Internet plays a major role in this transformation. Thousands of employment agencies operate on the Internet, and hundreds of thousands of employers advertise vacancies there. Applying for jobs has also become much quicker and far less cumbersome, as completing online applications can be done by copying and pasting from existing files. Communication between employers and candidates has also become easier and much more cost-effective because of email and other electronic communication tools.

The Internet offers the convenience of being able to plan, explore and arrange almost any trip. People can make potential savings by buying on the Internet, eliminating the need for travel agents and buying directly from the providers. Websites like Expedia.com, TravelSupermarket.com, CheapFlights.com and lastminute.com allow customers to buy flexible fares on the Internet, where they can compare different deals and make bookings. Other travel services, such as train tickets, coach tickets, cruises, hotels and various entertainment activities can also be searched for, compared and booked through the Internet. Services are also provided by all major airlines, providing considerable amounts of information on their websites. Some no-frills airlines such as easyJet conduct most of their business online due to the cost-effectiveness of such an approach. American Airlines, Air Portugal and some other airlines have held online auctions in which passengers can bid for tickets.

Property rental and sales are now common on the Internet. For example, the Yahoo search engine, loot.com and smartmove.co.uk make it so much easier for people to buy or rent a property by simply keying in a few words as to exactly what they are looking for. One can view many properties on the screen, saving one's own and the broker's time. One can sort and organize priorities according to one's chosen criteria and preview the exterior and interior design of the properties. Other property-related services such as inspections, repairs and valuations can also be arranged using the Internet.

5.6 Barriers to e-commerce

5.6.1 *Website design and operational functionality*

There is considerable weight attached to the appropriate design of websites. Poor design of website results in the loss of potential repeat visits. Poor design may include the use of inappropriate colours, contrast, font or navigation functions. Lack of proper functionality, excessive use of graphics or other similar factors can also deter customers from coming back to that website. Web usage barriers can also be attributed to vision, cognition and physical impairments associated with the normal ageing process. Vision changes include a decline in visual acuity resulting in inability to see objects on a screen clearly, decreased capacity to focus at close range or increased sensitivity to glare from light reflecting or shining into the eye. These physiological changes, and many others, impact the user's ability to see Web objects and read online content (Becker, 2005). These factors need to be taken into account when designing a website as an ageing population in most industrialized countries means that this segment is increasing in size. These are the people who might need the online services most due to mobility issues. Several software tools, including Dottie and Usability Enforcer, are available for senior-friendly websites. Numerous organizations, such as the National Institute on Aging (www.nia.nih.gov) provide guidelines for making senior-friendly websites.

Poor website design can also result in decreased trust in using online services, as look and feel often create a lasting impression. This issue is covered in greater detail below in the section on trust issues.

5.6.2 Regulatory issues

As the Internet is a global medium, it creates opportunities for trading on an international basis, but every country has its own laws and regulations concerning the provision of products and services. Buying things from a different country could mean that consumer protection is compromised as it is often not clear whether laws of the vendor's country or laws of customers' apply if anything goes wrong.

The Internet is also a major source of consumer intelligence (personal information, buying patterns and behaviour), which raises a number of privacy, security and data protection issues which regulators must address effectively. To do this, new regulations must be put in place more quickly than in the past, leading to constant changes in laws and regulations, and complicating compliance; again a major obstacle to the growth of e-commerce, especially cross-border e-commerce.

5.6.3 Information management

Good information management enables organizations to become more effective in their operations as it provides the information employees need to analyse and conceptualize information, thereby adding to the firm's store of knowledge and making their jobs more meaningful and efficient. This gives employees an opportunity to add value to the organization's products and services (Blount *et al.* 2005). In online services operations, good information can be a vital difference between success and failure. However, managing information has been a problem for organizations across many industries.

5.6.4 Outsourcing problems

Development or implementation of e-commerce-related systems and other technical tasks such as upgrading and integrating existing legacy systems are very complex. They require very high levels of technical and project management competence to carry out without outside help. Even the best companies need to recognize the limitations of their expertise and when to outsource certain e-commerce functions (Hirsh, 2002). Many organizations outsource all or part of their operations due to a lack of in-house expertise or simply to cut costs. Some aspects of outsourcing – for example, the type and number of partners – can present particular management challenges. Outsourcing works in some cases but can create a risk of an organization losing control of its critical functions. General good practice in planning, negotiating and actual outsourcing can minimize these risks.

5.6.5 Security

Security-related issues are a major concern for the future of e-commerce. E-commerce increases security risks, potentially exposing traditionally isolated systems to the open and risky world of the Internet. According to McDougall (2007), security problems can mainly be categorized as: hacking with criminal intent (e.g. fraud); hacking by 'casual hackers' (e.g. defacement of websites or 'denial of service' – causing websites to slow or crash); and flaws in systems providing opportunities for security breaches (e.g. a user is able to transact on other users' accounts). These threats have potentially serious financial, legal and reputational risks associated with them.

Information is a valuable asset and to fully utilize it requires wide availability, at least within an organization. However, security requirements might hinder wider information sharing. Therefore, organizational objectives of security and availability may be seen to pull against each other; the more confidential a set of information, the less available it would be. This has raised the question of 'available to whom?', and has led to a consideration of information as a human issue, as well as technological and managerial.

In an e-commerce environment, security threats largely fall into three categories:

1   *Login detail disclosure*: this is the most basic threat to the e-commerce system. Using a number of means, criminals acquire login details, such as a customer number or PIN and use it to access the account and steal money from it. This threat could be mitigated through promotion of good practice among consumers to keep their login details safe and harder to guess.
2   *Computer spy viruses*: these are computer programs that are circulated through email or other means. Once a customer opens a malicious email a program is automatically installed on his/her computer. These programs collect login data or other financial information, which is then used to conduct a range of criminal activities such as credit card cloning or unauthorized funds transfer.
3   *Dummy sites or phishing*: here, the customer is lured to the dummy or look-alike website. These websites look very similar to a genuine website, and when login details are entered, these are recorded and used for criminal activities.

Many technical and managerial solutions are available, and show various degrees of success. One of the main problems with implementing security solutions is customer resentment against several layers of security, which might lead to loss of custom. Another problem is the high cost associated with them; most sophisticated systems can be implemented only for the highest value parts of e-commerce systems. Hackers are not the only security threat – employees or contractors can do as much damage as a hacker can. Therefore, security provisions are also necessary for internal threats.

In the face of multi-faceted, multi-directional security threats, implementing ad hoc security systems may not be the best approach. McDougall (2007) suggests that organizations need, as a minimum, to have:

- a strategic approach to security, building best-practice security initiatives into systems and networks as they are developed;
- a proactive approach to security, involving active testing of security systems, controls (e.g. penetration testing), planning response to new threats and vulnerabilities and regular reviews of internal as well as external threats. Advice from financial regulators can be sought on how to do it;
- sufficient staff with security expertise and responsibilities;
- regular use of system-based security and monitoring tools. This may include use of digital signatures (a security option that uses two keys, one public and one private, which are used to encrypt messages before transmission and to decrypt them on receipt), or public key infrastructure (PKI) (policies, processes and technologies used to verify, enrol and certify users of a security application). A PKI uses public key cryptography and key certification practices to secure communications;
- continuity plans to deal with the aftermath of any security breaches.

It is impossible to have completely fool-proof systems; security breaches are always a possibility so organizations must have processes in place to deal with them. It is important to provide clear and simple guidelines to consumers so they know what to do if they become victim of fraud.

5.6.6 Loss of personal relationship

Another key barrier in e-commerce is a lack of personal contact between customers and organizations. E-commerce often erodes a direct relationship with customers as compared with traditional in-store interaction. To compensate, organizations must deliver higher quality services in order to compete with other service delivery channels. Another factor in the loss of personal relationships is the convenience of Internet shopping: it is much easier now to compare products and switch between different providers. This creates the need to offer high-value products and cut operational costs to remain competitive, which in turn may further erode the avenues for building personal relationships with customers. The solution to these problems appears to be offering a multi-channel experience that is better than that of direct competitors.

5.6.7 Trust issues

Lack of consumer trust is a major hurdle in the growth of e-commerce. Although winning consumer trust is more important in the online environment, online trust does share a number of characteristics with off-line trust. Wang and Emurian (2005) categorized these characteristics in the following four categories.

1 *Trust and trustees*: the two parties, truster and trustee, are vital for establishing a relationship. In an online environment, a website, or rather the trader behind it, is a trustee and a consumer is a truster.

2   *Vulnerability*: off-line traders usually have a physical presence, which reduces the sense of vulnerability, but the anonymity associated with the online world leaves consumers feeling more vulnerable. This is not just about vulnerability to fraud, but also loss of privacy, because every move made by a consumer can be recorded and analysed to assess their behaviour. In some cases, this information is sold to other parties without consumers' prior knowledge, further fuelling online mistrust.

3   *Produced actions*: a consumer action may include just visiting a website for information or purchasing a product, often providing credit/debit card information, as well as other personal data such as a home address. Both of these actions benefit traders in terms of a potential sale or an actual sale. To provoke these actions, a trader must do a number of things – discussed below – to create trust in the consumer's mind.

4   *Subjective matter*: trust is a subjective matter. Some people will trust easily while others will not trust no matter what. The majority of consumers, however, fall somewhere in between, and can be persuaded to trust even a virtual trader. Trust is a psychological state of mind when the person is willing to accept the risks involved. When the perception of benefits outweigh the risks in the relationship, the person may enter a trusting relationship. Therefore, the onus is on organizations to promote e-commerce benefits and minimize the related risks (by providing institutional and structural safeguards) to facilitate trust.

These characteristics of trust show that it is a complex issue needing careful consideration to understand what helps in formation of trust in an online environment. These elements can be described as: the integrity of a trader; his/her ability to deliver quality products and services; and owning up to the consequences of a near future failure (guarantees). The element of integrity also includes a trader being seen as making legitimate profits without undermining consumer interests. The presence of a privacy policy or statement on the website also inspires confidence.

Brand name plays an important role in the formation of trust, and as customers use a brand, if their experience is positive, they tend to come back for repeat purchases. Their recommendations, as well as carefully crafted marketing campaigns, play a vital role. Having some sort of physical presence or having an already established brand name often proves to be an invaluable asset in inspiring consumer trust. Consequently, organizations with well-trusted brand names which also keep high-street stores often perform better in e-commerce than their rival virtual organizations.

It appears that virtual organizations are relatively easy to set up in comparison to traditional physical stores. However, start-up costs are high, as establishing a trusted brand is costly and takes time. This is in addition to the purchase of expensive technology and integration costs. But it has to be done as an organization's strength and performance now very much depend on its ability and capacity to provide value by re-aggregating and tailor-making services to suit individuals and offering these services quickly, efficiently and securely.

Approval by third parties such as governments, regulatory authorities, professional associations or other trusted brands also plays a big part. However, organizations need to take active steps to promote trust in e-commerce. These steps may include:

• purchase of similar web domain names so it becomes difficult for fraudulent traders to set up similar websites;

- being proactive in combating online crimes and cooperating with other organizations and other regulatory/professional bodies to detect and prevent crimes;
- taking proper care in protecting consumers' information and taking particular care when using it for marketing purposes;
- providing appropriate guarantees against consumer losses in the event of fraud.

In addition to the above steps, website design can incorporate a number of features that contribute to the formation of online trust. Online traders can take many managerial measures to build and enhance trusting relationships before, during and after any online interaction. Online traders depend primarily on their electronic storefront or website to attract potential customers and to communicate their message. Applying trust-inducing features to the websites of online merchants is the most effective method of enhancing online trust. Wang and Emurian (2005) proposed a framework to explain these trust-inducing features. The framework classifies these features into four general dimensions: graphic design; structure design; content design; and social-cue design.

All of these dimensions have the potential to facilitate or undermine trust in a website. Simple things such as use of colour can steer consumers to decide whether to trust a trader or not. Generally speaking, an orange-coloured website may be taken to indicate a cheap/no-frills operation, whereas light blue may be taken as a high-end trustworthy business. Most consumers like a simple and easy to navigate structure as it creates a smooth and positive experience, which is a key dimension in winning trust. Provision of the human touch such as customer service representatives if things go wrong in online environments is now considered to be vital for winning trust.

5.6.8 Adoption/acceptance issues

Within this new set of market possibilities provided by the online environment, there are risks as well as opportunities for consumers. However, owing to the security and trust issues discussed above, consumer take-up of online services, including e-banking, has been much lower than expected. In addition, many customers lack the required IT skills or access to a computer or the Internet. From an organizational point of view, failing to successfully adopt e-commerce initiatives originates from a combination of unclear business vision for e-commerce and lack of technological expertise, among other factors. Other factors include: uncertainty of financial benefits; limited size of target market; lack of time/resources to start new projects; high costs of computing technology; and organizational issues like top management short-sightedness and longstanding internal barriers.

5.6.9 Clash with other service delivery channels

Although e-commerce promises to be more cost-effective and efficient than other channels such as physical stores, it may also cannibalize these other channels. In the short-term, a cheaper channel replacing an expensive one looks attractive, but in the long-run it may cost organizations an established and loyal customer base. For this reason many organizations treat e-commerce as only an extra channel, a factor in the slow growth of e-commerce.

Many organizations have invested huge resources in their high-street store networks, and in many ways view them as one of their core competencies. New technologies can enhance these core competencies, but at the same time may destroy them. This could mean that entry barriers for new entrants keep coming down and increasing competition from new and lower-cost rivals can erode profits. A recent example of this is the bankruptcy of the book shop Borders, which blamed competition with online book stores such as Amazon for their demise.

5.6.10 Change management issues

One of the main problems established organizations encounter when considering e-commerce adoption is organizational change. Technology adoption is usually slow if too much attention is paid to technical aspects rather than business processes and social issues. Some companies sell their e-commerce projects as 'pilot' or 'learning' vehicles and leave their development to the IT department; many senior executives equate 'going online' with a specific technology in mind rather than using digital technologies to implement their organization's strategic objectives.

Going online is about serving customers, creating innovative products and services, leveraging organizational talent, achieving significant improvements in productivity and increasing revenues. The high start-up cost of e-commerce also encourages some organizations to delay its implementation. Lack of a well-defined e-commerce strategy aligned with the general business strategy is also one of the most common problems. To minimize the effects of these issues an e-commerce initiative, just like any other business project, should be undertaken within a strategic framework.

5.6.11 Ethical issues

Consideration of the ethics of e-commerce has focused mainly on areas relating to the use/abuse of information collected through analysing online customer behaviour. In this context the main issues may include security/privacy of information about individuals, accuracy of information, ownership of information and intellectual property, accessibility of information held and what uses of this information are ethically acceptable.

One of the main benefits of e-commerce is that organizations can improve service and potentially generate more profits for shareholders and job security for employees. On the other hand, job losses are one of the methods of cutting costs, and this has numerous negative implications for those affected. The displacement of job opportunities away from face-to-face and back-office service roles to information system professionals is a common feature of the electronic commerce revolution (Turban et al., 2000). How organizations deal with this issue often raises ethical issues which may be mitigated by a careful and considerate approach to change management.

In business-to-business (B2B) e-commerce, access to sophisticated e-commerce often comes hand-in-hand with the need for 'plumbing in' of software and hardware, as is the case with Dell Inc., which means that business customers are locked into one big organization's facilities. This is a form of restriction of free choice. The main ethical issue here is that the business customer should be aware that a particular choice could mean there are significant implications for future freedom of choice.

Taking personal relationships out of all transactions may have the effect of dehumanizing the process. A client's relationship with an organization may have developed over years of loyal customer commitment. Reducing this to boxes ticked and computer-generated responses would, according to an ethic of care, result in the loss of the development of individual relationships, the human touch and the use of intuition. Such aspects may be viewed as necessary to the new electronic economy, but human networks are just as important a part of business practice as the efficiencies associated with e-commerce.

E-commerce also allows for the concealment of the real identity of suppliers of a product or service. This white labelling (products sold without clearly labelling the source/supplier) may offer extraordinarily misleading information about the source (Harris and Spence, 2002). This and many other ethical issues remain to be addressed, and progress seems to be slow.

5.7 Summary

This chapter covered what e-commerce is, the factors that contributed to its current shape and how it operates. It also discussed a number of benefits as well as problematic issues. This chapter serves as an introduction to e-commerce to facilitate understanding other e-commerce-related chapters (Chapters 10 and 17).

Potential benefits of e-commerce to organizations include: access to a wide market; cost savings; improved use of IT resources and business processes; better relationships with suppliers/customers; quick delivery of products and services; and a reduction in data entry and customer services-related errors. It is important to note that e-channels do not automatically bring these benefits, as other organizational issues also have to be dealt with.

Problematic issues in e-commerce implementation include:

- lack of proper integration of related systems;
- a culture of achieving only short-term targets;
- non-web-enabled business processes;
- lack of understanding and knowledge within the organization about e-commerce;
- lack of product differentiation and categorization;
- lack of understanding on the part of the customer community;
- difficulties in personalization of products;
- limited research and development;
- limited access to the Internet due to skills or connectivity issues;
- lack of understanding that the e-commerce initiative is a business critical area and not just a technical issue.

Existing organizational structure and unwillingness to change among employees is also often seen as one of the biggest hurdles in the implementation of e-commerce; we recommended a carefully planned and implemented change management strategy to address this.

These concerns are generic and reasonably well known. It is important that institutions embarking on e-commerce are fully aware of them, so that strategies can be developed to minimize their adverse effects. Additionally, each institution has its own set of organizational barriers that it needs to deal with when deciding to make a change in the way it operates in an online environment.

Glossary

Debit card   A debit card allows an account holder to access the funds in a current/ checking account electronically. Debit cards may be used to obtain cash from automated teller machines (ATM) or purchase goods or services using point-of-sale systems. The use of a debit card often involves immediate debiting and crediting of consumers' accounts.

Digital certificate   The electronic equivalent of an ID card that authenticates the source of a digital signature.

Digital signatures   A security option that uses two keys, one public and one private, which are used to encrypt messages before transmission and to decrypt them on receipt.

E-banking   In its very basic form, e-banking can mean the provision of information about a bank and its services via a homepage on the Internet. More sophisticated e-banking services provide customer access to accounts, the ability to move their money between different accounts and making payments or applying for loans via e-channels.

Electronic bill payment   An e-banking application whereby customers direct the financial institution to transfer funds to the account of another person or business. Payment is typically made by ACH credit or by the institution (or bill payment servicer) sending a paper cheque on the customer's behalf.

Encryption   A data security technique used to protect information from unauthorized inspection or alteration. Information is encoded so it appears as a meaningless string of letters and symbols during delivery or transmission. Upon receipt, the information is decoded using an encryption key.

HTML   Hypertext markup language: a set of codes that can be inserted into text files to indicate special typefaces, images and links to other hypertext documents.

Hyperlink   An item on a webpage that, when selected, transfers the user directly to another location in a hypertext document or to another webpage, perhaps on a different machine. Also simply called a 'link'.

Information management   Describes the measures required for the effective collection, storage, access, use and disposal of information to support business processes. The core of these measures is the management of the definition, ownership, sensitivity, quality and accessibility of information. These measures are addressed at appropriate stages in the strategic planning lifecycle and applied at appropriate stages in the operational lifecycle of the information itself.

Information systems   Organized collections of hardware, software, supplies, policies, procedures and people, which store, process and provide *access* to information.

Internet   A cooperative message-forwarding system linking computer networks all over the world.

Legacy systems   A term commonly used to refer to existing information systems and applications with which new systems or applications must exchange information.

Outsourcing   The practice of contracting with another entity to perform services that might otherwise be conducted in-house.

References

Becker, S.A. (2005). Technical Opinion: E-government Usability for Older Adults, *Communications of the ACM*, 48(2), 102–104.

Berger, S.C. and Gensler, S. (2007). Online Banking Customers: Insights from Germany, *Journal of Internet Banking and Commerce*, 12(1), 1–6. Available online at www.arraydev.com/commerce/jibc/2007-04/SvenBergerFinal_PDFVersion.pdf (accessed 20 August 2010).

Blount, Y., Castleman, T., and Swatman, P. (2005). E-Commerce, Human Resource Strategies, and Competitive Advantage: Two Australian Banking Case Studies, *International Journal of Electronic Commerce*, 9(3), 74–89. Available online at http://mesharpe.metapress.com/app/home/contribution.asp?referrer=parent&backto= issue,6,8;journal,14,32;linkingpublicationresults,1:106045,1 (accessed 20 August 2010).

Harris, L. and Spence, L. (2002) The Ethics of E-banking, *Journal of Electronic Commerce Research*, 3(2), 59–65.

Hirsh, L. (2002) The Case for E-business Outsourcing, *E-commerce Times*, 17 May. Available online at http://ecommercetimes.com/perl/story/17802.html (accessed 20 August 2010).

Kalakota, R. and Whinston, A. (1997) *Electronic Commerce: A Manager's Guide*. Reading, MA: Addison-Wesley Professional.

Kraemer, K. and Dedrick, J. (2001) *Dell Computer: Using E-commerce to Support the Virtual Company*. Available online at http://crito.uci.edu/papers/2001/dell_ecom_case_6-13-01.pdf (accessed 7 April 2010).

Krol, E. and Hoffman, E. (1993) *FYI on 'What is the Internet?'*. Available online at http://tools.ietf.org/html/rfc1462 (accessed 20 August 2010).

McDougall, P. (2007) Credit Suisse Outsources to BT in Deal Worth $1.1 Billion, *Information Week*, 13 February.

Pirakatheeswari, P. (2009) *Introduction to Electronic Retailing*. Available online at www.articlesbase.com/online-business-articles/introduction-to-electronic-retailing-1058777.html (accessed 7 April 2010).

Shah, M.H. and Siddiqui, F.A. (2006) Organizational Success Factors in E-banking at the Woolwich, *International Journal of Information Management*, 26, 442–456.

Turban, E., Lee, J., King, D., and Shung, H.M. (2000) *Electronic Commerce, a Managerial Perspective*. London: Prentice Hall.

Wang, Y.D. and Emurian, H.H. (2005) An Overview of Online Trust: Concepts, Elements, and Implications, *Computers in Human Behavior*, 21(1), 105–125.

Young, R.D., Lang, W.W., and Nolle, D.L. (2007) How the Internet Affects Output and Performance at Community Banks, *Journal of Banking & Finance*, 31, 1033–1060.

Further reading

Shah, M.H. and Clarke, S. (2009) *E-Banking Management: Issues, Solutions and Strategies*. Hershey: IGI Global.

Suggested activities

1 Based on any organization with which you are familiar, give reasons why they would trade online.

2 Discuss barriers that a traditional retailer might face if wishing to start trading online.

3 Consider possible future changes in technology and how they may affect e-commerce.

6 Quantitative methods

Caldico Ltd is a small firm that produces calendars and diaries for the UK and overseas markets. These include desk diaries, pocket diaries, wall calendars and so on. The diary operation is run separately from calendar production due to the different nature of the products. The diary production manager feels that better use could be made of resources, but finds it difficult to model operations, especially as there is very seasonal demand and other fluctuations. In particular, the costs of overtime and stock levels have been of concern. He thinks a different production plan might be able to help improve this. Without any suggestion for improvement it is likely that Caldico would continue to work in the same way.

Currently, the company works 12 four-week periods each year, involving administration, machine-minding, engineering, store-keeping, inspection and so on. Holidays total four weeks, one at Christmas and New Year, one at Easter and the first two weeks of August. Holiday pay is at the normal working week rate. The usual working week is 40 hours, and this costs a total of £2,400 per hour. Generally, administrative staff are not to work overtime, but when overtime is worked, a standing agreement between management and employees means that both the printing and binding machines will be staffed during any overtime working. Stockholding costs are valued at 1.8 per cent of average stock value per month. Overhead costs are around £200,000 per year.

The printing machine has ten parallel printing sections that operate independently of each other, but the machine can only produce one product at any one time. That is, it cannot simultaneously print different types of diary. Currently, the firm produces 14 different types of diary. In one hour, each section can print 100 business diaries, or 100 general diaries, or 60 of any other type of diary. The diary year can be changed instantly. The manufacturers give a set probability of any section breaking down and the firm has data on how long it takes to repair a section. The set-up time for changing from one run to another is 30 minutes.

The binding machine has seven parallel independent sections, but can only work on one product type at a time. Each section can bind 120 diaries per hour. The probability of section breakdown is known, as are repair times. If a section fails, it takes one hour to repair and is replaced at a cost of £60. There are currently 90 sections in stock in case of failure. If all seven sections are replaced in the same visit, it reduces time per section, which works out to be 3.5 hours for all sections, but each section is done one at a time, leaving six sections running (if just one needs repair). It may seem strange to replace sections that are not broken, but the management thinks this may sometimes be sensible as one worn section may indicate the others are due to fail. Setting up for a new run takes one hour. There has to be a minimum of a one hour gap between printing and binding.

Data on sales per diary, selling price per diary, contracts for the following year and the cost breakdown by materials is known, along with the average number of diaries made per unit of materials. Data on stock, supply orders and finished goods are also known. Initially, a spreadsheet was used to capture existing operations and model these to a level that satisfied management. By incorporating the known data with some 'what if?' scenarios, a better production plan was produced for the following year. This success led to management requesting a decision support system that incorporated all major operations, including production, sales and supplies. As a result, significant savings were made and Caldico's profit increased.

6.1 Intended learning outcomes

On completion of this chapter the reader should be able to:

1   use fractions, decimals, percentages, order of operations, simple algebra and indices;
2   employ descriptive statistics, such as centrality and dispersion;
3   create and interpret charts and graphs, including bar charts, line graphs and pie charts;
4   forecast with simple inference, including trends, moving averages and seasonal adjustments.

6.2 Introduction

This chapter provides an outline of some standard quantitative methods that should be sufficient for a non-specialist to gain an understanding of why these things are important and how they are addressed. Why are these things important to someone studying information systems (IS)? To manage resources it is essential that an organization can explain what is happening and can predict what will happen. Explanation and prediction can only be to a reasonable extent.

There is no such thing as perfect information. Given the data available, an organization that understands what is happening and attempts to forecast what will happen in the future will do better than one that doesn't, even though its forecasts will not be perfect. IS specialists must be able to work with people who are specialists in other areas. In fact, many people are employed in the area of decision support, and this requires a mix of skills, including knowledge of information technology (IT) and knowledge of how to use numerical data. Lots of decision support specialists started their career by taking a degree in business information systems (BIS) or business information technology (BIT). The key thing about these types of degree is that they are 'business' IS and 'business' IT, not just IS or IT. That means understanding both aspects and being able to use them together. Your knowledge and skills would be very incomplete if you could not relate the IS/IT side to business needs, and often those needs involve using the technology to help get the best use of available data. Finally on this point, you may aspire to be a manager. That involves budgets, forecasting, planning use of resources, reporting and so on. All of these will need a working knowledge of some basic mathematics and statistics.

6.3 Basic mathematics and statistics review

A manager who can interpret graphs and statistical data in the context of the business will be able to use resources more efficiently and effectively than one who cannot. There are some basic tools that are needed as a foundation. Without these, simple errors can be made that may have important consequences. This section will focus on fractions, decimals, percentages, order of operations, simple algebra and indices.

If you have the necessary background, this section could be skipped, but we suggest you look through it anyway, as you may find it helpful to review your knowledge. The order of operations in arithmetic is important. There is an old adage: 'Rubbish in, rubbish out.' We could add to that: 'Good data in, incorrectly processed, equals rubbish out.' In other words, you could have the most powerful computer and the most sophisticated spreadsheet, but if you use the tools incorrectly they are of less benefit than pen and paper used in the right way.

We normally think of numbers as 10 (ten), 6 (six), 3 (three) and so on. In fact, strictly speaking these should be 'plus ten', 'plus six' and 'plus three'. This is because they are what is known as positive numbers. As a convention, any number just stated as such (ten, six, three) is not preceded by the term 'plus'. We know it is positive, automatically, simply because we have not stated 'minus' in front of the number. For example, in the summer, the temperature might be 24°C. In fact, this is really +24°C. If you have not come across this concept before, just think about winter. Then the temperature might be below freezing and may be –3°C.

Simple fractions are really very intuitive and very easy to understand. If you have been frightened of 'doing fractions' in the past, read on! Let's start with something very simple. You have a cake. Each person is to get an equal amount of the cake (judged by the eye – in this case we are not worried about detailed accuracy by weight or volume). You cut the cake evenly in two, as shown in Figure 6.1. You now have two halves. If there were just two people each could have one-half of the cake. One-half is the same as $\frac{1}{2}$. This symbol simply means that there is a whole (the 1 on top, known as the numerator), and the whole has been divided into two (the 2 on the bottom, known as the denominator).

If you now cut the cake in two again, as in Figure 6.2, you could share between four friends and you would have one-quarter each or $\frac{1}{4}$ each. If two people shared the cake and one was hungrier than the other, one might have $\frac{3}{4}$, and one might have $\frac{1}{4}$. You could keep dividing the cake like this and have one-eighth each, one-sixteenth each and so on.

Let's suppose your cake is rectangular. You divide it into three equal pieces and two of these pieces are for you (shaded in Figure 6.3). Your amount is $\frac{2}{3}$ of the whole. The number of pieces you have (your share) is called the numerator. The number of pieces into which the whole is divided is called the denominator. In this case, '2' is the numerator and '3' is the denominator. In your friend's case, '1' is the numerator and '3' is the denominator. In Figure 6.4 the same cake has been cut into six pieces. If you take four pieces and your friend takes two, you have $\frac{4}{6}$ and your friend has $\frac{2}{6}$. But look at the cake – you have exactly the same proportion as before: $\frac{4}{6} = \frac{2}{3}$ and $\frac{2}{6} = \frac{1}{3}$.

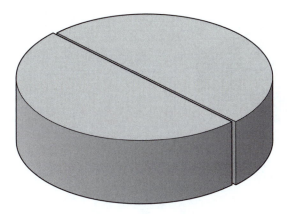

Figure 6.1 A cake cut in two.

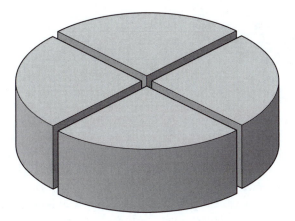

Figure 6.2 A cake cut in four.

Let's consider the first cake again. The cake has first been split into two, so each person could have 0.5 of the cake. When it is split into four, each person could have 0.25 of the cake. How does this work? Well, the decimal system simply takes the number 1 as a whole and divides this into ten parts, so if each person has half a cake they have half of the ten parts – five parts. The five parts are not five whole cakes though. They are five parts of a ten-part cake. The decimal point shows that the number '5' means 'five parts of something that has ten parts in total'. Half of 0.5 is 0.25. We have gone to a second decimal place. This means we have divided the whole into 100 parts. The number 0.25 means '25 parts out of a total of 100 parts'.

Dividing things into 100 parts is the basis of percentages. These are really very simple. When we divided the cake into two, we had $\frac{1}{2}$ or 0.5 each of the cake. In percentage terms this is expressed as 50 per cent each of the cake. The whole is 100 per cent. When we divided the cake into four, we had $\frac{1}{4}$ or 0.25 each (if four people had an equal amount each). This is the same as having 25 per cent each. Per cent actually means 'per 100 parts', so 25 per cent is 25 parts out of a total 100 parts.

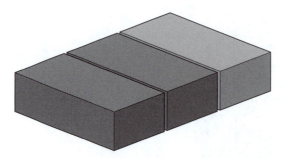

Figure 6.3 A rectangular cake cut into three.

Figure 6.4 A rectangular cake cut into six.

Why are we bothering with cakes? The cake example makes explanation very easy. In practice you would be more concerned with business concepts. Here are some examples. A firm wishes to increase productivity by 12 per cent next year. Last year IT expenditure rose by $\frac{1}{4}$ when compared with the previous year. A pay deal is proposed in which you would gain a 7 per cent increase over a three-year period, with a minimum increase this year of 2 per cent of your salary. If you do not know what these things mean, then how can you tell if your organization is doing well or if you are doing well?

Indices are also known as powers (indices is the plural of index). These powers are attached to a number and the number and power cannot be separated. That is, they are treated as a single item. For example, 3^2 ('three squared') means 3 multiplied by itself, which results in 9. Further, 5^3 ('five cubed') means $5 \times 5 \times 5$, which is 125. A square root of something is the number that, when multiplied by itself, will give that result. The square root of 100 is 10. The square root of 36 is 6. The square root of 49 is 7. A square root is sometimes denoted as a minus power. For example, 100^{-2} means 'the square root of 100'. In the case of $3 \times 3 = 3^2$, the 2 is the power or index. The 'normal' power of a number is 1. The number 10 is actually 10 to the power 1. The number 6 is 6 to the power 1. By convention, if we simply state a number then we assume it is to the power 1. If I wanted to tell you I have three eggs, I would not say 'I have three to the power 1 eggs', I would just say 'I have three eggs'.

The order of arithmetic operations is very important. There are a number of acronyms used to help us remember the correct order (BODMAS, BIDMAS, etc.). The order in which calculations are performed is:

Brackets
Index (or to the power Of)
Division
Multiplication
Addition
Subtraction

When we add or subtract numbers the order can be changed as long as the sign to the left of a number stays with it.

Example 1
$-5 + 7 = +7 - 5$
In this case the first + is dropped, so $-5 + 7 = 7 - 5$. (It is assumed that a number without a sign is positive.)

Example 2
$3 - 2 + 4 - 10 + 20 = 20 + 3 + 4 - 2 - 10$

(Notice 3 now has a + sign but 20 does not.)

Example 3
$2 + 3 \times 4 = 2 + 12 = 14$
(Multiply first.)

Align on the equals – here and elsewhere for similar layouts

Example 4
$3^2 - 5 \times 2 + 7 = 9 - 5 \times 2 + 7$ (index)
$= 9 - 10 + 7$ (×)
$= 16 - 10$ (+)
$= 6$ (−)

Example 5
$4 \times (5 + 3) = 4 \times 8$ (brackets)
$= 32$

Example 6
$2 + 5 - 8 \div 2 + 3 \times 4 - 2$
$= 2 + 5 - 4 + 3 \times 4 - 2$ (÷)
$= 2 + 5 - 4 + 12 - 2$ (×)
$= 19 - 4 - 2$ (+)
$= 13$ (−)

Note that $3(2 + 1)$ is the same as $3 \times (2 + 1)$. The × sign is usually left out if it is before brackets.

Algebra is something we use in everyday life. If you are someone who hated mathematics at school, algebra was likely to be one of the things about mathematics you hated the most, and you probably find it hard to believe we use it every day. It really is important and you cannot be a business-oriented person without it! Don't believe me? Try this. You buy ten apples and they cost 20p each. What is the total spent? Easy? Yes of course! You simply multiplied '10' (the number of apples) by '20' (the price in pence). The answer is of course 200p, or £2. Okay, let's now suppose that your friend bought ten apples and the total price was £2. You can calculate the price per apple to be 20p. This is algebra! Let's put these in algebraic formulations. First we have to define our variables.

a = number of apples – notice that a does not equal apples

t = total price

p = price per apple

$ap = t$

That means that the number of apples (a) multiplied by the price per apple (p) equals the total price (t). It is a lot quicker to put it in the algebraic form, isn't it?

If apples rise to 25p each and you now buy four apples, and you put these numbers into the formula, it will read $4(25) = 100p = £1$.

Let's go back to your friend who bought ten apples at a total price of £2 (200p).

We can transpose (switch round) the formula.

$t / a = p$

$200 / 100 = 20p$

This formula is a very basic one, but is very important. In economics it is:

$PQ = TR$

price $\times$ quantity = total revenue

We often use letters like X and Y to represent what are known as variables (things that can vary in quantity – apples, pay, inflation and so on). In economics a well-known equation is $Y = C + I + G + X - M$, where:

Y = national income (the income of a nation's economy, usually for a single year)
C = consumer expenditure
I = investment expenditure
G = government expenditure
X = income from exports
M = expenditure on imports.

If we know the values of almost all the variables, but we do not know the value of one of them, we can work it out by using simple algebra.

This section has provided a very brief review of fractions, decimals and percentages. If you do not feel comfortable with these things, then make sure you address them quickly. One thing is certain – these concepts will not go away. If you do not tackle them you will be caught out sooner or later.

6.4 Descriptive statistics

Very often when we look at data we want to know some key things. One of these is 'what is the middle value?' We have a number of possible middle values. These are known as measures of centrality. We usually call these the average value. We would also like to know how far the data is spread. For example, the average age of a group of people may be 25. This group may have ages ranging from three years old to 85 years old. Another group may also have an average age of 25, but with ages ranging from 22 to 27. Clearly, though they have the same average age, the groups are very different.

An average is a value that represents a middle point in the data. There are three main types of average: mean, median and mode. The mode is the most frequent value. The median is the middle value when the data is arranged in order of magnitude. The mean is the total of all values divided by the number of values. If we talk about the 'average' value of a group of data, without stipulating mean, median or mode, by convention we are generally referring to the mean value.

The number of goals scored by a football team in nine matches is:

3, 3, 0, 1, 2, 2, 0, 0, 1

The mean value = 14/9 (14 is the sum of the goals and 9 is the number of matches).

14/9 = 1.6 goals per match

The median value requires the data to be in order:

0, 0, 0, 1, 1, 2, 2, 3, 3

The middle value is 1 (the median).

The mode is the most frequently occurring value, which, in this case, is 0.

Sometimes data is grouped in frequencies (how often things occur). Suppose you were considering breakdowns of a printing machine, and you looked at weekly data. The following table shows that over a period of time, there were three weekly periods in which the machine broke down twice. There were five weeks during which the machine broke down three times (in each week). There was just one week in which the machine broke down six times. It did not break down more than six times in any week. What is the average number of breakdowns?

x	2	3	4	5	6
f	3	5	8	4	1

Note that x is the number of breakdowns in a week and f is the number of weeks that this number of breakdowns occurred. To find the mean value we need to sum (add up) the number of x values. This is done as follows:

$$3 \times 2 + 5 \times 3 + 8 \times 4 + 4 \times 5 + 1 \times 6$$
$$= 6 + 15 + 32 + 20 + 6$$
$$= 79$$

There are 21 occurrences (found by adding the frequencies $3 + 5 + 8 + 4 + 1$). The mean value is $79 / 21 = 3.76$. In other words, on average, the machine breaks down 3.76 times per week.

Now we can calculate measures of centrality, but what about comparing two lots of data and measures of dispersion (spread)? Suppose there are two football teams, A and B, and we need to choose one of them to take part in a competition. In this competition consistency is important. In order to make our decision we will use the number of goals they scored in their last 11 matches.

| A: | 4 | 7 | 0 | 1 | 2 | 0 | 6 | 7 | 4 | 2 | 0 |
| B: | 3 | 3 | 2 | 3 | 3 | 3 | 2 | 4 | 4 | 3 | 3 |

We will first consider the mean number of goals for each team:

Team A mean: $33 / 11 = 3$
Team B mean: $33 / 11 = 3$

The means are equal so we must use other criteria. As consistency is important we need to find some way of measuring the spread of the data.

The range is the largest value minus the smallest value.

Range A: $7 - 0 = 7$
Range B: $4 - 2 = 2$

As Team B has a lower range than Team A, we would choose Team B, but in general, although the range is very easy to find, it can be distorted by a very high or a very low figure, particularly if there is a large amount of data.

The interquartile range is an alternative. As you saw earlier, the median divides the data into two halves. If the two halves are then divided into two halves each, we now have four quarters. The middle value (half-way) is still the median. The value at the lowest quarter is the lower quartile and the value at the three-quarter point is the upper quartile. To find the median and quartiles the data must first be put in numerical order. Using Teams A and B again, we have:

A:	0	0	0	1	2	2	4	4	6	7	7
B:	2	2	3	3	3	3	3	3	3	4	4

The median and interquartile values are

A:	0	2	6	interquartile range: $6-0=6$
B:	3	3	3	interquartile range: $3-3=0$

This method reduces the impact of odd values that are out of the norm. Team B still appears to be the most consistent team using this method. The standard deviation uses all the values and gives a more useful measure of spread.

You need to learn some symbols. The sign for square root is √, but sometimes this has a line across the top so it is clear it includes all the numbers under the line. A square root is a number that, when multiplied by itself, gives another number (the square). The square root of 100 is 10. The square root of 64 is 8. The square root of 9 is 3.

Σ is used to mean 'sum' (add up), so if I had four quotes for a new computer, and I decided that each quote would be x (x_1, x_2, x_3, x_4), then Σx would mean add up all the values of x. I could then find the mean value by dividing by four (the number of quotes), and this would appear in a formula as: $(\Sigma x)/n$, where n is the number of quotes.

The formula for standard deviation is:

$$\sqrt{\frac{\sum (x-\bar{x})^2}{n}},$$

where $\bar{x}$ is the mean.

Using the football team data (mean = 3):

	A			B	
x	$(x-\bar{x})$	$(x-\bar{x})^2$	x	$(x-\bar{x})$	$(x-\bar{x})^2$
4	1	1	3	0	0
7	4	16	3	0	0
0	−3	9	2	−1	1
1	−2	4	3	0	0
2	−1	1	3	0	0
0	−3	9	3	0	0
6	3	9	2	−1	1
7	4	16	4	1	1
4	1	1	4	1	1
2	−1	1	3	0	0
0	−3	9	3	0	0
Σ	$(x-\bar{x})^2 = 76$		Σ	$(x-\bar{x})^2 = 4$	

Standard deviation for Team A:

$$\sigma = \sqrt{\frac{76}{11}} = 2.63.$$

Standard deviation for Team B:

$$\sigma = \sqrt{\frac{4}{11}} = 0.60.$$

Note the use of σ (sigma) for the standard deviation. The formula can also be written as:

$$\sigma = \sqrt{\frac{\sum x^2}{n} - \left(\frac{\sum x}{n}\right)^2}.$$

Many people can calculate a standard deviation, but many people do not have a clue what it means! Here is a secret! Don't tell anybody! We would like to know, how far away the data is 'on average' from the mean. The problem is that the mean is in the middle, so on average the data for Teams A and B would both be zero distance from the mean. This is because some of the values are above the mean and some are below, and because the mean is in the middle the negative and positive differences cancel out, so using a mean calculation will always give us zero. This is no help at all. In fact, the standard deviation overcomes this by getting the square of all values to start with.

A positive number, multiplied by another positive number, results in a positive, and a negative multiplied by a negative gives a positive result. If the individual numbers are above or below the mean, if we square the difference between the actual number and the mean it will therefore always give a positive answer. By doing this we can see how far away the data is from the mean, but this is in squared values.

The square root in the formula brings us back to original values. Here is the secret. Intuitively, the standard deviation tells us how far away the data is from the mean on average. It is no more than that, but it is a special type of average. From the above, we can see that Team B is the most consistent.

6.5 Charts and graphs

A graph is a diagram showing the relationship between two variables. It consists of two axes: the *x*-axis and the *y*-axis. The point where these two axes meet is called the *origin*.

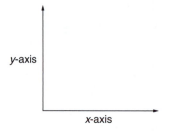

Figure 6.5 Two axes of a graph.

A point on a graph is given as a pair of coordinates: (x, y). The x coordinate is always given first as X comes before Y in the alphabet. The x coordinate is how far the point is along the x-axis and the y coordinate is how far the point is along the y-axis.

In Figure 6.6, the x coordinate of point A is 3; the y coordinate of point A is 2. Point A has coordinates (3, 2). Often it is necessary to extend the axes in order to allow our variables to take negative values. A point on the graph is given coordinates in exactly the same way as before. In Figure 6.7, point A has coordinates (5, 10); point B has coordinates (10, –10); point C has coordinates (–5, 5); point D has coordinates (–10, –10).

Line graphs may be used when data is continuous. For example, time can be split infinitely. In general, we tend to work to years, months, weeks, days, hours, minutes and seconds, but nuclear physicists might use millionths of a second as a norm. Time itself is continuous and we are merely limited by our ability to measure it. In Figure 6.8, it is reasonable to assume that the rate of inflation for each year can be connected to the previous or next year, as the rate would have varied over time and not jumped suddenly from one value to the next. This means that each point value can be joined to the next.

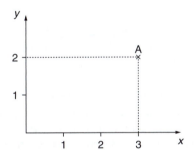

Figure 6.6 Coordinates.

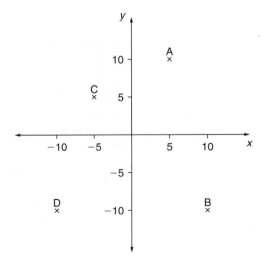

Figure 6.7 More coordinates.

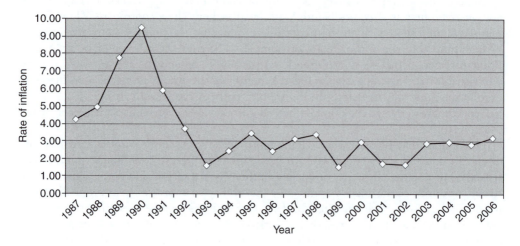

Figure 6.8 Rate of inflation, UK, 1987–2006.

A histogram may also be used for continuous data, but is generally used when the data are grouped to show frequencies. For example, if you took a sample of students' ages you might group data by those between 18 and less than 21, 21 and less than 24, 24 and less than 27, and so on.

If you did a survey of tourists in London and asked the respondents their country of origin, based on what is stated in their passports, you could show the results on a bar chart (Figure 6.9). It would not be reasonable to join the data, as it is not continuous. A respondent could not answer 'I am from half-way between Germany and France.' The same data could be shown as a pie chart (Figure 6.10).

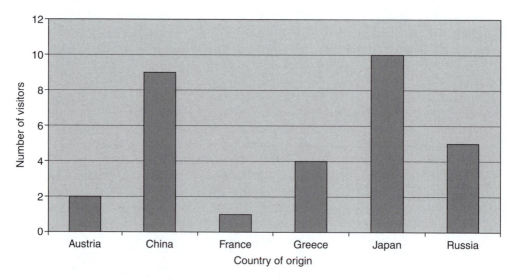

Figure 6.9 Number of visitors to London by country of origin.

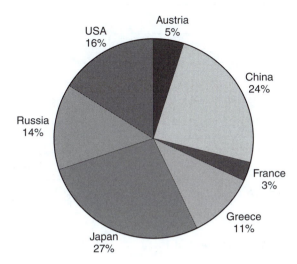

Figure 6.10 Percentage of visitors to London by country of origin.

6.6 Inference

Having used descriptive statistics to look at the past and present, we often want to consider the future. What happens if sales continue changing as they have been for the past few years? Would we need to increase the workforce? Would we need more production equipment? Would our cash flow enable us to sustain increases in sales because we would have to purchase more raw materials, and their prices have increased?

Let us look at an example of inference. Suppose we know that there is currently a shortage of trained nurses in the country. This shortage has increased over the past five years. Other things being equal (that is, without a major change in policies, the economy and so on) we can make an informed guess that if the changes over the past five years continue in a similar pattern, there will be even more of a shortage of trained nurses. This informed guess is a type of *inference*. We have inferred what is likely to happen. It is not fact, though it is based on fact. It is not opinion, such as 'I think painting A is much better than painting B'. It is inference.

Now let us take this example a bit further. Suppose we also know that, generally speaking, the elderly tend to need more medical care than the rest of the population. Let us also suppose that we know that over the past ten years the elderly population in the country has been rising. Other things being equal, we can infer what the size of the elderly population will be in five years time, and we can tell that it will be greater than it is today. If we couple this with our knowledge of the medical needs of the elderly, and our inference that in five years there will be an even bigger shortage of trained nurses, we can see that it would be useful to have more detailed ideas about numbers. How much will the elderly population increase? How much more will this require in terms of medical care? How many more trained nurses would we need to provide this care? Basic statistical inference can help address these questions.

One of the first things we would consider is a trend. There are many ways to do this. A simple one is by eye. Figure 6.11 shows how MBA salaries in the USA (in dollars)

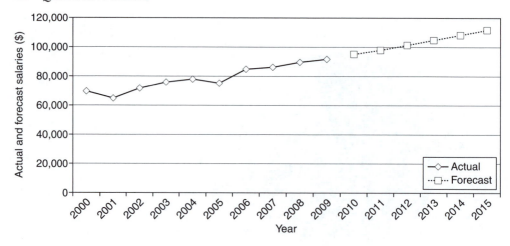

Figure 6.11 Actual and forecast USA MBA salaries 2000–2015.

have changed over the period 2000–2009. Notice that the changes are not the same every year. Despite fluctuations, we can see an upward trend. Simply by putting a ruler on the data line, we can get a good idea of this trend and use it to forecast future MBA salaries. Another way of doing this is to calculate the average increase per annum over the known period (2000–2009), and use this to forecast future salaries. In this case there is an average increase of 3.26 per cent. The forecast salaries are based on this figure.

A simple means of gaining a slightly more sophisticated trend, and of smoothing the data, is a moving average. This is a form of average that has been adjusted to allow for seasonal or cyclical components of a time series. It is often used to make the long-term trends of a time series clearer. When a variable, like the number of unemployed or the rate of inflation, is graphed against time, there are likely to be considerable seasonal or cyclical components in the variation. These may make it difficult to see the underlying trend. A suitable moving average can help make things clearer. Using the new car registration data shown in Table 6.1, we can construct a moving average for this highly seasonal data. Notice that it is fairly easy to see the seasonality by the way the data moves up and down from quarter to quarter, with similar patterns in each year. This is a well-known phenomenon, as spending on certain items may vary significantly according to the time of year.

The number of periods used to calculate the averaging process is based on judgement. The longer the length of the average, the smoother the series becomes, as each individual piece of information becomes less significant on its own; but the more periods used for the average, the less noticeable are changes in the underlying trend. If few periods are used, the smoothing becomes less effective.

With new car registration data, we want to remove the seasonality factor while still seeing the trend year-on-year. An average of this data every fourth period should enable us to achieve this. Having decided this, we then average the first four observations. This gives us the moving average for the mid-point of these four observations. In Table 6.1 this is 363,356. For the next moving average figure, we drop the first data value and pick up the next one. This continues until we no longer have four data figures available.

Table 6.1 New car registrations, UK, 2004 (Q4)–2009 (Q3)

Year/Qtr	Cars	Four-point moving average
2004 Q4	269,901	
2005 Q1	384,286	
Q2	355,678	363,356
Q3	443,560	364,414
Q4	274,132	376,423
2006 Q1	432,322	387,538
Q2	400,137	409,867
Q3	532,876	417,243
Q4	303,638	419,469
2007 Q1	441,224	419,469
Q2	400,137	420,853
Q3	538,413	425,070
Q4	320,507	428,849
2008 Q1	456,340	434,407
Q2	422,367	440,424
Q3	562,480	440,424
Q4	320,507	446,428
2009 Q1	480,358	451,986
Q2	444,597	459,387
Q3	592,084	

Source: based on data from SMMT (2010).

The calculations for the first two points of the moving average are as follows:

$$(269{,}901 + 384{,}286 + 355{,}678 + 443{,}560) / 4 = 363{,}356$$

$$(384{,}286 + 335{,}678 + 443{,}560 + 274{,}132) / 4 = 364{,}414$$

Having calculated the moving average we can plot this against the original data (see Figure 6.12).

To forecast one period ahead, we simply use the last moving average value that is known and add to it the seasonality factor. We do this by checking, on average for each quarter, how far above or below the trend (in this case moving average) the data values are. In this case, the average difference for each quarter between the data and the moving average is:

Q1: 29,211
Q2: 14,194
Q3: 107,544
Q4: –113,096

Based on this, we can now forecast a value for Q3 in 2009. Our moving average value for Q2 in 2009 is 459,387, and we use this as a starting point. We know that

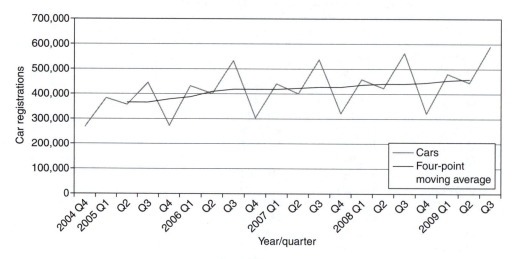

Figure 6.12 New car registrations, UK, 2004 (Q4)–2009 (Q3).

Q3 is on average 107,544 above the trend. We therefore add the two figures together to get a total of 566,931. The actual value was 592,084, so we did fairly well. No forecasts will be 100 per cent correct 100 per cent of the time. We may have improved the forecast a little by a small adjustment. We can see that there is an upward trend in the moving average, and we can calculate that this changes by an average of 6,002 per quarter. Adding this to our forecast gave us a value of 572,933, making it a little closer to the actual value. In fact, our final forecast is 97 per cent of the actual value. Most forecasters would be delighted with that level of accuracy.

There are other methods of finding and extrapolating the trend, such as simple linear regression. There are also some simple forecasting methods, such as exponential smoothing. These are not covered within this book, but may be part of your programme of study. The essence of the approaches is the same in every case. What is the general movement (trend)? What is the seasonal movement? What is the cyclical movement? We have not covered the latter here, but you should be aware that cyclical movements are to do with variations around a trend that form patterns, and which are not within a single year.

6.7 Summary

This chapter has covered some basic mathematics, descriptive statistics and commonly used graphs, and has given an introduction to simple inference. It outlined why these things might be important to someone studying IS. A case study was provided to demonstrate what kinds of improvements might be needed at an organization and how appropriate use of statistical techniques could help. It also indicated that IS can have an important role in such improvement.

The next chapter discusses accounting and finance.

Glossary

Average   Middle point of a data set.

Continuous data   Data that represents something that is joined continuously, such as time.

Discrete data   Data that represents things that are not joined, such as country of residence.

Dispersion   The spread of data.

Histogram   A type of graph, using bars to represent values, often used with frequency-grouped data.

Inference   The use of reasoned judgement to reach a conclusion.

Interquartile range   A measure of dispersion. The upper quartile minus the lower quartile.

Line graph   A graph used to represent continuous data.

Mean   A measure of centrality. The most commonly used form of average. Calculated by adding the data values and dividing the total by the number of data values used.

Median   A measure of centrality. The middle point of an ordered set of data.

Mode   A measure of centrality. The most frequently occurring value in a data set.

Pie chart   A chart used to show proportions.

Range   A measure of dispersion in a data set, found by subtracting the smallest value from the largest value.

Seasonality   Variation in data caused by seasons.

Standard deviation   A commonly used measure of dispersion.

Trend   The underlying general movement in a data set.

References

SMMT (2010) *New Car Registrations, UK, 2004 (Q4)–2009 (Q3)*. Available online at www.smmt.co.uk/dataservices/vehicleregistrations.cfm (accessed 4 September 2010).

Further reading

Leekley, M. (2010) *Applied Statistics for Business and Economics*. New York: Routledge.

Suggested activities

1   Using the example shown in Figure 6.11, based on the data below, calculate the average percentage increase in salary. Use this trend to forecast salaries across the period 2010–2015. Compare your answers with Figure 6.11.

Year	Salary ($)	Year	Salary ($)
2000	70,000	2006	85,000
2001	65,000	2007	86,000
2002	72,000	2008	90,000
2003	76,000	2009	92,000
2004	78,000		
2005	75,000		

2   Name four purchases for which sales are likely to be affected by seasonality, and name four items that are unlikely to be affected by seasonality.

3   For the new car registrations example, provide a forecast for Q4.

4   Think of five things that would be important for a large electronics business to forecast, and explain their significance.

7 Accounting and finance

Case study 7.1 Computers-R-Us

This fictitious case study was prepared by the authors to facilitate class discussion rather than to illustrate effective or ineffective management practices. It is not intended to refer to any real organization that exists currently or that has existed previously, and any resemblance to any such an organization is coincidental.

Your friend has completed a degree in computing. After working for someone else for three years, he set up a small business selling and repairing personal computers – Computers-R-Us. He shows you his accounts for year 1 and is pleased that he has made a substantial net profit of £20,300, which is very reasonable for a small business of this type in its first year of trading. Note: COGS is cost of goods sold.

Profit and loss account for year 1	£	£
Sales		151,000
Less COGS		110,000
Gross profit		41,000
Less Expenses		
Rent	15,000	
Electricity	3,000	
Advertising	1,200	
Depreciation (van)	1,000	
Other expenses	500	
		20,700
Net profit		20,300

Figure 7.1 A simple profit and loss account.

Despite the net profit, your friend is concerned that over the year he has often been overdrawn at the bank. Though technically very able, he has no background in accounting and finance, and asks you how it is that he makes a nice profit but runs up bank bills for overdrafts. Once you look through his books for the year you realize the problem – cash flow. He is allowing debtors longer to make their payments to him than he is allowing himself time to pay creditors. Also, the timings of payments through the year could be adjusted to be more favourable. With small adjustments there will be no need to overdraw at all next year!

Balance sheet as at the end of year 1	£	£
Fixed assets		
Van at cost		10,000
Less Depreciation		1,000
		9,000
Current assets		
Closing stock		5,400
Debtors and prepayments		4,700
Bank balance		1,200
		11,300
Less current liabilities		
Creditors and accruals		1,900
Net current assets	9,400	
Total net assets	18,400	
Capital		
Capital introduced		18,000
Add net profit		20,300
		38,300
Less drawings		–19,900
		18,400

Figure 7.2 A simple balance sheet.

7.1 Intended learning outcomes

On completion of this chapter the reader should be able to:

1   explain the differences between various organizational types;
2   outline the main sources of funds for organizations;
3   describe the nature and use of financial accounting, why accounts are prepared and how they may be used;

4   interpret the basic accounts of an organization;
5   use financial ratios to assess the performance of an organization;
6   provide an outline of the nature and use of management accounting.

7.2 Introduction

This chapter outlines basics of accounting and finance that should be sufficient for a non-specialist to gain understanding as to why these things are important and how they are addressed. *Gross domestic product* (GDP) is the total value of goods and services in a country over a specified time period. The United Kingdom's GDP totals around £1.5 trillion per annum; the USA's is around $14.3 trillion per annum; the European Union's is around €10.5 trillion per annum. Imagine if no one knew how much money organizations had spent and how that money was used. Imagine trying to look back and assess how well your firm had done over the past year if you had no basis to do so. Imagine everyone having a different base of accounting with no means of comparison. Imagine trying to forecast resource costs and sales for the coming year with no basis to do it. Accounting enables us to address these issues.

Financial accounting is mainly for external requirements, and includes recording transactions, summarizing transactions and reporting. It is subject to a regulatory framework that is authorized by the government. That is, all organizations have to meet certain national standards. Note that such standards are different from country to country. Management accounting is largely for internal (the organization's) requirements, and includes decision-making, planning, estimating and forecasting, measuring efficiency and capital expenditure. Management accounting is not subject to any regulatory framework.

In the United Kingdom there are a number of professional accounting bodies. The main ones are: the Institute of Chartered Accountants in England and Wales (ICAEW); the Institute of Chartered Accountants of Scotland (ICAS); the Institute of Chartered Accountants in Ireland (ICAI – a UK organization as it operates in Northern Ireland); the Association of Chartered Certified Accountants (ACCA); the Chartered Institute of Management Accountants (CIMA); and the Chartered Institute of Public Finance and Accountancy (CIPFA). Each has its own specialization and history, and each has a code of conduct for its members. There are similar professional bodies in many countries.

7.3 Organizational types

An organization may involve just one person, or it may involve many thousands. A sole trader (or sole proprietor) is an organizational entity that is just the owner (one person). The main sources of finance for a sole trader are capital introduced by the owner, loans from friends and family, bank borrowings through overdrafts or loans (often secured against the owner's personal and business assets) and profits put back into the business.

There is no distinction legally between the owner and the firm, and the owner's finances are the organization's finances, with all business debts deemed to be debts of the owner. Typical sole traders operate small shops, market stalls or small consultancies, for example. A sole trader may use an operating name that is different from the owner's legal name. For example, Fred Bloggs may trade under the name 'FB Autoparts', while Shamim Khan might use the trade name 'Flowers-R-Us'. Different countries have different rules about registering a trade name. Regardless of the trade name, the owner is not separate from the business in regard to financial and legal obligations.

There are a number of advantages to being a sole trader. Little or no work is required in terms of legalities to start the business or to dissolve it. As a sole trader, business is not separate from the individual so the accounts are simple. A sole trader can also react quickly to market changes without the need for lengthy consultation. The accounts for a sole trader are private. That is, they are not open to the public to view. There are disadvantages to being a sole trader. In particular, the individual's assets are at risk, which can include their car, home and anything else that may be of value. All the onus of managing and running the business falls on one person. Trying to raise finance may be difficult, as the only assets available are those of the owner. It is not possible to sell shares (as they do not exist for this type of business). A sole trader will not have the comfort of a company pension scheme. If they wanted a pension scheme this would have to be taken out privately, and would often be more expensive than for an employee in a company that had negotiated a bulk contract with a provider. If the owner is ill, the business may have to close for that time. Taking holidays may prove to be very difficult.

Another form of business is a partnership. In the United Kingdom a partnership is defined in the Partnership Act of 1890 as: 'The relation which subsists between persons carrying on a business in common with a view of profit.' In many ways being in a partnership is similar to being a sole trader. The typical sources of finance for a partnership are capital introduced by the partners, loans from family and friends, bank borrowings through overdrafts and loans (often secured against either the partnership's assets or the personal assets of individual partners) and profits put back into the business. Examples of typical businesses involving partnerships are small hotels, legal firms, accountancy firms, finance brokers and small insurance brokers.

A partnership means the problems and pleasures of running the business may be shared. It enables possible access to greater expertise and financial input, with two people bringing their own ranges of experiences and knowledge to the business.

Both losses and profits are shared, so the impact of difficult trading times may be lessened on each individual. Few legal formalities are involved, and usually a partnership agreement is drawn up to avoid misunderstandings. The legal rules relating to the accounts of partnerships vary from country to country. Typically, financial results do not have to be made public and accounting is fairly simple. In some countries the accounts must be open to show the financial implications of the partnership agreement. This would include items such as shares of profits and losses, capital introduced and withdrawn by each partner, drawings made by each partner, whether any partners are to receive a guaranteed salary, interest charged on drawings and interest allowed on capital balances.

Partnerships can have some disadvantages compared to being a sole trader. Personality clashes could threaten the business and may eventually result in the break-up of the partnership. In some cases – for example, if a married couple run a small hotel – such a business break-up can also mean a personal-break up. Partnerships may not have much more access to funding than that available to sole traders.

The next type of organization to consider is the limited company (UK terminology). Sources of finance for limited companies can include some of the things mentioned previously, but the common source is through issuing shares. A limited company is a separate (from the owners) legal entity, able to trade, own assets and owe liabilities (including taxes on profit) in its own right, independently from owners. The owner-ship of a limited company is divided into shares. Owners (known as shareholders or members) have limited liability for debts of a company. The management of the company is in the hands of directors, who might own only a small part of the share capital. Private limited companies (Ltd) cannot sell shares to the public. Public limited companies (PLC) can sell shares to the public. Directors are elected by shareholders. The major advantage of a limited company is that any debts are owed by the company as an entity, not by the owners.

Limited companies are required to publish their accounts, so there is a lack of secrecy about finances. There are extra costs involved in complying with legislation. In the United Kingdom, this includes the appointment of an auditor for large companies. Formal shareholder meetings must be held, and annual returns must be completed and sent to government. The accounting requirements for limited companies are more onerous than for sole traders or partnerships. Most shares are ordinary – the 'equity capital' of the company. Each ordinary share has equal rights to votes and dividends. Each share has a 'nominal' value, e.g. 25p. Some companies issue preference shares, which have a fixed dividend that is paid before the ordinary dividend. Some companies issue convertible shares or loans, which can be changed into ordinary shares in the future.

7.4 Financial accounting

The main financial statements prepared by an organization are the *profit and loss account* (sometimes called the *income statement*), the *balance sheet* and the *cash flow statement*. These are used to show the financial position of an organization at a particular point in time and its financial performance over a period of time, as well as to meet legal require-ments in completing them. To be able to understand financial reports requires under-standing of the terminology.

Assets are what an organization owns. They are split into fixed assets (sometimes called non-current assets) and current assets. *Fixed assets* are used within the organiza-tion and expected to be useful for longer than 12 months. They include land, build-ings, machinery, computers and vehicles. Note that these things are not bought with the main intention of being used for resale. They are there to help the firm produce its goods or services. *Current assets* are expected to be turned into cash within 12 months. They are purchased or manufactured for the purpose of resale. They include stock, trade debts, prepayments, bank balances and cash balances.

Liabilities are what an organizations owes (debt). They are split into current liabili-ties and long-term liabilities. *Current liabilities* are owed to suppliers for goods and services purchased on credit terms, and need to be paid within 12 months of the balance sheet date. They include trade credit, accruals, overdrafts and loans. *Long-term liabilities* are amounts owed which have to be repaid after an interval of time which is longer than 12 months. They include mortgages and other long-term loans.

Capital includes cash and any other assets introduced to an organization by the owners. It grows when profits are made. It reduces when losses are made. It may also be reduced by withdrawals of assets by owners or increased by additions by the owners.

Assets + expenses = liabilities + capital + income. This is known as the accounting equation and is the basis of the double-entry book-keeping system. It is known as a 'double-entry' system because each transaction is recorded in at least two accounts. Each transaction requires at least one account to be debited and at least one account to be credited with the total debits of the transaction equal to the total credits. The concept of debits and credits can be confusing because they are dependent upon perspective. If Company X sells something to Company Y and Company Y pays Company X by cheque, Company X credits the account 'Sales' and debits the account 'Bank'. Company Y debits the account 'Purchases' and credits the account 'Bank'. Expenses and income are summarized in the profit and loss account. Assets, liabilities and capital are summarized in the balance sheet. Table 7.1 shows some examples of assets, liabilities and capital in a firm that manufactures small metal toy cars.

In preparing accounts, certain adjustments have to be made. Accruals are expenses incurred, but for which the organization has not yet paid. These are added to expenses for the financial period. Prepayments are expenses paid in advance for a future period. They reduce expenses for the financial period. Depreciation is the loss in value of fixed assets; this must be estimated – for example, a van bought for £10,000 now will not be worth £10,000 in five years' time. There are two main methods of estimating depreciation. The *straight method* has equal depreciation over an asset's life. The *reducing balance method* has higher depreciation in earlier periods than in later periods. Unsold stock at the end of a financial period is valued at the lower of cost or net realizable value. The concept of prudence requires that stock is not valued at 'normal' selling price as profit must not be included before goods are sold.

Sales are the value of the year's sold goods or services, regardless of whether or not payment has been received. *Cost of good sold* (COGS) are the year's purchases, whether paid for or not, adjusted for unsold stock. Sales minus COGS equals gross profit.

Expenses are the 'overheads' of the business for the year, adjusted as needed for accruals and prepayments. Gross profit minus expenses equals net profit. Figures 7.1 and 7.2 show a simple profit and loss account and a simple balance sheet.

Table 7.1 Examples of assets, liabilities and capital

	Current asset	Fixed asset	Current liability	Long-term liability	Capital
Metal-forming machine		✓			
£7,000 owed by a customer	✓				
Boxes in which the cars are sold	✓				
Delivery van		✓			
£20,000 borrowed from a relative to be paid back over five years				✓	
£30,000 introduced by the owner					✓
Metal sheets used to make the cars	✓				
Bank account with an overdraft of £2,000			✓		
Cash of £500	✓				
Benches on which the toy cars are packed into boxes		✓			
Stationery for which payment has not yet been made			✓		

Notice that the profit and loss account is *for* Year 1, but the balance sheet is as *at the end of* Year 1. This is because the profit and loss account shows the flows of income and expenses into and out of the organization over a period of time, whereas the balance sheet shows the assets, liabilities and capital as a 'snapshot' at a fixed period in time.

The simple profit and loss account is fairly straightforward. The COGS is deducted from sales to find gross profit. COGS would be, for example, the cost of computers that someone buys to sell on for a profit. Expenses such as rent are deducted from gross profit to arrive at net profit. In the balance sheet the van is a fixed asset and its value is adjusted for depreciation. The net current assets are added to the fixed assets (after depreciation adjustment) to give total net assets. The capital introduced plus the net profit are summed and drawings are deducted – the owner has to live! The result should equal the value of net current assets. In other words, the balance sheet must balance!

All PLCs have to present cash flow statements as part of their published annual reports, and they are regarded as primary statements of equal importance to the profit and loss account and balance sheet. Table 7.2 shows Tesco PLC's cash flow statement for February 2008.

Cash flows are the lifeblood of a business and are different from profit and loss. Overall, a business could make a profit but may not reach that point because of a lack

Table 7.2 Tesco PLC's cash flow statement for February 2008

Year ended 23 February 2008	2008 £m	2007 £m
Cash generated from operations	4,099	3,532
Interest paid	(410)	(376)
Corporation tax paid	(346)	(545)
Net cash from operating activities	3,343	2,611
Net cash used in investing activities	(2,954)	(2,343)
Cash flows from financing activities		
Dividends paid	(792)	(467)
Other net cash flows on financing activities	1,204	(66)
Net cash from/(used in) financing activities	412	(533)
Reconciliation of net cash flow to movement in net debt		
Net increase/(decrease) in cash and cash equivalents	801	(265)
Net cash inflows from debt and lease financing	(1,827)	(268)
Short-term investments	360	–
Movement in joint venture loan receivables	36	38*
Other non-cash movements	(691)	18
Increase in net debt in the year	(1,321)	(477)
Opening net debt	(4,861)	(4,509)
Adjustment for joint venture loan receivables	–	125*
Adjusted opening net debt	(4,861)	(4,384)
Closing net debt	(6,182)	(4,861)

Source: adapted from Tesco (2008).

Notes
* The measurement of net debt has been revised to include loans receivable from joint ventures. Going forward net debt will be stated inclusive of the loan receivables from joint ventures. The reconciliation of net cash flow to movement in net debt is not a primary statement and does not form part of the Summary Group cash flow statement.

of cash. A cash flow statement summarizes the cash inflows and outflows over the past financial period. A cash flow forecast attempts to anticipate future cash flows. Cash flows are important to ensure that sufficient cash funds are available as and when needed for the business. Drawing up a cash flow forecast shows whether there is likely to be enough cash available to pay salaries and settle debts on time. It estimates the firm's reserves, which could be invested in expansion projects or new equipment. It helps identify when shortfalls are likely to happen, and surplus funds are likely to become available, and this helps plan for when the firm might need an overdraft, or be able to reinvest its reserves into the business.

Ratios may be used to interpret the performance of an organization. The *gross profit margin* is the percentage of gross profit to sales and is useful as a measure of production efficiency in a manufacturing company or sales efficiency in a trading business. If the gross profit margin is too low, it is unlikely to be able to support the overheads. *Net profit margin* is the ratio of pre-tax net profit to sales and is a measure of the firm's overall profitability. This is the main initial indicator of financial performance in the United Kingdom. Anything over 10 per cent is good, over 25 per cent is excellent, and anything below 5 per cent is questionable unless it is planned and short-term. Why? If net profit is too low the owners may be better off putting their money elsewhere. Economists call this *opportunity cost*.

The main indicators of solvency are the *current ratio* and its close relative, the *acid test ratio*.

Current ratio = current assets / current liabilities
Acid test ratio = current assets − stock/current liabilities

A current ratio of 1 : 1 means that cash available in current assets is sufficient to pay the debts listed in the current liabilities. If the ratio is less than 1 : 1 it could indicate that the firm might occasionally have minor cash flow problems. If the ratio is substantially less it could indicate that the firm may have serious financial problems.

The acid test ratio is bound to be less than the current ratio, but if it is substantially less it could indicate that the firm was unable to sell its stock sufficiently quickly to pay all of its debts and could have financial problems. It could also indicate that the firm is carrying too much stock.

A high *gearing ratio* shows that the firm is borrowing heavily. This indicates that the firm might be vulnerable to increases in interest rates.

Gearing ratio = bank borrowing / total assets

Return on capital employed indicates if the company is making efficient use of its finance.

Return on capital employed = pre-tax profit / net assets

The *interest coverage ratio* is used to determine how easily a company can pay interest expenses on outstanding debt. The ratio is calculated by dividing a company's earnings before interest and taxes (EBIT) by the company's interest expenses for the same period. The lower the ratio, the more the company is burdened by debt expense. When a company's interest coverage ratio is only 1.5 or lower, its ability to meet interest expenses may be questionable.

Interest coverage ratio = EBIT / interest expense

An example should help. Figures 7.3 and 7.4 show the ABC Ltd trading and profit and loss account and balance sheet for 2009 (note: WIP means 'work in progress'). ABC Ltd is a hi-tech company that makes electronic devices for the sports market and has been trading for three years. If you were considering investing in this company, there would be a number of questions you would ask:

- Are its sales and profits growing healthily?
- Is it planning ahead?
- How might its gross margin be improved?
- How might its net margin be improved?
- Are the company assets being used efficiently?
- Is the company solvent?
- How might its cash flow position be improved?
- How might its financial situation be improved?
- If the firm were to approach you as a potential business angel, would you be interested?
- What conditions might you make, as an investor?

You need more than two years' results to look at trends, so remember that this is a simplified example. Sales have almost doubled since the previous financial year and the company is still building stock levels, showing that it is planning for growth. Profits have also increased slightly and the working capital (net current assets) situation has improved, so all the trends are in the right direction.

The gross profit margin – $(120,497/240,013) \times 100$ – is not a great cause for concern, but may be considered a bit low for a manufacturing company at 50.2 per cent. The company needs to consider the elements of its production process to see what could be improved. Direct labour costs are 18.8 per cent of sales. Perhaps it would be possible to automate part of the process, but this ratio has already been reduced, so the firm is heading in the right direction.

Net (pre-tax) profit margin – $(4,311/240,013) \times 100$ – is 1.8 per cent, which is very low in comparison with the gross profit margin. Perhaps the company should examine its overheads, as these have almost doubled during the year.

Return (pre-tax profit) on capital employed – $(4,311/60,794)) \times 100$ – at 7.1 per cent is reasonably good, which indicates that the company is making efficient use of its finance. Keep in mind that opportunity cost should be considered here. If you can get a savings account at a bank that gives you a 10 per cent return, 7.1 per cent does not look as favourable.

ABC Ltd Trading and profit and loss account 2009

	2009		2008	
	£	£	£	£
Sales		240,013		145,976
Cost of sales:				
Opening stock	54,850		48,090	
Purchases	75,632		42,678	
Total pay	45,212		30,444	
Closing stock	[56,178]		[54,850]	
		119,516		66,362
Gross profit		120,497		79,614
Operating expenses				
Overheads	46,352		24,986	
Distribution	16,766		12,562	
Directors' fees	40,000		28,000	
Depreciation	5,984		2,956	
		109,102		68,504
Net profit		11,395		11,110
Interest payable		7,084		6,954
Pre-tax profit		4,311		4,156
Tax		936		1,076
Profit after tax		3,375		3,080
Ordinary dividend		0		0
Retained profit		3,375		3,080

Figure 7.3 ABC Ltd trading and profit and loss account for 2009.

ABC Ltd balance sheet 31 December 2009

	2009		2008	
	£	£	£	£
Fixed assets		58,538		57,975
Current assets:				
Stock and WIP	56,178		54,850	
Debtors	25,118		11,370	
Cash in hand	1,675		691	
	82,971		66,911	
Current liabilities:				
Trade creditors	26,919		13,062	
Hire purchase	15,690		11,740	
Bank loan	28,106		32,370	
Other loan	10,000		10,000	
	80,715		67,172	
Net current assets		2,256		[261]
Net assets		60,794		57,714
Capital and reserves:				
Share capital		10,000		10,000
Reserves		50,794		47,714
Capital employed		60,794		57,714

Figure 7.4 ABC Ltd balance sheet, 31 December 2009.

The current ratio – (82,971/80,715) – at 1.03:1 indicates that cash available in current assets is more than sufficient to pay the debts listed in the current liabilities. This means that theoretically the firm's liabilities are covered, provided it could sell stocks.

The acid test ratio – (82,971–56,178)/80,715 – is extremely low at 0.33:1. A rule of thumb is that the current asset ratio should be between 1.5 and 2.0. This is due to the idea that it is good to have about as much cash and near-cash as you have debts; an optimum ratio for the acid test is 1:1. The amount of money tied up in stocks should be kept to a minimum (as the money could be better used). This is likely to mean that the company could have severe short-term cash flow problems, especially if one of its customers is slow to pay, as most of its current assets are tied up in stock and (even worse) work in progress, which is completely unsaleable. The company may be growing faster than its finances will allow, a common situation known as *overtrading*. Alternatively, this may be standard for the industry, and some research would be needed to establish an informed view.

The gearing ratio – $(28,106 \times 100/(82,971 + 58,538))$ – is low at 19.9 per cent. This is good, except that the interest coverage ratio $(11,395/7,084)$ is also low (bad) at only $1.6:1$. This may be as a result of the low net profit margin, possibly compounded by high interest charges.

Based on the foregoing, the firm needs to improve its cash flow situation, either by chasing up debts more quickly or by factoring its debts to a third party. It also needs to improve its profitability. To improve its gross profit margin, it could reduce stock and work in progress, either by implementing better stock-control procedures or by improving its workflow to reduce manufacturing time, or by outsourcing part of the process. If finance is available, automation could help cut production costs.

To improve its net profit margin, ABC Ltd should investigate why its overheads are so high, and try to reduce them. It should try to reduce borrowing by paying off any fixed-rate bank loans at high interest rates, and possibly renegotiate a new loan on more favourable terms. Do the directors really need to take as much as £40,000 per year out of a new business? A potential investor would be looking for a share of the business, but would clearly not want to lose money.

A private investor in this company would probably want to know that the company intends to grow. A financial director may be needed, even if on a part-time basis, in order to improve the financial situation of the company, and to be able to increase its capital base in comparison with other similar companies. ABC Ltd is probably under-capitalized. A private investor would want to know that there would be a sensible exit route within five years in case things do not improve.

7.5 Management accounting

Management accounting is normally covered in the second or third year of a non-accounting degree such as Business Information Systems, and only a brief introduction will be provided here. It will be sufficient to enable understanding of what is covered in this domain and why it is important. Management accounting is concerned with three main areas: capital budgeting, capital structure and working capital management. *Capital budgeting* (investment appraisal) is about evaluating long-term investments. It considers what lines of business you should work and what sorts of buildings, machinery and equipment you will need. *Capital structure* is about where you get long-term financing to pay for your investment, such as bringing in other owners or borrowing money. *Working capital management* is about managing everyday financial activities such as collecting payments from customers, paying suppliers and deciding the amount of inventory to hold. In general, a firm's cash flows would look something like those shown in Figure 7.5. Management accounting is about getting the best from these flows, which means maximizing the market value of the existing owners' equity.

Maximizing value for shareholders can be done in a number of ways, but these are beyond the scope of this book, as they are in the realm of financial specialists. Three areas that are often covered by non-specialists are costs, inventory (stock) control and investment appraisal. A brief introduction to these will be provided here.

Costs may seem simple to the uninitiated, but in fact create all sorts of challenges. The main issue is what to do about overheads such as rent. Absorption costing spreads

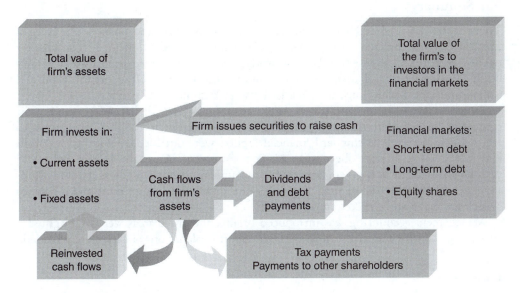

Figure 7.5 Typical cash flows for a firm.

such costs across activity areas, but this can lead to the conclusion that a particular line should be stopped because it may appear unprofitable. In fact, marginal costing may show the same line to be making a contribution to overheads and that it should be continued. Costing can become very involved and intricate; further discussion is beyond the scope of this text.

Stock control is about managing inventory to obtain the best financial advantage. Stock may be of three kinds: raw materials, work in progress and finished goods. Generally, introductory stock control is about the ordering of raw materials and goods for resale. Assuming no discounts for bulk purchases, a firm could order stock once per year, 12 times per year, 52 times per year and so on. Each order placed attracts a cost in terms of administrative charges. Thus, the fewer orders placed, the lower the cost. The solution would therefore be to order as few times as possible. Unfortunately, it is more complicated than this. Holding stock is a cost. Money is tied up that could be used for other things or that could be placed in an interest-bearing account. Thus, the less stock held, the better. The trade-off between ordering costs and holding costs is a very challenging area, and a starting point is what is known as the *economic order quantity*. This takes the total of the two costs (order and holding) and minimizes it. This introduction to the area is exactly that; it is beyond the scope of this text to go further on this subject.

Investment appraisal is about large-scale capital purchases – plant, machinery and equipment. There are many ways to consider how to use money in the best way for capital purchases, but essentially they fall into two types – discounting methods and non-discounting methods. Discounting methods take account of the rate of interest and consider future cash flows at today's value. This is known as *present value*. Non-discounting techniques simply consider the cash flows – typical methods are *payback* and *accounting rate of return*. Discounting methods normally used are *net present value* and *internal rate of return*. Investment appraisal goes beyond the scope of an introductory text, so will not be discussed further here.

7.6 Summary

This chapter has provided a basic introduction to accounting and finance. The roles of financial accounting and management accounting have been outlined. The chapter opened with the Computers-R-Us case study, which helped to demonstrate that successful business practice involves understanding the finances of an organization and some important distinctions, such as that between cash flow and profit.

Different types of organizations, their advantages and disadvantages and their sources of finance were discussed, ranging from sole trader, through partnerships, to limited companies. The standard financial reports were outlined, including the profit and loss account, balance sheet and cash flow statement. An example of a real-world cash flow statement was given. Some basic accounting terminology was given, including assets, liabilities and capital. Examples of a profit and loss account and a balance sheet were given and the content explained.

Management accounting was introduced briefly, and three areas were highlighted – costs, stock control and investment appraisal. Short explanations of each were provided.

Glossary

Accounting equation   Assets + expenses = liabilities + capital + income
Accrual   Expenses incurred but for which the organization has not yet paid.
Asset   What an organization owns.
Balance sheet   A snapshot of the organization's assets, liabilities and capital.
Capital   Cash and any other assets introduced to an organization by the owners.
Cash flow forecast   Predictions of incoming and outgoing cash and their timings.
Cash flow statement   Historical outline of cash that has come into and gone out of the organization.
Cost of goods sold   The direct costs of goods that have been sold.
Creditor   An entity that is owed money by the organization.
Current asset   An asset that is expected to be turned into cash within 12 months. Such assets are purchased or manufactured for the purpose of resale. They include stock, trade debts, prepayments, bank balances and cash balances.
Current liability   Debt owed to suppliers for goods and services purchased on credit terms and needed to be paid within 12 months of the balance sheet date. Examples are trade credit, accruals, overdrafts and loans.
Debtor   An entity that owes money to the organization.
Depreciation   The reducing value of a long-term asset.
Double-entry   Each transaction is recorded in at least two accounts. Each transaction requires at least one account to be debited and at least one account to be credited with the total debits of the transaction equal to the total credits.
Expenses   Costs that are indirect to the goods sold, such as rent and power.
Financial accounting   Accounting primarily for external requirements; includes recording transactions, summarizing transactions and reporting. Financial accounting is subject to a regulatory framework that is government-authorized.
Fixed asset   Assets used within the organization and expected to be useful for longer than 12 months. They include land, buildings, machinery, computers and vehicles. These things are not bought with the main intention of being used for resale.
Gross profit   Sales less cost of goods sold.

Limited company   A legal entity that is separate from the owners, able to trade, own assets and owe liabilities (including taxes on profit) in its own right.

Long-term liability   Amounts owed that have to be repaid after an interval of time which is longer than 12 months. They include mortgages and other long-term loans.

Management accounting   Accounting for internal requirements; includes decision-making, planning, estimating, forecasting, efficiency and capital expenditure. Not subject to any regulatory framework.

Net profit   Gross profit less expenses.

Partnership   Two or more people owning a business together.

Prepayment   Payment in advance.

Private limited company   A legal entity that has shares that cannot be sold to the public.

Profit and loss account   A financial statement of sales, costs and expenses over a period of time.

Public limited company   A legal entity that has shares that can be sold to the public.

Sales   The income generated from the goods or services produced by the organization.

Share   A part of the ownership of a company. Each ordinary share has equal rights to votes and dividends. Preference shares have a fixed dividend which is paid before the ordinary dividend. Convertible shares can be changed into ordinary shares in the future.

Sole trader   An organizational entity that is just the owner (one person). There is no distinction legally between the owner and the firm, and the owner's finances are the organization's finances.

Stock   Raw materials, work in progress, finished goods.

References

Tesco (2008) *Tesco PLC Annual Review and Summary Financial Statement.* Available online at www.investis.com/plc/storage/2008_TESCO_REVIEW.pdf (accessed 4 September 2010).

Further reading

Mott, G. (2008) *Accounting for Non-Accountants: A Manual for Managers and Students.* London: Kogan Page.

Suggested activities

1   XYZ Ltd manufactures cardboard boxes. List three things that are likely to be fixed assets and three things that are likely to be current assets for XYZ Ltd.

2   Explain why it is important that a manager of an IT department should have some understanding of accounting and finance.

3   Go to the Tesco corporate website and find the income statement and balance sheet. Consider what these are stating overall, and try to understand the items listed in them. www.tescoreports.com/areview08/financial.html.

4   Work out what the differences would be between the profit and loss accounts of a manufacturer, a trader and a pure service business.

8   Database management

Case study 8.1 Driver working hours

This case study was prepared by the authors to facilitate class discussion. Any resemblance to exist-ing organizations or people is coincidental.

This case study reports on a project initiated by a large UK company that has 1,764 drivers. The specification models how to capture, store and analyse drivers' working hours and can be used as a standalone application that can be integrated throughout an organization.

The European Union Working Time Directive (European Commission, 2003) for mobile workers and the Road Transport Directive (Department for Transport, 2005) require employers to monitor and implement regulations to ensure that mobile workers comply with all relevant directives. These regulations led to the development of a speci-fication to record, store and monitor large goods vehicle drivers' working hours. The specification suggests how to capture, store and analyse this data for use in a manage-ment information system related to the effective control and utilization of drivers and vehicle capacities.

This case study is concerned with a database and information system to deal with data relating to drivers of large goods vehicles (over 3.5 tonnes gross vehicle weight). The previous EU drivers' hours regulations covered the hours a driver spends controlling a vehicle and how much rest is taken daily, but did not cover total working hours.

At the start of the case study drivers were monitored via a tachograph that recorded driving hours onto paper disks (tachograph charts). Employers and drivers both have legal responsibilities to ensure that the drivers' hours laws are not exceeded. The challenge is in collecting working hours data and converting it to an electronic form.

The analysis concentrated on the early stages of a system development lifecycle for the purpose of preparing a specification that could be presented to software engineers for construction and coding or for the preparation of a simple database using a database management system. A simple high-level design diagram of the main requirements of the system can be found in Figure 8.1 and covers:

- deciding how drivers will capture working hours data;
- deciding how the transactional data will be collected and converted into a digital format;
- selection of a suitable storage architecture that collaborates with existing systems architecture;
- development of reports that allow users to view and query management information;

- development decision support tools for forecasting, driver capacity and balancing of hours;
- ensuring user interfaces for data capture, collection and interrogation of the system are simple and easy to use.

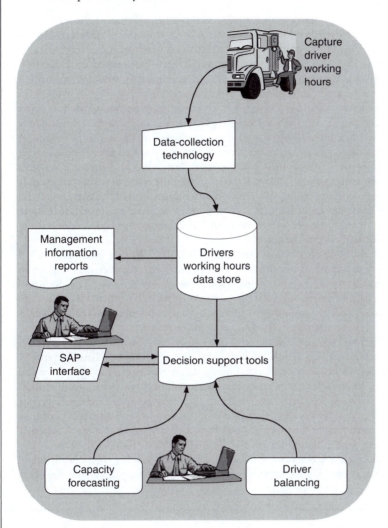

Figure 8.1 Simple high-level design of the main system requirements.

The most practical and cost effective data-collection method is optical mark recognition (OMR) because of the ease of completion of the optical mark cards by drivers and the accuracy of conversion into a digital format. The technology is affordable, and commercial packages enable users to create fully functional optical mark cards and provide the application needed to scan the information directly into a standard PC. Specialist optical card recognition scanners are also available. The major downside of this technology is that drivers still have to capture their working times before they complete the optical mark card, but this can be done using existing tachograph charts or some other system, such as the working hours log sheet. OMR is not the ideal solution when taking into account the introduction of digital tachographs. The investment in OMR software and hardware might be viewed as unwise, especially when mobile phone and Internet-based dual-tone multi-frequency (DTMF) signalling solutions are available on a flexible subscription basis. Using the DTMF infrastructure from another business could be a cost-effective interim solution.

The centre of the drivers' hours recording and management system is the data store. The choice of systems architecture is crucial if the client is to successfully exploit the drivers' hours data to improve vehicle capacity utilization and lower delivery costs. A relational database is the most suitable database architecture because of its flexibility, scalability and ease of maintenance. It would also integrate easily into the company's existing client–server infrastructure, allowing users to share data.

It could be argued that a flat file spreadsheet would be more cost-effective and easier to develop, especially as the data entities are simple, but the inherent data redundancy and scalability issues of a spreadsheet would cause increased maintenance problems. A relational database is more robust and easier to maintain because a database management system (DBMS) can be set to control users' access at different levels. Another issue with using a flat file spreadsheet is the usability of decision support tools. A prototype spreadsheet had limited use as a forecasting or driver hours balancing tool, but it provided a useful basis for the construction of the next iteration into a database platform. Also, more complex algorithms can be developed in relational database architecture to meet the decision support requirements of the specification.

The usability of the system is dependent on the ease of collecting data from 1,764 drivers every week and inputting it into the data store. If an incorrect data-collection system is implemented, the effect on staff workloads can be tremendous. The design of the user interface is critical in ensuring data is easily collected and inputted into the data store. Interfaces and specific reports are easier to design and construct in a DBMS than in spreadsheets, which rely on user-created macros for simple forms.

A major implementation issue was overcoming cultural attachments to spreadsheets and reluctance to use databases. Users tended to consider a spreadsheet solution as quick, cost-effective and easy to implement. A database solution was viewed as expensive and slow to implement. Nevertheless, the value of using a database was recognized and the company used an initial specification to construct a prototype relational database for testing. One of the main issues was to ensure that digital tachograph data could be imported via smart card readers and special USB flash memory sticks that were available from digital tachograph manufacturers. At the time of the case study, if the forecasting and driver hours balancing tools proved to give a business benefit, then the database would be written in *advanced business application programming* for integration into the company's SAP system.

8.1 Intended learning outcomes

On completion of this chapter the reader should be able to:

1 discuss the advantages and disadvantages of the use of databases over data files;
2 assign activities to each stage of database design;
3 differentiate between the database language components DDL, DML and DCL, and demonstrate an understanding of their roles in creating and maintaining a database;
4 describe the basic functions of a database management system, and their use in database management.

8.2 Introduction

This chapter begins by considering the questions: 'Why do we need to store data?', and 'Why is the need to store data increasing almost daily?'. This is followed by the related question: 'What are the properties we would most like our data storage mechanisms to have?'; or, in other words: 'What characteristics would we most like to see in the data we store, and the way in which we store it?'. We will then be able to examine two ways of storing data – namely, using files and using databases. We will explore the strengths and weaknesses of each of these methods, and will consider to what extent they meet the criteria we have identified. It will then be possible to judge how well each method satisfies our wish-list of desirable data storage properties.

8.3 The data explosion

The quantity of electronic data the human race is creating and storing is increasing at a truly explosive rate. One of the reasons for this is the falling cost of physical data storage. Most recently this has been magnetic media such as floppy or hard disks, and is now more often optical media such as CDs and DVDs, and solid-state devices. Prices have fallen to such an extent that, in business terms, they can now be considered to be almost insignificant.

At the same time, more and more data-intensive applications are being created, and existing software is generating more and more data. E-commerce (goods and services), online libraries, standards repositories, enterprise systems, social networking, educational software and search engines all contribute to an exponentially increasing volume of data to be stored, processed and retrieved. While we recently spoke in terms of kilobytes (10^3 bytes), megabytes (10^6 bytes) and terabytes (10^{12} bytes), now we must consider zettabytes (10^{21} bytes) and even yottabytes (10^{24} bytes).

8.4 A data storage wish-list

Clearly, very powerful storage mechanisms are needed to enable us to cope with these vast quantities of data. But we want to do more than just store it. Here are some desirable characteristics of any data storage mechanism:

Volume and cost: we want to store lots of data – cheaply!

Retrieval: there is little point in storing data if we cannot get it back– quickly, conveniently and reliably.

Sharing: we sometimes want to share our data with others – our colleagues or customers, perhaps – and would often like to be able to share their data too.

Flexibility: we want our data to be stored in such a way that it can be used by different people for several, or many, different purposes (probably at the same time).

Access control: while we might want to allow others to make use of our data, this does not mean that it should be freely available to all. First, we will probably want to limit access to certain individuals (or to certain computer programs or systems). Then we may want to restrict that access to particular parts of the data, and to limit the types of operation that may be performed on the data.

Security: data security is, of course, vital to business organizations, and maintaining security becomes a more complex issue when data can be shared between users. When we think of data security we tend to think of the danger from hackers, but there are many other ways in which the integrity of our data can be threatened. These include: malicious corruption from within our own company; the accidental deletion of data; the introduction of inconsistencies, errors or viruses; physical damage (for example, caused by fire or flood); and careless duplication and transportation.

Speed: although today's computers and associated digital equipment operate at amazing speeds, the number of operations per second of which they are capable is still relevant – because they process such vast volumes of data. Early relational databases could be very slow, and the speed at which they function can still be an issue today.

Compactness: the number of bytes needed to store an item of information is certainly becoming less important as the capacity of storage media expands, but is not yet completely irrelevant – again because of increased data volumes.

Complex, structured data: as the uses to which we put data become more complex, we need to store more complex types of data. Whereas we were once primarily interested in text and numbers, now we expect to be able to store images, sound and video, etc.

8.5 File-based data storage

Originally, virtually all computer data was stored as files – each program had its own file structure, which could not usually be used by other programs. This method is still widely used, and can be seen, for example, in popular Windows-based programs in which the file format is indicated by the extension (such as *.docx* and *.avi*). The main disadvantages of this way of working are that:

- data files designed for use with a particular program are unlikely to be useable for any other.
- This can result in data duplication and inconsistency.

Picture a large organization with several departments. The human resources department holds data on all of the organization's employees – for example: name, address, date of birth, telephone number, next of kin, highest qualification, training record and department. This is used by a program that simply maintains and displays employee information. The payroll department holds, for each employee, details which are similar but not the same: name, address, rate of pay, tax status, date of joining company and department. This is used by a program that calculates employees' wages or salaries.

Each department also holds data on its own staff: name, address and telephone number, so important information can be circulated to workers' homes using a mail-merge program. There are two obvious shortcomings to this situation. First, storing the same information in more than one place is a waste of effort and storage space. More importantly, if the information needs to be updated, then it may need to be updated several times. For instance, if an employee moves house, then the new address will need to be changed in the data files of the human resources department, the payroll department and the employee's own department. If for some reason one or more of these three is not updated, or if one or more of them is updated incorrectly, then there will be contradictory versions of the same data within the organization. The data will have become inconsistent, and in the future it may become unclear which version is correct.

Another flaw in file-based data storage is that in order to extract the data from files it is necessary to run the program for which they were written.

8.6 Advantages (and some disadvantages) of database storage

8.6.1 *Volume and cost*

A data file, written for a specific program, is likely to make more efficient use of storage space, and therefore to be less costly than if the data were stored in a database. However, the difference is marginal. Furthermore, data stored in a database can be used by many programs (and accessed interactively), so in the long-run a database can often be expected to be more cost-effective.

8.6.2 *Retrieval*

Databases store data in a highly organized and systematic fashion. Consequently, it can be manipulated and returned directly in response to queries from a user, or can be passed to programs for further processing.

8.6.3 *Sharing*

Data in databases can be shared by many users or programs simultaneously.

8.6.4 *Flexibility*

Data is stored in databases in a way that is independent of any particular purpose or program. It can then be retrieved in a format that matches the needs of any user or program.

8.6.5 *Access control*

Database management systems – DBMSs (see Section 8.9) – allow limitations to be placed on which users or programs can retrieve, change or delete data.

8.6.6 *Security*

Similarly, DBMSs have built-in features for protecting data from loss or corruption.

8.6.7 *Speed*

Databases often store vast quantities of data, so optimizing the speed at which they operate is important, and facilities are provided for this purpose. However, data storage and retrieval times can be greater than those achieved using purpose-written data files, and can be somewhat unpredictable. For this reason, the use of databases in time-critical applications may not be appropriate.

8.6.8 *Complex, structured data*

Data that is highly structured (often for use within engineering applications), and even elements of computer programs, can be stored within object-relational and object-oriented databases. Business information systems (BISs) generally use a simpler form of database – the relational database – which nevertheless can process a wide range of data types suitable for business purposes. Relational databases were introduced in the early 1970s, based largely on the work of a British computer scientist, E.F. Codd, while working for IBM.

8.7 Database design

Let us consider the design of a simple database. We will use as an example a library that lends books to members. It needs to store data on the books, its members and the loans it makes. This can be represented in the form of an *entity-relationship diagram* (E-RD), as shown in Figure 8.2.

In this E-RD there are three entities – member, loan and book. Entities can be defined as something about which we want to store data, and are represented in an E-RD by a box containing the entity's name (in the singular). Relationships are shown by lines joining the entities, and are named. There are several sets of notations used for drawing E-RDs. The one used here was devised by Gordon Everest, and uses the 'crow's foot' symbol to indicate cardinality. This refers to the maximum number of times an instance in one entity can be associated with instances in the related entity. So, in Figure 8.2, the diagram can be read: 'One member can take out many loans, but each loan can be taken out by one member only', and 'Each loan is for one book only, but a book can be loaned many times'. A database design shown in this way (i.e. representing the data requirements of a proposed system, without reference to how the data will be stored), is known as a conceptual design. This is the first of three design stages, as shown in Figure 8.3.

Figure 8.2 An entity-relationship diagram for a library.

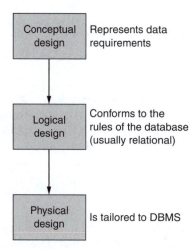

Figure 8.3 The three stages of database design.

8.8 Relational databases and logical design

All data within a relational database is stored as 'relations'. These can be represented as two-dimensional tables; the terms 'tables' and 'relations' are often used interchangeably. Figure 8.4 shows the 'member' relation for our library database, both in E-RD format and as a table. It is important to appreciate that the terms 'relation' and 'relationship' describe very different things. A relation is equivalent to a database table in a relational database, while a relationship describes the ways in which two (or more) entities are associated.

Figure 8.4 also shows attributes – which are the properties of entities to which we will allocate values. Let us now consider the rest of the data relating to the books in the library, and how it might be represented in the form of tables. This is shown in the E-RD in Figure 8.5a, and as a table in Figure 8.5b. As well as attributes, the table also shows some possible attribute *values*. We use the term 'row' to describe all the attribute values of a particular entity. Confusingly, they may not always be shown horizontally so, for example, the table in Figure 8.5b has three rows, shown vertically, and nine columns, corresponding to attributes, appearing horizontally.

The data in Figure 8.5b is not in 'normal form'. This means that although its meaning is clear on paper, it cannot be implemented in a relational database without some changes. First, let us look at the values of the 'Author(s)' attributes. We cannot predict in advance how many authors there will be for a particular book, but in a relational database we can accommodate no more than one value per attribute. We will in this case adopt an easy solution, and will only store the name of the first author. (An alternative approach would be to add extra attributes, say 'Author-2', 'Author-3', etc.)

The second problem concerns repeated values. We have said that one of the advantages of using databases for storage is to avoid data duplication and the resulting possible inconsistency. Clearly, we are defeating this purpose if every time we add an extra copy of a book to the database, in addition to the book number, we also have to add the title of the book, the author's name, the publisher and the category. For any particular book number, the other values will always be the same. Also, let us assume that there is only one copy of book number 2 in the library, and that it is accidentally destroyed, requiring us to remove its details from the database. As things stand, if we

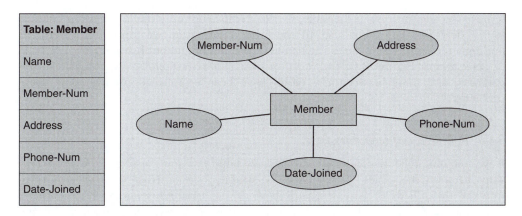

Figure 8.4 The member table and E-RD for the library database.

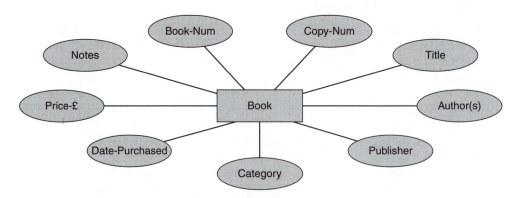

Figure 8.5a E-RD for part of database storing 'book' data.

Attribute	Value-1	Value-2	Value-3	
Book-Num	1	1	2	
Copy-Num	1	2	1	
Title	Garden Birds	Garden Birds	David Copperfield	
Author(s)	John Smith Trevor Jones	John Smith Trevor Jones	Charles Dickens	COLUMNS
Publisher	Routledge	Routledge	Higgins	
Category	Interests	Interests	Fiction	
Date-Purchased	08-Aug-2010	28-Aug-2010	14-Feb-2007	
Price-£	40.28	86.30	12.20	
Notes	–	Large print	–	

↑↑↑ ROWS ↑↑↑

Figure 8.5b 'Book' data for the library database, including possible attribute values.

remove the relevant row in the table, we will remove not only the information relating to the destroyed copy, but also all the other information we might find useful in finding a replacement – such as the names of the author and publisher.

Look now at Figures 8.6a and 8.6b, in which an extra table has been added to the database, and links between the tables have been established, to overcome these problems.

8.8.1 *Primary and secondary keys*

If we are going to store data in several database tables, we must also record the relationships between the tables – or we will be unable to reconstruct it as we originally intended. In an E-RD, relationships are shown by connecting lines between the entities; in the database tables we designate particular attributes as 'keys'. A 'primary key' is one which uniquely identifies a row in a database table (meaning that it must have a different

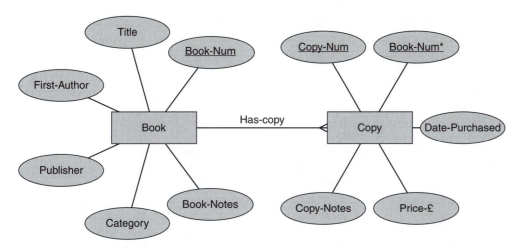

Figure 8.6a E-RD of normalized 'book' data.

Table: Book		
Book-Num	1	2
Title	Garden Birds	David Copperfield
First-Author	John Smith	Charles Dickens
Publisher	Routledge	Higgins
Category	Interests	Fiction
Book-Notes	Top-100	–

Table: Copy			
Copy-Num	1	2	1
Book-Num*	1	1	2
Date-Purchased	08-Aug-2010	28-Aug-2010	14-Feb-2007
Price-£	40.28	86.30	12.20
Copy-Notes	–	Large print	–

Figure 8.6b Normalized tables for 'book' data.

value in every row). The primary key in the 'Book' table is 'Book-Num'. This number will be allocated as each new book is added to the library. Primary keys are indicated in an E-RD or table by underlining (as in <u>Book-Num</u> in the 'Book' entity in Figure 8.6b). You will notice that there are two underlined attributes in the 'Copy' entity – <u>Book-Num*</u> and <u>Copy-Num</u>. This is because they are both needed to uniquely identify a row in the table, and this table is said to have a compound primary key. (There could be several books with the same value for Book-Num or with the same value for Copy-Num, but no book can have the same values for Book-Num *and* Copy-Num).

The attribute Book-Num belonging to the 'Copy' entity is shown in the E-RD and table followed by an asterisk (*). This indicates that it is a secondary key for this table. A secondary key for one table is always also the primary key for another table, to which it is linked. In this case, the primary key (Book-Num) in the 'book' table links to the secondary key (Book-Num*) in the 'copy' table to implement the 'has-copy' relationship. It is worth remembering that in a one-to-many relationship, the primary key is found in the table at the 'one' end, and the secondary key in the table at the 'many' end.

The full E-RD and tables for the library database, in a form that can be implemented in a relational database (known as *third normal form*), are shown in Figures 8.7a and 8.7b. This stage of the design process (i.e. the production of a design that adheres to the rules of a relational (or other) database) is known as the *logical design*.

8.9 Physical design

To recap – so far in our design of the library database we have decided what things we need to store data about (entities), and how the entities are related (relationships). We have also decided on attributes, corresponding to the characteristics of the entities, to which we can allocate values. This is our conceptual design.

We have decided to implement our database using the relational model, so our relations have become tables, and we have designated some of the attributes as primary and secondary keys. Primary keys allow us to identify rows in a table corresponding to instances of database entities. (That is to say, while the entity 'member' refers to members in general, rather than any particular individual, the row in the 'member' table with the number, say, '22', refers to one individual and no other.)

We have also linked the tables using a primary key in the table at the 'one' end of a 'one-to-many' relationship, and a secondary key in the table at the 'many' end. This completes our basic logical design.

We need to be able to create an electronic version of our database using computer software, and we will have to conform to the requirements of the software package that we will use to create the structure and store, retrieve and manipulate the data.

First, we must ensure that the names we have given to our entities and attributes ('identifiers') are acceptable. Some database software (especially older products) has strict rules – identifiers, for example, may be entered in upper or lower case only, the use of certain characters may be forbidden and some words may be reserved for use by the system.

It is only reasonable that if we expect a system to store and process data, we should tell it in advance what sorts of data it will be dealing with, and wherever possible, how much. The most common types of data are numeric, alphabetic and binary, but there are many subtypes within these major groupings. DBMSs are the software applications (such as Oracle, MySQL and Microsoft Access) that we employ to create and manage our databases. Some of the data types used by these DBMSs are shown in Table 8.1.

Decisions about which data type to use for each attribute of every entity in our database (or to put it another way, each column in every table), is part of the physical design of our database – because it depends upon which data types are provided by the DBMS we have chosen to use. Another aspect of physical design is that of indexing. If it is clear that when we come to retrieve data from the database, certain attributes/columns will be referenced more often than others, we can instruct the DBMS to index them. This enables the DBMS to locate them more easily on the storage device, which will increase the speed at which data is returned in response to our queries.

Let us now return to our library database and allocate data types to the columns in all of our tables (using Oracle DBMS data types). The result is shown in Figure 8.8.

Some explanations are necessary concerning the Oracle data types allocated to the columns in the library database tables:

- 'Book-Num' can be a whole number between 1 and 99,999,999.

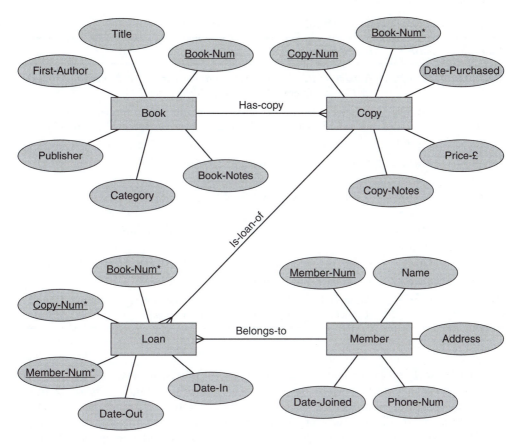

Figure 8.7a E-RD for the library database, including attributes.

Table: Book	
Book-Num	
Title	
First-Author	
Publisher	
Category	
Book-Notes	

Table: Copy	
Copy-Num	
Book-Num*	
Date-Purchased	
Price-£	
Copy-Notes	

Table: Member	
Member-Num	
Name	
Address	
Phone-Num	
Date-Joined	

Table: Loan	
Book-Num*	
Copy-Num*	
Member-Num*	
Date-Out	
Date-In	

Figure 8.7b Tables for the library database.

Table 8.1 Data types in popular DBMSs

Data type	DBMS	Description
CHAR(size)	MySQL	A fixed-length string (letters, numbers and special characters) of up to 255 characters. The size is specified in parentheses.
VARCHAR (size)	MySQL	A variable-length string (letters, numbers, and special characters) of up to 255 characters. The maximum size is specified in parentheses.
TEXT	MySQL	A string with a maximum length of 65,535 characters.
Integer	Microsoft Access	A whole number between −32,768 and 32,767.
Long	Microsoft Access	A whole number between −2,147,483,648 and 2,147,483,647.
Double	Microsoft Access	Double-precision floating-point, suitable for most decimals.
Date	Oracle	A date between 1 January 4712 BC and 31 December 9999 AD.
Timestamp	Oracle	As for date, but including fractions of seconds.
BLOB	Oracle	A binary large object – up to eight gigabytes of unstructured data, such as text, graphics, video and audio files.

- 'Titles' will consist of a string of characters (numbers, letters, spaces and some special characters such as punctuation), with a maximum length of 40 characters.
- 'First Author', 'Publisher', 'Category', 'Book-Notes', 'Copy-Notes', 'Name', 'Address' and 'Phone-Num' are strings of characters with the maximum length indicated. ('Phone-Num' is not stored as a number because telephone numbers sometimes include spaces, hyphens, etc., and numbers use more storage space than character data.)
- 'Copy-Num' is a whole number between 1 and 999.
- 'Date-Purchased', 'Date-Joined', 'Date-Out' and 'Date-In' are all dates.
- 'Price-£' is stored as a number that can have up to three figures before the decimal point, and two following the decimal point. In other words, any amount up to £999.99.

8.10 Database interfaces and SQL

Now that we have our final database design, there are three essential types of task we want to be able to carry out. We want to:

1   create an electronic version of our database;
2   enter data into the database;
3   retrieve data in a form that is useful to us.

In addition, there are some secondary 'administrative' tasks that will enable us to max-imize the usefulness of the database.

We may choose to interact with the database using a graphical user interface (GUI); most DBMSs include at least one GUI. It is possible to perform a wide range of tasks by using the features these provide, such as drag-and-drop, selection from menus and

Table: Book	
Book-Num	NUMBER(8)
Title	VARCHAR2(40)
First-Author	VARCHAR2(30)
Publisher	VARCHAR2(30)
Category	VARCHAR2(15)
Book-Notes	VARCHAR2(40)

Table: Copy	
Copy-Num	NUMBER(3)
Book-Num*	NUMBER(8)
Date-Purchased	DATE
Price-£	NUMBER(5,2)
Copy-Notes	VARCHAR2(40)

Table: Member	
Member-Num	NUMBER(7)
Name	VARCHAR2(40)
Address	VARCHAR2(40)
Phone-Num	VARCHAR2(20)
Date-Joined	DATE

Table: Loan	
Book-Num*	NUMBER(8)
Copy-Num*	NUMBER(3)
Member-Num*	NUMBER(7)
Date-Out	DATE
Date-In	DATE

Figure 8.8 The library database with oracle data types.

drop-down lists, etc. However, more powerful capabilities are provided by a textual language, known as SQL (structured query language). It was devised by IBM in the early days of relational databases, but is still (with a little subsequent updating) very widely used. It has the advantage that it can be incorporated into computer code written in other languages, so programs can be written that include the storing and retrieval of data using a database, and other facilities provided by the DBMS. SQL has three major components, which correspond to the tasks listed at the start of this section.

8.10.1 Data definition language

We use data definition language (DDL) to create the database tables in which we will store our data. The SQL to create the 'Member' table is:

```
CREATE TABLE Member (
Member-Num              NUMBER(7)           PRIMARY KEY,
Name                    VARCHAR2(40),
Address                 VARCHAR2(40),
Phone-Num               VARCHAR2(20),
Date-Joined             DATE();
```

(Note: versions of SQL differ. The code presented here is not guaranteed to run under any particular DBMS without modification.)

There are also SQL DDL statements to enable the copying and deletion of tables, and for making changes to existing tables.

8.10.2 *Data manipulation language*

We create databases so we can store and retrieve data, and we do this using the data manipulation language (DML) component of SQL. One way of inserting data into a table is:

```
INSERT INTO
    Copy (Copy-Num, Book-Num, Date-Purchased, Price-£, Copy-Notes)
VALUES
    (4, 1005, '21-may-10', 15.50, 'Slightly damaged');
```

Perhaps the most powerful SQL statements are those that we use to retrieve data matching a set of criteria that we specify. These are known as queries, and start with the keyword 'SELECT'. For example:

```
SELECT
    Member-Num, Member-Name
FROM
    Member
WHERE
    Date-Joined < '01-jan-2000';
```

This will return the membership numbers and names of all those library members who joined before 1 January 2000.

Queries can be complex and powerful. They can refer to data in more than one table, linking the tables using the primary and secondary keys. For example:

```
SELECT
    Name, Member.Member-Num, Address, Title, Date-Out
FROM
    Book, Copy, Loan, Member
WHERE
    Today() – Date-Out > 14
AND
    Book.Book-Num = Copy.Book-Num
AND
    Copy.Book-Num = Loan.Book-Num
AND
    Copy.Copy-Num = Loan.Copy-Num
AND
    Loan.Member-Num = Member-Num
ORDER BY
    Name;
```

This query will return an alphabetically ordered list of all members who have outstanding loans (more than two weeks), their membership numbers and addresses, the titles of the books borrowed that are now overdue, and the dates they were taken out.

DML can also be used to update data in the database, or to delete data (again, selectively according to the criteria supplied).

8.10.3 Data control language (DCL)

The final group of tasks that we need to carry out when using databases – especially ones that are large and/or have lots of users – can be regarded as secondary. This is because they concern the management or maintenance of the database itself, rather than its use to manage data.

We have seen that one of the advantages of using databases is that they enable data to be readily shared between users. One reason for this is that they store data in a 'neutral' format. That is to say, the way in which data is stored does not limit its use to a particular purpose or program, but lends itself to use as and when needed. Another advantage is that DBMSs provide facilities to enable owners of data to restrict its availability to those who have the necessary authority. This is known as access control, and some examples of access control statements in SQL are:

GRANT SELECT ON Book TO clerk5;
GRANT DELETE ON Member TO clerk2, clerk3;
REVOKE DELETE ON Copy FROM clerk 7;

The first of these allows a registered system user with the user name of 'clerk5' to access the 'Book' table (but only for the purpose of SELECTing data – i.e. the clerk will not be able to insert, change or delete data). The second statement allows clerk2 and clerk3 to delete rows (members) from the 'Members' table, and the third removes the privilege to delete rows from the 'Copy' table previously granted (one assumes) to clerk7.

Finally, access control can be applied in a similar way to computer programs and connected systems using the facilities of the database.

8.11 More database management tasks

There are many other tasks that must be performed to ensure the organization continues to gain maximum benefit from the database.

8.11.1 Creating views

A view is a virtual database table, created from real tables. A database manager can use views to limit users' access to highly specific data items within a database. Consider the following SQL statement:

```
CREATE VIEW
Member-Loan
AS SELECT
   Name, Member.Member-Num AS Num, Address, Phone-Num
FROM
   Member, Loan
WHERE
   Member.Member-Num = Loan.Member-Num;
AND
   Date-In = NULL;
```

The SQL from 'SELECT' onwards, would, if run as a query, return all the names, membership numbers, addresses and phone numbers of all members with outstanding loans. If the database manager were to grant to a user SELECT privileges on this view only, this would limit the user's access to this data, allowing them access to no other data within the library database.

Moreover, having created a view, we can query the data it contains further, e.g.:

```
SELECT
   Name
FROM
   Member-Loan
WHERE
   Num BETWEEN 1000 AND 1999;
```

This query returns only the names of library members with loans outstanding who have membership numbers within the specified range.

8.11.2 *Creating back-ups and snapshots*

While it is always important to back-up one's data, even when using small applications for personal use, the backing-up of business databases is vital – to the extent that businesses have had to cease trading because of lost data. But just what should be backed-up and when? Should copies be made of all of the data in the database or just the most important tables? Should only the latest copy of data be kept, or should 'snapshots' be taken at regular intervals? Should this be done manually or automatically? How many copies should be made, and for how long should they be kept? Where should they be kept – in the same building as the originals? In areas subject to earthquakes or floods one might even question whether they should be kept in the same region. And should the data be compressed (making it more difficult to retrieve), or perhaps be transferred to a data warehouse?

It is easy to see that the amount of backed-up data can greatly exceed that in the database itself. This has implications in terms of cost, physical storage space, security (the more data there is the more chance that it may get stolen), and the time and effort needed to organize the data in a systematic way (i.e. version control), so that the correct data can be retrieved if needed.

8.11.3 Data deletion

Individual database users may cease to use items of data, or even whole sections of the database, but may not feel that they can delete them in case they are still needed by someone else. In this way large parts of the database could become obsolete, without anyone noticing. Without centralized observation and control, the result could be a gradual degradation in DBMS performance, and a swamping or obscuring of legitimate data by the out-dated.

8.11.4 Restructuring and updating

The database may need to be restructured from time to time to reflect changes in the business organization. A particularly extreme instance can occur following company mergers or takeovers, when it may become necessary to combine previously independent databases, having completely different data structures and naming conventions. One or more of the databases, and large quantities of existing data may need to be changed, calling for corresponding alterations to programs that use the data.

8.11.5 Hardware and software upgrades

These are a fact of life, but can make life uncomfortable for a database manager. They are usually required at a point when an IT department seems to be running especially smoothly, and when the database manager is starting to relax! Hardware and software (e.g. DBMS) suppliers may release new versions of, or upgrades to, their products, and applications that interact with the database will also be subject to major change from time to time. In each of these cases, the database may at least require 'tweaking' to continue to function normally, and major adjustments will sometimes be needed.

8.11.6 Physical security

As well as the more technical aspects of databases, the database manager must be concerned with more mundane issues such as the control of access to buildings, security checks on employees and the prevention and detection of fire.

8.11.7 Legal and ethical considerations

Simply because we have the ability to store and manage vast quantities of information, it does not follow that we have the legal or moral right to do so. Laws relating to personal privacy, copyright and other forms of intellectual property rights, and conversely, to freedom of information, must be understood and adhered to. Not only organizations but individuals within the organizations can be held responsible and punished for breaches of the law.

8.12 Summary

It is difficult for an information systems specialist to imagine life without relational databases. Whether or not they are aware of it, ordinary members of the public make use of, or are affected by them on an almost daily basis. (Think of medical records, police and social security databases, online shopping, electoral registers and so on.)

Their power and convenience stem from the relational model, which eliminates the need for data files that can be used only for the specific purposes for which they were designed. This, in turn (together with the facilities provided by the DBMS), enables data to be shared, without duplication and inconsistency.

But there is no such thing as a free lunch. Large repositories of data must be managed, and they bring potential dangers and problems, such as access control, physical and electronic security issues and even legal considerations. The use of a database for all of an organization's data can be regarded as an 'all one's eggs in one basket' policy. While it has clear and substantial benefits, the failure of such a system can mean financial ruin for an organization.

Glossary

Attribute   A quality or characteristic of an entity, to which can be given a value.

DCL   Data control language – that part of SQL used to carry out secondary tasks on a database, such as access control.

DDL   Data definition language – that part of SQL used to specify the structure of a database, in the form of tables.

DML   Data manipulation language – that part of SQL used to query the contents of a database, and to return values.

DBMS   Database management system – a software system that enables the creation of a database and its population, and provides facilities for its maintenance and use.

Entity   An element in an E-RD corresponding to something about which we want to store data.

E-RD   Entity-relationship diagram.

Primary key   An attribute or column in a relational database by which a row can be uniquely identified.

Relation   Another name for a table in a relational database.

Secondary key   An attribute or column in a relational database table corresponding to the primary key in another table.

SQL   A textual language for the management and manipulation of relational databases and their contents.

References

Department for Transport (2005) *Road Transport (Working Time) Guidance: Brief Overview.* Available online at http://webarchive.nationalarchives.gov.uk/+/www.dft.gov.uk/pgr/freight/road/workingtime/rdtransportworkingtimeguidance?page=2 (accessed 22 September 2010).

European Commission (2003) *Directive 2003/88/EC of the European Parliament and of the Council of 4 November 2003 Concerning Certain Aspects of the Organisation of Working Time.* Available online at http://eur-lex.europa.eu/LexUriServ/LexUriServ.do?uri=CELEX:32003L0088:EN:HTML (accessed 22 September 2010).

Ford, R. (2010). Huge Rise in 'Hidden' Credit Card Crime. *Times Online*, 19 May. Available online at: www.timesonline.co.uk/tol/news/uk/crime/article7130209.ece (accessed 15 June 2010).

Further reading

Limeback, R. (2009) *Simply SQL*. Melbourne: Sitepoint.

Suggested activities

1   Suggest two application areas for which the use of databases would not be appropriate.
2   Consider how the library database used as an example in this chapter could be extended. Draw a conceptual E-RD to illustrate your ideas.
3   Consider the advantages and disadvantages of appointing a single individual within an organization with authority over all aspects of the database.
4   Consider how a database could be used unethically.

9　E-commerce 2

Case study 9.1　E-commerce in Nigeria

This case study was originally prepared by Dr Brian Lehaney and his student Eludinni Rotimi Omoniyi. It has been included by the authors to facilitate class discussion rather than to illustrate effective or ineffective management practices. It does not reflect any opinions of employees or management at any organizations mentioned.

The use of the Internet and mobile phone technologies are gradually penetrating African countries, especially Nigeria. This has led to increased availability of the Internet and mobile phones – thus, these technologies are used for various functions, such as entertainment, education, games, voice calls and research. Electronic commerce is continually rising as a significant business trend both for organizations and individuals. In Nigeria, little research exists to identify the needs of consumers or factors that can influence their use of e-commerce.

A study was attempted to ascertain factors that could help consumers in Nigeria conduct e-commerce transactions. Three hundred questionnaires were sent to recipients via email; 180 useful responses were received. Female respondents composed 22.2 per cent of the sample and male respondents 78 per cent. The majority of respondents are aged 20–40.

From the survey, electricity generation, government policy, insufficient technology and fraud were factors stated to be preventing consumers in Nigeria from engaging in e-commerce. Most of the consumers were hindered by irregular power supply. The awareness rate of e-commerce transactions for goods and services was not high, and there was low confidence in the potential of e-commerce transactions. However, 93 per cent of respondents felt they would conduct e-commerce transactions if other issues could be resolved. Respondents indicated strong preferences for using fixed-line means of accessing and conducting e-commerce, rather than using a mobile phone. This is because the speed of mobile phone connections is not as high as for fixed lines.

Bandwidth availability, access cost, ease of use of web content and security are major factors that influence the behaviour of consumers in conducting e-commerce. Most of the respondents selected the need for high bandwidth, followed by reasonable cost of access. The ease of use of web content is low because most respondents are already Internet users. Most respondents suggested that the lack of zip or postal codes in the country limits transactions.

At the time of the study, there was no trusted central payments facilitator available in Nigeria, such as PayPal. E-commerce transactions originating from Nigeria are therefore not always accepted or are blocked, despite the introduction of Mastercard and Visa. The majority of e-commerce transactions are therefore carried out within the country. Typically, these are for paying bills, often those for utilities. This means that only a small set of the potential e-commerce portfolio is being used.

9.1 Intended learning outcomes

On completion of this chapter the reader should be able to:

1 describe some of the most common e-commerce technologies;
2 explain why legacy systems pose the most challenging functionality and integration problems for e-commerce;
3 argue why systems integration is still a major technical challenge;
4 outline how services-oriented architecture may resolve some of the problems;
5 explain that business and organizational management is needed to gain the best use of technology in e-commerce;
6 consider critically major risks associated with e-commerce.

9.2 Introduction

Information and communication technologies (ICT) play very important roles in the advancements of commerce. Many organizations are now intermediaries that create added value by storing, manipulating and transferring purchasing power between different parties. To achieve this, they rely on ICT to perform many functions, including book-keeping, information storage, enabling customer communications and controlling and monitoring the delivery of goods and services.

E-commerce relies heavily on ICT to achieve its promise of 24-hours availability, low error rates and quicker delivery of products and services. When considering e-commerce technologies, commercial websites usually come to mind first, but e-commerce requires much more than just a good website. It needs back-end applications such as account systems, support applications and communication technologies, as well as middleware to integrate all these different systems.

There are two main forms of e-commerce system. This classification is based on the level of interactivity of the site (weak, average, strong) and on the type of opportunities pursued by the organization (informational, transactional, client relationship). The type of technology to be used evolves with the increase in interactivity and functionality of the organization's website. An informational site is primarily based on a brochureware model, while an e-commerce website oriented towards the management of client relationships requires more sophisticated technologies like customer relationship management (CRM) and knowledge management.

9.3 Software applications

Most organizations have several different computer applications for their products and/or services. In most cases these systems were developed decades ago, so they are often labelled 'legacy systems'. There are many problems associated with such systems, including integrating them with each other and with newer systems. They also suffer from inflexibility in terms of expansion or scaling down, and rising costs of maintenance due to the ageing process, as well as increasing scarcity of skills (such as first-generation language programming) needed to maintain them. These problems often affect even strategic-level business decision, such as forming partnerships with other organizations or mergers.

Legacy systems often fall short in provision of business intelligence for compliance, sales and management needs, or management decision-making. This is mainly due to the fact that the data formats used are often incompatible with modern data-mining tools, and without data from these core systems the resulting business intelligence would often be incomplete or even misleading. New product development can also be a problem, as the systems would have to be hard-coded even just to make simple product or price changes, which can be very time-consuming and costly. Good customer service is also difficult to achieve because the systems do not offer a consistent look and feel and are often too slow to respond.

One potential solution is replacement, but high costs and high business risks make this unattractive. Another alternative is to reengineer these systems first and then wrap them with new technology, which can provide functionality as a service to other systems and allow changes to the core systems without the need to redevelop all systems. Later systems can be divided and replaced/redeveloped on a piecemeal basis. This approach, if executed well, can help link an organization's infrastructure with modern business process-driven applications. To implement it, organizations may have at least partially to implement the middleware such as service oriented architecture (described later in this chapter). In addition, very good project management and support from top management in terms of provision of required resources would be crucial.

Another solution is outsourcing, as there are standard software packages available to manage most online products/services delivery. This option is often more risky and usually small- or medium-sized organizations choose it because they may not have enough resources to build these systems themselves. To mitigate the risks, software packages and vendors have to be chosen carefully to ensure best fit with the existing systems and business processes.

Integration with other systems that support different service delivery channels, such as stores/branches or the Internet, is also key to ensuring efficient enterprise-wide workflow information and to giving the organization a uniform look and feel, especially at the customer contact points. Security should always be a major priority when any changes in core systems are implemented. To this end, core systems may have to work with new biometric technologies, whether that takes the form of retinal scans, fingerprints or voice recognition.

Business continuity – that is, implementation of disaster recovery systems – is another fast-developing area, receiving much more attention now due to risks of events such as natural disasters and terrorism. In the USA, for example, many businesses were directly affected by the destruction wrought by Hurricane Katrina in 2005. They learned the hard way how unprepared they really were. The damage was so severe in certain regions that some organizations couldn't bring up systems until six months after the hurricane. Likelihood of this kind of event means that many organizations have renewed their focus on preparedness as they rethink their risk management strategies and bolster their business continuity plans (Amato-McCoy, 2006).

Continuity plans need to be revisited and updated every three months as a minimum, as one or more components of the continuity systems may not work when needed. Regular testing and simulation of disasters and mock recovery exercises are often needed to uncover any weak links. Every scenario and every possibility needs to be accounted for and drills need to be exercised and recovery plans put into action to keep them ready. This will ensure that organizations can get back to business quickly in the event of downtimes.

9.4 Customer relationship management systems

CRM systems are technology-enabled tools that help manage an organization's relationship with its customers. CRM systems help to gather/store customer data and analyse this data to enable customized marketing. They are often used to semi-automate customer services. The main purpose of CRM is often stated as enriching relationships with customers to gain greater loyalty, as well as revenues, though they have been used to cut the costs of customer services processes. In an e-commerce context, CRM software can help move customers from expensive branch- or phone-based services to self-help services via the Internet.

There have been numerous CRM successes and failures reported in the literature. As with other new technologies, success largely depends on how an organization manages the change process and implements new business processes. One example of successful implementation of CRM is at TotalJobs Group, a recruitment company based in the United Kingdom. The company originally introduced a hosted CRM system to the sales force, and two years later, it rolled the system out to the rest of the organization. The system presents each employee with a single view of the customer, so that important information can be obtained easily and quickly before contacting a customer. A useful indicator is the customer satisfaction survey, which has regularly shown continuing increases in customer satisfaction since the implementation.

Failures in CRM can often be traced to rigid corporate structures and cultures rather than technology itself. Vendors can also over-promise, so organizations planning to implement CRM systems need to evaluate their own needs first and then conduct a detailed evaluation of how these systems can meet those needs, rather than relying on the sales pitch of the vendors. A major reason CRM systems may disappoint is that they often cannot overcome integration problems, as they have to interact with problematic legacy systems.

9.5 Middleware

Lack of integration with other systems is one of the most common reasons for failures of the previously discussed technologies. There are many ways of tackling the problem of integration, such as re-coding parts of existing systems or replacing them altogether, but due to the related issues discussed above, middleware technologies have become popular. These technologies enable different types of systems to integrate with each other, and make it easier to integrate future systems. Potential benefits, such as reduced IT costs, systems integration and greater business agility have persuaded many organizations to adopt services-oriented architecture (SOA).

SOA is different from other computer applications development paradigms such as object-oriented software development. According to O'Donnel (2005), the advantages of SOA over other software development technologies is that by externalizing functionality into re-usable components and organizing them into a logical framework, it minimizes two of the greatest causes of delay. These are: the need for exhaustive communication between the business and IT; and the need for IT people to write code. In addition, unlike other IT paradigms, organizations can, in most cases, also re-use their legacy systems as SOA enables legacy systems to communicate with other systems.

In the context of SOA, services are self-describing, platform-independent computer programs that enable rapid and often low-cost composition of distributed IT solutions.

Services perform functions, which can be anything from simple requests to complicated business processes. As illustrated in Figure 9.1, services are offered by service providers or by brokers. To use these services, organizations need to build architecture based on universal standards so that new services can be added quickly. That architecture is SOA.

SOA builds on protocols such as extensible markup language (XML), simple object access protocol (SOAP), web services description language (WSDL), and on the concept of business process re-engineering (BPR).

Often viewed as a methodology rather than just a technology, SOA can be implemented across multiple projects, both internally and externally, eliminating the need to rebuild similar services for each project. Many vendors now offer SOA-related products such as messaging solutions or business process management tools (BPM) that help implement SOA. It is still a complex task that requires considerable upfront investment, a high level of technical expertise and very careful change management. Despite this, many organizations are adopting SOA because of the following benefits:

- integrating legacy systems
- service reuse
- shorter development cycle
- flexibility.

While such benefits will persuade many businesses to implement SOA, there are still many barriers, such as:

- large upfront investment
- complexity
- lack of mature development tools
- choosing a vendor
- governance
- adoption
- security
- service management
- website development issues.

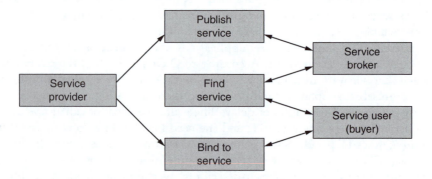

Figure 9.1 A simple model of service-oriented architecture.

9.6 Mobile e-commerce

Some organizations are making significant investments in mobile e-commerce systems to deliver several types of business value, from increased efficiency and cost reduction to improved operational effectiveness and customer service to gain a competitive advantage. A factor that has contributed to this development has been the extended availability and capacity of mobile communications infrastructure around the world.

The number of types of mobile devices has been increasing rapidly, and the functionality available has also improved dramatically over the last five years. The shrinking costs of data transmission and – due to the intense competition from suppliers – the reduced cost of devices have catalysed the distribution of mobile technologies and amplified the growth of the worldwide mobile market. In those countries where the traditional telecommunication infrastructure is not well developed, mobile technologies are transforming accessibility to Internet-based services.

M-commerce may be described as the newest channel to provide a convenient way of performing online transactions using mobile phones or other mobile devices. The potential for m-commerce may be far greater than typical desktop access, as there are several times more mobile phone users than online PC users. Increasingly 'mobile lifestyles' may also fuel the growth of anywhere, anytime activities.

There are two main types of technology available for use in mobile commerce: wireless application protocol (WAP) and wireless Internet gateway (WIG). WAP is an application environment and set of communication protocols for wireless devices designed to enable manufacturer-, vendor- and platform-independent access to the Internet and advanced telephony services. WIG is a short message service (SMS)-based service, in which a menu of available online products and services is initially downloaded from the organization to the phone device. This enables users to browse websites and perform purchase-related tasks.

Mobile commerce such as banking was offered in the United Kingdom by banks such as the Woolwich during the early 2000s, but it failed to achieve a critical mass of users. The same story has been repeated in many other countries with mixed results. The main hurdle in development of mobile commerce is low consumer adoption due to a number of factors, including:

- website development issues
- Internet connectivity costs
- difficult user interface
- lack of awareness amongst customers
- security concerns
- organizational changes
- small number of choices
- technology overload.

To promote adoption, customers need to be made aware of the advantages that m-commerce may offer over other channels. Customers should be provided with opportunities to try m-commerce or see demonstrations. This would raise awareness and give people a better understanding of m-commerce options. In addition, services being offered should be widely advertised to the target market, such as young people – who tend to be early adopters of innovative services.

Perceptions of risk, as with many innovations, need to be addressed by limiting customers' liability, as well as implementation of the latest security technologies and other procedures to minimize risks. New generations of mobile devices use encrypted digital signature and other related technologies to enhance security. The functionality and user interface of mobile devices is improving all the time, whereas the cost of Internet connectivity, at least in the developed world, is decreasing. These developments mean the prospect of widespread m-commerce adoption now looks brighter than ever.

An example of m-commerce is reported by Geach (2007). Named M-pessa, the system was developed by mobile phone operator Safaricom in Kenya. It was launched to improve the efficiency of microfinance by using mobile technology to make financial transactions cheaper, quicker and accessible to a much wider population. M-pessa is a fully operational service available to phone users in Kenya. The ideas and systems were adopted from South Korea, and proved to be especially useful for people with no access to the Internet through their computers. Basically, M-pessa is a financial service application installed on a mobile phone. A new-generation SIM card is needed, with M-pessa software embedded. Upgrades from older SIM cards are available free of charge and work on most mobile phone sets, so users don't have to buy a new handset to access it.

Similar systems could be implemented in advanced countries; the registered outlet could be a post office, bank, mobile phone retailer or local grocery shop. The main advantage is that a bank is not needed by either party. All that is needed is traditional cash (or card) to pay into the service provider's account by the person wishing to send the funds. This service would be especially useful for people without a local bank or without a bank account at all.

M-pessa provides fairly low-cost service in Kenya (18¢ to $1.24). Benefits for businesses are that the potential customer base is increased by providing another means of payment and easy access to funds that, for some people, currently do not exist. This has the potential, therefore, to help maintain and increase trade in local shops. Security of such a system could be a problem. The mobile phone itself could be stolen, potentially allowing the thief to transfer or withdraw funds. The phone could be hacked into, akin to what is done in desktop environments. In the case of a stolen phone, the built-in PIN and authentication provisions of mobile payments should mean that – provided these security details are not held with the phone – the thief should not have the chance to use the phone for fraudulent purposes. Extra security could come from CCTV at the registered outlets or the stolen/misused phone could be blocked by the network providers. Anti-virus software could also be provided at low cost to counter the threat of hacking and viruses.

Recent trends suggest that, with the arrival of more functionality and user friendliness in mobile technologies, these technologies might be ready for the delivery of m-commerce. To cash in on improved prospects, at least in the developed world, some banks such as Citibank in the USA have re-introduced mobile (or wireless device) banking. This service allows mobile phone or other wireless devices such as BlackBerry users to enter a six-digit PIN to access a wide range of online services, including online shopping.

Experiments are also underway – mainly in Japan, Norway and the USA – to turn these mobile devices into payment tools. Often called 'contactless payments', it involves swiping an enabled mobile phone near a point-of-sale terminal to make payments which could be a bill or purchase of goods. These efforts to develop such systems often have support from credit card vendors, who are looking for new ways to make payment processes more convenient.

9.7 Challenges in e-commerce technologies

Numerous technical challenges still remain to be tackled. Internet security is still one of the major issues hindering the growth of e-commerce. Owing to the structure and intention of the Internet to be an open network, purchase-related transactions are often exposed to many risks. Internet fraud is common, and related stories get considerable media attention, making some people hesitant to buy online. Different security methods (for both hardware and software) are being tested and employed continuously, but there is still some way to go to make online transactions secure and win the trust of many customers. The nature of security threats is evolving and changing continually, so e-commerce managers need to be aware of new security threats as well as new methods of combating those threats in order to stay on top of this challenge.

Managing information security is a very complex issue. Clarke (2007) argues that the domain is dominated by a set of practical controls that are seen as rigid, unclear and largely irrelevant to the business needs of most organizations. Even within some recent developments that have sought to provide a more accessible model for managing information security, most current practice is based around the needs of the technology and information rather than the needs of people in general and e-commerce users in particular. Where human issues are considered, it is to confer responsibilities and education on people to conform to the needs of the system, with the aim of regulating their behaviour.

Figure 9.2 summarizes the position reached so far, and gives some idea of the complexity of the issues. This model would be useful in planning for a comprehensive security provision.

Figure 9.2 helps in understanding the various dimensions in managing information security; Figure 9.3 helps provides some structure. Getting the basic controls in place is the highest priority because failure to do so would most likely undermine the whole security practice, irrespective of its social/technical biases. The next priority is to make sure the practice is regularly reviewed to check whether it is meeting the needs of its users and the business. Third, the evaluative model must be used to improve the practice towards a more socially aware approach. Underpinning all of this is the need to identify and deal with neutral, counter-productive and other-responsibility biased processes and controls. One way to deal with this is to remove neutral and counter-productive controls altogether and to reassign other-responsibility to the appropriate department within the organization, but clearly maintain such controls as dependencies for the information security practice.

There are numerous technological issues with regard to e-commerce. Lack of unified messaging standards is one of them. While Internet messaging standards are fast evolving towards unification, the problem of legacy systems still remains one of the main obstacles to e-commerce. Many large organizations still operate on large mainframe-based legacy systems for their core processing functions. While this is fine for some isolated functions, e-commerce requires capabilities such as the ability to integrate with other systems, which legacy systems are ill-equipped to provide. E-commerce systems are often complex, large-scale systems with demanding requirements for performance, scalability and availability, and even the most technologically sophisticated organizations are struggling to overcome all of these issues.

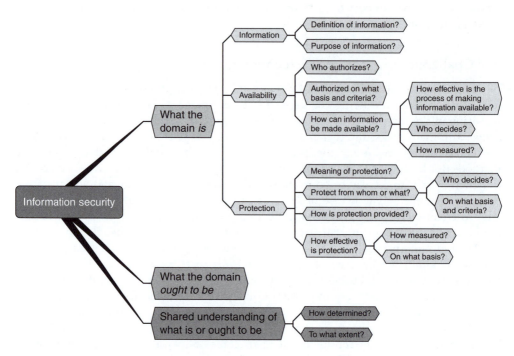

Figure 9.2 The complexity of information security (source: Clarke, 2007, p. 147 – used by permission).

Success in e-commerce often depends on how an organization has to re-shape itself to enable business online. An organization needs to have process-oriented and fully integrated systems to achieve the desired benefits from e-commerce. Even in cases of disparate applications, or where the company does not abandon existing applications (e.g. legacy systems), there are solutions to the problem. Several alternatives are available for increasing the level of systems integration. Data warehousing – discussed above – can provide a cheap alternative for data integration. Other technologies, such as enterprise applications integration (EAI) or SOA, may turn legacy systems (as well as other business applications) into strategic assets at a relatively low cost. EAI is a class of software that aims to provide an integration infrastructure for business applications. A similar approach is the development of middleware for systems integration.

One key technology management challenge is that systems must scale to accommodate business growth. Maintaining excellent performance across growing workloads is imperative. There is no greater customer inconvenience than a poor, unpredictable response – and in e-commerce competitors are only a few clicks away! The requirement for scalability goes beyond the ability to use more powerful servers, to distribute workload across a few server platforms or to balance communications traffic across multiple servers. Approaches to system architecture, software structure and workload distribution are needed to ensure scalability.

Availability of systems and security of data has always been an important issue, but is arguably even more critical in e-commerce, with 24 hours per day, seven days per week availability. Any unauthorized access to data or unplanned 'downtime' of systems

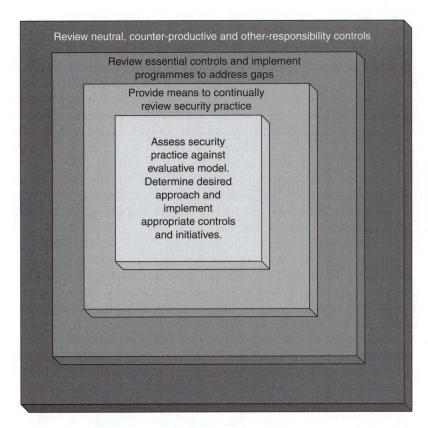

Figure 9.3 Framework for applying security practice (source: Clarke, 2007, p. 155 – used by permission).

can result in a public relations disaster. At the same time, threats from computer viruses, frauds and terrorism are commonly perceived to be increasing. This all means that a considerable IT budget is spent on fraud prevention and disaster recovery systems, which may include investment in encryption technologies, other security measures and maintaining two parallel sets of systems to ensure all-the-time availability. The following guidelines are becoming an integral part of e-commerce-related systems implementation.

1   Capacity and 'stress' testing should be done regularly, as prediction of demand for e-commerce systems can be more difficult than for traditional systems.
2   In the area of security, being online opens up systems to the outside world. Investments in security-related software/hardware will be a major expense.
3   Identity theft and fraud in online environments are one of the major threats to the existence of e-commerce. Firms need to keep up with new and evolving sources of threat.

Although many of these risks are unique to e-commerce, the principles of general good IT risk management apply in most cases.

9.8 Summary

This chapter has covered some of the most common e-commerce technologies. These technologies include product-related back-end systems, data warehousing, CRM systems and knowledge management systems, as well as middleware technologies such as SOA. Product-specific systems (legacy systems) are often the oldest systems in organizations, and pose the most challenging functionality and integration problems. These systems require considerable upgrading to support e-commerce. Data warehousing systems help organizations to gather, organize, store and analyse data for various operational and marketing uses. CRM systems are mainly used to enrich relationships with customers and to employ carefully targeted marketing strategies.

These systems become most useful when they work together. Integration is still a major technical challenge, and the arrival of integration technologies such as SOA is helping to resolve some of the problems. It is important to stress that technology is one dimension of e-commerce success, and careful management of social and strategic issues is also needed.

Website development-related issues are also growing in complexity, giving rise to the debate about technical versus social approaches to the development. As usual in any type of technology, technical views take higher priority in the beginning and related social issues gain recognition more slowly. The main challenge here is *not* to see web development and management as a problem to be solved by technical people. A framework (for example, of user groups) needs to be developed, from which the contribution from representatives of all stakeholders should be sought. Membership of participating groups or committees should not be fixed and, of course, should not be limited to managers or those in authority.

E-commerce also brings a new set of risks; organizations have to put in place structures to manage these risks. This structure may include an e-commerce risk management framework that enables controls to address the security, availability and adequacy of systems. The nature of those controls will depend on several factors, such as the extent of the technological dependency, sources of threat and extent of cross-industry collaboration to combat these threats. Organizations need to have a policy statement setting out the e-commerce risk management framework, and an organizational structure with clear responsibilities for the implementation of the framework and relevant processes and controls. Adherence to the principles of ISO Standard 17799, the international standard for information security management, is helpful in developing organizational structures and processes to manage e-commerce-related security risks.

Glossary

Content management system   A web-based CMS enables you to manage your site without knowing HTML, JavaScript or other web-related technologies. All you need to know is the content, what it should be, what it should look like and where it should go.

Customer relationship management   CRM defines a class of software applications which integrates the management of customer service, marketing and sales into a unified system. CRM systems provide an enhanced ability to share information, better tracking of customers and automation of routine services, and enable the customer to manage parts of their own data.

Data mining   The primary goal of data mining is to extract useful information from databases where tracking that extracted information was not the original goal of the database. Its practical application is to make better use of existing information in projecting sales and marketing efforts, and can also be very useful when trying to enter new, but related, markets.

Digital certificate   The electronic equivalent of an ID card that authenticates the source of a digital signature.

Digital signatures   A security option that uses two keys, one public and one private, which are used to encrypt messages before transmission and to decrypt them on receipt.

Enterprise resource planning   ERP systems are designed to consolidate all back-end systems across the enterprise into a series of interrelated software applications. Depending on the company, it is used to track and manage operations involving the manufacturing of goods, inventory control, accounting, human resources, marketing and long-term planning.

Encryption   A data security technique used to protect information from unauthorized inspection or alteration. Information is encoded so it appears as a meaningless string of letters and symbols during delivery or transmission. Upon receipt, the information is decoded using an encryption key.

Firewall   A firewall is a point on the network topography, generally between two disparate networks, that enforces rules on what types of data can pass thorough that point. In businesses, firewalls are generally used to prevent unwanted traffic from coming or leaving a private network.

HTML   Hypertext markup language. A set of codes that can be inserted into text files to indicate special typefaces, images and links to other hypertext documents.

Hyperlink   An item on a webpage that, when selected, transfers the user directly to another location in a hypertext document or to another webpage, perhaps on a different machine. Also simply called a 'link'.

Information management   Describes the measures required for the effective collection, storage, access, use and disposal of information to support agency business processes. The core of these measures is the management of the definition, ownership, sensitivity, quality and accessibility of information. These measures are addressed at appropriate stages in the strategic planning lifecycle and applied at appropriate stages in the operational lifecycle of the information itself.

Information systems   Organized collections of hardware, software, supplies, policies, procedures and people, which store, process and provide *access* to information.

Internet   A cooperative message-forwarding system linking computer networks all over the world.

Knowledge management   A framework (methodology) of enabling individuals, teams and entire organizations to collectively and systematically create, share and apply knowledge, using various tools, to better achieve their objectives.

Legacy systems   A term commonly used to refer to existing computer systems and applications with which new systems or applications must exchange information.

Middleware   Software that acts as an intermediary between different computer applications so they can communicate with each other.

Outsourcing   The practice of contracting with another entity to perform services that might otherwise be conducted in-house.

Service-oriented architecture   A flexible set of design principles used during the phases of systems development and integration.

Website   The service of providing ongoing support and monitoring of an Internet-addressable computer that stores webpages and processes transactions initiated over the Internet.

References

Amato-McCoy, D. (2006) *Planning For Continuity*. Available online at www.financetech.com/printableArticle.jhtml?articleID=181400621 (accessed 7 July 2010).

Clarke, S. (2007) *Information Systems Strategic Management: An Integrated Approach*, 2nd edition. London: Routledge.

Further reading

Chaffey, D. (2010) *E-Business and E-Commerce Management: Strategy, Implementation and Practice*, 4th edition. London: Prentice Hall/Financial Times.

Geach, N. (2007) *The Digital Divide, Financial Exclusion and Mobile Phone Technology: Two Problems One Solution? British and Irish Law, Education and Technology Association 2007 Annual Conference*. Hertfordshire, 16–17 April.

O'Donnell, A. (2005) Journey to Service-oriented Architecture, *Insurance and Technology*, September, 30.

Shah, M.H. and Clarke, S. (2009) *E-Banking Management: Issues, Solutions and Strategies*. Hershey, PA: IGI Global.

Stahl, B. (2008) *Information Systems Critical Perspectives*. London: Routledge.

Xu, L. (2007) *Frontiers in Enterprise Integration*. London: Routledge.

Suggested activities

1   Think about any organization you are familiar with; consider what e-commerce-related technologies they use and why.

2   Consider how knowledge management could be used to aid e-commerce.

3   Think about the advantages and disadvantages of using CRM to manage e-commerce-related customer services.

10 Organizational behaviour

Case study 10.1 Organizational behaviour in the public sector

This case study has been included by the authors to facilitate class discussion rather than to illustrate effective or ineffective management practices. Only publicly available material has been used to write this case study, and it does not reflect any opinions of employees or management at the organizations mentioned.

Globalization has led to a growing competitive environment, with new markets and deregulation. Efficient and effective use of resources is as important as ever, and organizations have to adapt quickly and need to be flexible. Managers have to lead strategic and organizational changes more often than at any other time, and organizational behaviour and change management are key factors in success. Initially, much attention was paid to the private sector, but understanding organizational behaviour and managing change are just as important in the public sector.

The Swedish Forest Agency's (SFA) mission is to make sure that Swedish forests, both public and private, are preserved and maintained so biological diversity can flourish and that sustainable growth of timber can be secured. The government is their main source of funding, but they also offer some services to private forest owners.

Previously the SFA consisted of ten autonomous authorities, but in 2006 it changed to a centralized organization divided into five geographical regions, with an average of nine districts in each region. There are also two supporting units, one providing expert knowledge to the districts and the other taking care of administration for all districts. The Swedish Tax Agency (STA) is in charge of all issues concerning tax, inventory of estate, national registration, economic crime and debt receivables of the state. In 2005 taxes collected by the government amounted to 51 per cent of GDP.

The general tax on labour in Sweden is 31 per cent (2005) and on average every Swedish citizen pays approximately 150,000 SEK in tax per year, including tax on labour, capital and consumption. Previously the STA was organized autonomously in each county, but in September 2005 it underwent an organizational change and now consists of seven tax regions serving people and small companies, with a separate office for larger companies. The organization also has an office in charge of administration and other supporting functions for local offices in all regions.

The Swedish Social Insurance Agency (SSIA) is the public welfare system that is intended to support people if they are unable to work due to illness, disability or adverse family matters. When people need help they apply to the SSIA, which decides upon what kind of help is needed. The SSIA spent approximately 15 per cent of the Swedish GDP in 2006, which amounted to 409 billion SEK.

The SSIA is organized in three main units. The national and local insurance centres that handle and take decisions on applications for support, and a self-service customer service centre that deal with simpler matters. The insurance centres have access to special units that assist and provide information requested by employees. This organizational structure is new as of 2008 and replaced the old structure, which consisted of three main units organized locally.

The Swedish Public Employment Agency (SPEA) serves as a link between employers and potential employees in order to make the labour market more efficient. They also analyse and evaluate how the labour market is changing, and in which segments there will be a lack of employees in the future, in order to help achieve a high rate of employment.

Previously the SPEA consisted of autonomous offices in each county. In 2008 the organization was divided into four main areas, which in turn were divided into 64 market areas based on where people live and where most companies recruit labour. The core organization also has supporting units which provide special help to the local offices.

10.1 Intended learning outcomes

On completion of this chapter the reader should be able to:

1   explain the importance of organizational behaviour, change management and human resource management;
2   describe the nature and scope of organizational behaviour;
3   summarize various types of organizational culture;
4   outline main factors in organizational development, change and teams;
5   select hard or soft approaches as appropriate to different situations;
6   describe main activities and issues in recruitment, employment relations and performance management.

10.2 Introduction

Organizational behaviour (OB) is about the behaviour of people within organizations, the context and process of management and the organization and activities of work. It is largely about intra-organizational relationships. The behaviour of people, the process of management, the organizational context, work processes and interactions with the external environment are all considered within the domain of OB. This means OB is concerned with individuals, groups, departments, the organization as a whole and the organization and its environment.

Organizations have some common factors that are integrated in various ways. The essentials are people, processes and technology. Within the integration of these factors, organizations will set objectives and create structures. Organizations exist to achieve their objectives, and these vary enormously, depending on the nature of the organization. Organizations are social constructs created by individuals and groups. An organization must have purpose, but each individual may interpret purposes very differently, and people may have their own agendas.

Factors in the internal and external environments can affect organizational behaviour and change management. Ineffective change can result in loss of time, resources, money and trust, and these can be disastrous for an organization. Organizational structures have changed radically in the last quarter of the twentieth century. During industrialization, structures tended to be bureaucratic, power came from the top, tasks were of a routine level and most employees were not supposed to take part in decision-making processes. This trend continued directly after the Second World War, when it was initially thought that methods of managing military operations could be used in civilian organizations. It soon became apparent that this was not the case. As Western economies shifted from industry to services, and knowledge workers became more common, different approaches to management had to be developed. Today, employees are not simply practitioners, they now have closer social relations with the external environment, and organizations need to consider employee satisfaction and commitment as a strategic element to increase participation, increase productivity and decrease employee turnover.

This chapter discusses concepts of organization structure and behaviour, the practice of organizing within the workplace and some of the human resource functions that relate to OB. Areas of interest include theories of organizations, approaches to management – including classical, scientific and human relations – and contingency theory. The nature of organizations, organizational goals, strategies and responsibilities, managerial behaviour and leadership are covered. Topics include design of structure, objectives, functions, span of control, chain of command, patterns of work, organization structure and change management. The chapter concludes with human resource aspects, such as the individual in the organization, work motivation and rewards.

10.3 Organizational culture

Organizational culture may be considered as a set of values, beliefs, understandings and ways of thinking that are shared by members of an organization. Such culture will be taught to new members of the group, and used to help face external problems together and to protect the group from outsiders – for example, to protect resources. Culture is also used to present a common image to those outside the group, to deter people the group may consider undesirable and to attract those the group considers desirable.

Sometimes culture is considered as simple as the difference between 'us' and 'them'. 'We' know our group and 'they' are not in it! Thus culture makes 'us' different from everyone else and forms boundaries to define the group. This boundary and grouping help give the group a feeling of strength and survival. Culture includes a pattern of basic assumptions and is invented, discovered or developed by a given group.

Culture may be positive as the group learns to cope with problems of external adaptation and internal integration, but it may also be negative and may result in inflexibility and ultimately the decline of an organization. A strong culture is one that has worked well enough over time to be considered valid, can be taught to new members and is considered by a group as the way to perceive, think and feel in relation to issues that arise.

As an example of culture, consider how people communicate. In one organization formal memos may be considered the norm, while in another, popping in unannounced to someone's office in order to resolve a problem swiftly may be what people do every day. A third form of common communication is via email; a fourth is by telephone. If you arrive at an organization that considers it the norm to pop into a colleague's office to resolve an issue, and instead you send a formal memo, you might find that word gets around very quickly and it becomes a very challenging place for you to work.

Culture has been likened to an iceberg, with no more than a third visible and the rest below the surface. The interesting thing about this is that the invisible layer may also be just as invisible to those within the culture as it is to those outside the culture. Cultural norms may be so ingrained that people assume these norms without considering that they may be cultural.

It is generally recognized that culture exists and may be very powerful, but you cannot see it, touch it or feel it. There are, however, artefacts that both influence culture and are influenced by it. This is a reflection of the continuing cycle: culture being formed by people; that culture influencing people; and people influencing culture. Artefacts include things you can recognize via your physical senses of hearing, sight, smell and touch. There is a distinctive cooking aroma from Indian restaurants that most of us would recognize if we were blindfolded. That aroma evokes thoughts of certain foods that you can almost taste and see without even having looked at the menu! Symbols, such as firms' logos are very powerful artefacts. Language, including jargon, can be used to help cement a group's identity and keep outsiders on the outside. Norms and behaviours may be used in similar ways. These artefacts are the equivalent of the part of the iceberg that can be seen.

If artefacts are the tip of the iceberg, what lies beneath the surface? Attitudes may vary enormously from organization to organization and from department to department. Consider two very different answers to one question: 'Hi John, I've got a bit of a problem with the photocopier. Would you give me a hand please?'

'Of course. What seems to be wrong?'

'Sorry, I don't have time, and anyway, it's not my job.'

Communication patterns have been mentioned previously. No one tells you to use email or phone or talk face-to-face. These things are part of the organization's culture. They will not appear on any organizational chart or promotional literature. Informal team processes reflect culture and can help define it. The personalities of people may be reinforced by culture: 'Go to the shop on the corner for that. They are always pleasant. Never go to the one in the high street. They are really miserable there.' Conflict may be ever present or may hardly exist. People may engage in political machinations and in what is sometimes called 'back-stabbing'. In another organization people may work together and may use the adage of never saying anything about someone else unless it is good. In one organization, members of staff may feel confident about their knowledge and skills and have a 'bootstrapping' culture of support. In another organization people may feel inadequate and resort to criticizing others in attempts to boost their own status.

Culture may often be a reflection of the values of the founders of an organization; once established, it is difficult and slow to change. It is reinforced by rites of passage, enhancement, renewal and integration. Rites of passage may include some form of initiation. In days gone past, apprentices at certain motor manufacturers were stripped, smeared with grease and hung from chains. This must have been a rather unpleasant experience, and hopefully not something that happens today. It did, however, confirm the new entrant as 'one of the lads' that had undergone a transition to the new job.

Rites of enhancement include establishing social identity and status – an example would be at an awards ceremony, say for sales person of the year. Rites of renewal help to refurbish social structures and functions, and include someone becoming more involved in organizational development, for example. Rites of integration are about reviving and increasing commitment, and could include helping to organize the office party and attending it. Note that some of the activities involved do not provide mutual exclusion of rites. For example, attending the office party might assist with two or three rites.

Stories are used to help establish and retain culture, and they are often about corporate or local heroes. Sometimes the stories are social and not directly work-related at all. They relate to work in the sense that the people involved will often be from the same department or site. An example is a bowling team. The activity is entirely social, but links to work because it is the work's team. The hero of the day could be someone who gets a series of strikes to win a close game. Another form of hero could be someone who steps in to buy a failing company, saves jobs that were at risk and turns around the company's fortunes. Legends and myths are often used to teach corporate values, and good leaders understand the power of narrative.

A culture that helps employees to feel valued and special may assist in gaining competitive advantage by fostering creativity, innovation, customer focus and open communication. A dysfunctional culture may assist in achieving competitive disadvantage by fostering resistance to change, lack of creativity, inertia and a lack of customer care. Have you ever been to a supermarket checkout and had to wait while two employees discuss their work situation, such as when their breaks are due, which days they will be working and so on? Have you ever waited while they discuss what was on the television yesterday evening?

You should recall from Chapter 2 that managers engage in planning, organizing, leading and controlling. How does culture affect these activities and how do these activities affect culture? The answers depend on how 'things are done around here'. In planning, how much risk should be involved? Are planners risk averse, risk neutral or risk lovers? Are plans developed by individuals or teams? How much effort is put into considering external factors?

When organizing, how much is centrally controlled and how much is devolved? Should tasks be done by individuals or teams? How much do managers interact with each other and with other members of staff? In leading, are managers concerned with increasing employee satisfaction? What leadership styles are used? Are challenges welcomed or dismissed? In controlling, is imposition the norm or do employees tend to take responsibility for their own actions? What criteria are important in employee performance evaluations?

10.4 Types of culture

There are many types of culture and many ways of classifying them. Tables 10.1 and 10.2 indicate some of the things that reflect culture and are part of it. Table 10.1 shows some of the important things that comprise culture. Table 10.2 shows how adaptive and non-adaptive cultures relate to core values and common behaviours. Note that cultural types are not mutually exclusive and there can be mixed cultures within a single organization. Different departments may have different cultures and groups may exhibit traits from a number of cultures.

Table 10.1 Some elements of culture

Element	How important are these?
Attention to detail	Analysis and precision
Outcome-focused	Results
People-focused	Relationships
Team-focused	Groups and co-operation
Aggressiveness	Intra-organizational competition
Stability	Status quo
Innovation and risk	Change

Many of us would feel that we have come across bureaucratic cultures, especially in dealing with large organizations and intransigent 'customer services' staff. Such a culture tends to occur in organizations where there is little or no feedback and where feedback is not welcomed. In this case, people often become bogged down with how things are done, not with what is to be achieved. This is also known as the difference between doing something right (such as making sure you use the correct form) and doing the right thing (such as making sure the customer gets what is needed). Such cultures are often criticized for being very traditional, very hierarchical, and for being 'wrapped up in red tape'. It can be argued that they produce consistent results, and if you consider a wartime situation, an army would work like this.

A power culture concentrates power among a few people, which can result in swift decision-making. Sometimes this culture is considered to be like a spider's web, with control radiating from the centre. Power cultures tend to have few rules and little bureaucracy, and they often occur in small enterprises.

A blame culture tends to cultivate distrust and fear. The most important thing in a blame culture is to make sure that you are not held responsible for things that go wrong, as opposed to focusing on achieving the goals of the organization. People blame each other to avoid being reprimanded or put down. This may result in no new ideas or personal initiative because people do not want to risk being wrong.

A tough guy or macho culture often includes quick feedback and high rewards. It is often associated with fast-moving financial activities such as brokerage, but could also apply to the military, a police force and athletes competing in team sports (such as a football team). This can be a very stressful culture in which to operate. This culture is similar in some ways to the 'work-hard-play-hard' culture, but this culture is

Table 10.2 Adaptive and non-adaptive cultures

	Core values	Common behaviours
Adaptive	Managers care about stakeholders	Value people and pay attention to comments. Change is seen as an opportunity to innovate and improve.
Non-adaptive	Managers care about themselves and are risk averse	Poor communication. Change is seen as a threat and is therefore resisted. Comments are not welcome.

characterized by few risks being taken, though it does have rapid feedback. It is typical of some large organizations that strive to give high-quality customer service. It is often recognized by the use of team meetings, jargon and buzzwords.

In a brand-congruent culture people believe in the product or service of the organization. They feel good about what their company is trying to achieve, and they cooperate to achieve it. People are passionate and seem to have similar goals in the organization. They use personal resources to actively solve problems, and while they don't always accept the actions of management or others around them, they see their job as important. Almost everyone in this culture is operating at a group level.

These are just some examples of culture types, and should not be construed as an exhaustive list.

10.5 Organizational development, change and teams

There are many different types of area of interest or problem situations within organizations. Some are technical and require what are known as hard approaches. Some are about human interaction and require what are known as soft approaches. Table 10.3 highlights the main features of these approaches.

Organizational development involves people in human activity systems, and therefore suits soft rather than hard approaches. Organizational development needs to consider things such as power bases, organizational culture, leadership styles and changes in the organization's environment. These are beyond the scope of hard approaches.

There are many ways to consider rationality in organizations. Some economic theories postulate that firms try to maximize profit. Others suggest that firms try to maximize revenue or market share. Another view is that managers try to maximize shareholder wealth. The view taken here is that people within organizations have their

Table 10.3 Hard and soft approaches

Hard approaches	Soft approaches
Clear goals and objectives	Organizations are human activity systems
Quantifiable data	Goals need negotiation
Control mechanisms are clear	Pluralistic perspectives
Power is clear and known to work	Power is diffuse and maybe unknown
Unitary view of the organization	Consensus view and conflict views of organizations
Evolved first to meet needs of the engineering and industrial systems	
Aims to solve problems	Evolved later as responses to difficulties in using hard approaches
The analyst is detached from the system being considered	Aims to appreciate and improve understanding and relationships
Provides an answer to a problem	The analyst is part of the system being considered
	Provides improvement from a messy situation to another messy situation

own rationality. Like the previous example of an iceberg, we may be aware of what is on the surface, but cannot know what lies beneath. This is partly because people do not always understand their own reasons for doing things.

Human activity systems involve people and therefore involve individual rationality and emotions. As a result, organizational development and change are complex and involve what are known as 'messes' or messy situations. While hard approaches are often geared to optimization, soft approaches are about considering a mess, gaining improvement, moving to another mess, gaining other improvements, and so on. A hard problem has a solution. A soft problem (or mess) has resolution. People are not machines, robots, sheep or computers. Hard systems approaches will not be appropriate if the area of interest is defined differently by different people (stakeholders) in the situation, quantitative criteria cannot easily be agreed or where systems are complex.

An example of a hard problem is the determination of the materials required for a bridge to carry particular loads. A soft problem situation would be determining where to site the bridge to take account of physical factors, the wishes of the local community on side A of the bridge, the wishes of the local community on side B of the bridge, the financial constraints and the legal constraints. Within the two local communities there will be residents, business owners and people who work in either community but do not live there. Some of the residents will also be business owners. The local authorities on each side of the bridge will also have views about where it should be sited, as will various groups within the communities.

Change is only effective when people's feelings, hopes, needs, perceptions and ways of doing things are addressed. If these are not considered, resistance to change can be extremely strong, and even if change is eventually accomplished, it may require huge efforts and resources to achieve. Messy situations require managers to dissolve existing problems by challenging underlying purposes and assumptions.

Organizational development is about trying to achieve improvements that are beyond day-to-day activities. For example, if a foreman swaps two workers on two machines so that worker A works on machine A and worker B works on machine B, because each is more skilled and more efficient on the respective machines, this would be a tactical or operational change. If senior management decides to use new machines of a different type and run processes in new ways, this is strategic and requires consideration of change. It is about organizational development. Organizational development is therefore about strategic changes and their implications and implementation.

Organizational development is long-term, and needs to be properly supported by senior management. It is about improvements at the strategic level to vision, values, culture and problem-solving processes. It requires ongoing collaborative management and teamwork and emphasizes processes. As it is strategic it involves medium- to long-term change. It is about people, recognizes their worth and emphasizes the concept of a change agent or facilitator. It involves the organization as a whole, as well as its parts, and it uses action research as a means of intervention. It is participative, drawing on theory and practices of the behavioural sciences, while subscribing to a humanistic philosophy of openness. Given the previous discussions about culture in this chapter, it should be apparent that organizational development is likely to be easier to achieve in some organizations than in others.

If we consider why people may be resistant to change, it can help in managing a change programme. People need to be motivated to want to do something different from what they have been doing. Successful change management involves trying to overcome resistance to change by communication, empathy and support, participation and involvement. Creating a clear vision that people understand and recognize as positive is important. This can involve setting out a mission statement with valued outcomes and midpoint goals. It is important to make a true and accurate assessment of your political power that includes your knowledge, skills and personality. It is also necessary to identify and influence key stakeholders.

Managing the transition is a challenging task. Activity planning with a road map for change can help, and it is vital to gain the commitment of people and groups. This can be assisted by structuring to manage the change process, which includes using a task force, having the full support of senior management and ensuring that the management hierarchy is used to help with the transition. Sustaining momentum can be aided by providing suitable resources for the change, having relevant staff development and reinforcing new behaviours.

Change is not necessarily positive for everyone. A change project might threaten jobs in some parts of an organization. External pressures may mean that if the change were not implemented, the organization might fold and all jobs would be lost. Usually, if jobs are lost in a particular area there are often increased opportunities elsewhere. Employees may feel that the introduction of a new system would make their jobs less interesting or satisfying. In addition, a project may have enemies within the management structure of the organization. Not all managers have the interests of an organization at heart. Their goals may be very selfish. It is common for people to state that a new system will not work in practice. They may be right! In managing change it is important to listen and to weigh the arguments. If senior management feel that a new system will work, it needs to be explained and understood by participants. Sensible projects will always have organizational benefits and changes usually have benefits for significant numbers of people. In these cases, opposition is likely to diminish over time.

Team building is an important part of change, and the momentum gives the opportunity to form new teams. This is often considered as forming, storming, norming, performing and adjourning. *Forming* is the first stage in which members of a team get to know each other and establish ground rules. *Storming* is the stage in which conflicts arise as team members try to obtain leadership. High levels of conflict may be positive at this stage, as this may reduce conflict later in the project. During the *norming* stage, conflicts are largely settled and a team or group identity is established rather than a collection of individuals. People have become members of a team. In the *performing* stage, focus is shifted to undertaking the specified tasks. In the *adjourning* stage the team disbands and the project comes to a close.

Belbin (1981) suggested that there are typical team roles, though one person may undertake more than one role. The following provides a brief summary of some of the roles. The *Chair* is good at running meetings rather than being a brilliant leader. The *Plant* is good at growing ideas and potential solutions to problems. The *Monitor/Evaluator* is good at appraising ideas and potential solutions. The *Shaper* directs the team's attention to important issues and helps avoid people going off at tangents. The *Team Worker* (also known as the *Social Secretary*) is good at helping to create a pleasant working environment. The *Resource Investigator* does 'what it says on the tin', and is good at finding resources. The *Completer/Finisher* is good at seeing tasks through, including those started by others. The *Company Worker* is a good team player and willing worker. The *Specialist* is single-minded, self-starting, dedicated, and provides knowledge and skills in rare supply.

Team work should consist of both active work and reflective work. *Active work* means finding the right tasks and allocating them. Active work is performing adequately and effectively in a certain situation. All the team members should actively fulfil their tasks and contribute information to the team. Active work is the work that brings the actual results. *Reflective work* is mostly focused on the work already done. Through reflective work it is possible to learn from the process, to make generalizations and generate theories. The team members review their work styles, but reflective work is also a new seed for the future in asking questions such as 'How can we work together more creatively and effectively?' Reflection is often neglected because of a lack of time, and this is often cited as the reason that teams have failed. The time reserved and spent on reflective work is as important as the active and productive time. It is important to agree this together as a team. Figure 10.1 provides a checklist of activities that help in building teams.

10.6 Human resource management

Human resource management (HRM) covers key areas such as recruitment, employment relations, performance management, appraisal systems, pay and benefits, training and human resource development.

☐ Getting to know each other as people
☐ Getting to know each other as professionals
☐ Getting to know the special skills of each partner
☐ Getting to know the motives of the participants to work in the project
☐ Getting to know the motives of each institution to work in the project
☐ Giving the team a name
☐ Defining the main concepts and aims of the project
☐ Setting the evaluation criteria and methods
☐ Working with motivated and committed individuals and institutions
☐ Clearly defining roles and responsibilities
☐ Agreeing how to handle conflict situations
☐ Sharing the ownership of the project
☐ Agreeing on basic rules for the team's work
☐ Reflecting on the work and progress of the team
☐ Using a suitable communication system
☐ Employing variable working methods at the meetings
☐ Recognizing and sharing individual expertise
☐ Encouraging reserved members
☐ Celebrating milestones
☐ Dedicating enough time to social events
☐ Preventing isolation – through politics, age, economic circumstances, competence within the project or linguistic skills
☐ Guiding and leading – showing sensitivity to the feelings of others

Figure 10.1 A team-building checklist.

Recruitment is the process of attracting, short-listing and selecting qualified people for a job. The stages in recruitment include seeking candidates by advertising or other methods, and screening and selecting potential candidates using tests or interviews. Typically, a specification will be prepared by the relevant line manager in conjunction with the HR department. This spec will vary according to the level and nature of the job. For a professional-level post it would normally include an introductory statement that outlines the need for the post and how it fits within the organization. This would be followed by a list of expected responsibilities. After this the reporting lines would be stated to show to whom the person would report and for whom they have line management responsibility. It would also indicate other major contacts.

The main section is next, and it is this against which candidates will be assessed. This is the person specification. It will normally have two sections for essential and desirable attributes, sometimes as a two-column table. These are often sub-divided into areas such as qualifications, knowledge, experience, skills and personal attributes. The specification will include the main conditions of service, such as holiday entitlement and an outline of any sick pay scheme, and it should also include the salary range. If an advertisement is to be used, this will be based on the job specification, and would list main duties along with main requirements, such as qualifications. The advertisement and the job specification should note the deadline for applications and should indicate how the application should be made – by application form, submission of curriculum vitae (CV) or perhaps a mix of both.

Qualifications, knowledge, experience, skills and personal attributes can be indicated using CVs and application forms. From the applications received, a line manager may select a long-list or may simply leave the total number of applicants as the long-list. At this stage, other members of the department may be asked to give views on the candidates, and a short-list is produced. It is important to have a structured feedback system for candidates who have failed to make the short-list, and clear reasons should be given to candidates not selected. The short-listed candidates would normally be invited to the next, and usually final, stage of the selection process. This would almost always involve a formal interview, prior to which candidates may be asked to solve problems (individually or in groups), engage in role play, take tests (including psychological tests) or give presentations.

References may be taken up at any time, but it is usual to ask for a candidate's permission to do this prior to interview. The interview itself should be semi-structured, based on themes, with similar questions being asked of each candidate, and similar time being allowed. Structured feedback should be given, as this is especially important for those who are not appointed.

The process of helping new employees become productive members of an organization is just as important as recruitment. Many organizations have an induction programme in which new employees learn about the structure of the organization, their role within it, health and safety procedures and so on. A mentor may be assigned to give ongoing support. Part of this process is about cultural induction, and the belief that this will aid retention. The costs of engaging a new employee are high, and an organization does not want to recruit to a professional position only to find the new employee going elsewhere after six months.

The term 'employment relations' (ER) was previously known as 'industrial relations', but the name has changed to reflect changes in economies and changes in emphasis, understanding and scope. 'Industrial relations' can have connotations of large organizations in the manufacturing sector with unionized employment situations.

ER may be considered in a theoretical way, and links strongly to OB and models of management. In practice, ER is the arm of HRM that is about the creation of policies and procedures, the implementation of law and understanding of government legislation relating to employment. Large organizations will typically have statements of ethical principles in regard to employees, and these may be part of mission statements or value statements.

Employment relations may be considered from three theoretical perspectives: unitarism, pluralism and radicalism.

Within *unitarism* the organization is depicted as one that has goals that are supported fully by all, with all members of staff – from managing director to shop-floor worker – sharing common purpose and engaging in mutual cooperation. Concomitantly, there is a notion of benign dictatorship, with a paternalistic approach by management and high employee loyalty. On this basis trades unions are considered unnecessary because the loyalty between employees and organizations achieves synergy.

The *pluralist* perspective perceives the organization to contain divergent sub-groups, each with its own culture and loyalties and each with leaders and visions that may not match the overall objectives of the organization. Traditional industrial relations views the two major sub-groups as management and trade unions. Consequently, the role of management would lean less towards enforcing and controlling and more toward persuasion and coordination. Trades unions are deemed as legitimate representatives of employees, conflict is dealt with by collective bargaining and, if managed effectively, can lead to positive change.

The *radical* perspective is sometimes considered as Marxist or structuralist. It examines the nature of capitalist society and considers it to have a fundamental division of interest between capital and labour. This perspective sees inequalities of power and economic wealth as having their roots in the nature of the capitalist economic system. Conflict is therefore seen as inevitable and trade unions are a natural response of workers to their exploitation by capital. A major critique from this perspective is that trade unions serve to strengthen the status quo and to legitimize the position of management. In practice, trade unions are in decline and ERs have been subsumed within HRM as a whole.

Performance management (PM) is about trying to ensure that goals are achieved effectively and efficiently, which can be at the level of an organization, division, department or individual. PM relates to career advancement, leadership and management, culture, organizational change and motivation. The purpose, customers, product and scope of what is trying to be achieved (based on the strategic plan) are used to develop a commitment analysis, and a mission statement is created for each job. This indicates the objectives and tasks, which are used with a detailed job description to create performance criteria.

Early approaches to performance management were often solely focused on the financial aspects of an organization, especially in regard to increasing profit margins or reducing costs. They were not always successful; for instance, driving down costs could sometimes be at the expense of quality, staff (lost expertise) and customers. Why would this be? Very often it is a matter of long-term versus short-term perspectives. In essence, profit is the difference between costs and revenue. Other things being equal, increasing revenue or decreasing costs increases profit. An easy way to decrease costs is to cut staff development and marketing. In the short-run, profit would increase. Over time, revenue would decrease because of the reduction in marketing, and effectiveness and efficiency would decrease because of lack of training. Thus, actions that result in immediate profit gains are not always beneficial to an organization in the long-run.

One well-known approach to PM that attempts to address such issues is the balanced scorecard (BSC) (Kaplan and Norton, 1996). The BSC provides measures that give a comprehensive view of an organization. The BSC enables both financial and non-financial aspects to be linked to business strategy and cascaded throughout the organization, culminating in strategically linked objectives for individuals.

The BSC has four interdependent perspectives:

- financial
- internal
- learning
- customer.

From the financial perspective, the focus is on how the company should position itself to be considered an attractive and exciting investment to its owners. For a profit-maximizing organization this is the prime reason for being, at least in theory. The financial perspective considers things such as profitability, growth, shareholder value, market share, operating costs and asset turnover.

To achieve the financial objectives, an organization will have to bring some kind of value to its customers, value the customer considers to be worth the price the organization charges for goods or services. The customer perspective focus is, therefore on how to position the products in order to produce this perceived value. This may incorporate things such as time, quality, service and cost.

In order to achieve those customer objectives, the organization will have to excel at certain internal processes. These objectives are described in the internal processes perspective and include things such as quality processes, cycle time, operations, employee skills, productivity, decisions, actions, coordination and resources and capabilities.

Finally, in order to excel at these processes, the company has to provide an infrastructure and the necessary human capital to pull it off. These issues are addressed in the learning and growth perspective, which covers things such as the creation of new products and services, greater value for customers, increased operating efficiencies and improvements in staff development.

Notice that some of the points are covered in more than one perspective. This is an important principle of the BSC and is deliberate. Two other important (but often forgotten) principles of the BSC approach are:

1 A manager should only be measured on things over which that manager has direct control. In other words, responsibility has to be associated with authority.
2 There must be a clear strategy.

The BSC has some limitations. One of these is not inherent in the BSC itself, but in its implementation. Some organizations have attempted to use the BSC, without success. On closer inspection it is clear that in many cases they have taken bits of the approach but have not subscribed fully to its principles. Other issues include lack of a clear strategy, limited support from senior management, over-emphasis on financial measures, poor data on performance, inconsistent or inappropriate terminology and over-emphasis on the implementation of software rather than emphasis on process and principles.

10.7 Summary

This chapter started with a case study that showed the importance of OB, change management and HRM. The nature and scope of OB have been discussed, and noted to be largely about intra-organizational relationships. OB covers the behaviour of people, the process of management, the organizational context, work processes execution and interactions with the external environment.

Organizational culture was outlined as a set of values, beliefs, understandings and ways of thinking that are shared by members of an organization. The impacts of culture were discussed. Examples of different types of culture were provided. Organizational development, change and teams were considered, and the differences between hard and soft approaches were summarized.

Finally, HRM was considered as covering recruitment, ER, PM, appraisal systems, pay and benefits, training and human resource development. Of these, recruitment, ER and PM were discussed in more detail.

Glossary

Employment relations The arm of human resource management that is about the creation of policies and procedures, the implementation of law and understanding of government legislation relating to employment.

Hard approach An approach with clear goals and objectives, quantifiable data and control mechanisms are clear.

Human activity systems Systems involving people that therefore involve individual rationality and emotions.

Organization A social construct with a purpose, created by individuals and groups.

Organizational behaviour Intra-organizational relationships incorporating the behaviour of people within organizations, the context and process of management and the organization and activities of work.

Organizational culture A set of values, beliefs, understandings and ways of thinking that are shared by members of an organization.

Organizational development Improvements in an organization's processes and structure that are beyond day-to-day activities.

Organizational structure The way in which an organization is configured.

Performance management The process of trying to ensure that goals are achieved effectively and efficiently.

Recruitment The process of attracting, short-listing, and selecting qualified people for a job.

Soft approach An approach that views organizations as human activity systems in which goals need negotiation and pluralistic perspectives.

References

Belbin, R. (1981) *Management Teams: Why They Succeed or Fail*. Oxford: Butterworth-Heinemann.
Kaplan, R. and Norton, D. (1996) *Balanced Scorecard: Translating Strategy into Action*. Boston, MA: Harvard Business School Press.

Further reading

Champoux, J. (2010) *Organizational Behavior, Integrating Individuals, Groups, and Organizations*. New York: Routledge.

Suggested activities

1   How would the objectives of a large local government differ from those of a large private sector firm of similar size? Find from any sources you can as much of the following for a public sector organization and a private sector organization: mission statements, values, objectives, strategy, corporate plan. What differences will these things make to organizational behaviour and human resource management?
2   Describe three cultural norms you have experienced within present or previous employment, or that you have observed at any organization.
3   Think about the Belbin characters (p. 143). Do you recognize any of them? In what situations have you encountered these and what happened? How do they differ? Is one specification better than the others in terms of clarity, etc.?
4   Consider the costs associated with an employee leaving and employing a replacement person.

11 Systems analysis and design

The Child Support Agency (CSA) is a body that was launched in 1993, with responsibility for implementing the UK 1991 Child Support Act and related legislation. Child support is the monetary contribution provided by a non-resident parent towards the cost of raising a child. This is paid to the person who has day-to-day care and control of the child. The CSA was created in an attempt, as far as possible, to remove child support disputes from courts of law. As the CSA was not given court powers, it was criticized, among other things, for its ineffectiveness, as it had no authority to trace absent parents. The basis for calculating payment was complicated (sometimes requiring over 100 pieces of data) and in 2003 it was simplified. Even with simplification, the new approach was not easy for everyone to understand.

A new computer system was implemented, but in 2010 not all cases have been transferred across; of around 40,000 old-rule cases, nearly 20,000 are still on the old system (though 13,000 of these have been suspended). It costs the CSA around £12 million per year to take legal actions, but it manages to collect only £8 million per year, and it outsources some of its debt to a number of third-party debt collection agencies.

In 2005 Liberal Democrat MP David Laws tabled a parliamentary question asking how many cases had been held up in the CSA's computer system since it was introduced. The CSA deputy chief executive Mike Isaac responded that in the past 6–8 months approximately 32,000 cases had the required technical intervention work carried out by supplier EDS to make them available again to CSA staff. He added that from June 2005 the number of additional cases that required such intervention each month was approximately 1,200 and that the CSA was investigating the underlying system faults that gave rise to cases that were temporarily unable to pass through the system.

This would be concomitant with drafting of plans to enable such cases to be scheduled and managed in a controlled and efficient manner. In 2006 the National Audit Office reported that the CSA had a backlog of 300,000 cases, with each case taking an average of nine months to process instead of the six-week target. The IT system developed by EDS was highlighted as the main problem. It had so far cost £539 million, was expected to rise to £768 million by 2010.

Adding a £321 million rescue plan means the total cost by 2010 would be £1.1 billion. At this point an estimated 36,000 new cases had become stuck in the system due to IT failures, and each required manual intervention by CSA staff. Around 19,000 continued to be progressed manually outside of the IT system.

Sir John Bourn, head of the National Audit Office, said

> These problems will have caused genuine hardship and distress to many parents and their children. From design to delivery and operation, the programme to reform the Agency has been beset with problems which the Department for Work and Pensions, the Agency and its IT supplier EDS, have struggled to deal with.

Edward Leigh, chairman of the Public Accounts Committee, stated that it was one of the 'worst public administration scandals in modern times'. He added:

> Ignoring ample warnings, the DWP, the CSA and IT contractor EDS introduced a large, complex IT system at the same time as restructuring the Agency. The new system was brought in and, as night follows day, stumbled and now has enormous operational difficulties.

In 2006 it was announced that the CSA was to be scrapped and replaced by a new system. At that time around £3.5 billion of outstanding maintenance was uncollected, and only one in three parents were receiving payments to which they were entitled. The net taxpayer cost was more than £200 million per year.

A review of the CSA by Sir David Henshaw stated:

> The legacy of past failure is significant and cannot be allowed to put new arrangements at risk. Responsibility for failings has often been unfairly placed upon staff who have done their best to deliver for children and parents while coping with, among other things, poor systems architecture and significant IT problems. The CSA brand is severely damaged and its credibility among clients is very low.

The Henshaw Report noted that any new IT requirements will be considered in the run-up to the end of the existing IT contract with EDS in 2010.

In 2008 the government stated that inputting all child-maintenance-claim cases into the new CSA computer system would not be completed before 2013, ten years after it was created. It also emerged that the computer system had needed 130 changes in eight years in attempts to get it working properly.

Richard Steel, vice president of local government IT user group Socitm, said

> When designing a complex IT system, a prerequisite is fundamental review of the relevant business processes before the detailed specification can be produced. A high number of changes may be an indication that this did not take place, and that the customer is attempting to skew the system design to suit the ways in which they are used to working.

Socitm development services manager, Dilip Chudgar, added: 'A high number of complex changes certainly suggests something has gone fundamentally wrong in the process design.'

11.1 Intended learning outcomes

On completion of this chapter the reader should be able to:

1   describe the main generic components in information systems development;
2   explain some of the main information systems development methodologies;
3   outline the main roles and features of design, coding, realization and maintenance;
4   explain why usability of human computer interfaces is important;
5   apply recognized criteria to assessing the usability of human computer interfaces.

11.2 Introduction

The activities comprising the early stages of information systems (IS) development were introduced in Chapter 3 – these included business analysis, project initiation and requirements capture. Figure 11.1 shows the core activities in IS development as a whole, together with typical outputs at each stage. There are many ways of building information systems, some of which we will examine later in this chapter, but they all involve the activities in this diagram in some shape or form. Further on we will examine various ways in which they can be modified, combined, re-ordered and applied to form IS development methodologies, but first we will continue our discussion of the core activities.

11.3 Design

11.3.1 Outline

If we regard requirements capture as the identification of a problem to be solved, then we can see the design of an IS as a plan for solving the problem. The term 'design' is used to describe both the process of formulating this plan and the document or documents that constitute a record of the plan. The overall design can be broken down into three components: functionality, data and interfaces.

Functionality

Functionality describes what the system will do, and how it will do it, and can be described in terms of system architecture and detailed design.

The system architecture is a high-level view of the design, showing the overall structure – i.e. the most important components and how they interact. This is further decomposed into the detailed design of individual components. This must be in sufficient detail to allow programmers to convert it to program instructions during the coding stage.

Many different techniques are used to document functional design, such as flow charts, data flow diagrams and activity diagrams. All use a combination of text and graphics, and as we will see, different methodologies tend to favour (or require) particular documentation techniques.

Data

The design of data and data structures (the way data is organized and stored) can be as important as functional design, especially for data-intensive applications, such as

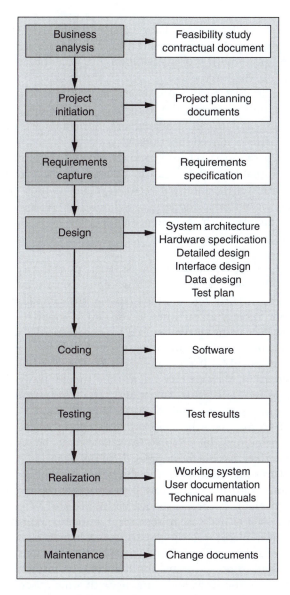

Figure 11.1 The waterfall model of IS development.

transaction processing and database systems. Good data design can minimize the need for storage space, maximize the speed of access and improve flexibility and compatibility with linked external systems.

One of the measures of good system design is modularity. This is a measure of how easy it is to make changes to one part of a design or program (i.e. a module) without the need for corresponding changes elsewhere. Designers aim for 'cohesion' (meaning the functions and data within a module all contribute to a single well-defined task) and try to avoid 'coupling' (in which functions and data are shared across modules).

Interfaces

Many systems nowadays are highly inter-dependent. They must communicate with other systems, which may already exist within the organization or may not yet be built. They may also need to communicate with systems belonging to other organizations or those publicly available, such as the Internet.

An interface is a mechanism that enables such communication, and which relies heavily on agreed communications standards (protocols). Interfaces must be designed to ensure that messages can be exchanged, data can be shared and, in many cases, that one system can call upon another to perform agreed functions.

Another aspect of communication is that between an IS and its users. A system that fulfils its functional requirements admirably may still fail to be used (or may not be used to the full extent of its capabilities) if the interface between it and its users (the human–computer interface (HCI)) is second-rate. The term *usability* is used to describe the ease of use of a system and the quality of the experience undergone by its users. General principles of good HCI design include:

- Consistency – a consistent interface not only avoids confusing the user, it inspires confidence – leading him/her to believe the system as a whole is up to standard and the data will be processed consistently too. So, for example, the same format should be used for data input and display at all times. If the date is input or displayed in the form 'dd/mm/yyyy' when the system is used for one particular task, then it should take this form when used for all other tasks. Similarly, screen layouts should be as consistent as possible. If error messages are displayed at the bottom of the screen on one occasion, then that is where they should always be displayed. Colour coding, such as red for error messages and yellow for warnings, should be consistent, as should menu positions and the use of function keys.

- Feedback – it needs to be clear to the user when processing is taking place, and when he/she must wait before continuing. This provides reassurance that the system has not crashed, or that the wrong key has not been pressed, and is often indicated by an hourglass, or some sort of moving graphic. In the absence of such an indication, the user is likely to become impatient and press keys or jiggle the mouse, causing errors or unexpected behaviour. Feedback should be immediate. When it takes the form of an error message it is of little use to the user if it appears long after the action causing the error has taken place (as in the case study in Chapter 3).

- Intuitiveness – given that users of IS are notoriously reluctant to read manuals, we should minimize the need for them to do so by making our HCIs as intuitive as possible. One way of doing this is to use icons and symbols with which users are familiar from their existing everyday knowledge and experience. Most people will associate an hourglass with waiting, a trash can with disposing of something or an envelope with mail – whatever language they speak – and if they don't know what a symbol means they can at least make an intelligent guess. Similarly, an icon that is a representation in miniature of an action or process (such as a letter 'A' followed by an arrow and the letter 'Z', meaning 'sort alphabetically') is normally understandable without further explanation. The way items within menus and sub-menu are arranged should also be based on logical and intuitive principles. So within a word-processing application, users will naturally expect all functions concerned with inputting and outputting ('Open', 'Save', 'Save as ...', etc.) to be grouped together within a single menu, without having to give it much thought.

- Help – there will of course be times when intuition is not enough, and the user needs some assistance. Information systems normally provide help in three forms – context-sensitive, searchable and tutorial. Context-sensitive help relates to what the user is doing at the time help is requested. In many Microsoft Windows-based applications, pressing the function button 'F1' will invoke help on the topic related to the current screen. On the other hand, it may be necessary to search the help available to find assistance on a topic unrelated to the current task: 'How do I share a document with my colleagues?'; or 'What is the maximum number of records I can store?', for example. If a user is going to make regular or extensive use of a system, or of a system function, then it may be worthwhile for him or her to become adept in its use by working through a tutorial – which is the third form of help that may be provided by an IS. In addition to this built-in help, external support and assistance may be available – from a user group, for example, or perhaps from an online help-desk, links to which may be built into the system for easy access.
- Error messages – even a highly intuitive interface with an extensive help system cannot prevent the occasional error from occurring. The use of ISs can be a stressful experience, so when things do go wrong, error messages should be polite and meaningful, and should tell the user how the error can be corrected. Examples of the type shown in Figure 8.2a–c are not at all uncommon, and definitely do not contribute towards a good user experience.

System developers should be careful to employ the language and terminology of system users when they are designing error messages, rather than the jargon they might use on a day-to-day basis with their colleagues. Messages such as 'Failed to initialize data stack' or 'Level 8 floating point exception' might be useful to IS professionals, but are unlikely to mean much to the 'man in the street'.

Shackel (1990) defines four criteria by which we can judge the usability of a HCI:

- learnability – the time and effort needed to reach a specified level of performance;
- throughput – the speed of accomplishing tasks, and the frequency of errors;
- flexibility – the ability of the system to handle changes to the tasks performed;
- attitude – of users towards the system.

Hopefully this section has demonstrated that if we want to meet all of these criteria it is by no means enough to understand only the technical aspects of system development. We very much need to consider the capabilities and characteristics of our users, and to cater for their capabilities and characteristics. Designing a HCI is as much about understanding human beings as it is about understanding computers.

11.3.2 Coding

We have seen how the requirements for a system can be identified, and how a plan for meeting these requirements (a design) can be devised. Later sections will discuss various approaches to the documentation of these activities and their outputs.

Converting the plan into instructions (or 'code') that can be executed by digital equipment (computers, networks, printers, communication devices, etc.), is the job of computer programmers. Coding is a specialist occupation, and programmers tend to be a rather special breed. The qualities they must possess include an aptitude for

Figure 11.2 Error messages and degrees of helpfulness.

problem solving and attention to detail, and the ability to get to grips with abstract or unfamiliar concepts and complex logic. Programmers may or may not also play a part in other stages of system development. It is certainly possible to be an IS specialist without being a programmer. Readers who are interested in programming should refer to the further reading section at the end of this chapter.

11.3.3 Error prevention, detection and correction

In any human endeavour, it is most unusual to get everything right first time, and IS development is no exception. Systems are often large and complex; they require the communication of unfamiliar and difficult concepts between people of different backgrounds; they are put together by fallible human beings; they often embody new technology and new – if not experimental – ideas. It is not surprising that errors occur, but it does mean that developers must spend a great deal of time and effort reducing their number, and minimizing their detrimental effects. Ideally, of course, we would like to eliminate all errors, but in practice we cannot expect to do so, nor can we be sure how many errors remain undetected.

Errors can be built into an IS at the requirements capture and/or implementation stages (or, as we will see later in this chapter, can arise when the system is in use).

Requirements capture errors ('building the right system')

It goes without saying that systems developers need to ensure the systems they build are the ones that users and other stakeholders want. In other words, the system requirements should be met. But this by no means always happens. Requirements can be misunderstood or poorly communicated. Sometimes system developers fall into the trap of making incorrect assumptions about what is wanted. Sometimes the problem is poor communication, perhaps caused by the misunderstanding of technical terms or by poor documentation. Sometimes the initial requirements are correctly collected and understood, but are subsequently poorly communicated between system developers, with the result that they become corrupted. Once again this may be because they have been poorly documented.

It is not unusual for the initial system requirements to change while development is underway. If these changes are not communicated, or are improperly or incompletely passed from person to person, then once more we will have a system that does not do what the users want.

Implementation errors ('building the system right')

Even when system requirements have been correctly understood, it is still quite possible to incorrectly translate them into a working system by errors in design or programming. Computer code incorporates complex logic, often employs obscure notations, and in any non-trivial system will be written by several, if not many, individual programmers. Each programmer's contribution must be integrated with the whole, which must function like a complex machine. (Hence the term 'software engineering'.) It is easy to understand how errors can occur, and how difficult it can be to detect and correct them. The result of such errors may be that the system will crash or that it will function incorrectly. The worst that can happen is that an error will remain unnoticed, and the system will malfunction, perhaps producing incorrect output. In the early days of business ISs it was not unusual, for example, for bills for negative amounts to be sent to customers, or for bills to be sent to customers who had long since died. ISs have come a long way over recent decades, but instances of this type have not been totally eliminated.

Whatever the cause or causes of errors, it is clearly highly desirable to prevent them wherever possible, and/or eliminate those that do occur before they can do harm.

One way to eliminate errors is to re-use existing (tried and tested) system components — whether design elements, sections of code or whole programs. Of course, this also saves time and expense. It cannot always be assumed, however, that components that function correctly in one environment or situation will do so in different circumstances. The use of IS development methodologies contributes to the elimination of errors by ensuring that systems are built in a systematic and controlled way, and that all developers within a team go about their jobs in a similar fashion. This enables developers to benefit from the experience (and mistakes) of experienced practitioners, and to coordinate their activities effectively.

If errors do occur, then we very much want to detect and correct them, which is normally achieved by various forms of testing. Most testing will be done by the developers themselves – by following a test plan and using test data. Both of these are normally written at a fairly early stage in system development, and certainly before program code is written. Both are also often designed by someone other than those responsible for writing code. This is because coders can be subconsciously influenced by the code they have already written, and errors or incorrect assumptions in this code may be repeated in the test data they also produce.

Table 11.1 shows part of a test plan for a small piece of code that converts temperatures in Celsius (only whole numbers between −2,743 and 5,000 inclusive) to degrees Fahrenheit.

The test plan shows the system's required responses to user actions, which often means what the system outputs in response to user input. In use, it would have an additional column for recording actual responses, so that all detected errors can be ironed out.

Consideration needs to be given to what system functions need to be tested, and what test data should be used. It is certainly not enough to test only those user actions or input data that appear to be sensible. Users can behave in the most unpredictable (and apparently foolish) ways, and these actions must not cause a computer to behave in a similarly unpredictable fashion or to crash.

The example in Table 11.1 is very simplistic. Additional aspects of the system that we might also want to test include:

- the behaviour of interfaces, both

    - HCIs – e.g. how text and graphics are arranged on the page, and how they respond to user actions;
    - interfaces with other systems or sub-systems such as databases.

Table 11.1 Test plan and test data for a temperature conversion program

User action	Input data	Expected response
Input	0	32°F
Input	10	50°F
Input	−273	−459°F
Input	−274	'Error: temperature out of range (below absolute zero)'
Input	−100	−148°F
Input	5,000	9,032°F
Input	100	212°F
Input	'Twelve'	'Error: please enter numbers only'
Input	10,000,000,000	'Error: temperature out of range (above 5,000)'
Input	'' (no data)	'Error: no data entered'
Input	13.8	'Error: only whole numbers please'
Press 'F1'		Open new window containing help search facility
Click 'HELP' button		Open new window containing help on temperature conversion facility
Click 'EXIT' button		Close temperature conversion window, display main menu

- the provision of help;
- navigation between pages of a website or between display screens or windows;
- the storage and retrieval of data;
- printing;
- responses to combinations of user actions (e.g. if the user attempts to book a single hotel room for two people).

When designing test data we need to ensure we include both valid and invalid data so we can be confident that our system processes valid data correctly, and rejects invalid data, taking appropriate action such as generating error messages. Invalid data includes:

- data in the wrong format, such as:
  - alphabetic data where numeric data is required;
  - numeric data with the wrong degree of precision (e.g. too many decimal points);
- data outside of a naturally valid range (e.g. a date of 32 January 2015);
- data outside of the range that can be processed by the system (e.g. a travel booking system may not process bookings more than one month in advance);
- data that contradicts other data (e.g. a maiden name for a man).

Valid data should include:

- values at the limits of valid ranges (e.g. a date of 31 January). Together with data outside of a valid range this is known as 'boundary data'.

The system should also be tested to ensure that if data items *must* be input (this is often the case with items such as contact details – name, address, telephone number, etc.), then their absence is detected and reported to the user.

Testing can be carried out at various times by different people using a wide range of techniques (only a few of which are mentioned here).

WHEN

Many IS development methodologies incorporate continual testing throughout the development process, in particular during the design, coding stages and around release time.

Alpha testing is carried out by potential users of a system after development is complete, but before the system is declared fit for purpose. It is often at the developer's site and is normally used before beta testing

Beta testing involves release of a non-final version to some users who provide feedback before the final version is implemented. Beta testing is used to ensure as far as possible that the product has no faults or bugs. Sometimes beta versions are made available to the open public to increase feedback.

Acceptance testing is carried out by the client(s) before the system is signed off as meeting the requirements.

WHO

System developers will obviously want to test their own products to ensure they are of the expected quality.

Specialist testers may be part of the development team, or may be external. External testers do not have to consider the cost of correcting any errors they uncover, so they may be expected to be more thorough.

Users can play an invaluable part in making sure the system meets their requirements. In the early stages of development this is likely to be by ensuring that 'the right system is being built' (validating the requirements), and in the later stages by helping to eliminate implementation errors ensuring the system has been 'built right' (implementation verification).

TECHNIQUES

Black box testing concerns itself with the comparison of inputs and outputs to a system, without regard to how they function internally, as previously described for the example test plan.

White box testing requires a more intimate knowledge and understanding of the internal operation of a system. It usually refers to the testing of program code, and attempts to test all possible pathways through the code. This is more time-consuming and costly than black box testing, but the more thorough approach means that we can have greater confidence in the final product.

Unit and integration testing refer to the division of program code or of a system into relatively small, largely independent units (program code or sub-systems) to simplify the testing process. Having tested these units it then becomes necessary to join them together again and to perform more tests to ensure they work together as expected.

Stress testing is the exposure of a system to heavier use than would normally be expected. We might expose it to greater data volumes or a greater number of simultaneous users than it would realistically have to deal with in operational use. It is reasoned that if it can cope with this sort of 'pressure', then it will be able to cope with anything it will meet when used in earnest.

Usability testing refers to the testing of the user interface, especially for the desirable characteristics discussed in Section 11.1.2.

Automated testing enables systems to be tested with larger volumes of data or for longer periods of time than would otherwise be practical.

When deciding which types of testing to carry out, and the amount of testing to be undertaken, the developer must balance the desire to eliminate errors (and the consequence of them remaining undetected) against the time and money that the process will consume. Critical systems such as those regulating medical equipment or aircraft control systems could be expected to undergo more rigorous testing than a system that prints business cards.

Finally, some errors that occur when ISs are in use are totally or partially outside of the control of the system developer. Hardware or operating system failures, the failure of an interconnected system, power outages and unpredictable actions on the part of users (such as trying to save data to a disconnected drive) are all things the system developer can do little to prevent. Users may even misuse the system deliberately in an attempt to bring it down or cause damage. But even when errors are not the fault of the developer, he/she can usually build in measures to minimize their effect if and when they arise. We have seen how we can design HCIs to minimize the likelihood of user errors taking place. Similarly, we can design systems to be 'resilient' so that even in the event of errors we cannot prevent, we can keep their harmful effects to a minimum, meaning little or no data is lost and the system does not crash or hang; instead the anomalous situation is detected and reported to the user. Ways in which resilience can be built into a system include the scheduling of automatic back-ups, the provision of 'undo' features to allow users to correct mistakes and regular status checks to detect abnormal situations.

An IS that does not function in the required manner, or that contains errors that have not been ironed out ('bugs') causes, at best, frustration and, at worst, disaster. The lack of errors is one of the most important measures by which quality is measured. A system that does not work properly can be worse than no system at all.

11.3.4 *Realization*

There are many important issues to be considered before a new or upgraded system can be used for the first time. If the system is complex, or if its functionality or interface have changed significantly, then it may be necessary to provide instruction or training. This may take the form of courses and/or the provision of user or technical manuals. Advisors may need to be made available for some time – in person, by telephone, email or online query.

There may be large quantities of data that need to be transferred from previous systems (known as 'legacy systems') to the new one. This process ('data migration') can be far from simple, and will probably need conversion programs to be written to translate data to new formats.

It may be necessary to adapt existing business processes, or to adopt new ones, to be able to make effective use of a new IS. On the other hand, a well-managed organization will have considered how its ISs strategy meets its business needs and will integrate the design of ISs and business practices to complement each other.

There are always risks involved when introducing changes – and this is especially so when we replace or make significant alterations to ISs. This is because they often embody new ideas and new technology that have not been subjected to long-term testing to uncover their shortcomings or to prove their reliability. The right ISs, introduced in the right way at the right time, certainly present significant opportunities for efficiency gains, novel business ideas and models, and consequent competitive advantage. But at the same time their centrality to so many business functions can mean disaster if they go wrong.

One way in which we can decrease our exposure to risk and minimize the harmful effects of system malfunction is by introducing new systems gradually. This is, of course, not always possible or desirable – sometimes the nature of the system makes the 'all-in-one-go' method the only option. There are several variations on the staged approach to system changeover or introduction. A pilot scheme may be adopted, whereby a new system is 'trialled' in a single department or at a single location of a large organization. If problems occur, then any potential damage will be confined to the area in which the system has been introduced. This area will, of course, have been carefully selected to ensure that unwanted outcomes can be isolated and will have limited effects on the business as a whole. If and when the system is running satisfactorily in the experimental area, and any 'glitches' have been resolved, then it can be rolled out to the rest of the organization.

Alternatively, it may be possible to introduce system changes incrementally – a small change one week, another the following week, and so on. This will avoid a single point in time when there may be considerable disruption and a significant risk of problems. However, the result will be a period of constant change, which employees and or system users may find extremely unsettling. They may prefer to brave the changes all in one go (like having a tooth pulled rather than suffer continual nagging pain).

Parallel running is a strategy whereby old and new systems are run side-by-side until it can be determined that the new system is working properly. This can be very effective, but the extra resources (such as staff, hardware and accommodation) may not be available, and even if they are, then their duplication is likely to be costly.

It may be viable for an organization to shut down its operations (or that part of its operations for which the new system will be used) for a short time while the change-over takes place. Although this may sound extreme, and would be out of the question for many companies, there are business sectors that are highly seasonal (such as tourism, agriculture and sport) for which this approach would be practical.

There are, of course, many ways in which these strategies can be combined. For example, the best policy for a particular company might be to introduce parallel running of a new system at just one of its locations. This could then be used as a pilot scheme, so that if it was successful, it would subsequently be implemented throughout the organization.

11.3.5 *Maintenance*

System development is not complete when a system has been installed. Despite all the care taken to ensure a smooth introduction, most systems can be expected to be subject to teething problems in the first few weeks or months of operation, which may be major and may require immediate attention. The need for repairs and minor improvements may be uncovered long after initial installation.

After the system has been in use for some time the need for upgrades and updates may arise – not necessarily because of any shortcomings in the original system, but because of changing requirements. These can be brought about by new technical developments or fresh business ideas presenting opportunities the system must accommodate. Changing customer profiles or actions on the part of competitors may bring about the need for further adaptation. A well-designed system should first of all be flexible, so that changes in its use are possible without changes to the system itself. However, unpredictable events and circumstances are likely to mean that sooner or later system modifications will be needed. So a well-designed system is also one that can be modified with the minimum of time, effort and disruption to the activities of the business.

11.4 Methodologies

11.4.1 *Overviews*

Methodologies are standardized or agreed ways of doing things; our interest is in ways of building ISs. But they are more than just 'methods', although the words are sometimes used interchangeably. An IS methodology (of which there are very many) includes at least most of the following:

- perspective
- phases
- procedures
- lifecycle
- techniques
- guidelines
- models
- documentation.

We will consider these aspects of methodologies, and will look at some examples of how they are implemented in practice, but first let us examine the benefits of the use of methodologies in general.

11.4.2 *Why we use methodologies*

In the early days of ISs, when systems were comparatively simple and were created by individuals or small teams, there was little need for conformity – developers 'did their own thing'. As systems grew in size and complexity it became necessary to coordinate the work of many analysts, designers, programmers, testers and all the other individuals involved in system development. Teams also needed to ensure that ideas, designs, programs and working systems were documented thoroughly (and in a manner that they all could understand), and to manage the large quantities of documentation produced.

When using a methodology, developers follow an agreed set of well-defined procedures. Common modelling and documentation techniques enable them to communicate ideas in a way they will all understand. Standardized and comprehensive documentation also means that system maintenance is made much easier.

Embedded within the procedures of a methodology are tried and tested techniques and methods, which are based on the expertise of experienced practitioners. These help to ensure tasks are performed to a consistently high standard, and that no essential tasks are omitted.

Staff trained in a particular methodology have skills that are readily recognized by employers. This is good for employees in terms of their ability to find work and develop their careers. Equally, it can benefit employers, who can advertise for and employ staff skilled in a particular methodology – without having to train them in practices that are peculiar to their company.

Some methodologies are associated with particular project management methods – for example, SSADM (structured analysis and design method), and PRINCE2. These are concerned with wider issues such as:

- the planning of the use of manpower and other resources;
- the monitoring and coordination of activities between participants;
- budgeting and expenditure;
- legal and contractual issues.

Organizations that employ recognized IS development methodologies and project management methods can significantly enhance their credibility. In some cases (especially for projects commissioned by government departments), only those companies that can provide evidence of their competence in a particular methodology and project management method will be allowed to bid for IS development contracts.

11.4.3 *Perspectives*

Methodologies can be grouped according to their particular perspectives on ISs and IS development. The concept of perspectives is similar to that of abstraction in modelling – in which we look at the subject or situation to be modelled, and focus on the aspects that we consider to be most important, at the expense of others. Just as there are modelling techniques in which we emphasize the importance of data, functionality or communication, we can do the same for whole methodologies. However, IS development perspectives are often broader, and may take on a more philosophical nature, and may stress aspects such as user involvement, risk minimization or flexibility.

The list in Table 11.2 is far from exhaustive, but includes some of the most widely adopted perspectives and some methodologies that embrace them.

11.4.4 *Lifecycles*

It is quite possible to build a system by carrying out the activities described in the previous sections in the order shown in Figure 11.1 – i.e. by working from the top of the diagram to the bottom. This was indeed the common practice in the early days of IS development, and is still appropriate for some systems and in some situations today. This top-to-bottom approach, often known (for obvious reasons) as 'the waterfall' lifecycle, has limitations, however. In particular, it assumes that the early stages

Table 11.2 Methodologies and perspectives

Perspective	Example	Emphasis
Process-oriented	STRADIS	Top-down functional decomposition
Data-oriented	IDEF1X	Data used by the business (limited in scope – perhaps more of a technique than a methodology)
Hybrid	SSADM	Combines both the above approaches
Object-oriented	Booch, RUP	Objects corresponding to real-world equivalents, having associated processes and data re-use
Business-oriented	Information engineering	Meeting business needs, on time and within budget
Agile	XP, Scrum	Speed of development, flexibility of requirements and user participation in development
Web-based	WISDM	Web-based systems
Human-centred	SSM, ETHICS	The influence of humans on information systems and vice-versa

(especially the requirements capture stage) will be carried out to such a degree of accuracy that there will be no need to revisit them. It also assumes that the user requirements gathered at the outset will not change over the lifetime of the development project. Other approaches may involve some sort of iteration. Some include the building of prototypes – limited versions of systems or sub-systems, created for test or demonstration purposes, and not used subsequently. Some provide for incremental delivery, in which larger systems are handed over a bit at a time. This enables users to benefit from the new system (or parts of it) at an earlier stage, and can reveal errors or changes to requirements earlier. Many methodologies are designed to cover only part of the IS development lifecycle. Soft systems methodology (SSM), for example, is intended to assist the identification of 'problem situations' (characterized by complexity and lack of agreement as to their precise nature), before requirements capture can begin.

11.4.5 *Techniques*

IS development methodologies typically recommend, or require the use of, a particular set of techniques, for activities such as requirements capture and analysis, modelling or coding. SSADM, for example, uses relational data analysis – a technique for producing a formal model of an organization's data, which is consistent and eliminates duplication. XP (extreme programming) uses pair programming, in which two programmers work together at a single computer. Many methodologies rely on particular diagramming techniques and notations (as can be seen in the following section on SSADM). Note, however, that these techniques are not necessarily unique to a particular methodology. Many methodologies, like SSADM, make use of relational data analysis, even if they do not use that term to describe it.

11.5 An example methodology: SSADM

SSADM is a highly prescriptive, rigorous, document-led approach to system development. It is prescriptive in that it provides detailed instructions for all the activities to be carried out in the stages (analysis and design) of system development for which it is intended. It adopts the waterfall lifecycle, demanding that each stage be documented and signed off before the next is begun. SSADM is an 'open standard', meaning that anyone can use it, and has been adopted by the UK government. All information systems developed by government departments (or for government departments by external contractors) must use SSADM. It also has an associated project management method – PRINCE2 (PRojects IN Controlled Environments).

The methodology employs three key modelling techniques throughout all of the stages.

11.5.1 *Logical data modelling*

Key data requirements of the business are ascertained, and logical data structures (LDS) are created (Figure 11.3). (These are essentially equivalent to entity relationship models). Entities are the things about which the organization needs to store information, attributes represent their qualities and relationships describe the ways in which they are connected, correspond or interact with each other.

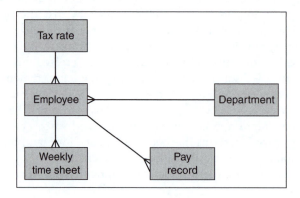

Figure 11.3 A logical data structure.

11.5.2 Data flow modelling

Key processes are identified, along with the data that flows between them, and data stores. External to the system, the origins of data ('sources') and destinations ('sinks') are recorded. Data flow diagrams (DFDs) are drawn (see Figure 11.4), in which processes are shown as boxes joined by lines to represent data flows. These diagrams are hierarchical, so the processes within a top-level diagram (known as a context diagram) can each be represented as another DFD, and so on, until the required level of detail is attained.

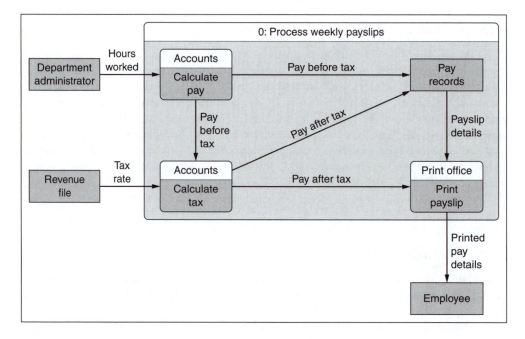

Figure 11.4 A data flow diagram.

11.5.3 *Entity/event modelling*

The events that can happen affecting each entity (as identified in logical data modelling), and the order in which they may take place, are represented diagrammatically in an entity life history (ELH) diagram (see Figure 11.5). Optional and repeated events can also be shown, indicated by the * and ° symbols, respectively.

The three views presented by these modelling techniques complement each other – i.e. data-oriented (logical data modelling), functional (data flow modelling) and time-based (entity/event modelling). Proponents of SSADM claim that between them they are able to represent all the essential components of an IS, and that checking for consistency between models helps to ensure their correctness.

The methodology is divided into 'modules', as shown in Table 11.3.

SSADM modules are further divided into stages, steps and tasks, each with detailed instructions, checklists, and rules. Elsewhere in this book we will see how other methodologies take quite different approaches to system development, and the importance of selecting the right methodology for a particular organization, situation or purpose.

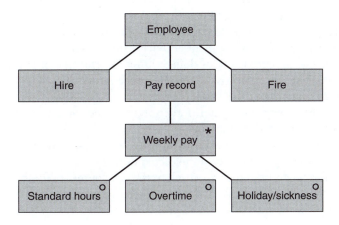

Figure 11.5 An entity life history.

Table 11.3 SSADM modules

Module	Activities
1 Feasibility study	Compare costs vs benefits (actual and intangible) Determine the ability of the organization to implement the solution
2 Requirements analysis	Investigate and document current system; produce business system options (BSOs) to meet new needs; document selected option
3 Requirements specification	Refine and add detail to the selected option
4 Logical system specification	Produce technical system options and a logical design
5 Physical design	Create a physical database design and a set of program specifications

11.6 Summary

This chapter builds on the introduction to the domain found in Chapter 3. It has continued with a description of the main generic components in IS development. The main generic components in IS development have been discussed and some of the major IS development methodologies have been explained. An example methodology, SSADM, has been described in more detail.

Important roles and features of design, coding, realization and maintenance have been outlined. The important area of the usability of HCIs was covered and criteria for assessing the usability of HCIs have been given.

Glossary

Data migration Moving data associated with an existing system to the one that replaces it. This may require conversion to a new format.

GUI Graphical user interface.

HCI Human–computer interaction (or interface).

Interface Something that is interposed between objects, entities or systems, to enable them to communicate or work together.

Legacy system An existing system alongside which a new system must function.

Lifecycle The order in which system development activities are carried out.

Methodology A recognized or accepted way of doing things. In the case of ISs this may include the use of shared perspectives, phases, procedures, lifecycle, techniques, guidelines, models and documentation.

Module A self-contained component (of a system), the internal functioning of which can be changed without affecting other modules.

Resilience The ability of a system to continue to operate, with the minimum of disruption or data loss, following failures or unpredicted events.

Software engineering A formal and rigorous approach to the development of software, which is especially suitable for large systems and safety-critical systems.

System architecture A high-level view of a system, consisting of the key components (especially the software and hardware) and their interactions.

References

Shackel, B. (1990) Human Factors and Usability, in Preece *et al.* (eds) (1990), *Human–Computer Interaction*, 2nd edition. Reading, MA: Addison-Wesley.

Further reading

Brookshear, J. Glenn (2008) *Computer Science: An Overview*. Reading, NY: Addison-Wesley.

Laudon, K. and Laudon, J. (2004) *Management Information Systems: Managing the Digital Firm*, 8th edition. Upper Saddle River, NJ: Prentice Hall.

Suggested activities

1 Consider Shackel's HCI usability criteria and decide which of these can be measured, how this can be done, and what units of measurement can be used.

2   Look at the test plan in Table 11.1 and identify which data items are of the following types:

    a   boundary data;
    b   data outside of a naturally occurring range;
    c   data outside of system processing capabilities;
    d   data in an incorrect format.

3   Critically appraise the CSA case in the light of this chapter.

12 Data warehousing and business intelligence

Case study 12.1 Qualcomm

Parts of this case study were excerpted from TDWI's What Works: Best Practices in Business Intelligence and Data Warehousing, *Volume 28 (published at tdwi.org). Reprinted with permission.*

This case study has been included by the authors to facilitate class discussion rather than to illustrate effective or ineffective management practices. Only publicly available material has been used to write this case study, and it does not reflect any opinions of employees or management at the organizations mentioned.

Qualcomm is a wireless telecommunications company based in San Diego, California. The company was founded in 1985 by Professor Irwin Jacobs, Andrew Viterbi, Harvey White, Adelia Coffman, Andrew Cohen, Klein Gilhousen and Franklin Antonio.

The following outlines some of the major activities of Qualcomm since its inception:

- produced the OmniTRACS satellite locating and messaging service;
- in 1990 began the design of the first code division multiple access (CDMA) based cellular base station;
- in 1992 started producing CDMA cell phones, base stations and chips;
- in 1997 paid $18 million for the naming rights to the Jack Murphy Stadium in San Diego, renaming it to Qualcomm Stadium (rights till 2017);
- in 1999 sold base station business to Ericsson and cell phone manufacturing business to Kyocera;
- focused on developing and licensing wireless technologies and selling application-specific integrated circuits that implement them;
- in 2000 acquired Snaptrack, the inventor of the assisted-GPS system for cellphones, branded as gpsOne, with technology that reduces the searching time for geolocation from minutes to around one second;
- in 2004 acquired Trigenix Ltd, a mobile user interface software development company based in Cambridge, UK;
- in 2006 purchased Flarion Technologies, the creator of the Flash-OFDM wireless base station, and the inventor of the flash beaconing method;
- is the inventor of CDMAone (IS-95), CDMA 2000 and CDMA 1xEV-DO, which are wireless cellular standards used for communications;
- participated in the development of the Globalstar satellite system along with Loral Space & Communications;
- owns significant number of key patents on the widely adopted 3G technology, W-CDMA;

- products include tracking devices, semiconductors, satellite phones, operating systems, speech codec and server software.

Understanding how internal applications are used is vital to Qualcomm. The company has a number of business intelligence (BI) systems, so obtaining information on the use of applications may appear to be straightforward. In practice, employees from the product development services team found they could not easily use these tools to obtain this information. They had the necessary technical skills to use the tools available, but they did not have the time and resources needed.

Steve Rimar, Qualcomm senior programmer analyst, used QlikView to enable access to a large data set that provided analysis on the number and profiles of employees using the system, along with specifics on peak usage time, system performance and speed, average product turnaround time and bottlenecks in the process. With Qualcomm's existing BI solutions, development time for the same application could have taken weeks or even months. Although the new system was originally intended for reporting within Qualcomm's product development services organization, use grew organically as employees recognized its potential for analysis of functions outside of IT.

More than 100 dashboards and reporting applications have been deployed across 15 business units. These applications have given employees one-click access to information that had previously taken them hours or even days to find and access. As a result, Qualcomm has increased efficiencies in the chip-testing lifecycle and ultimately improved throughput time.

Previously, each group had to compile and distribute individual spreadsheets, with one group having nine different subdivisions and employees in both the USA and India. Today, that department's 40 users share a single view of how each chip feature is testing against each phone, with trending analysis of coverage percentage, automation complete and other key testing metrics. Qualcomm has been able to save one day each month previously spent generating reports. The same application also enables Qualcomm to optimize staffing to meet timing commitments to the company's manufacturing suppliers.

In addition to increased reporting and staffing efficiencies and the associated cost savings, Qualcomm is able to provide its engineers with the intelligence to improve quality control processes. Before this, a quality technician spent at least four hours each week preparing reports for eight different Qualcomm product families. This was an exhausting and time-consuming five-step process that included querying data from the company's Manufacturing Execution System using Qualcomm's former BI software product, exporting to Microsoft Excel, creating a pivot table, refreshing the existing chart and manually calculating yield and defects per 100 units to complete the chart. Today, the weekly reporting process has been completely eliminated, saving the quality technician 16–20 hours each month.

12.1 Intended learning outcomes

On completion of this chapter the reader should be able to:

1 explain what data warehousing is;
2 explain what business intelligence is;
3 describe the main potential benefits and drawbacks of data warehousing and business intelligence;
4 report on relevant trends and suggest possible outcomes;
5 argue possible syntheses between data warehousing and business intelligence.

12.2 Data warehousing

A data warehouse stores organizations' data electronically to assist ease of access, input, analysis, querying and reporting. The vast majority of storage is for transaction data. Transaction data describes changes that occur with events, and the description would normally state the time/date of the transaction, the object involved and a quantity of some kind. Examples of transactions include work activities (absences, pay and so on), financial activities (payments, invoices, etc.) and logistics (goods in, goods out, deliveries, etc.). This is just a sample of the many types of transactions that are possible. A record management system is used to record, store and retrieve transaction data. A data warehouse often has larger amounts of data than a standard records management system, and may be geared to ease of use for accessing aggregated data.

Data warehouse output is generally provided as virtually unformatted tables or as reports that have tailored formatting. Data warehousing may be used to inform BI, but not all data warehousing is used this way and not all BI uses data warehousing. The two are linked, but are separate.

A data warehouse is often designed to enable queries and reports to be written by non-technical employees, and organizations want transactions and processing to be completed in reasonable time. Reports and queries, run on the servers/disks used by transaction-processing systems, can lower the probability that transactions complete in an acceptable amount of time. Organizations may therefore decide to implement data warehousing architecture that uses separate servers/disks for some querying and reporting. There are server technologies that may speed up query and reporting processing, but may slow down transaction processing. Conversely, there are server technologies that may speed up transaction processing but which slow down query and report.

A data warehouse often performs data cleansing, which involves detecting, correcting and, where necessary, removing corrupt or inaccurate records. Anomalies may arise because data is inaccurate, incomplete, incorrect or no longer relevant. Data may also not be consistent with other data sets, and part of cleansing is to rectify this.

A data warehouse may be used to store records of transaction processing that contain data over a relatively long period of time, and generally longer than would be dealt with effectively and efficiently by a transaction-processing system. A key issue of a data warehouse is security. Members of staff who legitimately need access to data need to be able to retrieve it quickly and in the right format. The challenge is in facilitating ease of access for legitimate users while denying or restricting access to others.

A typical architecture for a data warehouse is layered. A data access layer provides the interface between the operational and informational access layers, and has means to input, change and extract data. An informational access layer is used to enable reporting and analysing, and this is often linked to business intelligence. A metadata layer holds the data directory, which includes data warehouse dictionaries. An operational database layer provides the source data for the data warehouse, and this links to enterprise resource planning systems.

There are various stages of data warehousing. An off-line operational database uses data that is simply copied from an operational system to another server. This prevents the processing load created using the data impacting on the performance of the operational system. An off-line data warehouse is regularly updated from the operational system, and uses a data structure designed to facilitate reporting. A real-time data warehouse is updated whenever a transaction occurs in the operational system. An integrated data warehouse is also updated whenever a transaction occurs in the operational system. In addition, it passes data back to the operational system.

The normalized approach to storing data uses, to an extent, database normalization rules. Tables are grouped by subject areas that cover general data categories, such as accounts, customers, products and so on. Normalization enables information to be added easily to the database. There are, however, many tables, which can make it less easy for an end user to join data from different sources into meaningful information and also to access the information. It may require technical database understanding of databases to do these things, and that adds to resource needs.

The dimensional approach partitions transaction data facts (numeric data) or dimensions, which give the reference information that provides context for the facts. For example, a financial transaction may have numerical facts about the total cost, the number of items, the price per item and so on. It can also have dimensions, such as an invoice date, the name of the customer or supplier and so on. The dimensional approach tends to make it relatively easy for an end user to understand and retrieve data quickly. It is difficult to modify the data warehouse structure if an organization changes the way it does business. It is complicated to load data from different operational systems while maintaining integrity of facts and dimensions.

Data does not all conform to particular styles. For example, a mortgage firm may record whether or not someone holds mortgage protection insurance. This may be entered in one operational system as 'Y' or 'N'. On another it may be entered as 'Yes' or 'No'. It may seem trivial, but in fact a lot of data warehouse work is about making similar-meaning data consistent when they are stored in the data warehouse. There are particular tools used to extract, transform and load.

Although data warehousing is almost exclusively about transaction-processing data, this chapter would not be complete without a discussion of master data management (MDM). MDM has the aim of conforming non-transactional data that could be considered as dimensions by using processes and tools that consistently define and manage the entities of an organization, which may include reference data. MDM provides processes for organization to ensure consistency and control in collecting, aggregating, matching, consolidating, quality-assuring, persisting and distributing data.

MDM attempts to avoid multiple versions of the same master data in different parts of its operations, partly because of the potential for inconsistency. This can happen for many reasons, with a common one being an acquisition or merger. Two organizations will usually not have the same data structures, and any duplication and inconsistencies need to be resolved. Database administrators will attempt to do this, but trying to reconcile several master data systems can be challenging, because applications will be dependent on the master databases. Consequently, two or more MDM systems are not actually fully merged, and a reconciliation process is used to ensure consistency between the data stored in the two systems. If more mergers occur, the issue is exacerbated, possibly to the extent that data-reconciliation processes become extremely complicated, unmanageable and unreliable. If this happens, there could be 50 or 60 master databases that are not integrated or badly integrated. This can result in operational problems that affect effectiveness, efficiency and, probably most importantly, customer satisfaction.

MDM solutions often have processes such as data collection, data transformation, identification of sources, normalization, rule administration, error detection and correction, data consolidation, data storage, data distribution and data governance.

Tools include data networks, file systems, data warehouses, data marts, operational data stores, data mining, data analysis, data federation and data visualization, customer data integration product and product information management. Administrators adapt descriptions to conform to standard formats and data domains, making it possible to remove duplicate instances of any entity. Such processes generally result in an organizational MDM repository, from which all requests for a certain entity instance produce the same description, irrespective of the originating sources and the requesting destinations. MDM has suffered some criticism because of claims of large costs and low returns on investment.

Data warehousing has also been criticized for a number of reasons. Systems often store historical data that has limited value. Data gained from internal transaction-processing systems may be of little use in making decisions about the future. Data warehousing systems can complicate business processes, and something that should be relatively simple can become very complicated, resulting in a system that services itself rather than its customers. There are large learning costs for an organization that is new to using data warehousing. Typically, responses will be slower initially, and customers may be adversely affected. As a result, the payback period may be significantly longer than may have been thought. Finally, data warehousing may be considered to be of strategic value and end up being used solely for operational and tactical purposes, with simple reports taking longer to produce than previously, and at greater cost.

12.3 Business intelligence

BI has developed from the decision support systems (DSS) that began to be developed in the mid-1970s, and, like DSS, BI incorporates ideas from organizational theory with information systems in order to support decision-making. BI technologies provide historical, current and predictive views of business operations and activities, including online analytical processing, data mining, business performance management, benchmarking, text mining and reporting.

BI may be distinguished from competitive intelligence (CI) because it tends to be considered as the analysis of internal, structured data and business processes (using information technology), while CI is considered as the collation and analysis of internal and external information (structured and unstructured) with or without support from technology. This distinction is not universally accepted, and BI may be used to gather information about the market and market rivals. Thus, BI is sometimes considered to include market analysis, sector analysis and competitor analysis. BI applications may be integral to an enterprise's operations or occasional to meet a special requirement; organization-wide, or local to one department; centrally initiated or more locally determined.

BI terminology has a diverse history and is still in its infancy; new terms are emerging, with the following being common:

- business intelligence
- competitive intelligence
- competitor intelligence
- corporate intelligence
- environmental scanning
- market intelligence.

Organizations may undertake their own business analysis or they may use an outside agency. Performance information is collected from inside the company and potential improvements are considered. Either following this or concomitantly, outside sources are considered; these can include publicly available accounts and other information on other businesses in the same sector, reported market analysis and customer surveys. The internal and external information is reviewed and decisions made as to any further specific information that may be required and how this relates to business strategy. This may be to improve implementation or to inform any possible revisions.

BI may be contrasted to traditional information gathering by the interdepartmental focus and the focus on business performance. BI is distinguished by the use of advanced technology and techniques such as data mining. Market analysis may help provide understanding of a particular issue, but it does not help with detailed understanding about specific competitors and the inner management of the organization. A BI model incorporates internal and external information, broad sector information, detailed competitor information, structured data and unstructured data, all with a view to improving performance. Effective BI should result in (for example) speedier data collection, innovative business initiatives, targeted marketing, clearer understanding of customers' needs and greater knowledge of the sector and competitors within it. Business agility is a desired outcome, and this enables an organization to adapt quickly to changing market conditions – it is the ability of a business to adapt rapidly and cost-effectively in response to changes in the business environment. This involves adapting goods and services to meet customer demands, adjusting to the changes in a business environment and using resources effectively and efficiently.

BI may make use of data warehousing, but the latter is not a prerequisite. BI may include data sourcing, data analysis, situation awareness, risk analysis and decision support. Data sourcing relies on many different sources of data, such as formatted tables, images, text documents, sounds and webpages. Data includes estimating trends, forecasting and summarizing. Situation awareness is about filtering out irrelevant information (while ensuring relevant information is kept), and setting the remaining information in the context of the business and its environment. Risk assessment considers what is feasible and what is desirable; it is also about laying out sensible options. From these options, decision support helps in choosing actions.

BI projects may be costly because disparate business data must be extracted and merged from a variety of data sources, including online transaction-processing systems, batch systems and external syndicates. Also, many BI decision support initiatives require new technologies, new tasks and new roles and responsibilities. In addition, analysis and decision-improving applications must be delivered promptly and with high quality. BI may be difficult to implement, and as a result may fail due to mistakes and resistance to change. Common factors in failure include inadequate planning, missed tasks, missed deadlines, poor project management, undelivered business requirements, low-quality deliverables, inappropriate focus on technology and lack of attention to organizational behaviour and change management.

Davenport (2008) concludes that there are ten BI needs to evolve:

1 Decisions are the unit of work to which BI initiatives should be applied.
2 Providing access to data and tools isn't enough if you want to ensure that decisions are actually improved.

3 If you're going to supply data to a decision-maker, it should be only what is needed to make the decision.

4 The relationship between information and decisions is a choice organizations can make – from 'loosely coupled', which is what happens in traditional BI, to 'automated', in which the decision is made through automation.

5 'Loosely coupled' decision and information relationships are efficient in terms of provision of information (hence many decisions can be supported), but do not often lead to better decisions.

6 The most interesting relationship involves 'structured human' decisions, in which human beings still make the final decision, but the specific information used to make the decision is made available to the decision-maker in some enhanced fashion.

7 You cannot really determine the value of BI or data warehousing unless they're linked to a particular initiative to improve decision-making. Otherwise, you'll have no idea how the information and tools are being used.

8 The more closely you want to link information and decisions, the more specific you have to get in focusing on a particular decision.

9 Efforts to create 'one version of the truth' are useful in creating better decisions, but you can spend a lot of time and money on that goal for uncertain return unless you are very focused on the decisions to be made as a result.

10 BI results will increasingly be achieved by IT solutions that are specific to particular industries and decisions within them.

BI may be seen either as something only for the management of an organization or as process-enhancing organizational learning for the entire organization. BI may therefore be seen as a process or quality that is within an organization, rather than as a division or department in a structure. Concomitant with this view is the notion of BI as being there to identify and solve problems and challenges, and BI informing and helping decide in the business planning process, as well as being an initiator of a discussion about results with other functions within the company. Within this scenario, BI is a social function, so communication skills become crucial.

BI may be considered as a process of prognosis or explanation, as well as activities for understanding the need for information and activities to gather, arrange, analyse and distribute information about competitive market factors. Together these enable an organization to identify and solve problems and challenges of the future. Therefore, intelligence may be considered as refined information that better enables looking into the future.

BI has a clear connection to strategy, both as a concept and as an ideal prerequisite for decision-making. The need to have a high degree of flexibility has effects on strategy and information handling – and information needs analysis. These have to do with what is meant by the basic concept of 'intelligence'.

Figure 12.1 shows a common depiction of the intelligence cycle. The intelligence cycle is of course a simplification of reality, used for description and to aid understanding. The model depicts an ideal flow of information within an organization, but it does not indicate what actually happens. In fact, it is difficult to know how intelligence affects an organization and how any effects may be quantified.

The intelligence cycle is derived from the military arena, and the techniques of CI may be linked to political and military intelligence agencies, particularly within the

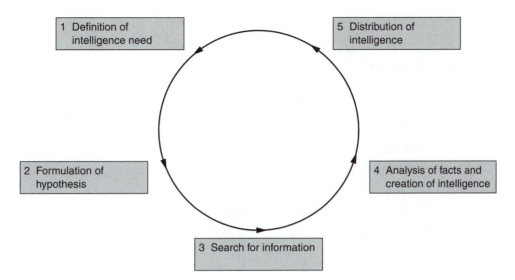

Figure 12.1 The intelligence cycle.

Cold War era. In this context, CI was about gathering and analysing information about the adversaries' activities. Civilian organizations have more complex and politically affected decision and power structures, making the decision process more difficult to capture.

While the term 'intelligence' in this context is military-derived, the use of BI stems from consultancy agencies. The term 'business intelligence' was promoted by Howard Dresner of the Gartner Group in the late 1980s, and described as a set of concepts and methods to improve business decision-making by using fact-based support systems. BI tools have also had a strong influence on the development and defining of the subject. They often refer to types of application software designed to report, analyse and present data. This has led to some perceiving BI to be a solely technological development. There is thus some confusion about what BI is, and while consultancy agencies have been innovative in promoting the term, they have also contributed to its obscurity by using it in different ways in different contexts.

Gilad and Gilad (1988) propose a three-fold usage for the term: to denote a process; as an organizational function; and as a product. They state that the BI product is 'processed information of interest to management about the present and future environment in which the business is operating' (Gilad and Gilad, 1988: 1). This broad definition captures the notion that *processed* information is a key factor (not just information), and it highlights the fact that management has an essential role in BI. Management decides what will be in the scope of BI by determining what information they want and what the BI process is expected to produce. The result has to be real intelligence rather than a mere addition to an ever-growing library containing nothing but gathered useless data.

Given the diversity of perceptions and some of the broad meanings attributed to BI, it has sometimes been considered as an umbrella term. Taking this kind of perspective, BI may be considered as something like that shown in Figure 12.2. A problem

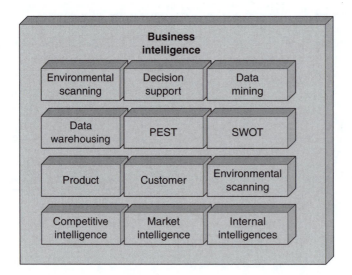

Figure 12.2 An umbrella view of business intelligence.

with broad definitions and broad perspectives is that they can appear to encompass everything and are indistinguishable from other areas. Thus, the umbrella view of BI may also be seen as strategy or knowledge management. Conversely, a problem with a narrow definition or perspective is that it can exclude important elements that should be included.

Gilad and Gilad (1988) distinguish between *operational BI* and *strategic BI*, with operational BI being about the present organizational environment, while strategic BI is about the future organizational environment. The object of a formalized BI system is to shift the focus from short-term tactical intelligence to better use of strategic intelligence for the decision-making process. This kind of aspiration has been evident many times before within business and management, with fads coming and going. Expert systems and executive information systems were also perceived to have strategic potential, but in practice have tended to be used at operational levels (Coakes *et al.*, 1997; Xu *et al.*, 2003).

Case study 12.2 Marketing intelligence trends 2015

This case study has been excerpted from MI Trends 2015 – The Future of Market Intelligence. GIA White Paper 3/2010. Global Intelligence Alliance, www.globalintelligence.com. *Reprinted with permission.*

This case study has been included by the authors to facilitate class discussion rather than to illustrate effective or ineffective management practices. Only publicly available material has been used to write this case study, and it does not reflect any opinions of employees or management at the organizations mentioned.

The intelligence industry, heading towards 2015, is moving to more sophistication, integration to business processes, impact on decision-making and visibility. Market intelligence (MI) (frequently used interchangeably with competitive intelligence or business intelligence) is a distinct discipline by which organizations systematically gather and process information about their external operating environment (such as customers, competition, trends, regulation or geographic areas).

The results provided here are based on an MI trends survey conducted by GIA among 146 executives and intelligence professionals globally during May 2010, of whom 83 per cent were intelligence professionals and 17 per cent end users. The respondents were asked 19 questions related to the six key success factors of world-class market intelligence: scope, process, deliverables, tools, organization and culture.

Not surprisingly, the survey results suggest the emerging growth markets such as China, Asia Pacific, Latin America, the Middle East and Eastern Europe are rapidly becoming part of the geographic scope of most companies' intelligence programmes. The primary focus in these areas is gradually shifting from looking at investment opportunities and market entry strategies to continuously keeping the areas under the radar screen. Many Western companies already have an established presence in the growth markets, and they now need to stay on top of the local market dynamics both on an everyday basis and in the future. As a result, processing and translating local language business information will most likely consume more resources than before.

Which areas in the business environment will be under the heaviest change and therefore have the most significant impact on MI efforts?

Increase significantly (+2)
Increase moderately (+1)
Remain the same (0)
Decrease moderately (+2)
Decrease significantly (+2)

From a value-chain perspective, customers, end consumers and competitors will continue to be the primary focus of the intelligence efforts for most surveyed companies. Customers and end users drive the business, whether in the mature markets or emerging ones,

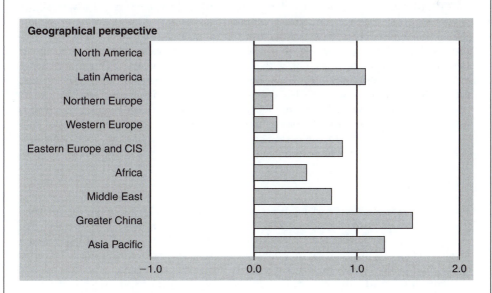

Figure 12.3 Anticipated changes in the regional scope of the intelligence programme.

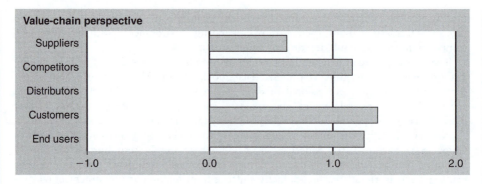

Figure 12.4 The dominant focus of MI efforts continues to be on the front end of the value chain.

and competition typically influences pricing and differentiation strategies. Suppliers and distributors, in turn, tend to be heavily under the radar screen in industries undergoing rapid changes in the value chain. Changes may include mergers and acquisitions, partnerships and joint ventures on the supplier side or, for instance, shifts in manufacturing technology or distribution strategies.

Risk management emerging as an application area of MI

The scope of the intelligence efforts is initially determined by the MI-needs analysis that should be repeatedly revisited even if the company is not expanding to new geographic areas, or the value chain that it belongs to remains stable. User groups to the intelligence programme are also part of the scope of the activity, and the existing intelligence infrastructure can be leveraged to serve additional corporate functions and activities, of which risk management is an emerging example.

With the Sarbanes–Oxley Act in force since 2002 and the more recent major failures in corporate risk management, it is becoming increasingly important for (especially public) companies to comply with strict risk control measures, both financially and qualitatively. From the MI perspective, this means that, for instance, sizeable strategic investment decisions should be backed up with sound research and analysis. This is not only to ensure business success in the first place, but also to avoid management being held liable afterwards for bad decisions made based on improper or missing information.

MI can bring an external point of view to the risk management discussion (which is typically internally focused). On top of internal business risks, management should consider risks originating from the customer base, competitive dynamics, macroeconomic factors, political environment or technological shifts.

Intelligence process

'Intelligence process' refers to the process of gathering, analysing and reporting information about specified topics to users. The intelligence process should always be anchored to the existing corporate processes (strategic planning, sales, marketing, product management, etc.) within which information will be used. In practice, the output delivered by the intelligence process should find its place as part of the strategic planning process, sales meetings, marketing reviews and innovation management, or as part of simply maintaining current awareness in the organization about the developments in the external operating environment.

Needs analysis leads to information gathering from both secondary and primary sources, after which the information is converted into analyses and conclusions, followed by delivery, utilization and feedback. The concrete output of the process provides inputs to decision-making, backed up by intelligence products of different purposes, formats and levels of analysis, depending on the user groups.

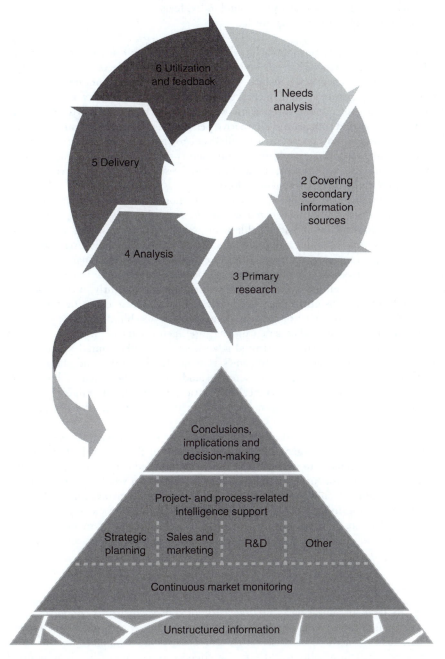

Figure 12.5 Intelligence process and the role of their output as part of business processes.

The survey results suggest that social media applications will be used increasingly for collecting and sharing information for MI purposes. Three perspectives were specifically brought up in the survey:

- internal use of features from social media applications;
- information collection and analysis around individuals;
- cultural shift triggered by social media.

By monitoring the activities in social media of some key people at customer, competitor and supplier organizations, it will be possible to identify projects, new competence areas, travel plans, business relationships and open positions that, combined, tell a lot about the company's strategy and initiatives. Competitor and customer wikis will be created in order to enhance the internal knowledge about them. Blogs will be used in order to provide internal context and alternative perspectives to relevant business signals, and crowd forecasting will emerge as a parallel tool to traditional forecasting methods. As people get used to both networking virtually and communicating on the go through smartphones and pocket computers, it should become easier to engage different parts of the organization in the daily intelligence efforts.

The survey results give strong support to co-creation as an emerging trend in the corporate world. That is, intelligence deliverables are created jointly by MI professionals and various decision-makers and stakeholders. In practice, MI professionals will need to increasingly often give briefings and presentations and engage in facilitating workshops such as scenario planning, war gaming, crowd forecasting and trend seminars.

From the MI perspective, the co-creation trend means two things. Decision-makers (the end users of the intelligence deliverables) will engage more tightly in the process of actually producing the insights. This is typically rewarding and motivating for intelligence professionals who, in turn, get to be involved in reaching the often strategic decisions that the company takes based on the intelligence efforts. However, to claim their position as the management's trusted advisor and co-worker, intelligence professionals must truly understand the company's business fundamentals and the management's mindset, and to incorporate this understanding into their deliverables in an analytical and thought-provoking manner. In practice, co-creating intelligence deliverables with management does not mean less work for the intelligence professionals, but more.

The results also suggest that, ideally, in the future, the intelligence team needs to use their time on taking the intelligence deliverables to a high analytical level, after which it is time for the management to get involved and reach the final conclusions jointly with the intelligence team. Not surprisingly, the analysis process as a whole is not something that many companies would see being outsourced; nor would management be using much time on turning information into analyses. Outsourcing other parts of the intelligence process than analysis will, on the other hand, be considered by many of the surveyed companies in the interest of liberating the in-house resources to concentrate on working closely with the management and decision-makers.

How do you anticipate the analytical output of the MI process developing?

Typically, in large organizations, intelligence efforts first emerge in regional units, without any significant central coordination that would ensure uniform research approaches, analysis methods or presentation templates. Many companies have realized, however, that building a solid world-class intelligence programme that is recognized company-wide requires an HQ-centric approach to ensure the local units have a common platform to base their own efforts on. By at least partly standardizing the presentation

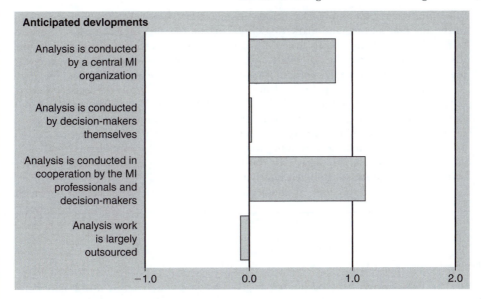

Figure 12.6 Anticipated developments in the analysis process.

templates, analysis frameworks and sourcing of data, companies will achieve cost savings, avoid doing double work, facilitate cross-functional cooperation, and maximize the benefits of the intelligence programme for the entire organization.

One of the frequently mentioned topics in the survey – and indeed in any MI-related discussions lately – is the integration of MI to decision-making and corporate business processes. Considering the popularity of the topic, it is surprising how few companies to date can honestly say that their decision-point intelligence is in good shape, i.e. that all strategic decisions are being backed-up with timely and well-prepared analyses.

Two conclusions can be drawn:

- Intelligence teams still need to work further on proactively understanding the business fundamentals and growth drivers of the company – and the related decision-making processes.
- Decision-makers need to understand that the intelligence teams will need continuous visibility not only to the concrete assignments that are requested from them, but to the decision points in the background from which the intelligence needs are derived.

Summary of other findings

In general, MI deliverables will become increasingly sophisticated in the future, with increased analytical depth, online availability and still greater future-orientation. The sophistication of the intelligence deliverables ties in with the overall stage of development of the intelligence programme. By combining experience with tools and resources it is possible to concentrate on increasingly analytical and future-oriented intelligence output, such as analytical deep-dives, scenario analysis and war-gaming workshops, while in the early stages there is typically more emphasis on rather basic deliverables.

Intelligence culture is essentially the glue that keeps the entire intelligence operation together, and by the very definition of culture, it is born and nurtured inside the organization. Perhaps the most important element in gradually generating an intelligence culture in any organization is senior management's articulated support of the activity.

Other important building blocks include demonstrated benefits of the activity and successful internal training and marketing efforts. These together typically take the organization from first being merely aware of the intelligence programme, through accepting it and recognizing its value, to finally assisting the intelligence team in co-creating the insights the company needs in order to stay competitive in the marketplace.

An intelligence culture, like culture in general, is much about social cohesion, common beliefs and common behaviour. The fundamentals such as management's support and marketing efforts will continue to drive the intelligence culture, but an interesting addition will be brought not by the social media tools themselves, but by people growing familiar with exposing their thoughts and views to large virtual audiences. The survey results indicate that this trend might bring significant changes to the cultural side of corporate intelligence activities, going forward.

The full report on the survey contains much more information and detail of responses.

12.4 Summary

This chapter has provided a basic introduction to data warehousing and business intelligence. The chapter opened with the case study, which helped to demonstrate that successful development and implementation of BI systems can have quantifiable results. The concluding case study reported on a survey that indicated views on market intelligence and its future.

The data warehousing section outlined the main features of data warehousing and some benefits and drawbacks associated with its implementation. The BI section discussed the main features of BI, some common terms used, and why BI is considered to be important in competitive environments.

Glossary

Business intelligence   The analysis of internal, structured data and business processes (using information technology).

Competitive intelligence   The collation and analysis of internal and external information (structured and unstructured) with or without support from technology.

Data access layer   The interface between the operational and informational access layers; it has means to input, change and extract data.

Data cleansing   Detecting, correcting and, where necessary, removing corrupt or inaccurate records.

Data warehouse   Storage of an organization's data electronically to assist ease of access, input, analysis, querying and reporting.

Dimensional approach   An approach that partitions transaction data facts (numeric data) or dimensions, which give the reference information that provides context for the facts.

Informational access layer   Enables reporting and analysing; this is often linked to business intelligence.

Integrated data warehouse   A data warehouse that is updated whenever a transaction occurs in the operational system; also passes data back to the operational system.

Intelligence cycle   A model that depicts an ideal flow of information within an organization, but which does not indicate what actually happens.

Master data management Data management that has the aim of conforming non-transactional data that could be considered as dimensions by using processes and tools that consistently define and manage the entities of an organization, which may include reference data.

Metadata layer The data directory, which includes data warehouse dictionaries.

Off-line operational database A database that uses data that is simply copied from an operational system to another server.

Operational database layer The source data for the data warehouse; this links to enterprise resource planning systems.

Real-time data warehouse A data warehouse updated whenever a transaction occurs in the operational system.

Record management system A system used to record, store and retrieve transaction data.

Transaction data A description of changes that occur with events; it would normally state the time/date of the transaction, the object involved and a quantity of some kind.

References

Coakes, E., Merchant, K., and Lehaney, B. (1997) The Use of Expert Systems in Business Transformation. *Management Decision*, 35(1), 53–57.

Davenport, T. (2008) *10 Principles of the New Business Intelligence*. Available online at http://blogs.hbr.org/davenport/2008/12/10_principles_of_the_new_busin.html (accessed 4 January 2010).

Gilad, B. and Gilad, T. (1988) *The Business Intelligence System: A New Tool for Competitive Advantage*. New York: American Management Association.

Global Intelligence Alliance (2008) *MI for the Strategic Planning Process*. Available at: www.globalintelligence.com (accessed 2 February 2010).

Power, D.J. (2007) *A Brief History of Decision Support Systems*. Available online at http://DSSResources.COM/history/dsshistory.html, version 4.1 (accessed 15 January 2010).

Xu, X., Lehaney, B., Clarke, C., and Duan, Y. (2003) Some UK and USA Comparisons of Executive Information Systems in Practice and Theory. *Journal of End User Computing*, 15(1), 1–19.

Further Reading

Kimball, R., Ross, M., Becker, B., Thornthwaite, W., and Mundy, J. (2010) *Kimball Group Reader: Relentlessly Practical Tools for Data Warehousing and Business Intelligence*. Chichester: Wiley.

Suggested activities

1   Find out (provide sources):

    a   the names of any organizations that use data warehousing;
    b   the names of any organizations that use business intelligence;
    c   job titles in these areas.

2   Discuss the benefits and drawbacks of using data warehousing and business intelligence in three different economic sectors and for different sizes of organization.

3   In your own words, summarize how organizations' internal information systems relate to data warehousing and business intelligence.

4   Discuss the Qualcomm case study in light of this chapter.

13   Strategy and information systems

Case study 13.1 East Slovakia coal industry

This case is drawn from Lehaney et al. *(2008). It was previously published in Bali* et al. *(2009).*

This case study has been included by the authors to facilitate class discussion rather than to illustrate effective or ineffective management practices. Only publicly available material has been used to write this case study, and it does not reflect any opinions of employees or management at the organizations mentioned.

The initial issues in this case were to do with physical processes, and a particular manager who wanted to improve production. In fact, the case turned out to relate more to strategy, operations management in a wider sense, information flows and culture. The investigation revealed misunderstandings and poor communication that wasted resources.

The manager had difficulties in meeting targets set by the marketing department. He had tried to use forecasting, without much success, and wondered if simulating the processes would be of help, and if some combination of approaches would be useful. What was clear was that the management desire was for a technical solution, and it was apparent that issues such as culture and knowledge sharing were not initially on the management agenda. Plant managers wanted quantitative models and quantifiable solutions.

The Upper Nitra Basin is the richest and largest brown coal basin in Slovakia. Upper Nitra Mines (UNM) was founded on 1 July 1996 by the transformation of a former state-owned set of mines. Under state planning, coal demand was highly stable. Mine managers were told what to produce, and there was no need to change production, since demand was secured by government order. After the fall of communism in 1989, UNM faced the new and uncertain conditions of the free market. UNM was forced to renew all previous sales contracts and try to win customers within the competitive market. In this new situation, the newly formed Czech Republic suddenly became a competitor, as did other East European coal producers such as Poland and Ukraine. Piped Russian gas began to be delivered cheaply to increasing numbers of homes throughout Slovakia. In the face of such competition, UNM had to re-evaluate its situation and decide if it was willing and able to find new markets, or at what points it should downsize and possibly close.

The effect of closure would be multiplied across East Slovakia, as direct and knock-on employment in many areas depends upon the coal mines. Currently there is no possibility of alternative employment, since the Russian piped gas requires relatively few local operatives and the Slovakian government is unwilling or unable to provide further financial assistance. Gas heating installation in villages has been growing rapidly, to replace traditional coal heating. The gas heating is as cheap as or cheaper than coal heating, but is clean and easily controlled; the gas may also be used for cooking. In addition, unlike the past when village youngsters worked locally on the land or in mines, today's young people are moving into towns and cities to seek employment. This reduces local demand for coal, and the central heating systems of the cities tend to use gas or electricity.

District heating is the dominant method of heat supply in Slovakia, where almost 100 per cent of city accommodation is supplied with heat from district heating, which represents approximately 49 per cent of all households in Slovakia. Approximately 39 per cent of primary energy source consumption is used for heat production in industry, service sectors and households either for space heating or for production purposes. The fuel base of district heating plants includes mainly natural gas (71.3 per cent), followed by coal (16.4 per cent), fuel oil (6.7 per cent) and others (5.6 per cent). Approximately 970,000 households are supplied by individual heating, of which 870,000 households are family houses with electric heating, coal stoves, gas ovens or wood stoves.

There are three major companies, located in five different regions, producing coal in the Slovak Republic. The first (and major) one is UNM, which has three subsidiaries: Mine Cigel, Mine Handlova and Mine Novaky. The second is Mine Dolina and the third is Mine Zahorie. In 2004 these three companies employed 8,774 people and produced 3.746 million tonnes of coal. The Novaky electric power station is the only one in the Slovak Republic that passes Western European emission standards. Novaky used over 2.5 million tonnes of coal in 2004. Households and community used 618,000 tonnes of assorted sized coal; the bulk of the remainder was used by the chemical industry.

With a skilled and competitively priced labour force, strong manufacturing tradition and proximity to European markets, Slovakia's prospects may appear to be favourable. Previously state-controlled sectors, such as energy (coal, gas), have now been opened to competition however, and raw materials firms can no longer rely on obtaining long-term government contracts. In the light of this competition, information flows and information management are now extremely important. In these new, unstable and dynamically changing conditions, managers need effective decision support methods and ways to reconsider their systems so that market advantages can be realized in production and sales.

Historically, the production manager had been told to process as much coal as was delivered from the mines. In the new market environment he would have liked to know what demand existed, for which products, in what timescales, and be able to react to these and be proactive in the processing operation. Coal that is processed and not bought by the market on the same day has a very short lifespan and thus is a waste product. Although having moved to a market situation, the processing plant continued to be managed as if in a planned economy. Regardless of market demand, the mine produced coal to levels that related purely to current ability to produce. This coal is taken to the processing facility, which is forced to receive all coal from the mine.

The market requires specific amounts of different types of coal, and the processing manager was under enormous pressure to meet this demand, yet there was no direct link between market demand and coal production at the mine. The authors proposed that the process would work much more effectively if mine production were influenced directly by market demand. While in a market economy this suggestion might be seen as obvious, it was a suggestion against the current culture. Nevertheless, it was difficult for those who resisted to offer rational arguments against the proposal. Those who resisted were, however, in the majority and strongly influenced decisions. Eventually, after much debate, it was agreed that if it could be shown that the proposed model would be more efficient, it would be adopted. A proxy for improved efficiency was agreed: the amount of waste coal produced.

It was also agreed that a simulation model should be developed to demonstrate the effects of the proposed new policy. The model showed vast improvements in reducing physical coal waste, which was a direct result of market knowledge feeding into information flows. The value of this knowledge may be estimated by the cost savings that were due to the reduction of coal waste. The structure of various units and their interactions with each other were the primary issues that needed to be addressed. The key change was when participants began to discover more about their own systems, and to realize that the issue of information management is vital in addressing this situation. Thus, what had started out as a possibly straightforward operational research modelling situation became an intervention in which the major issues were ones of cultural change and management of information.

Despite the demonstrated advantages for operational planning, successful implementation would require some strategic changes, altering established practices and relationships with other segments of the company; in particular, with the coal extraction site and marketing division. The proposed scenario has been discussed extensively and clearly demonstrates improvement by using forecast market demand rather than fixed deliveries dictated by the mine. This approach requires an investment in culture change, modelling and information management. While everyone at the mine accepts the logic of the solution, there is still huge resistance to change, and this resistance comes from some of the more senior management.

As the case developed, the issues of information management and the need to change existing practices highlighted personal, strategic, cultural and societal issues. After exploring the problem situation it became apparent that the production manager's problem was not the need for modelling techniques, but one of change management. In order to further that case, he needed to demonstrate the value of market knowledge. All the information needed to address the issues was available, but the organization and its information flows had to be considered in new ways if the issues were to be addressed successfully.

13.1 Intended learning outcomes

On completion of this chapter the reader should be able to:

1   explain the differences between corporate strategy, business strategy, organizational strategy and information systems strategy, and how business strategy may be supported by IS/IT strategy;
2   synthesize material to argue the strategic value of information;
3   evaluate the setting of an organization within its sector and the wider macroeconomic environment;
4   analyse an organization's competitive position by applying approaches for analysis such as PEST, SWOT, and the five competitive forces;
5   appraise and compare major strategic models.

13.2 Overview of strategy

You may often hear the word 'strategy' used in general conversation. Its meaning in that context can be variable. In business it is to do with long-term planning, high-level decisions and large-scale activities. What do we mean by long-term? A traditional view from the discipline of economics works quite well for this in many ways. Consider the three traditional factors of production: land, labour and capital. Note that capital in this context does not mean lots of cash. Capital refers to plant and machinery, such as factory buildings, production line equipment, tractors and so on.

The very short-run covers periods where no variation to any factors of production is possible. In the short-run, just one factor of production may be varied (typically, this has been considered to be labour). In the long-run, all factors of production can be varied. The very long-run covers periods in which technology can change. Strategy is concerned with the long-run and very long-run.

Figure 13.1 illustrates an overview of corporate and business strategy. Corporate strategy deals with the biggest decisions about the types of markets in which an organization wishes to operate. Business strategy is about achievements, such as profitability, competitiveness and market share.

The organization has internal interactions and it also interacts with external environments. The latter includes the industry (micro-environment) and the national and international economies and structures. This relationship is shown in Figure 13.2.

In the micro-environment we are concerned with the criteria that are specific to the organization and the market in which it operates. It is important that the specific segment of that market is also recognized. For example, Mercedes Benz are not in the same market segment as Skoda. With some companies it is also important to identify that they may produce ranges of products that are spread across market segments. Sometimes these will be separated into different businesses. Until recently, Ford owned Jaguar, Aston Martin and Land Rover, the markets of which were very different from the standard Ford product. This is not unique to the automotive industry. Supermarkets are another example where there may be a cheaper economy-range product, a standard product and a premium product for the same kind of item, such as baked beans.

In general, a strategy is a kind of plan, and a business strategy is a structured and clear outline of an organization's goals and means to achieve them. As indicated by Figure 13.2, strategy should be informed by many things, including market forces, consumer patterns, organizational capacity and capabilities and government legislation. There are many approaches to business strategy. Two of the most well-known are Porter's generic strategies framework (Porter, 1980) and D'Aveni's hypercompetition model (D'Aveni, 1994).

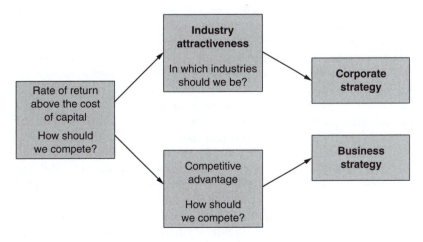

Figure 13.1 An overview of corporate and business strategy.

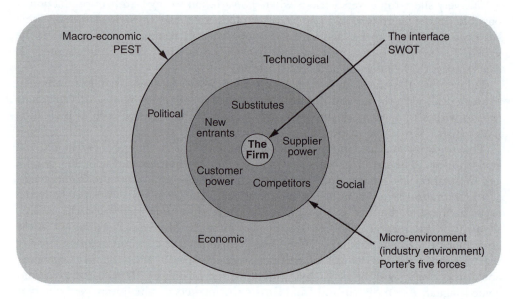

Figure 13.2 The organization and its environment.

In the *generic strategies framework* firms face competition in trying to sell their products, and each firm tries to gain the competitive advantage. Porter distinguishes three major strategies for achieving competitive advantage:

- cost
- differentiation
- focus.

Cost leadership is about being the lowest-cost producer in the marketplace; by keeping costs to a minimum the organization can achieve above-average performance, providing that products are of comparable quality to those of competitors. In other words, cutting costs while producing an inferior product will not gain this kind of competitive advantage. Within a perfectly competitive market, with many small firms, any cost advantage will be short-lived, as competitors will follow suit very quickly. In a market with very few large competitors, one cost leader exists and, as a result of price wars, may drive higher-cost organizations out of the industry. Lower cost equates to the ability to offer lower prices to consumers.

Differentiation is uniqueness of products. An organization attempts to identify the non-price characteristics that are most important to customers, and it tries to appeal to customers by increasing the appeal in at least one of these characteristics. It is always the case that customers will consider price, so enhancing the quality of a differentiating characteristic will not achieve competitive advantage if the price is too high. This is a challenge for a firm, because creating differentiation in a qualitative way adds costs. As an example, a large economy loaf of white sliced bread may cost as little as 50p from a large supermarket chain. A loaf of sliced bread that is perceived by customers to be of superior quality may cost as much as £1.50 from the same store.

This is the maximum consumers will pay for the perceived quality difference. Therefore, additional costs through further product differentiation cannot be passed on to the consumer, and would eat into profit margins.

A firm may limit its scope to a narrow section of a market and may tailor its products to meet the demands of a particular consumer group; this approach has two variants, cost focus and differentiation focus. Focus may achieve local competitive advantage, but may not achieve overall marketplace competitive advantage.

D'Aveni's *hypercompetition model* is based on the concepts that competitive advantage cannot be maintained and, as a result, speed and aggression will quickly erode any short-term advantages. Within this model, attempting to sustain an advantage can distract from gaining new ones and, ultimately, may be fatal for an organization. Advantage should therefore be about a series of temporary disruptions rather than sustainability, with it being important to start creating the next advantage well before the erosion of any current advantages. Under hypercompetition there are four possible areas of advantage:

- cost/quality
- timing/know-how
- strongholds
- deep pockets.

The first arena is competition based on cost and quality in which product positioning can be a source of strategic advantage. Usually, firms compete by offering differing levels of quality at different prices. When quality is not a factor, firms are forced to engage in price wars because this is the only dimension in which they can compete. As hypercompetition escalates, firms use new dimensions of quality and service to differentiate themselves. Some firms try to cover all the ground between being a high-priced, high-quality differentiator and low-priced, low-quality cost leader by becoming full-line producers.

One way to escape this cycle of competition on price and quality is to enter a new market or launch a new product. Timing of market entry and the know-how that allows entry form the second arena for competitive interaction. A first-mover can seize control of the market but often invests heavily in establishing a product or service that can be imitated and improved upon by competitors. To foil imitators the first-mover may create impediments to imitation, but the followers then attempt to overcome these impediments. The followers become faster at imitation, forcing the first-mover to change tactics. The first-mover may then use a strategy of leapfrogging innovations, building on large technological advances that require entirely new resources and know-how. This makes it harder for an imitator to develop the same resources, but eventually the imitators catch up. This forces the first-mover to seek new leapfrog moves, which become more expensive and risky with each leap. These cycles of innovation and imitation eventually lead to a market in which the last available leapfrog move is exploited and imitated, and continuing the leapfrogging strategy becomes unsustainable because the cost of the next-generation leapfrog is too high. At this point, even if a new technological leapfrog jump can be made, it takes so long that competitors have time to catch up.

As the move towards ultimate value and rapid imitation tends to level the playing field, competitors seek to gain advantage in the third arena, by creating strongholds that exclude competitors from their turf. By creating entry barriers around a stronghold in a certain geographic region, industry or product market segment, firms try to insulate themselves from competitive attacks based on price and quality or innovation and imitation. While firms build entry barriers that keep others out of their markets, this tactic is rarely sustainable over the long-run. Entrants eventually find ways to circumvent entry barriers. After building a war chest in their own strongholds, competitors can fund forays into the protected strongholds of others. These expeditions usually provoke a response from the attacked companies. Such responses often go beyond defensive actions in the attacked market by leading to a counterattack against the initiating firm's stronghold. These attacks and counterattacks often erode the strongholds of both players. This process can be seen on a large scale in globalized markets, where huge businesses based on one continent attack the strongholds of large companies based on other continents until it becomes hard to tell whether competitors are American or Japanese (or any other nationality). As entry barriers have come down and markets integrate, the playing fields again begin to level out, and the old competitive advantages provided by having a protected stronghold are no longer viable.

After firms exhaust their advantages based on cost and quality, timing and know-how, and after their strongholds have fallen, they often rely upon their deep pockets. The fourth arena in which firms try to develop strategic advantage is based on financial resources. Well-endowed firms can use their brute force to bully a small competitor. These large firms have greater endurance, using their resources to wear down or undercut their opponents, but the small competitors are not completely defenceless. They can call upon government regulations, develop formal or informal alliances, or step aside to avoid competition with the deep-pocket firm. With these moves and counter-moves, or even with the erosion of resources over time, the large firm eventually loses its deep-pocket advantage. When small firms build their access to resources through joint ventures or alliances, power tends to balance out and eventually the deep-pocket advantage is neutralized.

D'Aveni's *seven Ss framework* describes how firms may be able to disrupt competition. The seven Ss provide a useful model for identifying different aspects of a business strategy for helping an organization to be competitive in a hypercompetitive market. The framework helps firms to evaluate and assess competitors' strengths and weaknesses, as well as to inform strategy. The model may help managers to create and identify new organizational responses, especially in markets where the rate of change makes sustaining a business strategy and its advantages difficult. The seven Ss are:

1   superior stakeholder satisfaction
2   strategic soothsaying
3   speed
4   surprise
5   shifting the rules of competition
6   signalling strategic intent
7   simultaneous and sequential strategic thrusts.

The seven Ss are concerned with the ability of the company to create disruption, seize the initiative and create a series of temporary advantages. The first two of these, stakeholder focus and strategic soothsaying, are concerned with establishing a vision for disrupting the market. This includes setting goals, setting the firm's disruption strategy and identifying some core competencies necessary for the firm to create specific disruptions. The second two, speed and surprise, focus on key capabilities that can be applied across a wide array of actions intended to disrupt the status quo. The final three, shifting the rules, signalling and simultaneous and sequential strategic thrusts, are concerned with disruptive tactics and actions in hypercompetitive environments.

Superior stakeholder satisfaction is the key to winning each dynamic strategic interaction with competitors. The process of developing new advantages or undermining those of competitors begins with an understanding of how to satisfy customers. By discovering ways to satisfy customers, the company can identify its next moves to seize the initiative, but customers are not the only stakeholders that must be satisfied. By empowering employees, the company can gain the internal motivation and vision needed to carry out those moves.

Strategic soothsaying is a process of seeking out new knowledge necessary for predicting or even creating new temporary windows of opportunity that competitors will eventually enter but that are not now served by anyone else. These opportunities can be found by creatively combining products, understanding trends in the business environment that will open up new opportunities, and serving new customer markets with the existing capabilities of the firm.

These first two Ss differ from conventional thinking about advantage in that they argue that the source of advantage is the ability to win each dynamic strategic interaction with competitors. This is achieved by finding how to satisfy the customer in a way that is new or superior to old methods. This requires two competencies: motivated, empowered workers at all levels of the organization; and knowledge of the future or an ability to create the future. Together, these enable the organization to satisfy customers in ways that are new or superior to old methods.

Speed and surprise are self-evident factors. The final three Ss are concerned with tactics or punches/counterpunches used in a hypercompetitive environment. These three Ss suggest that winning a dynamic strategic interaction has to do with how the traditional interaction between competitors is attuned to using signals, new competitive methods that shift the rules and simultaneous and sequential actions that manipulate or mould the actions of competitors.

Shifting the rules of competition is concerned with actions that redefine the battlefield. By shifting the rules of the game, the company creates new opportunities to satisfy customers. The company finds new ways of satisfying customers that transform the industry, such as adapting the personal computer to serve the mainframe computing industry, or inventing the disposable razor to transform the market for standard razors.

Signals are announcements of strategic intent that are important preludes to more powerful actions. Signals can stall the actions of competitors or create uncertainty that erodes their will to defend against attacks. They can preannounce or fake aggressive offensive moves that alter the behaviour of competitors. Thus, signals can be used to disrupt the status quo and interactions between companies, thereby creating an advantage.

Simultaneous and sequential strategic thrusts are the use of a series of actions designed to stun or confuse competitors, disrupting the status quo to create new advantages or erode those of competitors. Whereas traditional strategic actions have been treated one at a time, actions in hypercompetition are used in combinations that are difficult to unravel and difficult to defend against. These thrusts move on several geographic or market fronts simultaneously. By manipulating competitors' reactions using a series of simultaneous or sequential actions, they result in the initiating company's advantage. Hypercompetitive firms who wish to harass, paralyze, induce error or block competitors use simultaneous and sequential strategic thrusts.

Organizational strategy is about the design of the organization, as well as the choices it makes to implement that design and carry out its operations. The *business diamond* (Hammer and Champy, 1994) presents a clear and relatively simple model to help identify crucial components of an organization's plan (Figure 13.3).

Cash *et al.* (1994) produced a framework for organizational strategy based on managerial levers that comprise the best combination of control, cultural and organizational variables. At the hub of this model are people, information and technology. Control variables include data availability and quality of performance measurement systems and planning processes and quality. Cultural variables are about the values held by individuals and groups within an organization. Organizational variables include business processes, decision rights, formal reporting relationships and informal networks. Managers may use the levers to help develop and implement organizational strategy in order to achieve and improve organizational effectiveness and efficiency.

13.3 Some approaches to strategic analysis

PEST stands for *political, economic, social* and *technological*. These factors affect market growth or decline, and therefore the strategies an organization may adopt. There are variations on the acronym, such as PETS and STEP. Also, PEST is sometimes extended by adding *ecological* (or *environmental*), *legislative* (or *legal*), and *industry* analyses, which are used in the PESTEL and PESTELI frameworks. It can be argued that such extensions to the basic PEST model are unnecessary, as the four factors within PEST can be used to cover all the others. In this chapter the basic PEST model is used.

SWOT stands for *strengths, weaknesses, opportunities* and *threats*. SWOT will be discussed subsequently, but it may be useful to note for now that PEST analysis is usually used to evaluate the wider industry, market and economy, whereas SWOT analysis is used to assess a business unit, project or objectives. PEST tends to be used before SWOT, because without knowing the market it would be difficult to analyse the strengths,

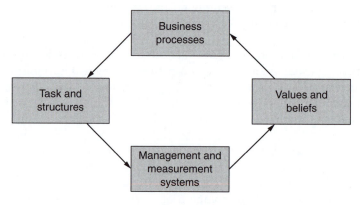

Figure 13.3 The business diamond (source: adapted from Hammer and Champy, 1994).

weaknesses, opportunities and threats of a particular proposition, so PEST helps to inform SWOT. There will be some overlap between PEST and SWOT, but this should be seen as positive interaction rather than repetition, as the two approaches are different.

It may be difficult at first to understand PEST, but keep in mind that it is about considering how the market is affected by the wider national and international contexts. As mentioned previously, a market needs to be defined carefully, and you need to consider whether you are looking at products, organizations, brands or something else. Is a firm considering its market? Are you looking at one particular product, the firm as a whole, one particular brand (with maybe many products), a possible takeover or merger, or maybe a new investment opportunity?

Figure 13.4 shows some examples of factors that may be considered when conducting a PEST analysis. These are by no means exhaustive, and you should think of other factors that may be considered under the four main headings.

An overview of SWOT is shown in Figure 13.5. Sometimes people get confused between strengths and opportunities and between weaknesses and threats. It is important to keep in mind that strengths and weaknesses are internal to the organization. Opportunities and threats are external.

It is also important to note that some things may appear more than once. For example, in considering a business, it may be considered to be a strength that the head of that unit is very focused and determined to achieve goals. This may be considered as a weakness if viewed from a different perspective. The head may be considered to be oblivious to things outside of the immediate objectives and may be thought to be obstinate. Context is therefore vital in carrying out a SWOT analysis.

The SWOT framework helps sort ideas into a logical format that may help analysis, understanding, discussion, planning and decision-making. In a group, SWOT helps to surface underlying views, and helps avoid making decisions that are purely based on

Political factors	Social factors
Ecology	Image – brand, organization, product
Funding	Consumer trends – e.g. leisure/work balance
Government policies – local and national	Demographics
International pressure groups	Ethics
Legislation – current, future, national	Family values
Trade unions and pressure groups	Media
Wars	Religion
Economic factors	**Technological factors**
Domestic economy – current and trends	Competing technologies
Interest and exchange rates	Disruptive technologies
International trade/monetary issues	Global communications
Market and trade cycles	Intellectual property rights
Overseas economies – current and trends	Linked technologies
Seasonal variations	Research and development funding
Taxation – firms, consumers, products	Technology legislation

Figure 13.4 Some examples of PEST.

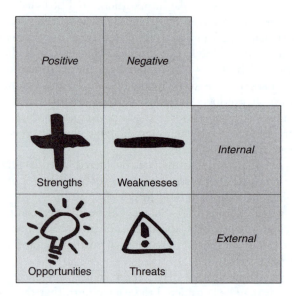

Figure 13.5 An overview of SWOT.

instinctive reactions ('gut feeling'). SWOT analysis helps review strategy, but this can only be done properly in the context of objectives. Things that may be considered include: how products may be marketed; whether a new brand is likely to be viable; if an acquisition should be pursued; and if a supplier should be changed. This list is by no means exhaustive. Figure 13.6 lists some things that may be considered under each SWOT heading. Again, these are just examples, and there are many more factors that may be relevant.

Porter's five forces provide a means to consider the market strength and competitive position of an organization. The five forces are represented in Figure 13.7, and examples are given in Figure 13.8. New entrants to an industry can increase competition, thus making the industry less attractive, as increased competition can result in reduced profits. Many industries have barriers to entry that deter potential rivals from entering that market, and which therefore protect high-profit companies within the market. An example of an entry barrier is high start-up costs, as is the case for car manufacturing.

The threat of substitutes is often the most disregarded of the five forces, but can be the most harmful factor of strategic decision-making, since businesses must evaluate their direct competition. Substitutes are a direct result of industry competition, which can reduce products and profitability because they limit price levels, meaning industry attractiveness can be reduced. Examples are: different brands of cola; different brands of cornflakes; and different brands of baked beans. It is a personal choice as to whether something is considered to be a substitute or not.

The cost of items bought from suppliers, such as raw materials, can impact on the profitability of a firm. If suppliers have high bargaining power then the company's industry is less attractive, because the firm may have to absorb supplier price increases, for example. The bargaining power of suppliers may be reduced by adopting new technology quickly, reducing the cost of inventory (by using just-in-time, for example) and using information about customer needs and wants effectively and efficiently.

Strengths	Weaknesses
Culture	Poor organization
Financial reserves	Poor communication
Management skills	Limited cash flow
Quality of product	Unreliable information system
Technical skills	Low morale
Training schemes	Little or no staff development
Unique selling points	Bureaucracy
Opportunities	**Threats**
Market developments	New entrants
Government grants	Macro-economic downturns
Industry trends	Competitor developments
Technology development	Legislative effects
Global factors	Loss of key staff
New geographical locations	Market demand
Fashions	Supplier weaknesses

Figure 13.6 Possible factors in a SWOT analysis.

Buyers are the people or organizations who create demand in an industry (the customers). The stronger the power of buyers the more they can affect the selling price of products. The bargaining power of buyers decides how much pressure customers can enforce on margins and volumes. The bargaining power of buyers may be reduced through increasing loyalty and by adding features or branding to the product.

Rivalry and competition between companies can cause reduction in profits. In pursuing a competitive advantage over their rivals, companies can use a number of techniques such as lowering prices (for short-term advantage), or developing advantageous relationships with suppliers.

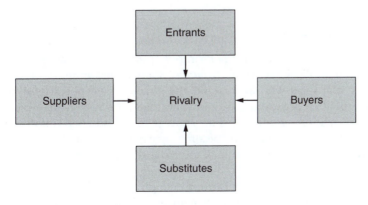

Figure 13.7 Porter's five forces (source: adapted from Porter, 1980).

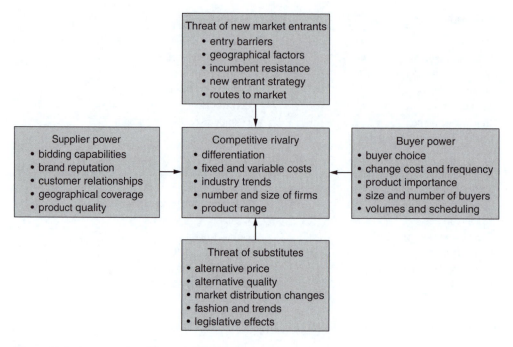

Figure 13.8 An example of Porter's five forces.

The five forces combined help determine the long-term profitability and competitiveness of businesses, and make up the industry environment. The framework provides information that may inform SWOT analysis and assist in comparisons within a competitive environment. There are similarities with PEST, but PEST can be used to consider the wider national and international contexts, including government legislation.

There are some limitations to the five forces model, and there have been criticisms of it. It is, however, appealing in various ways, not least because it offers a relatively easy starting point for managers to begin thinking about industry composition, and to use this for further analysis.

13.4 Information systems strategy

Business information systems students are not simply studying information technology or information systems. They are studying *business* information systems, presumably aiming to become managers who understand the strategic and operational roles that information may play in organizations, and how that information may best be managed using the technology available. Put another way, business information systems graduates should be well placed to become managers who are able to communicate successfully with the people who look after the technical side of the organization's information systems (IS).

For many reasons, managers should be informed enough to be able to engage in IS decisions, such as procurement, use and so on. If managers do not participate in these activities, they leave such decisions to technicians. The latter may be extremely knowledgeable about the technology, and may make excellent decisions based on that knowledge alone. They should not, however, be as knowledgeable about the business as the managers running it, and a good technological decision may not be the best business decision.

ISs should be there to support business goals and organizational systems, not for their own sake. This may seem a silly statement, as it is so obvious, but there are many cases of ISs that have failed because they did not address those fundamental points.

You will recall that there are two main ways in which an organization may be viewed: the functional view and the process view. The functional view considers an organization as a set of parallel and separate areas; typically these would include accounting, marketing, operations and so on. The process considers the firm as a set of ongoing activities, such as management, product development and so on. Both views are important in considering IS strategy. In developing and implementing such strategy it is important to remember that managers at different levels require different information, and they require it to be presented in different ways. Senior managers need highly aggregated information that helps inform strategic decisions. Day-to-day management of operations requires internally focused information that is useful for short-term decisions.

The *information systems strategy triangle* (Pearlson and Saunders, 2009) links business strategy, organizational strategy and information strategy. An overview of this is shown in Figure 13.9.

The triangle indicates that the three points should be in balance. If they are not, it may lead to problems in an organization. It is business strategy that drives the other two strategies, and both organizational strategy and information strategy should complement business strategy and each other. If one corner of the triangle changes, the other two corners must be reviewed.

Having previously discussed business strategy and organizational strategy, what is involved in IS strategy? Table 13.1 (extended from Pearlson and Saunders, 2009)

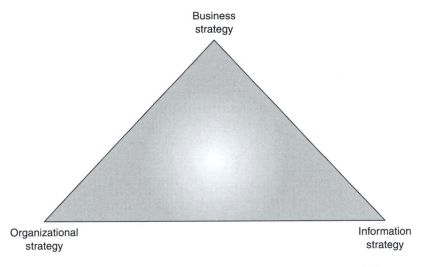

Figure 13.9 Information systems strategy triangle (source: adapted from Pearlson and Saunders, 2009).

Table 13.1   Some considerations for IS strategy

	Data	Hardware	Networks	Software
How	Physical or electronic entry and retrieval?	In-house or sub-contracted?	In-house or sub-contracted?	In-house or sub-contracted?
What	Items to be input, stored and retrieved	Physical components	Physical and wireless links	Applications, programs
When	Runs needed to meet deadlines?	Needed now or later?	Needed now or later?	Needed now or later?
Where	On-site or off-site, on personal machines or network?	In one location or in many?	For whole organization or groups?	Available to all or specialist software for a few?
Who	Need for access, security clearance, skills	Need for access, security clearance, skills	Need for access, security clearance, skills	Need for access, security clearance, skills
Why	What happens if it is not there? What happens if it is?	What happens if it is not there? What happens if it is?	What happens if it is not there? What happens if it is?	What happens if it is not there? What happens if it is?

Source: extended from Pearlson and Saunders (2009).

shows some things that may be considered. These are not exhaustive, and other factors such as cost, local skills, availability and so on, must be addressed in the planning and decision-making process. Table 13.1 helps a manager to have a high-level view of four major IS infrastructure components and to consider them in a structured manner.

13.5 Summary

This chapter gave an overview of strategy and distinguished between corporate strategy, business strategy, organizational strategy and IS strategy. A case study highlighted the strategic value of information. The setting of an organization within its sector and the wider macro-economic context was discussed

Three common approaches for analysis were discussed – PEST, SWOT, and the five competitive forces. Two major strategic models were outlined, Porter's generic strategies framework and D'Aveni's hypercompetition model.

The information systems strategy triangle showed the link between business strategy, organizational strategy and information systems strategy. The business diamond and managerial levers were discussed. Some areas that are covered by information systems strategy were highlighted.

Glossary

Business diamond   A system used for organizational strategy to help identify crucial components of an organization's plan.

Business strategy   Planning and decisions about how a firm competes.

Corporate strategy   The choice of businesses in which to engage.

D'Aveni's hypercompetition model   A model based on the concept that competitive advantage cannot be maintained. Speed and aggression are used to attain short-term advantage in four areas: cost/quality, timing/know-how, strongholds, deep pockets.

D'Aveni's seven Ss framework   A model that describes how firms may be able to disrupt competition through superior stakeholder satisfaction, strategic soothsaying, speed, surprise, shifting the rules of competition, signalling strategic intent and simultaneous and sequential strategic thrusts.

Information systems strategy   High-level, long-term decisions and planning about the best ways to use information.

Managerial levers   The best combination of control, cultural and organizational variables, linked with people, information and technology.

Organizational strategy   The design of the organization and the choices it makes to implement that design and carry out its operations.

PEST   Political, economic, social and technological factors that affect market growth or decline.

Porter's five forces   Buyer power, supplier power, threat of substitutes, threat of new entrants – these combine to produce competitive rivalry.

Porter's generic strategies framework   A model in which competitive advantage is achieved by cost, differentiation and focus.

Strategy   Long-term planning, high-level decisions and large-scale activities.

SWOT   Strengths and weaknesses (internal to the organization), opportunities and threats (external to the organization).

References

Bali, R., Wickramasinghe, N., and Lehaney, B. (2009) *Knowledge Management Primer*. New York: Routledge.

Cash, J., Eccles, R., Nohria, N., and Nolan, R. (1994) *Building the Information Age Organization*. Homewood, IL: Richard D. Irwin.

D'Aveni, R. (1994) *Hypercompetition: Managing the Dynamics of Strategic Manoevering*. New York: Free Press.

Hammer, M. and Champy, J. (1994) *Reengineering the Corporation*. New York: Harper Business.

Lehaney, B., Malindzak, D., and Khan, Z. (2009) Simulation Modelling for Problem Understanding: A Case Study in the East Slovakia Coal Industry, *Journal of the Operational Research Society*, 59(10), 1332–1339

Pearlson, K. and Saunders, C. (2009) *Managing and Using Information Systems: A Strategic Approach*. Chichester: Wiley.

Porter, M. (1980) *Competitive Strategy*. New York: Free Press.

Further Reading

Clarke, S. (2007) *Information Systems Strategic Management: An Integrated Approach*. London: Routledge.

Suggested activities

1   Given that the three traditional factors of production are land, labour and capital, how does the more recently recognized factor of production, knowledge, fit with the traditional view, with strategy, and the notions of short- and long-runs?

2   Think of factors that may be added under the main headings in Figure 13.4, then think about how the factors in the figure, including those you have added, may be sub-divided and what issues may arise from them. Find some real-world examples of things that have happened that would fit within a PEST analysis.

3   Think of one thing not listed in this chapter that may sensibly be considered by SWOT, and use the cells shown in Figure 13.5 to produce some discussion points and questions.

4   Discuss what barriers to entry might exist within the computer manufacturing industry.

14 Project management

Case study 14.1 Channel Tunnel

This case study has been included by the authors to facilitate class discussion rather than to illustrate effective or ineffective management practices. Only publicly available material has been used to write this case study, and it does not reflect any opinions of employees or management at the organizations mentioned.

The now familiar Channel Tunnel (or 'Chunnel') that was opened to passengers and freight traffic in 1994 is not a new idea. In 1802 Albert Mathieu put forward a cross-Channel tunnel proposal, followed by proposals in the 1830s by Aimé Thomé de Gamond and in 1865 by George Ward Hunt. In 1881 British railway entrepreneur Sir William Watkin and French Suez Canal contractor Alexandre Lavalley began a project for a channel railway tunnel. Work commenced on both sides. On the English side 1,893 metres were dug, on the French 1,669 metres were dug. In 1883 the work stopped after an injunction was served against Watkin.

After various failed attempts over the years, interest in a tunnel dropped, but re-emerged in 1985, and four proposals were submitted, following encouragement by both the French and UK governments. A rail proposal was based on a scheme previously suggested in 1975 by Channel Tunnel Group/France–Manche (CTG/F–M); Eurobridge was proposed as a 4 km span suspension bridge with roadway in an enclosed tube. Euroroute was to be a 21 km tunnel between artificial islands approached by bridges. Channel Expressway was to be large diameter road tunnels with mid-channel ventilation towers. The cross-channel ferry companies opposed all four proposals. It appeared that public opinion strongly favoured a drive-through tunnel, but ventilation issues and concerns about accidents led to the only short-listed rail submission, CTG/F–M, being awarded the project.

At several times during the work, the company that was funding the tunnelling work (Eurotunnel) ran out of money and had to return to the stockmarket and its banking financiers to seek new funds. There were reports of how the tunnel, dug simultaneously from the UK and French sides, did not meet in the middle. Ten people died during the tunnel construction and there was heated debate about high-speed trains running through residential areas of Kent.

At the outset of the project, the technology involved and the sheer scale of tunnel digging meant it would not be possible for it to be undertaken by one company. A consortium of ten companies (five French and five British) was formed and had to coordinate the digging of three tunnels (one each way and one service tunnel), as well as the 1,200 suppliers and 15,000 workers. Once this had been achieved, the tracks (over 130 miles in total) were laid, and the control system for the running of the trains was installed. When the two tunnels met (one dug from France and one from the United Kingdom) there was less than two-thirds of an inch of error. Huge pistons were installed to control the air pressure build-up caused by trains operating at 100 mph in an enclosed space. There are 300 miles of cold-water piping in the tunnel to dispel heat caused by air friction. On the UK side more than 90 acres of land reclamation occurred due to the chalk that had been dug out. The tunnel is 31 miles long, with an average depth of 150 feet below sea level.

From an engineering point of view, the scale of the project and the fact that it has been achieved at all may be argument for it to be considered as an immense success. There are other arguments, however. Tunnelling commenced in 1988, and the tunnel began operating in 1994, several years late. At 1985 prices, the total construction cost was £4.6 billion, which amounted to an 80 per cent overrun. At the peak of construction 15,000 people were employed, with daily expenditure over £3 million.

By the start of 1995, the service being provided was getting good press reports, and the passenger transport side of the business was running ahead of predictions. Many of the earlier operating problems appear to have been rectified. The Eurostar service is the passenger carrier, with each of the high-tech trains carrying the equivalent of two jumbo-jet loads of passengers at one time (over 800 people). It is owned by a consortium of British, Belgian and French railways.

Each train is over one-quarter of a mile long and fitted out to resemble the interior of an aircraft rather than a train. The chairs recline and individual reading lights are provided. The train can travel at 186 mph on specially adapted tracks in northern France and around 100 mph through Kent. The engines for the trains were developed by GEC-Alsthom, an Anglo-French company, and can run on the four different power systems the trains will come across – French, Belgian, British and the tunnel itself. Much of the rest of the train design comes from the highly successful French TGV (train à grande vitesse).

Le Shuttle is the part of the service for cars, caravans and coaches, which has box-like carriages that transport vehicles with their occupants remaining in the vicinity of their vehicles during the journey. Unlike ferries, this service is virtually weather-proof and only takes 35 minutes from platform to platform.

The safety systems (especially for fire) are where the greatest application of technology has occurred. The fire breaks, detection systems and procedures for dealing with an outbreak are far in excess of anything previously related to a train. The freight service for taking lorries and containers through the tunnel runs on different trains from the passenger and car services.

14.1 Intended learning outcomes

On completion of this chapter the reader should be able to:

1 describe the main phases in a project;
2 summarize the main features of each stage;
3 produce and interpret Gantt charts;
4 produce and interpret PERT diagrams;
5 explain why large projects are complex.

14.2 Introduction

Project management is an important concept in information system (IS) development, as well as in the implementation of most other business initiatives. Often, the development or implementation of information technology (IT) or the management of change will be run as a project, and will be accomplished using various well-established project management techniques and tools. IS development and implementation are often treated as a large-scale project and broken into several smaller projects for managing various different aspects (called project portfolios). These might range from business process change for making the organization ready for new technologies to implementing the technologies themselves.

Project management methodologies offer a systematic approach to all stages of a project by providing guidance on how to plan, monitor and measure every step in a project. Project management is defined by the Project Management Institute (PMI, 2008) as the application of knowledge, skills, tools and techniques to a broad range of activities in order to meet the objectives of a project. A project is temporary and its timeframe may vary from a few days to several years, depending on the scope of the project.

Traditional project management methodologies offer structured, low-risk and rigid approaches to project management, but may not be the most appropriate in the implementation of new technologies such as e-commerce, which are often implemented in external, customer-facing environments. In such circumstances, e-commerce managers often seem to be willing to take greater risks and to adopt flexible and unorthodox approaches. This is mainly because e-commerce projects are close to the core activity of the organization (promoting and selling their services), so they are likely to use an approach that leaves a greater number of options open and allows for quick adjustments to enable a quick response to fast-changing technologies, the market place and customer preferences.

14.3 Planning

There are some techniques for helping to manage complex and large projects, and these will be discussed further on. Before that, let us look at some of the basics about planning goals. Goals may be about personal targets or trying to achieve organizational objectives. Some people say things such as 'My goal is to get a private pilot's licence.' If that person has no plan as to how to achieve that, then it is not a goal in the sense that is meant here. It is a desire or a dream, but nothing more. To plan to achieve goals you need to take into account what is desirable and what is feasible. You also need to consider necessary and sufficient conditions. Another consideration is realism about what is in your control and what is not.

Here is a simple example. On a particular day I would like to attend a football match and watch Tottenham Hotspur beat Manchester United. The outcome of the match is not within my control, so that cannot be a goal (please excuse the pun). I have a desire to attend the match but I have to pay for transport and tickets and I have to be free from other commitments that would take priority. If all those things are satisfactory, attending the match is both desirable and feasible. It is necessary that I have enough money to pay for a ticket, but it is not sufficient, as all the tickets may have been sold. This is a very simple example, but imagine building something like the Channel Tunnel, with all the planning involved. The concepts just discussed are equally valid in this situation, so being able to apply goal-setting at a simple level is vital to being able to manage more complex situations.

Good plans tend to have certain common factors. These are: a clearly defined aim; linked phases; explicit statements of things such as resources, actions and knowledge;

and relevant and achievable scales and timings. A simple way of considering these things is by use of a table in which you list each goal; the measures of success you will use; the timescale for each goal; the resources needed; and outside factors that may impinge on achieving your aim. If we move from personal goal planning to managing a larger project, the preceding principles can be developed a little further.

Developing ISs is often a large-scale business initiative requiring large-scale financial investment as well as the availability of a pool of human resources with a range of specialist skills such as technological, marketing, change management and project management. IS projects often proceed through three generic phases: pre-development, development and post-development. In the pre-development stage, the idea of implementing a new IS may attract top management, and the benefits or pressures of doing so may become irresistible.

The development phase includes actual development, the implementation or updating of related systems, and making necessary changes in the organizational structure and culture. This phase must address many managerial and technical issues, as discussed elsewhere in this book. The last phase, post-development, includes a number of activities such as system maintenance, continuous updating and implementing any necessary changes. For this phase, management needs to understand a range of new marketing, product development and innovative delivery methods to ensure the success of the project.

In the case of large-scale systems, development, implementation and management activities (such as those shown in Figure 14.1) may become independent projects themselves so that an organization requires programme management rather than just project management. For example, the IS adoption process has to be carefully planned and executed and is often seen as a project in its own right. From an IT project point of view, time and budget constraints could prove to be serious problems, as would be the handling of any organizational transformation processes. To deal with these issues, support from top management is seen as a key ingredient in the success of a project. It often needs a champion amongst top management (generally on the board of directors). Lack of senior management support can lead to failures because, without it, obtaining the required resources to bring about the necessary changes in an organization can prove impossible.

In the late 1990s there was an acute shortage of people with IT-related skills, and this still persists in some areas, partly owing to continuous changes in technologies. The situation is worst in developing countries, owing to the lack or poor provision of education, training and exposure to these technologies. Dealing with these issues is an integral part of any project management process.

14.4 Managing projects

Figure 14.2 shows an overview of the generic project management process.

The *terms of reference* provide a clear and precise description of the project aims, the success criteria, the budget, the scope, the resources, the milestones and the timescale. Although a later phase mentions communication explicitly, that is not to say that communication is not important throughout. It *is* important, and especially so when developing terms of reference. Typically, the first attempt is a draft that will be discussed and reworked many times before agreement is reached. At this stage it is very important to distinguish between the things that are under the direct control of the project manager and those that are not.

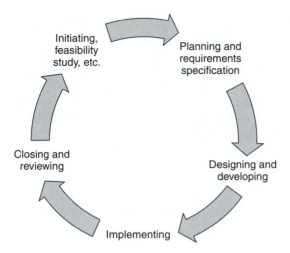

Figure 14.1 An IS development lifecycle.

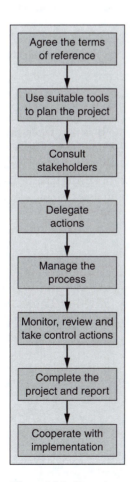

Figure 14.2 Generic project management.

In planning the project it is common to work in reverse order, starting with the intended outcome and going to each preceding stage to assess what needs to be achieved and what resources are required. As an example, in house construction it is usual to order the furniture well before the house is built. In this case, 'furniture' does not mean beds and sofas. It is a construction term used to mean things such as door fittings (handles, locks, etc.). If the furniture is ordered only once the house is built, it may not arrive till a month later, meaning the project will not complete on time. The project team should be involved in developing plans.

For IS projects (which includes most e-commerce projects) Avison and Torkzadeh (2009) recommend the following steps:

1   aligning the IS projects with organizational goals – this may seem obvious but too many IS projects are technology-driven rather than being based on a sound business case;
2   defining project scope;
3   selecting an appropriate project management methodology such as PRINCE2 to help complete the tasks that follow;
4   developing a detailed project plan – estimating project costs and benefits and assessing risks;
5   building a multi-disciplinary project team to ensure quality;
6   if developing the system in-house, using an established IS development methodology and lifecycle (such as that shown in Figure 14.1);
7   measuring project success;
8   project closure.

These steps are not necessarily linear and can be used or re-iterated as and when necessary. In this chapter we describe traditional project management methods, but with a flexible approach used in IS-related projects. Each IS project will have unique features in terms of size, market environment and technological or organizational change needs. Having said this, they will also have a number of common aspects, and the following is a guide to the typical phases an IS project will go through.

14.4.1 Feasibility study

Higher management may be convinced that a new IS will bring many benefits to the organization, but may not be clear about return on investment, the ability of the organization to undertake its introduction or the availability of required resources. Consequently, they conduct a feasibility study to address these issues.

14.4.2 Decision to go ahead

This decision is often taken by higher management and is followed by the drawing up of initial top-level plans.

14.4.3 User requirements definition

The customer service department and IS department may collaborate in the creation of customer surveys and interviews which will be used to determine project requirements. This is discussed in some detail in Chapter 3.

14.4.4 Risk analysis

An analysis of potential risks to the project will be carried out in collaboration with all the stakeholders. The aim is to identify events that could jeopardize the project, to estimate the damage they could cause and to adopt strategies to minimize them.

14.4.5 Project planning

Detailed project plans are created for the development of systems and subsystems, and for testing, deployment and handover. Dealing with organizational change management issues will also be planned at this stage.

14.4.6 Pilot project

Pilot systems may be developed and evaluated within a small part of the organization. Overall project plans and systems requirements may then be refined as a consequence.

14.4.7 System development

Systems will be developed in-house or by an outsourcing vendor under the guidance of the organization. The organization and the outsourcing vendor often conduct the acceptance and/or functionality testing jointly.

14.4.8 Training

Training in the use of the new IS will probably be conducted in parallel with system development, but should be completed before services go live.

14.4.9 Evaluation

Regular evaluations are required, especially when services begin to go live, to address any problems, assess benefits and learn from experience so that the next iteration brings better results.

14.5 Some project planning techniques

14.5.1 Overview

Approaches such as brainstorming and Ishikawa diagrams (fishbone diagrams or cause-and-effect diagrams) can be very useful at the planning stage. It is essential to consider which activities can be run in parallel and which are sequential. Most large projects would warrant a feasibility study. *Gantt charts*, *critical path analysis* (CPA) and *project evaluation and review technique* (PERT) may help with detailed project planning, scheduling, costing and reporting.

14.5.2 Gantt charts

A Gantt chart illustrates a project schedule in the form of bars. The chart shows start and finish dates and the main components of a project. Gantt charts can also show dependency of one activity upon another. Although a spreadsheet may be used to create a Gantt chart, if the project is complex and CPA or PERT are going to be used, then it is probably more convenient to use dedicated project planning software. Regardless of the application used, Gantt charts have some common factors. Each activity has a separate line that shows its duration. For large projects this is likely to be weeks or months. Colour coding or shading may be used to indicate different activity types. Gantt charts are fairly simple to construct and use, but are very useful. They have certain limitations, such as not easily showing the importance of related parallel activities, nor their inter-dependence.

Figure 14.3 shows a Gantt chart a student prepared to help plan the project component of a programme of study. This is a task that you are likely to be asked to do for your own study. As you can see, even for a simple project, it becomes difficult to see the activities. Figures 14.4–14.6 show the task list, chart and key separately so they can be read more easily. Remember that this is a simple project. A slightly more complicated Gantt chart is shown in Figure 14.7. This was for a project funding bid. The tasks on the left are *work packages*. Now imagine producing a Gantt chart for the Channel Tunnel project!

14.5.3 *CPA and PERT*

A Gantt chart is one way of depicting a work breakdown structure, but it has limitations and does not show critical paths, for example. The critical path is the longest complete path of a project. If any activity on this path were delayed, the whole project would be delayed. A critical task is one that is on the critical path. A non-critical task has slack time available. While CPA shows activities that have no slack and those that do, a Gantt chart does not show these things. CPA diagrams, however, have no illustrative scale for duration, and that means the observer cannot immediately and intuitively grasp how long activities take. Table 14.1 shows the activities in a small IT project and Figure 14.8 shows a CPA diagram based on Table 14.1.

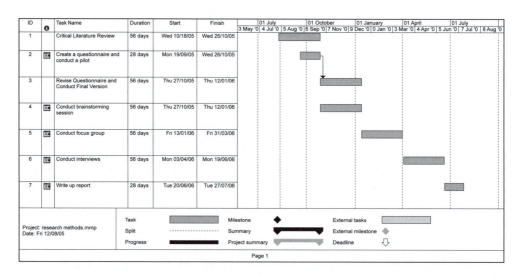

Figure 14.3 A Gantt chart for a student's dissertation.

ID	ⓘ	Task Name	Duration	Start	Finish
1		Critical Literature Review	56 days	Wed 10/18/05	Wed 26/10/05
2	▦	Create a questionnaire and conduct a pilot	28 days	Mon 19/09/05	Wed 26/10/05
3		Revise Questionnaire and Conduct Final Version	56 days	Thu 27/10/05	Thu 12/01/06
4	▦	Conduct brainstorming session	56 days	Thu 27/10/05	Thu 12/01/06
5	▦	Conduct focus group	56 days	Fri 13/01/06	Fri 31/03/06
6	▦	Conduct interviews	56 days	Mon 03/04/06	Mon 19/06/06
7	▦	Write up report	28 days	Tue 20/06/06	Tue 27/07/06

Figure 14.4 The task list for Figure 14.3.

Table 14.1 Activities in a small IT project

Task	Duration in days	Parallel or sequential	Dependent on
A Needs analysis	7	Sequential	
B Change management programme	25		A
C Choose hardware	1	Sequential	A
D Purchase and install hardware	14	Parallel	C
E Analysis of core modules	14	Sequential	A
F Analysis of supporting modules	14	Sequential	A
G Program core modules	14	Sequential	E
H Program supporting modules	21	Sequential	F
I Quality assurance of core modules	7	Sequential	G
J Quality assurance of supporting modules	7	Sequential	H
K Initial training on modules	1	Parallel	B, I, J
L Creation and QA of management information system	7	Sequential	K

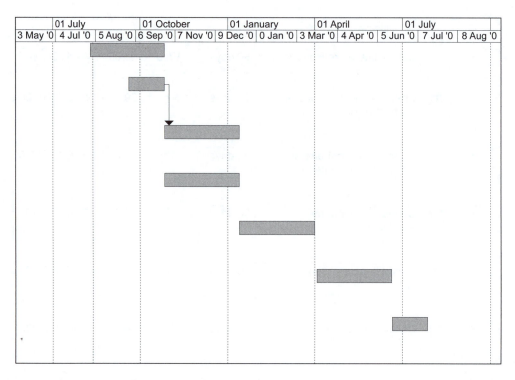

Figure 14.5 The chart from Figure 14.3.

Figure 14.6 The key from Figure 14.3.

For ease of explanation, this example has no days off for weekends. Each box shows the activity title, planned start date, planned end date, slack and the dates that could be used given that slack. The bold route is the critical path. It is the longest path through the network, and if any activity is delayed on this path it would delay the whole project. For example, *purchase and install hardware* has a duration of 14 days and slack of zero. If this activity were delayed by one day, the start of the following activities would be delayed by one day, and this would result in the project not being completed on time. Thus, the planned start and finish dates for *purchase and install hardware* are fixed at 12 September 2010 and 25 September 2010. *Change management programme* takes 25 days. It could start directly after *needs analysis*, in which case it would begin on 11 September 2010 and finish on 5 October 2010. It is required before *initial training on modules* can begin, but the *initial training* cannot start until 24 October 2010, as it is dependent on other modules finishing. That means *change management programme* has slack of 18 days.

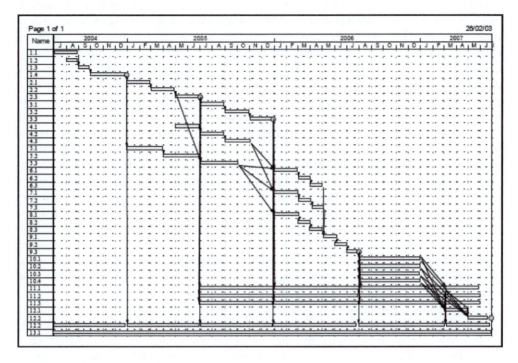

Figure 14.7 A more complicated Gantt chart.

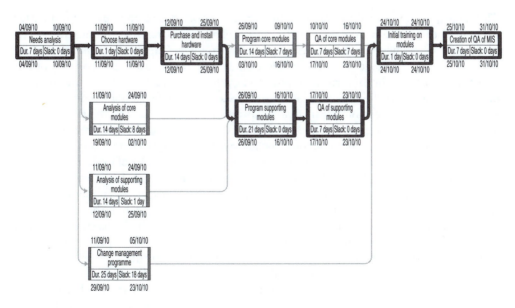

Figure 14.8 A CPA diagram based on Table 14.1.

There are many ways of drawing CPA diagrams, but nowadays the activity on node method (precedence diagram) is used almost exclusively. Within this, there are various approaches that can be taken, and this example is just one. If you understand the example you will be able to understand other CPA approaches. *Programme evaluation and review technique* (PERT) is very similar to CPA. One of the main differences is that it adds a cautionary element in regard to activity durations. To do this it sums the shortest predicted duration, four times the most likely predicted duration, and the longest predicted duration. It then divides this total by six to give a weighted average.

The critical path method makes dependencies visible between the project activities by using project network diagrams or precedence diagrams. It helps in organizing large and complex projects, enabling a systematic and transparent approach to project planning and scheduling, project execution and risk management. It also enables the calculation of the slack (or float) of each activity. CPA may help encourage the project manager to reduce the project duration by optimizing the critical path and making the most efficient use of resources. It increases visibility of impact of schedule revisions, which are usually necessary when major milestones have been missed or when the risk of missing a major milestone looms large. It provides opportunities to respond to the negative risk of going over schedule by identifying the activities that are most critical.

For large and complex projects, there will be thousands of activities and dependency relationships. This requires specialist software and specialist users to operate it. A large project would have to be split into portions for printing, and this detracts from some of the value of being able to see the critical path on one diagram. If the plan changes during project execution then the precedence diagram will have to be redrawn.

14. 6 Setting success criteria

The success of an undertaking can be a matter of perception, so formal project evaluation is essential to identify and assess the key aspects of a project that make it either a success or failure. Assessment of a systems project's outcome is important to most of those involved in development projects – whether as a developer, customer, manager or any other stakeholder – for different and, possibly, conflicting reasons. For example, a developer may regard good functionality of a system as a success, whereas for a senior manager, the impact of a project on organizational productivity may be the main measure of success. In practice, systems development projects are often deemed failures upon completion because few are completed on time and within budget. There is a clear need for some comprehensive success indicators to be agreed before the start of projects.

Shenhar *et al.* (2001) propose a multi-dimensional framework for assessing project success. In this approach, projects are classified according to the technological uncertainty at the project initiation stage and their system scope, which is their location on a hierarchical ladder of systems and subsystems. The approach is presented in Table 14.2. It has 13 success measures, arranged into four dimensions: project efficiency, impacts on customer, business success and preparing for the future.

The first dimension is concerned only with efficiency of the project management effort. This is a short-term dimension expressing the efficiency with which the project has been managed. It simply tells how a project met its resource constraints, and whether it was finished on time and within the specified budget. The second dimension relates to the customer, addressing the importance placed on customer requirements

Table 14.2 Project success framework

Success dimension	Success measures
Project efficiency	Met project schedule
	Stayed on budget
Impacts on customer	Met functional performance
	Met technical specifications
	Addressed most customer needs
	Solved a customer's problem
	The product is used by customers effectively
	Customer satisfaction
Business success	Commercial success in terms of profit or growth
	Creating a large market share
Preparing for the future (long-term benefits)	Creating a new market or segment
	Creating a new product line
	Developing a new technology (or new type of system)

Source: adapted from Shenhar *et al.* (2001).

and on meeting their needs. The third dimension addresses the immediate and direct impact the project may have on the organization. In the business context, did it provide sales, income and profits as expected? Did it help increase business results and gain market share? The last dimension is aimed at measuring long-term benefits from a project; it addresses the issue of preparing the organizational and technological infrastructure for the future.

14.7 Project management methodologies

14.7.1 *Overview*

A typical project will involve hundred of activities that would roughly fall into the following categories:

- cost estimating and preparing budgets;
- planning for effective communication and deciding on which communication tools will be used. Some project management tools such as PRINCE2 offer group working facilities to enable effective team working;
- setting goals for individuals and project teams;
- implementing change and process improvement;
- quality assurance and controls;
- risk assessment and management;
- scheduling and time management.

Without a proper project management methodology, different stakeholders such as top management, project managers, users, workers, etc., will have different ideas about how things should be organized and when the different parts of the project should be completed. All of the stakeholders need to know how much responsibility, authority and accountability they have and, because of the complexity of IS projects, there may often be confusion surrounding these issues. Project management methodologies help developers to plan and keep track of these activities. A good project management method can guide the project through a controlled, well-managed, visible set of activities to achieve the desired results. There are many project management methodologies and tools, but the most commonly used are PRINCE2 and Microsoft Project.

14.7.2 PRINCE2

PRINCE2, or PRojects IN Controlled Environments, is a comprehensive methodology for project management. It was developed and is owned by the Office of Government and Commerce (OGC) in the United Kingdom. PRINCE2 has a dedicated accreditation body (APM Group Ltd) with over 15 accelerated consulting organizations.

PRINCE2 describes eight components which need to be present for a successful project:

1   Business case: describing the business reasons and objectives for the project.
2   Organization: helping in planning the roles and responsibilities of the stakeholders.
3   Plans: defining the project's products, how the work should be carried out, when and by whom.
4   Controls: how the project managers exercise control.
5   Management of risk: identifying and managing risk.
6   Quality in a project environment: managing quality issues and procedures.
7   Configuration management: how the project's products are developed and configured.
8   Change control: how to manage changes to the specification or scope of the project or product.

PRINCE2 can provide projects with:

- a controlled and organized start, middle and end;
- regular reviews of progress against plans and against the business objectives;
- flexible decision points;
- automatic management control of any deviations from the plan;
- the involvement of management and stakeholders at the right time during the project;
- good communication channels between the project management team and the rest of the organization;
- agreement on the required quality at the outset and continuous monitoring against those requirements.

PRINCE2 is a process-driven methodology rather than one that is rigidly staged, so it offers the systematic flexibility required for IS projects. It contains a complete set of concepts and project management processes that are necessary for a properly run and managed project. However, the way in which PRINCE2 is applied to each project will vary considerably, and tailoring the method to suit the circumstances of a particular project is critical to its successful use.

14.7.3 *Microsoft Project*

Microsoft Project is another common project management methodology, as well as a software tool. It is a useful and popular project management tool used for business project planning, scheduling tasks, managing resources, monitoring costs and generating reports. Its main features include:

- help for defining the content and building the project plan;
- a calendar to reflect the work schedule;
- task allocation;
- the ability to add sub-tasks, link related tasks and set task dependencies;
- milestones for the identification of significant events;
- calculation and representation of lag and lead times and constraining dates;
- a resource list and created resource calendars;
- critical path analysis;
- comprehensive reporting tools to keep track of the progress.

The latest version of Project, called MS Project Professional 2010 (see www.microsoft.com) is easy to use and very comprehensive in terms of its coverage of different aspects of project management. The user interface is similar to that of the widely used MS Office suite, and everyday project management tasks such as resources control and communication between different stakeholders are easy to accomplish.

Details of other similar tools can be obtained from www.pmi.org. Additionally, we recommend a systems approach to project management (see Clarke (2007) for an example of its implementation), which can be used in conjunction with the above described tools and techniques.

14.8 Other issues

14.8.1 *Risk*

There are many risks associated with IS projects. Risks need to be identified during the planning stage, and a risk log should be created as early as possible. To create a risk log, each risk identified should be allocated a number, the type of risk and a summary of status and analysis. There should be an owner for every risk.

The risk log is used to identify all risks, to assess the probability that they will be encountered and their potential impact on the project. The document is revised at every stage to identify any new risks, and to determine whether any changes will affect the continuing viability of the project. At the end of the project, any remaining risks to the operational system must be assessed.

Risk analysis activities can be categorized as:

- prevention (don't do it);
- reduction (what can be done to reduce it? At what cost?);
- transference (can someone else do it better?);
- contingency (what do we need? Should this happen?);
- acceptance (can we live with it or is it very unlikely to happen, or too expensive to counter?).

Risk management includes planning for risks (and identifying countermeasures), and identifying any resources needed to counter the risks. Risks should always be monitored for early indications and assessed for the impact of any changes. All risks should be controlled to make the plan succeed.

14.8.2 Human factors

An IS project can have significant economic, organizational and social impacts on the organization. Well-defined goals combined with a communication strategy can reduce any resentment among the organization's staff. Such resentment could create a negative atmosphere, with considerable consequences on the progress of the project. Other social issues and ways to deal with them, discussed in Chapters 5 and 15 , are also relevant here.

In multinational companies, cultural differences often exacerbate communication problems. For example, a message from someone where communication tends to be more direct might seem rude to someone from a different background. Misalignment of expectations can be the source of major problems in large-scale projects, but can be minimized by effective communication, which can build trust; this greater trust can often lead to improved formal and informal communication levels. Hence, meaningful communication is a necessary antecedent of trust. There are two types of communication: formal and informal. Formal communication is often about hard data such that relating to legal, technical or commercial areas. Informal communication is more personal and requires a greater degree of trust and understanding between different stakeholders in a project.

IS projects often have a significant impact on the organization, and require people throughout the organization to learn new behaviours and skills. Negative effects of change are often inevitable when people are forced to adjust to change at a fast pace. Organizations need to proactively recognize the effects of change and develop skills among their staff to enable the change. Without this proactive approach, the risk of resistance to change increases significantly and reduces the chances of achieving the expected benefits.

Change management is a well-developed concept and a number of methods exist for managing technology-related changes. Detailed discussion of these change management methods is outside the scope of this book. Most common themes include:

- create a vision to inspire people;
- create a plan to manage change;
- communicate the changes to all affected parties;
- cultivate motivated and empowered affected parties using training as well as incentives to embrace change;
- cement the change in the organization's culture gradually.

Managing social issues must be taken seriously as mismanagement of these is often cited as a key reason for the failure of projects.

14.9 Common reasons for failure of IT and IS projects

It has been argued that few information systems can be considered a success. The reasons for claiming success, it is said, are largely based on erroneous methods of its measurement. These methods, it is claimed, are usually focused on the extent to which a system meets the requirements specification agreed at the start of a project. The main measures of success are often negative in nature, based on the so-called 'correspondence failure' principle, whereby the system objectives are stated in advance, and success or failure is defined in terms of whether these objectives have or have not been achieved. Lyytinen and Hirschheim (1987) suggest the notion of expectation failure, or the failure of the system to meet the expectations of stakeholders and propose four dimensions of failure (presented in Table 14.3).

Having mentioned the types of failure, it is also important to briefly cover some of the most common causes of IS projects failure. These are summarized in Table 14.4.

Table 14.3 Types of information systems failure

Failure type	Explanation
Correspondence	The failure of the final system to correspond with the requirements and objectives determined in advance
Process	Failure in the development process, usually in the form of a cost/time overrun or inability to complete the development
Interaction	Users fail to use the system sufficiently or effectively
Expectation	Failure of the completed system to meet the expectations of participants

Source: adapted from Lyytinen and Hirschheim (1987).

Table 14.4 Some of the most common causes of IS project failure

Failure factors	Examples
Human issues	• Employee turnover – people leaving the project. It is often difficult to find suitable replacements • Conflicts – between individuals, teams, departments or outsourcing partners • Motivation – lack of motivation during development or at the usage stage
Technical issues	• Hardware and software issues such as difficulties in integration, scalability or robustness • Data integration issues due to differences in formats or transfer limitations
Political issues	• Too much competition between different stakeholders • Too much or too little control or authority • Conflicts in terms of expected benefits and/or project objectives
Financial issues	• Errors in estimates • Poor budget control • Cost overruns
Lack of leadership	• Lack of vision and ability to inspire • Poor people, technology or processes management

Source: adapted from Avison and Torkzadeh (2009).

14.10 Summary

The management of organizations, and in particular of strategic change within those organizations, is often achieved via projects or project portfolios (i.e. programmes).

A very high number of technological projects fail because of poor project management. To gain competitive advantage and create value through the adoption of change management strategies, companies can implement business processes that allow efficient and effective enterprise project management.

It is important to understand that success in projects is largely a subjective concept. Any success evaluation should take into account both the hard (tangible and measurable) and soft (subjective and difficult to quantify) dimensions of success. Success is perceived differently by different stakeholders, and success criteria must be prioritized to address any possible conflicts. Success is also affected by time, with some measures being short-term and others long-term. Finally, success may be partial, as some criteria may be successfully met while others may not.

Project managers must agree the criteria for success with the stakeholders as early as possible. The rate of success may also be improved if all parties involved keep expectations at a realistic level. Quality review processes with user involvement throughout should ensure that all acceptance criteria are achieved and measured.

To be successful, any complex project needs to work across departments at both the planning and operational levels. Staff from different departments need to be brought together to work together towards common objectives. Stakeholders' participation in decision-making from the earliest stages of a project is needed to ensure that there is a common will to collaborate, rather than resistance.

Glossary

E-commerce   Conducting business using the Internet.
MS Project   A project management methodology and a software tool to help manage the project.
Outsourcing   The practice of contracting with another entity to perform services that might otherwise be conducted in-house.
PRINCE2   PRojects IN Controlled Environments; a comprehensive methodology for project management.
Project   A task with specific objectives and pre-fixed timeline and resources.

References

Avison, D. and Torkzadeh, G. (2009) *Information Systems Project Management*. Los Angeles, CA: Sage Publications.

Clarke, S.A. (2007) *Information Systems Strategic Management: An Integrated Approach*, 2nd edition. London: Routledge.

Lyytinen, K. and Hirschheim, R.A. (1987) Information Systems Failure: A Survey and Classification of the Empirical Literature, in Zorkoczy, P.I. (ed.) *Oxford Surveys in Information Technology*, 4th edition. Oxford: Oxford University Press, pp. 257–309.

PMI (2008). *What is Project Management?*. Available online at www.pmi.org/Pages/default.aspx (accessed 8 March 2008).

Shenhar, A.J., Dvir, D., Levy, O., and Maltz, A. (2001). Project Success: A Multidimensional Strategic Concept, *Long Range Planning*, 34, 699–725.

Further reading

Shah, M.H. and Clarke, S. (2009) *E-Banking Management: Issues, Solutions and Strategies*. Hershey, PA: IGI Global.
Stahl, B.C. (2008) *Information Systems: Critical Perspectives*. Abingdon: Routledge.
Xu, L.D. (2007) *Frontiers in Enterprise Integration*. London and New York: Routledge.

Suggested activities

1   Consider a project with which you are familiar, and identify the key success factors.
2   There are many risks involved in managing an IS project. Discuss five common risks, explaining what steps can be taken to reduce the likelihood that they will derail a project.
3   Why is it important to define success criteria at the beginning of a project?
4   What are the key attributes of a good project manager in an IS context?

15 Digital society

It was reported in the *London Times* (Ford, 2010) that the number of victims of card fraud in England and Wales had increased by 40 per cent between 2008 and 2009, to more than 2.4 million people. People were three times more likely to fall victim to plastic card fraud than to have their homes burgled.

There is a wide range of credit and debit card crimes that can be perpetrated. First, there is the physical theft of the cards. This is less common now that 'chip and PIN' protection is widely used, which means that possession of a card may be not enough for a criminal to be able to make use of it – it is also necessary to know the PIN number, which may be obtained by 'eyeballing' (watching over someone's shoulder as they use an ATM, or by simple deduction if an obvious number (such as the holder's birth year) is used. Cards may be cloned if out of the user's possession for even a short time (as in a restaurant), and the details obtained may be bought and sold, especially over the Internet. Sometimes criminals will apply for cards in the name of an existing individual, and will then use them for a short time as though they were that individual. This is known as identity theft.

In March 2010 Albert Gonzalez, from Miami, received the longest US prison sentence given for a crime of this type. He was jailed for 20 years for leading a group of hackers that stole tens of millions of credit and debit card numbers from TJX and other retailers. Gonzalez pleaded guilty to multiple charges of conspiracy, computer fraud, access device fraud and identity theft for hacking into TJX, which owns T.J. Maxx, BJ's Wholesale Club, OfficeMax, Boston Market, Barnes & Noble and Sports Authority. He was also charged with hacking into the payment card networks of Heartland, 7-Eleven and Hannaford Bros. supermarket chain to steal more than 130 million credit and debit card numbers.

The severity of the sentence was not only proportional to the profit that can be made by this sort of crime, but is also an indication of the threat to society that it poses. It has been suggested that unless the forces of law and order, financial institutions and retailers get to grips with credit and debit card fraud, within five years the system will become completely unusable.

15.1 Intended learning outcomes

On completion of this chapter the reader should be able to:

1   explain what is meant by the term 'digital society';
2   analyse the effects of computers on society;
3   evaluate the limitations, potential hazards and unwanted side-effects of innovations in the field;
4   critically appraise the benefits to society, and the potential for profit.

15.2 Introduction

A friend asked me whether the 'digital society' was a club for computers. No – it's not a club for computers, but it is, of course, related to computers – and all the other forms of digital technology that are entering our lives at an increasing rate – mobile phones, camcorders, printers, networks, PDAs, digital TV and radio, portable music players, cameras and so on. All of these devices process information electronically, and most of them are connected with communication in some way too, although the purposes for which they are employed may be quite different from each other. That's the 'digital' bit taken care of. 'Society' is harder to define. Dictionary definitions differ considerably, but they all tend to include phrases of the type 'structured system of human organization', 'group of people sharing ideas and values' and 'humankind generally'.

So we can say that society is about groups of people rather than individuals. Essentially, it's about 'us' – the ways in which we interact and the rules and customs (whether or not they are explicitly stated) that govern or influence the ways in which we interact. Whatever you regard society to be, it is clear that the impact of digital technology on society is growing rapidly, and can be expected to continue to do so. We will see plenty of evidence to support this claim later in this chapter.

But does the digital society matter? And should it be of particular concern to students of business information systems (BIS) and business information technology (BIT)? Students of any discipline are understandably interested first and foremost in the value of their studies to their forthcoming career. Why, then, should they study these 'soft' issues? Will they really be of use in their work? Well, the answer to the last question is: 'most probably'. None of us today can be oblivious to the effects on society of what we do for a living – even if only because the rest of society (and probably the market) won't let us. So we can't dispose of our old computing equipment in a way that will damage the environment, because there is a risk that our actions will be uncovered and made public. Then we may be prosecuted, and financial (and perhaps more serious) penalties may be imposed, and the reputation of our business will suffer. Equally, we must make sure that data relating to our customers is maintained securely, or we may face similar consequences. Most of us will also possess more altruistic motives for behaving ethically – we are interested in the common good, and we prefer to make a positive contribution to society, rather than being a millstone around the necks of our fellow citizens. And, of course, we want to be sure that other members of society behave in a responsible manner too.

Furthermore, unless we are university lecturers, we do not spend all of our time working, and ISs and IT impinge on many areas of our lives other than our jobs. Our health, education, personal safety, individual freedom and culture – and that of those around us – are all greatly affected by digital technology. If we not only understand the technology, but also appreciate the social issues arising from its use, then we are better able to take control of our lives and our destinies.

15.3 Let's be negative

It could be argued that the motor vehicle and the computer are by far the two inventions that have had the greatest impact on modern civilization. (It could of course also be denied – but let us not enter into that debate at this point.) Let us instead agree that the impact of both has been tremendous, and that they are analogous in many ways. They have both significantly changed our way of life, and while most would agree that this has been generally for the better, this is by no means exclusively so.

Motor cars were invented towards the end of the nineteenth century, and seat belts a few decades later. Nevertheless, it was not until the 1980s that most countries made the wearing of seat belts compulsory. Clearly, it would have been wise to investigate the potential dangers of motoring at an early stage, and to devise ways in which they could be minimized, rather than concentrating on the development of faster and faster machines. Indeed, in retrospect, it now appears to have been stupid in the extreme to pursue greater speed without paying proper consideration to safety issues. The wearing of seat belts, if introduced earlier, could have saved many thousands of lives. But is it being alarmist to compare this example with the use of IT? Well, perhaps not, as we will see later.

In this chapter we will often be taking a fairly circumspect view of new developments in computing and IT, and their effects on society. This is not because we are Luddites – not because we oppose change and think that anything new must be harmful or dangerous. This is not an attitude that IS scientists or technologists could possibly support. But stepping back from our day-to-day activities and thinking about what we are doing, and considering whether there may be any unwanted consequences of our actions, can have many benefits.

First, identifying potential problems at an early stage in IT and ISs – whether they be those that might lead to real physical or financial harmful effects, whether they be dangers or shortcomings, or merely inconveniences or annoyances, can help us to forestall them and perhaps to prevent potential disasters. (This can be seen in the case of seat belts in cars, and in the well-publicized examples of thalidomide and asbestos.) This way of thinking may not come naturally to younger people, especially those working in IT-related fields. Such people tend to have a positive attitude towards their speciality. They are optimistic and enthusiastic about their profession, and one would not want it any other way. Moreover, businesses are keen to take advantage of new developments. They naturally want to make use of them to increase their competitive advantage over their rivals. They will tell you that you don't make a profit by adopting a 'stick in the mud' attitude. However, an idea that goes wrong because of overenthusiasm or premature product release, leading perhaps to a product recall or the issue of software 'patches', can soon destroy a company's reputation for high-quality products and services.

In short, recognizing potential problems, especially in the area of digital technology and its effect on society – and then taking actions to deal with them before they become unmanageable – is not being negative at all. It is evidence of a highly positive and constructive attitude, which will increase the chance of a successful outcome to any venture or enterprise, without adversely affecting the society within which it must exist.

15.4 Computer crime

Are you out of work? Are your job prospects dismal? Do you want a high income for doing very little? Then why not consider computer crime? There has never been a better time to take up this exciting opportunity. Just look at the advantages:

- Low entry costs – gone are the times when you needed a getaway car, gun, crowbar and swag bag. All you need are a PC, a broadband connection and no conscience.
- High rewards are possible – there are millions of suckers out there waiting to give you their money. With a decent scam just a few pennies from each of them will make you a fortune.
- No national boundaries – not only do you have access to victims all over the world, but once you've got their money it's very difficult for them to track you down. Even if they manage to find out who you are they are not going to bother to prosecute you from overseas. If you just take a little from each one it's not worth their time, effort and cost.
- Easy money – there's no manual labour involved.
- No physical risk – there's no need to worry about falling off the ladder as you break into an upstairs window, no need for dangerous explosives to crack the safe, and no night watchman, policeman or angry victim will be around to apprehend you.
- Home working – you can work in the comfort of your own home, at a time that suits you.
- No tax to pay – declaring your earnings to the tax man is not recommended.

It has to be admitted, there are certain drawbacks to a career in computer crime, such as the lack of a pension scheme and sickness benefits. And, of course, society takes its revenge on the unsuccessful criminal by imposing penalties that can be quite severe!

Computer crimes can be regarded as falling into two groups. Some were already taking place, but can now be automated or committed more easily using digital technology. Others are possible only because of its availability or widespread use. Some crimes fall into both groups.

Many criminal activities have become much easier now that the technology exists to support them. It was always possible to copy printed material belonging to someone else and to distribute it, but it has never been as easy as it is now. Similarly, audio and video recordings can be duplicated almost at the touch of a button. The copying of such material for one's own use has now become so widespread that many people believe the practice is legal, or that it is a very minor offence that is never punished, and therefore acceptable. However, without the protection of copyright, authors, publishers and performers may cease to be creative, and society will be poorer for it. In practice, many have had to change their business models (for example, by selling music online), or have been forced to accept a reduced income from their work.

Similarly, content that is original, but that is still illegal, can be published easily using digital technology. This includes material that is libellous or pornographic, or that incites citizens to break the law. A wide range of media, including websites, emails, SMS messaging and peer-to-peer communications, may be used for such purposes. Many have the advantage that material can be posted anonymously or using a false identity.

Blackmail, threats, various scams or con tricks, demands for money, online fraud – none of these are new, but computers enable them to be undertaken from home, anonymously and in bulk.

The second group of criminal activities is concerned with the misuse of ISs, and clearly could not take place before the advent of such systems. So, rather than the utilization of computers to commit crimes, this refers to a new category of offence in which the computers themselves become targets. In order to use an IS to his/her advantage, the criminal must first gain access (commonly known as 'hacking'). This is usually followed by stealing, manipulating or destroying information. Systems dealing with money directly are obvious targets, and online banking can be particularly prone to abuse. ATMs can be rigged with devices that capture the personal details of individuals using them, and stolen credit cards (or credit card details and user identities) can be used to make online purchases, as discussed in the case study at the start of this chapter.

Systems that process other types of information can also have value to the criminal.

Business espionage is believed to be common, but its extent is unknown. This is because businesses are reluctant to reveal details of attacks they have suffered, which may be damaging to their image. Their customers may be reluctant to do business with an organization that has information security problems. Criminals have even been known to blackmail victims – threatening to reveal a security breach unless payments are made.

Of course, there are also those who take delight in hacking into systems to which they have not been given access, and maybe causing damage; or in creating viruses to inconvenience the public, for the sheer joy of doing so. This form of 'electronic vandalism' costs us all money, because we have to employ firewalls and anti-virus software to protect our systems and data, and because the businesses with which we deal have to do the same, and they pass the costs on to us. More importantly, it wastes time – including that of those whose time is particularly valuable to society, such as the medical professions.

It is worth noting that the most common perpetrators of computer crime are employees or ex-employees of the companies that are the victims.

Happily for the more law-abiding members of society, it's not just the criminal who can take advantage of digital technology. Computers and other digital devices are now widely employed in the prevention and detection of crime, and on the whole, the forces of law and order still seem to have the upper hand.

Software to combat unauthorized access to systems, and to prevent or remove infection by viruses and worms, is now usually powerful enough to keep the hackers at bay. Occasionally, a new virus will appear and may cause a panic (whether or not it does any real harm) until a defence is found. Novice or infrequent computer users, however, may not appreciate the need to protect themselves and their equipment, or may not have the necessary understanding of the safeguards available, and may become victims. Penalties for hacking vary enormously from country to country (and from state to state in the USA), and according to the nature of the offence. The cases considered to be most serious usually involve more than simple access to a system, such as a threat to national security, or theft (as in the case study at the start of this chapter).

Digital CCTV (closed-circuit television) is one of the most visible recent additions to the digital armoury of those who combat crime, whether they be police, business organizations or private individuals. Whereas the previous generation of analogue devices could be used to monitor premises or vulnerable areas, their capabilities were limited to providing surveillance (live or recorded), which could be viewed at a remote location. The main advantage of *digital* CCTV cameras is that the images they receive can be processed electronically, enabling a wide range of added functionality. Video content analysis can be used to detect people carrying guns or knives, and the authorities can be alerted. Facial recognition software, linked to a database of images, can be used to scan a crowded street or sports arena to identify wanted criminals in a crowd. Number-plate recognition software, again linked to a database, can pick out motor vehicles that are stolen or that belong to drivers without insurance. Suspects roaming a city can be tracked automatically by a central computer passing control from one camera to the next. Images can be transmitted over the Internet so householders who have digital CCTV installed in their homes can keep a watch over their belongings from any Internet-enabled computer.

The use of CCTV does not attract universal approval. There are many who believe it constitutes an invasion of privacy, because it monitors the actions of the innocent as well as the guilty. Some claim that, rather than deter criminal activity, it just moves it from one place to another – from the places where there are cameras to the places where there are none. Others point to the fact that much of the image processing is built on error-prone artificial intelligence techniques, and that mistakes can lead to serious injustices. And, of course, criminals can themselves make use of CCTV. One way they do this is with hidden or disguised devices in ATMs, used to record the keying in of customers' PINs.

There are many computerized techniques for verifying the identity of individuals (which the criminal fraternity are constantly trying to circumvent). Using the method known in the United Kingdom as 'chip and PIN', a microchip is embedded into credit or debit cards. When presenting a card to make a purchase or withdrawal, the user must enter a number (usually four digits) into a terminal, which is checked against the content of the microchip before the transaction is allowed to go ahead. This system will not work unless the card holder keeps the PIN number secret. When the chip and PIN scheme was first introduced in the United Kingdom, some banks maintained that it was infallible, and refused to compensate customers who claimed to have been subject to card fraud, saying that it must have been caused by the customers' own negligence. Following a change in the law, banks must now reimburse customers for fraudulent use, unless they can prove that the customer was at fault.

Biometric devices enable individuals to prove their identity using characteristics of the human body that are unique to them. These include iris or retina scanners, electronic fingerprint recognition, voice analysis, hand geometry and palm vein authentication. None of these mechanisms are universally accepted as infallible. Critics are particularly concerned about their use in situations that could result in someone losing their liberty. The possibility of an error occurring can be reduced by using more than one method for each instance of identification. But problems remain in relation to the disabled, for some of whom individual biometric identification methods are unusable.

Other digital technology used in the fight against crime includes various tracking devices based on GPS (global positioning system). This enables offenders or suspects to be continuously monitored by fitting them with 'tags' – devices which cannot easily be removed, and which transmit a signal revealing the wearer's location. The same technology can be used in motor vehicles, so they can be tracked and recovered if stolen. Both uses are controversial – the former raises questions related to human rights, and the latter is open to abuse because it can be used to track vehicles with or without the knowledge of their owners.

The extent to which tracking devices and other means of electronic surveillance (such as the monitoring of computer communications and phone tapping) are used by the security services is unknown to all but a few, and will vary greatly from country to country.

All technology can be used for the good of society, by those wanting to profit from it at the expense of society, and by those trying to protect or undermine society. In this respect, digital technology is no different.

15.5 Digital technology and ethics

Ethics deals with questions of what is right and what is wrong, and as such is subject to many different interpretations and disagreements. It is usually assumed that all (or most) criminal activity is unethical, but many would say that in some instances illegal actions (perhaps in an attempt to change the law) can be ethically justified. However, most would agree that it is possible to behave unethically without breaking the law. Societies in which unethical behaviour is common are generally regarded as being poorer as a result.

As with criminal activity, the advent of digital technology has provided extra scope for unethical behaviour. The ability to communicate with large numbers of people – cheaply, quickly and over huge distances – is one of the main benefits of the digital age. But it also provides a greater pool of 'victims' for those who would abuse the opportunity. All sorts of undesirable content can be made public via websites, email and mobile phone in particular, and in many cases it can be broadcast anonymously. So we see pornography, malicious rumours and accusations, extremist propaganda and an abundance of embarrassing, undesirable or simply unwanted material. Often this is communicated in an intrusive manner – such as in spam emails or browser pop-ups – so that it is difficult or impossible to avoid (or costs us money to do so).

So, while we have increased opportunities to express our opinions, and to learn the views of other members of society, this is at the cost of being subjected to inappropriate and often objectionable material. To a certain extent we can use software to filter out the unwanted stuff, and ISPs (Internet service providers) can censor content so we are not aware of its existence. This itself raises more ethical questions. Who is to say what material should be censored? Should the government of a country decide what its citizens can and cannot view, or should they be able to decide for themselves?

The copying and unauthorized distribution of text, music, software, databases, etc., as discussed earlier in the chapter, constitutes breach of copyright and is illegal. Sadly, students at all levels have been tempted to 'copy and paste' content from websites, and to present it as their own work. This crude attempt at plagiarism is easily detectable, and anti-plagiarism software is now available to automate the process. But plagiarism is not limited to direct copying. It can be defined as claiming, or leading people to believe, that something is your own creation, when it is not. This 'something' can be almost anything – text, drawings or diagrams, photographs, graphics, websites, stories and – in particular – ideas. For example, to describe an experiment, survey, theory, sequence of events or business process, or almost anything of interest in an academic context that was created or devised by someone else, and not make it clear that it is not your own, is plagiarism. Plagiarism is considered to be a serious offence in the academic and scientific domains – equivalent to cheating in exams – and has not been limited to students. From time to time high-profile instances of plagiarism by researchers and academics (who should know better) come to light, with highly damaging consequences for the careers of those concerned.

An issue that is particularly topical and highly contentious is that of Internet gambling. There are those who would say that an occasional speculation is perfectly harmless. Indeed, many people have been placing small bets on horse races, football matches and the like for years, have enjoyed doing so, and appear to be undamaged. Others oppose the practice, and declare that trying to obtain money without earning it is inherently immoral, or perhaps that gambling is forbidden by their religion. But gambling over the Internet raises ethical issues in addition to those relevant to the practice in general. Those who are opposed to it make some or all of the following claims. The reader can decide on their validity.

- Internet gambling is extremely convenient. You do not need to go to the news-agent for a lottery ticket, or to the betting shop, racecourse or casino. You can lose your money in the comfort of your own home, with no effort at all, at any time of day or night. Perhaps it is too convenient.
- Internet gambling sites sometimes provide enticements for new customers. A size-able welcome bonus or free bets are offered for those who sign up. Weak-willed individuals are tempted to begin gambling because of this, and then find it diffi-cult to stop (especially if they do well initially).
- Sites accept credit cards. To some gamblers, 'credit card money' does not seem like real money, so they may spend more than they can afford, getting into debt.
- Gambling can be addictive. Sufferers can squander vast amounts of money, and can lose families, homes and jobs as a consequence.
- Some sites do not keep a check on the amount of money lost by individuals, and do not limit their losses.

There are many other types (perhaps an unlimited number) of unethical activities and behaviours to which digital technology can be applied. As in the case of crime, the technology is neutral; the way it is used reflects society's ethical standards rather than the technology itself.

15.6 The digital divide

Many ethical questions are concerned in one way or another with fairness and equality. So, the question of whether the digital society is one that is fair or equal is an import-ant one. Associated questions include whether digital technology tends to improve inequities or make them worse, who the winners and losers in the digital society are, and just how important are fairness and equality anyway? The term 'digital divide' has been used to describe the difference between those who have access, or easy access, to digital technology and those who do not, and the affects this has on their standard of living and opportunities in life. It is worth noting that in addition to access to the technology itself, people also need to know how to use it effectively, and to have the freedom to do so. The following paragraphs describe a point of view, which of course is open to challenge.

There are 'divides' that have existed throughout the history of humanity. The most obvious right now are those between rich and poor, old and young, the educated and uneducated (or less educated), those who live in the West and Third World residents, and inhabitants of cities and of the countryside.

15.6.1 *Rich vs poor*

On the global level, the difference in per capita income varies enormously between nations. As a consequence, digital technology is simply beyond the reach of individuals in many countries. In this situation even the wealthy are limited in their ability to make use of it because of the lack of infrastructure, such as broadband provision and ISPs. Moreover, there are fewer other local users of the technology with whom to communicate or do business, and fewer websites and providers of services and information that is relevant. But the disparity between rich and poor also exists within national boundaries. To a varying extent depending on the country concerned, and the 'flavour' of politics prevailing, significant differences in income can be seen between those in employment and those who are unemployed, those who have inherited wealth and those who have not, and between those in jobs that pay well and those that do not. In some countries there are more variations – for example, between genders, tribes, castes, land owners and tenants, and religious or political groups.

15.6.2 *Young vs old*

The extent of the divide between young and old again varies between countries and cultures. To generalize (probably excessively), in many countries older people living on pensions (or without pensions) may have less money to spend than the young on digital technology. Even if they can afford it, they find it difficult to understand and make use of. They often lack confidence in their ability to cope with what they regard as highly technical matters, and less support is provided to them than the young, because the return on investment is seen to be lower.

15.6.3 *Educated vs uneducated (or less educated)*

It is not enough simply to have access to digital technology (i.e. to be able to afford it). To use it effectively (and profitably) calls for knowledge, understanding and skills that are difficult to gain without formal education of a relatively high standard. This is simply not available to some, although, ironically, digital technology is an excellent mechanism for the delivery of education, once a basic familiarity has been established. Lack of education is often a consequence of belonging to one of the other disadvantaged groups (poor, elderly, etc.).

15.6.4 *City dwellers vs countryside dwellers*

In addition to the often reduced income of residents, the infrastructure in remote areas may be significantly inferior to that of towns and cities. However, recent developments in mobile technology (wireless broadband, wi-fi, GPS, etc.) could greatly reduce this problem.

15.6.5 *The problem compounded*

Those on the wrong side of the digital divide – the poor, the old, the uneducated and those who live in the Third World or lack access due to being in the countryside, who are already disadvantaged as described above, now find that they are deprived of the advantages of digital technology – access to information, education, a wider market (if in business), goods and services that are more convenient and less expensive, employment opportunities, and so on. This may well have the effect of reducing their income, with the result that they are unable to afford to purchase or update their digital equipment. Thus the divide continues to widen, unless steps are taken to bridge it.

15.6.6 Does it matter?

There are certainly people who are not concerned about the digital divide, and see no need to bridge or even narrow it. This includes the selfish, who simply do not care as long as they are on the 'right' side of the divide, and do not suffer as a consequence. Then there are those who might be termed 'economic right-wingers'. They believe in what has been called the 'trickle-down effect'. To simplify, this idea supposes that the benefits enjoyed by the privileged will gradually be transferred to the less fortunate members of society as the former spend their money. So, although the divide will remain, all members of society will be better off than they were. There are also those on the 'wrong' side of the divide, who are living in extreme poverty, who are more interested in day-to-day survival than technological progress. Access to clean water or health services is more important to them than a new computer. Of course, in the long-run, the use of digital technology by their governments and local authorities could probably increase their access to these essential services, and could improve the country's economy, so these things could be afforded.

15.6.7 What can be done?

If we decide that the digital divide is undesirable, and if we want to change what we don't like, then we need to decide what, if anything, we can do about it. That's a lot of 'ifs', but it is sadly often the case that recognizing problems is easy – finding solutions is more difficult.

On the international scale, economic aid can be provided to developing countries by governments. This can then be used, for example, to improve the electronic infrastructure of a country, to train teachers or to provide schools with computers. Charities can do the same, as can businesses that have an altruistic outlook (or that want to improve their public image). In the United Kingdom, Computer Aid International appeals for donations of used computing equipment (from organizations and individuals), refurbishes it where necessary, and distributes it to developing countries. However, while such efforts make an important contribution towards tackling the problem of the digital divide, it does not seem to be going away.

Governments can target education at those most in need, and can introduce social policies (such as the provision of computing clubs for the over-50s and installing computers and Internet access points in libraries). However, the amount of money governments can spend on such initiatives is limited by what the public will stand. In democracies and dictatorships alike, and in all shades of administration in between, nothing is more likely to bring a government down than an increase in taxation. Perhaps the real need is for a change of attitudes, so that the digital divide is recognized as unacceptable, and that it must be bridged in spite of the cost. A difficult task indeed.

15.6.8 *Should we be trying to bridge the digital divide?*

Finally, it can be argued that the digital divide is a phenomenon rather than a problem, and that there is no need to do anything about it. It is reasoned that as new technological developments come along, they are taken up first by those with the most money to spend. (Being an 'early adopter' of digital technology in this way is not necessarily a good business strategy. It may turn out to be profitable, but exposes organizations to considerable risk because such innovations are prone to failure, or simply do not 'catch on'.) If the technology is successful, more and more people will buy it, and eventually the price will fall because it becomes cheaper to manufacture in bulk. Thus the digital divide becomes a digital delay, and the have-nots become have-laters.

15.6.9 *Disabilities and the digital divide*

The reader might be surprised that there has so far been no discussion in this section of physical disability, and its affect on employability. This is because it might be one area in which digital technology is helping to narrow the divide rather than widen it. Increased automation means that the proportion of jobs that are physically demanding is falling. As intellectual ability becomes relatively more important, those with physical disabilities are more able to compete in the marketplace for jobs. In addition to this, significant advances are being made in improving the accessibility of the technology, and in allowing its users greater independence. Just a few devices and services available are mentioned here. Readers with a particular interest should refer to Robitaille (2009).

Blindness or visual impairment

Screen-readers convert text to speech, and incorporate special features to deal with the difficulties that webpages can present, such as tables, illustrations and captions and frames. (The World Wide Web consortium, and others, have devised accessibility standards to minimize such problems with websites, and software has been written to check sites' levels of conformity.) Software is available to magnify parts of a computer screen, and is now incorporated within Microsoft Windows. There are Braille readers and printers, and tactile devices for communicating images. Services provided (sometimes by community websites, sometimes by commercial organizations) include audio description on TV and Braille translation.

Deafness

A variety of purpose-built or adapted telecommunications devices are available, which may simply amplify a telephone, signal an incoming call with a light instead of a ring-tone, or incorporate speech-to-text. The deaf may find text messaging on mobile phones, instant messaging and emails via computer particularly useful. Digital hearing aids offer increased quality and extra functionality, including wireless connection to external devices, such as a computer or telephone.

Restricted movement

Alternative or modified input and output devices can enable the use of computers by those who would find the standard type difficult or impossible. These include undersized or oversized versions of keyboard and mouse, and keyboards designed for operation with one hand. An eye-gaze system uses a camera mounted on a computer monitor and focused on the user's eye. The user can select characters, symbols or words with a quick glance, and the equivalent of mouse clicks is achieved with a slow eye blink. Similar devices can use head tracking as an input device, and a foot mouse can substitute for the hand-operated type.

15.7 IT law

As more and more business is carried out electronically, it becomes increasingly important for IS specialists to be aware of their obligations under the law, and of the protection it affords. As ISs become larger and more complex, and attract more users, it becomes easier to commit offences unintentionally, and the consequences of errors or omissions can be increasingly costly. As business becomes global, international law and the law of foreign administrations become relevant.

Furthermore, what is legal does not always correspond to what we instinctively feel to be right – but ignorance of the law is often not an excuse for breaking it, and the penalties can be severe. It is a good time to be a lawyer! Lawyers, of course, are an expensive commodity, so we don't want to employ them unless we have to. On the other hand, the consequences of not taking legal advice when we should can be disastrous. A reasonable aim for an IS specialist is to understand enough about the law to be able to judge when to consult an expert.

Caveat – almost everything that follows is an over-simplification! The law is hugely complex, and to discuss or describe these topics without a little artistic licence would result in a longer publication than the author wants to write or you want to read. This is why lawyers are so wealthy!

Laws vary from country to country, and even within national boundaries (for example, different US states have some very different laws, and within the United Kingdom, Scotland has a quite different legal system). Additionally, there are laws that apply within groups of countries, such as the European Union, and international law. Whatever the jurisdiction, the following legal topics are important.

15.7.1 *Data protection*

Data protection is concerned with protecting the rights of individuals with regard to information that is held about them. Generally speaking, the obligations of information holders include ensuring that it is obtained with the consent of the data subject (i.e. the person about whom data is held), that it is correct, up-to-date, held securely, not disclosed without the permission of the data subject, is not excessive, and not kept longer than necessary.

15.7.2 *Intellectual property rights*

The term intellectual property rights (IPR) refers to creations of the mind rather than physical objects. Such creations are still property, however, and things such as industrial designs, patents, trademarks and copyright can be bought, sold, inherited, given away and 'stolen'.

Individuals and organizations have the right to prevent others from using their intellectual property without their permission – the two main mechanisms being patents (which protect ideas and inventions) and copyright (which protects the sorts of things that can be published, whether or not they already have been. We will briefly discuss copyright here, as it is most relevant to the area of ISs.

There are some variations between countries, but in general copyright protects:

- literary, dramatic, musical and artistic works
- sound recordings
- films and videos
- broadcasts
- computer programs and data
- databases
- material published on the Internet.

One should assume that all 'works' of the above types are subject to copyright, whether or not it has been 'claimed' using a phrase of the type:

© Phil Lovett 2010 – All rights reserved.

This is because in most countries, copyright exists the moment a work is created, and the owner (who is usually the author, but may be his/her employer, or someone who has purchased the copyright) does not need to register it or bring it to anyone's attention.

The term 'infringement' is used to denote a copyright (or other IPR) offence. It can result in the award of damages proportionate to the loss suffered by the owner, or in fines or jail sentences imposed by the state. There are exceptional circumstances in which copyright does not apply – especially in the case of academic use – but this does not mean that students, lecturers, professors, etc. can copy material without limit. You need to be aware of just what you can and cannot copy according to the laws that apply where you live.

15.7.3 Computer misuse

Computer misuse refers to what is commonly known as hacking (gaining unauthorized access to ISs, possibly followed by further offences) and has already been discussed.

15.7.4 Laws relating to electronic and mobile commerce

The law provides protection to those buying 'at a distance'. This includes transactions via the Internet, digital television, mail order, telephone and fax. Sellers are required to supply consumers with clear information about the goods or services on offer, and about delivery arrangements and payment. This usually includes such things as the price of items, delivery costs, the customer's right to cancel the agreement and return the goods (including for how long this right lasts and who bears the costs of carriage) and arrangements for paying by credit or debit card. It is important that the seller provides an accurate description of goods and services – although a special law for online selling may not be required – as this is the same as for bricks-and-mortar concerns. Online retailers are also required to supply their geographical location.

A lack of understanding of the law can be very costly to those doing business online. In a well-publicized incident in 2001, Kodak offered a digital camera for sale on its website for £100. This was an error – the price should have been £329. About 2,000 cameras were ordered, and customers received confirmation of their orders, which referred to a contract having been formed. When the pricing mistake was realized, Kodak originally tried to deny that contracts were in existence, but eventually decided to honour the orders. Similarly costly errors were made by other online retailers in the early days of e-commerce. Nowadays, companies make it clear in their terms and conditions (which customers must acknowledge having read), that contracts are not formed until the goods are sent out.

15.7.5 *Other laws*

Depending on the nature of their jobs, IS practitioners may also need to have some knowledge of the law relating to employment contracts, health and safety issues, freedom of information, human rights and libel. They should also be aware that they may be legally responsible not only for their own actions, but also for the actions of their employees.

15.8 Employment

Digital technology has without doubt affected dramatically the employment status and conditions of many individuals, social groups and nation states. However, while most may have been affected, the nature and extent of the changes have varied greatly. Some jobs virtually no longer exist (there are now very few typewriter repairers – once a common occupation). Many completely new careers have materialized as a result of digital technology (there were even fewer website designers in 1980 than there are typewriter repairers now). But perhaps one should be careful when using the word 'career', which implies an occupation will last a lifetime, or at least a significant portion of it. That is often no longer the case. Some jobs have become extinct because the human input has been totally automated; others have been transformed, as workers have been required to master new technologies. As an example of the latter, those in the medical professions may now have to cope with extraordinarily complex equipment – an intensive care unit could almost be mistaken for the set of a science fiction movie.

Just as individual employees may have been winners or losers in the digital society, the effect on organizations has differed widely too. Some have even disappeared completely, and new ones have risen to take their place. The full reasons for the downfall of F.W. Woolworths (1997 in the USA, 2008 in the United Kingdom), TWA (2001) and the General Electric Company (2005) are too complex for discussion here. But the advent of digital technology and more effective use of that technology by the competitors of these companies was probably a significant contributory factor.

On the other hand, there have been some spectacular successes by companies specializing in IS and IT – Microsoft (initiated in 1975), Cisco (1984) and Google (1998) being obvious examples. In addition, many smaller companies working in these and similar areas (with nevertheless very many employees between them) have prospered. Companies that do not specialize in the production of digital goods or services, but who have adopted or adapted business models to exploit IS/IT fully, have also been extraordinarily successful; Amazon, Lastminute.com and Nissan are in this category. Many people are unhappy about the power (economic and political) that companies such as these possess, pointing out that they are wealthier than some nation states. This, they argue, gives them the power to influence governments, and can lead to a weakening of democracy.

As well as whether or not an individual is employed, digital technology can also affect the character of that employment, and the characteristics, knowledge and skills needed by employees. More technology implies fewer manual jobs, and more jobs that are clerical, administrative, managerial, service-oriented, scientific, technical, media-based and so on. While the need for physical skills is reduced, workers often need a higher standard of formal education. They may need to update their abilities regularly, and to be more flexible in the range of duties they are prepared to undertake. They may find themselves working from home, and working irregular hours, and while their duties may be less physically challenging, they may consider themselves to be subject to greater mental stress.

15.9 And so on ...

Lack of space has precluded a fuller discussion of some areas that are, however, worth mentioning in brief.

15.9.1 Culture

In the digital society we read less, and spend more time browsing, chatting electronically and engaging in social networking. We attend fewer live events, but download and view more digital material. We are less likely to take part in sporting activities, and more likely to play computer games.

Our language is changing. English is the language of the Internet, and as a consequence other languages are disappearing or becoming of secondary importance. Many fear the increasing dominance of Western values as a result. English itself is changing – 'American English' is becoming more common, and the use of the abbreviations and conventions of 'texting' are insinuating themselves into situations where more formal language was previously expected.

15.9.2 Education

Various forms of distance learning have become increasingly common, which means that a higher standard of education is generally more widely available. However, some would argue that more extensive use of computers within universities has been at the expense of increased student–staff ratios, and less personal contact.

15.9.3 The environment

Improved communications mean there is less need for people to travel to work, so in theory we should expect less pollution caused by transport. Whether this is in fact so, or whether it will become or remain so, is unsure. The disposal of old computing equipment is also an issue. Often it is discarded, not because it is faulty or worn out, but because it has been superseded by faster or more powerful technology, or even just because it is out of fashion. Nowadays, we are becoming increasingly conscious of the need to dispose of it in an environmentally responsible manner. Recycling is becoming more common, including the passing on of unwanted equipment to charities or Third World countries. Other relevant questions include whether our use of electricity to power digital technology is excessive, and whether it will ever bring us the 'paperless office', as once predicted.

15.9.4 Health issues

This is surely a matter of swings and roundabouts. Lack of exercise contributes to our becoming obese and unfit. Long sessions sitting at a computer can cause physical and mental stress, perhaps leading to RSI and mental health problems. On the other hand, digital technology has brought us tremendous advances in the diagnosis and treatment of diseases and improved access to health advice.

15.10 Summary

This chapter has explored some of the profound effects that digital technology has had, and continues to have, on society. Hopefully it has demonstrated that those who study and work in this area need to be aware of the limitations, potential hazards and unwanted side-effects of innovations in the field, as well as the benefits to society and the potential for profit.

Glossary

ATM   Automatic teller machine, otherwise known as a cashpoint – a publicly located machine that provides remote access to individuals' bank accounts so they can withdraw cash and carry out other basic financial transactions.

CCTV   Closed-circuit television.

Ethics   The branch of philosophy dealing with, or the study or consideration of, what is right and what is wrong.

GPS   Global positioning system – a satellite-based system, built and maintained by the USA, that provides location information worldwide.

IPR   Intellectual property rights – the rights of an individual or a corporate body relating to 'creations of the mind'.

ISP   Internet service provider.

PIN   Personal identification number – an individual number issued to holders of credit and debit cards to prevent fraudulent use.

RSI   Repetitive strain injury – a term used to describe one of several musculoskeletal conditions (such as tenosynovitis, carpal tunnel or tendonitis) caused by repeated actions, which can be initiated or exacerbated by extended use of a computer keyboard.

Reference

Ford, R. (2010) *Huge Rise in 'Hidden' Credit Card Crime*. Available online at www.timesonline.co.uk/tol/news/uk/crime/article7130209.ece (accessed 15 June 2010).

Further reading

Robitaille, S. (2009) *The Illustrated Guide to Assistive Technology and Devices: Tools and Gadgets for Living Independently.* New York: Demos Medical Publishing.

Suggested activities

1   Discuss some types of unethical behaviour made possible by the advent of digital technology, other than those already mentioned in this chapter.
2   What is your opinion about Internet gambling? Should it be:

   • banned?
   • permitted?
   • controlled?
   • encouraged?

   Provide evidence and arguments to justify your opinion.
3   Discuss with your friends, colleagues or fellow students whether the digital divide exists, and if so:

   a   Does it matter?
   b   Can anything be done about it?
   c   Should anything be done about it?
   d   Will anything be done about it?

4   Identify three jobs or careers that are under threat from digital technology, and three new areas in which digital technology offers good prospects for future employment.

16 E-commerce 3

Case study 16.1 Bank A

This case study has been included by the authors to facilitate class discussion. Any resemblance to existing organizations or people is coincidental.

Bank A is one of the United Kingdom's leading providers of personal financial services and products. It is one of the medium-sized banks in the United Kingdom, with over 400 branches nationwide. Initially it was opened as a small building society, but it grew rapidly and became a bank in the late 1990s.

It is a very innovative company and its enthusiasm for new technologies means it is at the forefront of providing financial services through new service delivery channels such as e-banking and mobile banking. Bank A was one of the first financial institutions in the United Kingdom to network its branches, using countertop online terminals linked to the central mainframe – this happened during the 1980s. For this reason most of the financial services at Bank A were readily accessible through a variety of different channels such as branches, telephone, the Internet, digital televisions and mobile phones, as they evolved into credible channels.

This gives convenience and flexibility to customers to manage their finances wherever they are, and whenever they want, instantly. To provide good access and flexibility to customers, Bank A invested heavily in technology and has gone through many organizational changes (outlined below). Since becoming a bank, their strategy has been focused on adapting to the new world of multiple distribution outlets beyond the traditional branch network. The main reason behind this was top management's belief that winners would be those organizations that combined new technologies with traditional business to provide integrated solutions. Another reason was the fast-changing environment in the retail banking industry, with new entrants such as Egg, Smile and even supermarkets providing financial services using innovative business models and technologies.

Increasing customer retention through depth of relationship and service was also an important objective. Internet technology was seen as a key enabler for this purpose because it can provide rich information about customers. This enabled Bank A to personalize financial services according to the needs of individual customers, thus enriching the relationship and, as a result, achieving greater loyalty and creating cross-selling opportunities. They invested heavily in relevant technologies, which enabled them to gather and analyse extensive customer information.

Very early into the e-banking implementation, they noticed they were also getting customers from the remote areas of the United Kingdom, where they had no penetration in the past.

Bank A had to change considerably in terms of departmental structures to become more business process-oriented in order to web-enable itself. There were many processes that were totally integrated and automated, such as printing and sending cheque or deposit books on customers' request. Staff numbers were not reduced; instead, their role was changed and most of them geared towards sales. The ability to focus on sales has resulted in 3.6 products held by each customer, which is much higher than its competitors. This radical transformation from being a mortgage-centred building society to a customer-focused and integrated bank was seen by many in the industry as an example of best practice.

Bank A is aware of the power and uniqueness of the Internet medium. E-channels opened up a whole new way of communicating with customers and they dedicated an area within their marketing function that dealt with the e-channels. Now the focus was on understanding customers and using that understanding to enrich relationships with them. This profiling ability also enabled them to assess the requirements of individual customers and offer services accordingly. The main idea behind this was to replace high-margin products with smaller margin, multi-product relations with customers.

Bank A used a middleware layer for the integration of different systems and channels, which allowed a host of different clients (front-end systems) to access a whole lot of back-end systems. This middleware layer provides a common interface to all existing systems, enabling them to add new systems quickly, as the interface has to be implemented just once, to the middleware rather than to the whole range of different systems. In addition, this middleware enabled them to implement a component-based architecture. This makes the channels interchangeable and allows the bank to add new channels or services without disrupting core services. This architecture also allows Bank A to add new off-the-shelf systems to quickly increase the capacity of the systems.

Having an established brand name was an important factor in their success. The main reason for this given by most informants was that a household name such as Bank A gives customers added confidence to conduct business online. Other reasons may include their previous positive experiences with the company and the non-substantial nature of the online medium, which makes trust in a well-known name as well as high street presence even more important than when more traditional channels such as the telephone are used.

To utilize multiple channels to full advantage, channel integration was achieved. This included sharing of business rules and other components across channels, a common set of interfaces into core systems for use across all channels, high-quality, customer-centred functionality across all channels, ability to deliver all products and services through all channels and customer services which are able to support all channels. Bank A uses the highest levels of encryption to secure their system. Costs of this high level of security are very high, but they saw it as a necessary evil, and no compromises were made in this regard.

Bank A paid special attention to change management from the beginning. They consulted most of the employees on major decisions. E-banking was quite aggressively promoted within the organization in a number of ways. This strategy helped make staff feel an important part of the change and eased their resistance to it. Another major benefit of this strategy they experienced was useful feedback from staff members as customers, which was invaluable for improving services and system interface, especially at early stages.

16.1 Intended learning outcomes

On completion of this chapter the reader should be able to:

1   explain major challenges and issues in e-commerce management;
2   evaluate the role of e-marketing in relation to e-commerce;
3   analyse the ways in which ethics and trust affect e-commerce;

4   explain why models that include human factors are important in e-commerce;
5   assess the role of information security in e-commerce.

16.2 Introduction

As a direct consequence of the emergence of the digital economy, customers are increasingly demanding more value, with goods customized to their exact needs, at less cost, and as quickly as possible. To meet these demands, businesses need to develop innovative ways of creating value, which often require flat enterprise architectures, integrated IT infrastructures and different way of thinking about doing business. This transformation of business from an old company to a new agile electronic corporation, and from an electronic business to an innovating learning organization, is not easy and requires a lot of lateral thinking, planning and investment. This chapter will cover many of these management issues in e-commerce, along with some suggestions for how to address e-commerce-related issues.

16.3 Strategy development

Companies involved in e-commerce face uncertainty about the future of their business models and how they impact on their business as a whole. This uncertainty requires proper strategic planning in order to fully utilize opportunities and minimize threats. Strategy development often requires a methodological approach. In a corporate environment, strategy is an organized decision-making process that helps organizations to match resources with opportunities. The external environment has a strong influence on the strategy-making processes, as has the internal resources of the organization.

Strategy can be divided under two headings: strategy by design and strategy by discovery. Strategy by design encompasses systematic approaches, whereby plans are derived through reductionist methods. Strategy by discovery, by contrast, requires a systemic, holistic approach, favouring participative methods covering the whole system of interest.

In the context of e-commerce, both views have a place, with a perceived need for a mixture of approaches, premised, at least in part, on the organizational context encountered. Furthermore, in respect of corporate strategy as applied to e-commerce management, strategy by discovery may be seen as long-term, concerned with planning for the unknown, or forecasting discontinuities. The design approach may be seen as short-term, and concerned with carrying out the IS strategy through the application of information technology. Corporate strategy cannot therefore rely on any one approach, but must craft a combination of strategic methods to fit the organizational form and context.

E-commerce should be considered more as a business project rather than a technological initiative (Shah and Siddiqi, 2006). In this context, cost–benefit analysis may be very useful. Offering online services is very expensive because of initial technological, human and marketing costs. A detailed investment appraisal may save a company from a costly pitfall. Moreover, a number of studies may take place in order to find answers to the following questions.

*   To what extent will business strategy be affected?
*   To what degree will the transformation of business strategy impact on the competitive advantage of the company?

- How is the enterprise strategy changing against competitors?
- What will be the return on investment?

Change resulting from e-commerce implementation affects many people in organizations. In a participative approach, uncertainties resulting from changes are usually addressed by getting as many employees involved as possible at all stages of a project lifecycle. This may lengthen the project duration, but the benefit can be immense. It is also important to keep the communication going and to keep all stakeholders, including users, informed of the progress for the entire duration of the project.

E-commerce initiatives should be business-driven and not technology- or trend-driven. The project should be customer focused, making it easier to conduct business. E-economy partnerships with other organizations are more important than ever, as a group of companies is better placed to offer competitive goods under one roof than is an individual company. The integration of technology and business processes from suppliers to customers to provide real-time (or close to it) business decision-making ability, and management of information and knowledge are the keys to understanding customers and offering customized products/services according to segment or individual needs.

16.4 Customer service

In recent years, legislation has increased customers' rights, and the Internet and global competition have increased the range of products and providers. The increasing amount of information on the Internet and changes in social behaviours has decreased the loyalty factor considerably. These changes have resulted in a growth in users with sophisticated needs and anywhere/anytime availability requirement. Users increasingly do not tolerate inadequate websites. Information must be instantly available for all products, along with stock and delivery information.

The increasing popularity of the Internet as a business medium brings numerous opportunities for organizations, as well as threats. It is now much cheaper to serve customers compared with other channels, such as high-street stores, and it also offers access to previously inaccessible markets. On the other hand, it can result in lower switching barriers, so that cross-selling will become more difficult and information about customers will become harder to obtain (due to loss of face-to-face contact). Thus, organizations often have to compete product by product.

One way of improving customer services is use of existing call centres to build rich relationships. If the call centre can respond to other forms of enquiry, such as emails, they become a 'contact centre' rather than just a 'call centre'. If these 'contact centres' are equipped with data mining and customer relationship management (CRM) systems, they can be used to track customers' preferences and enrich relationships with existing customers, therefore increasing the products-per-customer ratio, as well as help to develop new products by utilizing feedback from customers.

In practice, it needs a database system that is able to hold data from external sources, and can be integrated with all e-commerce applications. Various software tools are needed to collect this data, process it to turn it into usable information and deliver it to the point where it is needed, such as the CRM system or sales force. Needs of modern customers are constantly changing, so it is important that these systems are able to monitor individual customer preferences and update the database on a real-time basis. If this kind of integrated system can be implemented – and some organizations have achieved it – it becomes possible to target individual customers with greater accuracy and to come closer to niche marketing. Integrated information therefore makes it possible to employ a number of marketing concepts like niche marketing, database marketing, micro marketing, interactive marketing, relationship marketing and mass customization.

Another possible use of modern technologies to serve customers better is utilizing Internet picture telephone/video conferencing to offer one-to-one discussion and advice. In this way, e-commerce may be used for strengthening cross-selling and price differentiation. It might be an expensive option, but organizations offering these video link-based customer services may be able to forge closer relationships with customers.

Another method of enriching relationships with customers is the development of virtual communities. A virtual community is an Internet-based group of users who share a common interest. The members of a virtual community usually contact each other by different communication platforms such as newsgroups, web forums, web chat, online notice boards and blogs. Commercial organizations can use this to facilitate discussion between its customers and, as a result, improve their services and loyalty factor.

16.5 Security

Security is paramount for the growth of any sort of online trade. Security in this context includes transactions, as well as front-end and back-up systems. Internet security is still one of the major issues hindering the growth of Internet-related trade. Owing to the structure and intention of the Internet to be an open network, Internet fraud is common, and related stories get immediate media attention, making people hesitant to buy online.

Managing information security is a very complex issue. Clarke (2007) argues that the domain is dominated by a set of practical controls that are seen as rigid, unclear and largely irrelevant to the business needs of most organizations. Even within some recent developments that have sought to provide a more accessible model for managing information security, most current practice is based around the needs of the technology and of information rather than the needs of people. Where human issues are considered, it is to confer responsibilities and education on people to conform to the needs of the system, with an aim to regulate their behaviour.

Figure 16.1 summarizes the position reached so far, and gives some idea of the complexity of the issues. This model would be useful in planning for comprehensive security provision.

While Figure 16.1 helps in understanding the various dimensions in managing information security, implementation requires more practical guidelines. Sha and Clarke (2009) suggest the procedure outlined in Table 16.1.

Getting the basic controls in place is highest priority, because failure to do so would most likely undermine the whole security practice, irrespective of its social/technical biases. Next priority is to make sure the practice is continually reviewed to check whether it is meeting the needs of its users and the business. Third, use the evaluative model to identify opportunities to improve the practice towards a more socially aware approach. Underpinning all of this is the need to identify and

Table 16.1   Adapted approach to information security

Number	Step	Comments
1	Assess presence of essential controls. If there are gaps they should be addressed unless there is a good reason not to.	Absence of essential controls puts the organization at risk of loss of information and access in a way that cannot be addressed through application of sociologically biased controls.
2	Assess security practice of organization against evaluative model and create security profile map. Compare this profile with another organization of similar size, industry sector, complexity, etc.	As more organizations are assessed the baseline of organizations' security profiles will grow and provide this additional dimension of analysis.
3	Determine whether any implemented system-biased controls can be easily converted to by changing context, environment, people involved, means of capturing feedback, etc.	This represents the easiest step to moving the very common goal-attainment-focused security practice to a real-world-focused one.
4	Determine whether any of the controls identified above have not been implemented but could be deployed reasonably easily.	If an organization has built its practice around audit requirements and/or functional concerns, it is quite likely that not all controls have been implemented.
5	Reassess security profile and compare with the previous practice of target organization, along with other organizations of similar size, industry sector, complexity, etc.	This gives a new baseline from which to measure improvements. Other specific measures such as user satisfaction, number of security incidents, etc. should be formulated on a case-by-case basis. Have regard for the outcomes that are sought by the organization.
6	Identify Neutral (N), Counter-productive (C) and Other-responsibility (O) controls and eliminate or reassign.	It is critically important that N and C controls are not just dropped and ignored. Careful thought should be given to determine whether they are correctly classified and consideration of whether they are important to some other organizational function (in which case, presumably, they would be reassigned as O). If O controls remain a dependency after they have been reassigned the dependency must be surfaced and appropriate service levels agreed and documented.
7	Use the action loop through public and private spheres to drive the security practice towards a human-centred focus.	This action step is key to maintaining a focus on both technical and human-centred issues throughout the life of an information security system.
8	Reassess security profile and compare with last baseline. Redo action loop at action step 6.	This becomes a long-term (perhaps continual) process to achieve desired outcomes and sustain the required focus.

Source: Shah and Clarke (2009).

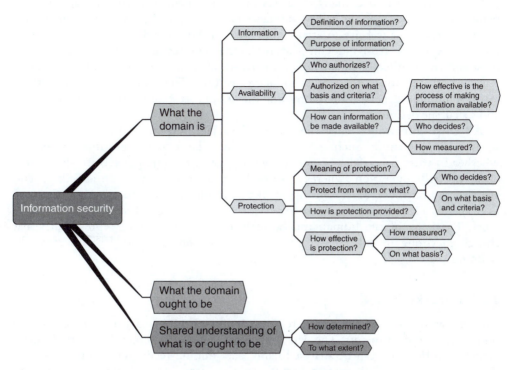

Figure 16.1 The complexity of information security (Clarke, 2007, p. 147 – used by permission).

deal with neutral, counter-productive and other-responsibility biased controls. One way to deal with this is to remove neutral and counter-productive controls altogether and to reassign responsibility to the appropriate department within the organization, but maintain such controls as dependencies for the information security practice.

16.6 Winning customer trust

Managing security itself is often not enough to win the trust of customers. Approval by third parties such as governments, trading authorities, professional associations or by other trusted brands also plays a big part. Organizations need to take active steps to promote trust in e-commerce by:

- purchase of similar web domain names so it becomes difficult for fraudulent traders to set up similar websites;
- being proactive in combating online crimes and cooperating with other organizations and regulatory/professional bodies to detect and prevent crimes;
- taking proper care in protecting consumers' information and taking particular care in using it for marketing purposes;
- providing appropriate guarantees against consumer losses in the event of fraud and providing help and advice to customers when they do become victim of these frauds.

Online traders can take many measures to build and enhance trusting relationships before, during and after any online interaction. They depend primarily on their electronic storefront or website to attract potential customers and to communicate their message. Applying trust-inducing features to the websites of online merchants is the most effective method of enhancing online trust. Wang and Emurian (2005) proposed a framework to explain these trust-inducing features. The framework classifies these features into four general dimensions: graphic design, structure design, content design and social-cue design.

All these dimensions have the potential to facilitate or undermine trust in a website. Simple things such as use of colour may be used by consumers to decide whether to trust this trader or not. Generally speaking, orange websites indicate a cheap/no frills operation, whereas use of light blue may be taken as a high-end trustworthy business. Most consumers like a simple and easy to navigate structure as it creates a smooth and positive experience which is a key dimension in winning trust. Provision of the human touch, such as customer service representatives if things go wrong in online environments, is now considered to be important for winning trust.

16.7 E-marketing

The interactive nature of e-commerce creates opportunities to gain a much deeper understanding of customers. The data gathered about the customer during their interaction with the bank can be analysed using data-mining techniques. This marketing decision support capability often determines the success of the Internet channel. In addition, there is a growing realization among corporations that the Internet has forever changed the traditional paradigm of marketing and remote customer contact. The new e-channels, if backed up by data capture and analysis capabilities, have made it possible to focus on building relationships with individual customers and to make direct and personalized contact with each customer. E-commerce has the potential to be a rich experience for customers, with the foremost goal being to increase the depth of the relationship between the customer and the organization. As technology evolves, the opportunities to extend and enrich the relationship with customers also grow.

Traditionally, both direct and mass marketing, were aimed at a large number of customers, but the arrival of the interactive channels has changed the marketing dynamics. New marketing paradigms are about allowing customers to browse, explore and compare products before a marketing message is customized to suit their needs.

Talha *et al.* (2004) argue that dramatic changes in marketing have resulted in an addition to the traditional '4 Ps' (price, product, place, promotion): 'personalization', which means the process of customizing products according to a customer's needs, has become a cornerstone of marketing efforts. In addition, the nature of traditional Ps has changed significantly. For example, new pricing strategies need to be much more sensitive to the marketplace as any unjustifiable price increase can damage sales figures, especially since price comparisons are much easier. At the same time, subtle changes in pricing that are sensitive to the online marketplace can be made on a dynamic basis to respond to changes in the marketplace or to suit different target markets (market segments). The Internet enables organizations greater precision in setting prices, more flexibility/adaptability in terms of responding to market changes and the ability to gather richer information for effective market segmentation.

The second P of new marketing strategy is *products* (or services). Online products/services can be modified or developed from scratch in a matter of days to respond to the dynamic marketplace. This has also resulted in shortened product lifecycles, and many organizations are offering new services or withdrawing weak products much more frequently than in the past. This means that the process of traditional product development often needs to change considerably to accommodate this new requirement of dynamic flexibility. E-commerce also enhances the ability of an organization to bundle related products on the basis of individual needs. Bundling is a sales approach in which two or more complementary services are offered as a bundle at a discounted price. With the Internet, bundling of information is easy because of hyperlink and other related capabilities.

The third P of marketing mix, *personalization*, has also changed due to the arrival of e-commerce. Now it is possible to create so much flexibility in a product/service that customers can customize it, within pre-defined limits, to meet their exact needs. The case of Bank A, given at the start of this chapter is also a useful demonstration of how consumer data can be used to personalize marketing and services. Advanced databases/data-mining tools and Internet cookies provide detailed insights into a customer's behaviour when they are online, and new communication technologies make it easy and cost-effective to mass market personalized services, because the whole process of personalization can be automated.

The fourth P of the e-marketing mix, *promotion*, has perhaps changed most. Traditional promotional campaigns used to rely on high-street stores/branches, newspaper and radio/TV advertising. However, new advertising mediums such as Internet banners, mobile texting and interactive marketing have significantly changed promotion operations. Internet marketing takes various forms. First, there is the mass broadcasting model, in which direct emails and TV is used to broadcast an advertising message. The target audience depends on availability of email addresses or viewing numbers for a particular programme on TV. This type of marketing can use multimedia contents, but the message has to be very brief, as long messages will not get the desired results. One main drawback of direct emailing is increasing spam and junk mail, which can turn customers away.

The fifth P of e-marketing, *place*, has had many of its key features changed over the last decade or so. Traditionally, most products/services were delivered via high-street stores or branches. This system worked well for large organizations as it was difficult for smaller organizations to get full access to the market and for new players to enter into the market due to the high cost associated with developing or maintaining a bricks-and-mortar network. The arrival of e-commerce has changed this. Now it is relatively easy for smaller organizations (such as Bank A in the case study) to offer their services countrywide or even worldwide. Entry barriers to the market have diminished significantly, so that organizations with a much smaller base of resources/skills, such as supermarkets, have started offering a variety of additional services.

Changes in all the Ps discussed above have resulted in a greater emphasis on interactive marketing. Interactive marketing is not just about promotion of products to customers by the suppliers, but also includes customer interaction with each other via email, chat room, electronic bulletin boards and virtual communities. These interactions create relatively new forms of relationship between consumers, marketers and suppliers of products and services. They can enable exchange of an unprecedented flow of information in all directions. Effective exploitation of this information and its flow might be the main source of competitive advantage in the future.

Another aspect of successful e-marketing is brand management. Owing to security issues and perceived fraud threats, many customers only deal with trusted brands in online environments. For this reason, well-established organizations often outperform new Internet-only, virtual organizations. For new entrants to e-commerce, building a trusted brand may therefore require considerable effort and resources. To build a new e-brand, an appropriate logo and key message should be developed. Customers can be focused on a range of services related to the site. Usage can be made accessible and easy to operate. Developing an e-brand is not just a management challenge; all levels of the organizations, its customers and intermediaries need to be involved in the process.

16.8 Channel integration

An important decision faces organizations when they want to trade online, due to increase in channel choices. Arrival of new e-channels has offered organizations new opportunities and new dilemmas about which channels offer the best return on investment in the long-run in an increasingly volatile business environment. In the financial sector, there has been a steady reduction in the number of branches since the late 1980s. Arrival of e-channels is causing further downsizing of the branch networks. However, the question remains whether these new channels will make the old physical channels redundant? The most common strategy traditional organizations have pursued is a dual strategy offering both old channels and new e-channels. Branch or high-street stores are likely to survive for a long time as organizations are slowly changing their role from routine sales-driven to customer service centres or evidence of credibility, which a physical store provides to an organization.

At first sight the advantages of establishing new distribution channels with respect to costs, market-reach and potential penetration seem to be promising. However, a 'blind' investment in novel forms of distribution can also have some disadvantages. A traditional organization offering lower margin/cost products/services online could suffer negative externalities by cannibalizing their traditional market and jeopardizing overall profits. On the other hand, competitors will also consider how to make best use of various distribution channels, including the question of whether or not it might be advantageous to combine innovative forms of distribution channels with traditional ones. This all means that use of different channels and how best to mix them has become a complex strategic issue in the need for careful analysis and decision-making.

If an organization adopts a multi-channel strategy, the Internet should be integrated with other service delivery channels such as high-street stores and internal systems to increase its effectiveness. Processing across the channels has to be real-time too to avoid inconveniences to customers. Best-practice institutions have a clear strategy for how the Internet will fit with their other channel offerings. Many organizations use the Internet as an additional channel of distribution and keep their traditional channels such as high-street stores intact. This gives the organization the opportunity for a gentle transition from a traditional bricks-and-mortar service delivery strategy to an online strategy.

Branding is a transferable resource across physical and social barriers to entry for customers in a new and perceptibly daunting online environment. The importance of brand factor is increasingly recognized, and many virtual organizations open some high-street stores to enhance their brands. However, this trend is limited to just a few organizations.

Usage of the major delivery channels is split and changes with time. High-street stores remain the most heavily used channels. All channels are useful to customers for the specific purpose each serves. For example, in the context of banks, e-banking may be good for checking balance or transferring funds between different accounts; ATMs for withdrawing cash; and branches for discussing mortgages and so on. For this reason, Bank A in the case study is using multi-channel strategy successfully. In the electronic goods industry, some large retailers such as Argos allow customers to buy products online and then pick them up at the nearest store location.

16.9 Media and contents

The richness of the medium's content has been a critical success factor in attracting a sharply growing number of website visitors and commercial users. Organizations usually feed their websites with contents such as corporate profile, product and pricing information, ordering procedures, etc. However, they need to look beyond usual contents and make their websites far richer to attract larger numbers of visitors.

Poor website design can result in decreased trust in using e-commerce as look and feel often creates a lasting impression. Appropriate design of websites is very important in e-commerce success. Poor design may include use of inappropriate colours, contrast, font or navigation functions. Lack of proper functionality, excessive use of graphics or other similar factors can also deter customers from coming back to that website. Web usage barriers can also be attributed to vision, cognition and physical impairments associated with the normal ageing process and certain medical conditions.

Vision changes include a decline in visual acuity, resulting in inability to see objects on a screen clearly, decreased capacity to focus at close range or increased sensitivity to glare from light reflecting or shining into the eye. These physiological changes, and many others, impact the users' ability to see Internet objects and read online content (Becker, 2005). These factors need to be taken into account when designing a website as the ageing population in most industrialized countries means that this segment is increasing in size. Several software tools, including Dottie and Usability Enforcer, are available for senior-friendly websites. Numerous organizations, such as the National Institute on Ageing (www.nia.nih.gov) provide guidelines for making senior-friendly websites.

16.10 Web-enabling the technological infrastructure

There are numerous technological issues with regard to e-commerce. E-commerce systems are often complex, large-scale systems with demanding requirements for performance, scalability and availability, and even the most technologically sophisticated organizations are struggling to manage them. Success requires a comprehensive approach to predict future demands and building systems to handle quick surges in use.

Upgrading current technological infrastructure is often essential to bring it up to speed with e-commerce. Technology failures such as website failure often lead to lost custom. Any organization hoping to make a successful future in online markets must test the technology thoroughly before releasing it on customer accessible websites. Most front-end and back-end systems often need to be integrated to offer multi-channel trade.

E-commerce is about how an organization has to re-shape itself to enable commerce online. An organization needs to have process-oriented and fully integrated ISs to achieve the main benefits of e-commerce. Even in the case of disparate applications, or in case the company does not abandon existing applications (e.g. legacy systems), there is a way to solve the problem. There are several alternatives available for increasing the level of systems integration. Data warehousing, a bundle of technologies that integrate data from multiple source systems for query and analysis, provide a cheaper alternative for data integration. Other technologies, such as enterprise applications integration (EAI) and service-oriented architecture (SOA) may turn the legacy systems (as well as the rest of business applications) into strategic assets at a much lower cost.

16.11 Managing change and user issues

When considering the implementation of e-commerce, a question to think about is the existing structure, as well as the organizational culture. This requires focusing on an organization's business structure and business processes with the existing IT systems, as well as examining new processes suitable specifically for e-commerce. Existing processes often have to be re-engineered in order to align them with the new processes, which requires major changes in the way business is organized or operates, hence the need for change management. Change management is the process of planning, controlling, coordinating, executing and monitoring changes that affect business. It requires considerable emphasis on the management of change skills and responsibilities. There are three main aspects of managing change:

1   use of the initial, vision-creating phase to unfreeze the organization and make employees 'change prone'; at the same time, attention should be paid to the potential causes of resistance and these are minimized;
2   placing of duty on all staff for appropriate aspects of change to create a sense of ownership;
3   placing of specific responsibility on one or more senior executives (a change champion) to facilitate the process of change.

The process of effective change management starts with quick recognition of a need for change in response to a new threat, changes in the market place or simply the implementation of new business plans or technologies. Change resulting from e-commerce implementation affects many people in organizations. Uncertainties resulting from changes are usually addressed by getting as many employees involved as possible at all stages of a project lifecycle. When considering the implementation of e-commerce, changes in organizational structure as well as the organizational culture often result. This requires focusing on an organization's business structure and business processes with the existing IT systems, as well as examining new processes designed specifically for e-commerce. Existing processes often have to be re-engineered in order to align them with the new processes. Therefore, companies should be ready to face this challenge; strategic planning is required to manage ongoing changes.

E-commerce systems will be used by a number of different types of people, including customers, executives and management staff, as well as other interested parties such as trade partners and even competitors. Many systems fail simply because one or more types of user refuses to use a system or uses stealth tactics to undermine the new system. This phenomenon is often referred to as *user resistance*. To minimize user resistance it is important to understand the main causes. Generally speaking, there are many underlying complex issues of cognitive and motivational factors which give rise to improved quality or improved acceptance by users.

The first phase in dealing with user resistance is to ensure that users from all hierarchical levels are involved in consultations about the need for the new technologies. Consultations should include the choices an organization has, and should continue throughout the development stage, including training and incentives for adopting new technologies or working practices. Ayadi (2006) argues that implementation failures of new technologies often occur because the executives focus on financial and technical feasibility rather than organizational or social feasibility. An organizational or social feasibility study would have dealing with user issues at its core. It is also essential in e-commerce to get customers (arguably the most important users of the system) involved, but this is much more complex than the implementation of internal consultation, and requires different strategies. Customer involvement in feasibility studies, systems testing and so on requires a higher level of incentives than is required where the users are employees. Focus groups that include users from different customer segments are useful in addressing this issue.

At implementation stage, internal users may fear job losses, or loss of power or status, which may result in a demoralized workforce. In extreme cases, some employees may even try to sabotage the new system in order to avoid the perceived negative consequences. This issue can be addressed by implementing a comprehensive human resources management strategy covering changes in working practices, job appraisal and training programmes.

The size of an organization is one of the key factors affecting the adoption of new technologies. The larger the organization, the more resources and capital need to be allocated to facilitate adoption. The existence of a new technology's champions also influences the adoption. Champions are needed among top management as well as at middle and lower ranks of an organization to keep people around them motivated. Perceived usefulness is also widely believed to be a key facilitator of adoption. If people in an organization get convinced that a new initiative is good for the organization as well as for themselves, they become more motivated to adopt the new technology and related changes.

Many customers will also be reluctant to adopt e-commerce. Understanding the rationale in resisting e-commerce is of value to companies in enabling the development of plans to achieve widespread adoption. What motivates someone to use e-commerce for their buying needs? Often there has to be an added value (lower cost or convenience, etc.) in using the Internet. Many would only use it if they perceive e-commerce to be of higher value.

If lack of awareness is causing people to hesitate or resist Internet-based services, the organizations can launch a properly planned communications campaign to give information tailored to help in this situation (Kuisma *et al.*, 2007). The feelings of insecurity and learning issues that are common barriers to adoption could be avoided by proper marketing campaigns, communication with customers, customer training and user-friendly website design. To facilitate adoption, organizations also need to adopt a systematic approach to customers' learning processes and adopt their tutorials and other training material according to the learning needs of their customers.

Technology adoption is usually slow if too much attention is paid to technical aspects, rather than business processes and social issues. Some companies sell their e-commerce projects as 'pilot' or 'learning' vehicles and leave its development to the IT department, and many senior executives equate 'going online' with a specific technology rather than using digital technologies to implement their organization's strategic objectives. Going online is about serving customers, creating innovative products/services, leveraging organizational talent, achieving significant improvements in productivity, and increasing revenues.

16.12 Ethical issues

Consideration of the ethics of e-commerce have mainly focused on areas relating to the use/abuse of information collected through analysing online customer behaviour. In this context, the main issues may include security/privacy of information about individuals, accuracy of information, ownership of information and intellectual property, accessibility of information held and what uses of this information are ethically acceptable. These relate to: freedom of choice; transparency; facilitating fraud (ethical/illegal activities of others).

One of the main benefits of e-commerce is that organizations can improve service and potentially generate more profits for shareholders and job security for employees. On the other hand, job losses are one of the methods of cutting costs, and this has numerous negative implications for those affected. The displacement of job opportunities away from face-to-face and back-office service roles to IS professionals is a common feature of e-commerce. How organizations deal with this issue often raises ethical issues which may be mitigated by a careful and considerate approach to change management.

Fraudulent activity by individuals and businesses is both illegal and unethical, but what about the *facilitating* of fraudulent activity? How much responsibility do organizations have to prevent their services being used to aid unethical or illegal activities such as money laundering or spending money online made through corruption? How about balancing the need for revenues with policing and ensuring compliance with ethical standards? All these are tricky questions that face many organizations, and are even more difficult to deal with in the online environment.

Taking personal relationships out of business processes has the effect of dehumanizing the process. A client's relationship with an organization or an employee may have developed over years of loyal customer commitment. Reducing this to boxes ticked and computer-generated numbers/models would, according to an ethic of care, result in the loss of the development of individual relationships, the human touch and the use of intuition. Such aspects may be viewed as necessary to the new electronic economy, but human networks are just as important a part of business practice as the efficiencies associated with e-commerce.

E-commerce also allows for the concealment of the real identity of suppliers of a product or service. This white labelling (products sold without clearly labelling the source/supplier) may offer extraordinarily misleading information about the source (Harris and Spence, 2002). This and many other ethical issues remain to be addressed, and progress seems to be slow.

16.13 Human resource management

Human resources (HR) management is a key factor in the success in e-commerce. E-commerce HR requires special skills because HR functions such as HR planning, job analysis and job design, recruitment and selection, job progression, appraisal process, training and compensation would be different from other traditional business areas. Often, e-commerce professionals need special skills, and as a result they are still in short supply so e-commerce brings a special set of challenges for the HR function. To succeed in this, the HR function must recognize the inherent differences between e-business and traditional bricks-and-mortar business, and adapt to these changes.

The most obvious changes for human resources may include the need to identify employees with skills different from those found in more traditional organizations. People working in e-commerce are often doing jobs that did not exist before and are working in an organization or division that did not exist before. Therefore, basic HR problems are exaggerated for e-commerce environments. For a typical e-commerce project, HR needs to recruit employees with a wide range of skills, such as:

- technical staff like Internet architects, designers and developers, infrastructure specialists, website managers, Internet security experts and a team administrator;
- business-focused staff like content experts for marketing or sales and specialists like website graphics designers;
- IT-related staff such as programmers and analysts;
- managerial staff for strategic planning, relationship management, project management, content creation/management and process integration.

In addition to the above specific skills, knowledge, aptitudes and other characteristics are desirable and combined in a proper way so they can work together to accomplish the desired goals. A good understanding of these job roles, skills and issues would be required to recruit, retain, organize and develop an e-commerce department or team.

Employees with relevant skills are aware that they can easily find an attractive job in an active job market where their skills are highly valued. Problems in HR could mean that organizations lose these valuable employees. A related HR problem concerns organizational design. Some firms find that the changes resulting from e-commerce can be best managed by a new organizational design. Some choose to create a separate 'online unit' division that handles the e-commerce operations. This separate entity is usually expected to be integrated with the rest of the operation after some time. These separate entities often have a more entrepreneurial and informal culture which is suitable for online business operations so they are better able than their parent companies to attract the type of talent needed.

16.14 Summary

This chapter covered a number of challenges and issues in e-commerce management. We discussed consumer issues, employee management, some aspects of change management and HR management. E-marketing and how it helps in e-commerce was covered in detail, as were the ways in which organizations can win online customer trust. We also covered the ethical issues in the online environment. These include use of consumer data for marketing purposes or prevention of money laundering, etc.

Online trust is an important aspect of e-commerce. Although trust in e-commerce shares many common elements with off-line trust, it is different in that technology rather than just the organizational entity is an object of trust. The consequences of breach of trust include loss of stakeholder satisfaction, loyalty and ultimately loss of customers. Information security management is another area covered in this chapter. Information security in e-commerce is very much dominated by technologically biased, operationally focused, pragmatic controls. Human considerations are largely ignored, so we have suggested an approach informed by social theory. The approach gains its credibility from an explicit basis in social theory, from which an evaluative model and method of implementation have been crafted.

Glossary

Customer relationship management (CRM)　CRM defines a class of software applications which integrate the management of: customer service, marketing and sales into a unified system. CRM systems provide an enhanced ability to share information, better tracking of customers, automation of routine services and enabling the customer to manage parts of their own data.

Data mining　The primary goal of data mining is to extract useful information from databases where tracking that extracted information was not the original goal of the database. Its practical application is to make better use of existing information in projecting sales and marketing efforts, and can also be very useful when trying to enter new, but related, markets.

Enterprise resource planning (ERP)　ERP systems are designed to consolidate all back-end systems across the enterprise into a series of interrelated software applications. Depending on the company, it is used to track and manage operations involving the manufacturing of goods, inventory control, accounting, human resources, marketing and long-term planning.

Encryption　A data-security technique used to protect information from unauthorized inspection or alteration. Information is encoded so it appears as a meaningless string of letters and symbols during delivery or transmission. Upon receipt, the information is decoded using an encryption key.

Firewall　A firewall is a point on the network topography, generally between two disparate networks, that enforce rules on what types of data can pass through that point. In businesses, firewalls are generally used to prevent unwanted traffic from coming or leaving a private network.

Information management　This describes the measures required for the effective collection, storage, access, use and disposal of information to support agency business processes. The core of these measures is the management of the definition, ownership, sensitivity, quality and accessibility of information. These measures are addressed at appropriate stages in the strategic planning lifecycle and applied at appropriate stages in the operational lifecycle of the information itself.

Information systems　Organized collections of hardware, software, supplies, policies, procedures and people, which store, process and provide *access* to information.

Internet　A cooperative message-forwarding system linking computer networks all over the world.

Knowledge management   Knowledge management is a framework (methodology) of enabling individuals, teams and entire organizations to collectively and systematically create, share and apply knowledge, using various tools to better achieve their objectives.

Legacy systems   A term commonly used to refer to existing computer systems and applications with which new systems or applications must exchange information.

Middleware   Software that acts as an intermediary between different computer applications so they can communicate with each other.

Outsourcing   The practice of contracting with another entity to perform services that might otherwise be conducted in-house.

Service-oriented architecture   A service-oriented architecture is a flexible set of design principles used during the phases of systems development and integration.

Website   The service of providing ongoing support and monitoring of an Internet-addressable computer that stores webpages and processes transactions initiated over the Internet.

References

Ayadi, A. (2006) Technological and Organisational Preconditions to Internet Banking Implementation: Case of a Tunisian Bank, *Journal of Internet Banking and Commerce, 11(1)*. Available online at: www.arraydev.com/commerce/jibc (accessed 12 May 2010).

Becker, S. (2005) Technical Opinion: E-government Usability for Older Adults, *Communications of the ACM*, 48(2), 102–104.

Clarke, S.A. (2007) *Information Systems Strategic Management: An Integrated Approach*, 2nd edition. London: Routledge.

Harris, L. and Spence, L. (2002) The Ethics of E-banking, *Journal of Electronic Commerce Research*, 3(2), 59–65.

Kuisma, T., Laukkanen, T., and Hiltunen, M. (2007) Mapping the Reasons for Resistance to Internet Banking: A Means–End Approach, *International Journal of Information Management*, 27, 75–85.

Shah, M. and Clarke, S. (2009) *E-Banking Management: Issues, Solutions and Strategies*. Hershey, PA: IGI Global.

Shah, M. and Siddiqui, F. (2006) Organisational success factors in e-banking at the Woolwich, *International Journal of Information Management*, 26, 442–456.

Talha, M., Shrivastva, D., Kabra, P., and Salim, A. (2004) Problems and Prospects of Internet Marketing, *Journal of Internet Banking and Commerce*, 9(1). Available online at www.arraydev.com/commerce/jibc/0402-02.htm.

Wang, Y.D. and Emurian, H.H. (2005) An Overview of Online Trust: Concepts, Elements, and Implications, *Computers in Human Behavior*, 21, 105–125.

Further reading

Chaffey, D. (2010) *E-Business and E-Commerce Management: Strategy, Implementation and Practice*, 4th edition. London: Prentice Hall/Financial Times.

Rust, R. and Oliver, R. (1994) Service Quality: Insights and Managerial Implications from the Frontier, in Rust, R.T. and Oliver, R.L. (eds), *Service Quality: New Directions in Theory and Practice*. London: Sage, pp. 1–20.

Stahl, B. (2008) *Information Systems Critical Perspectives*. London: Routledge.

Xu, L. (2007) *Frontiers in Enterprise Integration*. London: Routledge.

Suggested activities

1   Summarize the e-marketing strategy of a real organization.
2   Discuss the ethics of using customers' information for marketing and customization of products.
3   Discuss trust issues relating to e-commerce and what organizations can do to win the trust of customers.
4   Develop a strategy for an online book-selling company and outline their channel strategy, as well as ways in which they can maximize profits.

17 Knowledge management

Fujitsu is the third largest information technology (IT) company in the world. Their headquarters is in Japan and they have large divisions in the USA and the United Kingdom. They deal with many different types of industries, including financial services, retail, government, health care and utilities. The company spans markets that include computing products, telecommunications, microelectronics and IT services.

Fujitsu UK (uk.fujitsu.com) provides a knowledge management (KM) consulting service, which is an important part of their portfolio. Fujitsu UK has an interesting philosophy to KM that is different from many other companies. Fujitsu UK believes KM should have two areas of concern. There should be a global strategy and local implementation (Brompton, 2002). This means there should be organizational benefits realized that affect the company as a whole that fit different aspects of the organization. This produces a hybrid of top-down and bottom-up approaches.

The hybrid theory seems to be an ideal. Whether or not it is an ideal in that it seem to be for the best but cannot be attained, or it is the best because it must be obtained, is the dilemma. It is not difficult to argue that if a knowledge management system (KMS) does not have support from the people who are going to fund and guide it, and from the people who are going to implement it, it will not reach its full potential and will eventually fade out.

The way Fujitsu UK approaches KM is focused on how the knowledge should be used. This deals with transferring the knowledge to the point of performance. This is just a fancy term for using the knowledge to get a specific task done. Where the knowledge is used to perform a task is the point of performance.

Fujitsu UK believes that transferable knowledge is the most important. This type of knowledge can be used directly at the point of performance, without additional reflection, analysis or consolidation. This kind of knowledge is, however, hard to obtain because almost any kind of knowledge probably has to be reflected on at some level, or even analysed, so that it may be used effectively for a particular situation. Fujitsu UK notes that there are four dimensions of using knowledge that need to be taken into consideration. These dimensions are: people, processes, organization and technology.

One important use of KM to Fujitsu UK is in value management, which is about making business decisions by being better informed, especially helpful in the area of investing. Fujitsu UK argue that by managing the knowledge gained from real-world experience and client scenarios, they can help companies make better business decisions.

Fujitsu UK also realizes that e-learning is a significant contributor to knowledge management. This means knowledge that is attainable by collaboration with experts and other team members via email, e-forums or telecommunication in general can enhance the knowledge of an organization. This is a quick and effective way to learn about knowledge or create and capture knowledge in the organization, because it is more easily accessible.

Fujitsu UK believes that too heavy an emphasis on technology can overshadow the importance of how a KMS will be used to benefit the organization. Being an IT company, Fujitsu UK obviously recognizes the importance of technology, but feels that it should not take precedence over knowledge use when developing and evolving a KMS. Fujitsu UK realizes the importance of a sharing culture and that the lack of one is one of the biggest impediments to a successful KMS.

Fujitsu UK implemented a KMS for the UK Department of Health. The Department of Health realized that there was an enormous amount of knowledge within the organization, but much of it was disorganized, with no structure. Fujitsu UK helped create a top-down framework and build it upon the bottom-up framework of knowledge-sharing initiatives that Fujitsu UK had helped create earlier.

Fujitsu UK also helped jurors to be more knowledgeable about the UK court system before jury duty, which assisted jurors in becoming more focused on the case itself rather than being concerned about how the justice system works. As part of this, Fujitsu UK developed Juror Online, which provides a virtual tour of the UK justice system. A juror that is knowledgeable about the justice system can possibly make better decisions when it comes to the deliberation process.

17.1 Intended learning outcomes

On completion of this chapter the reader should be able to:

1   explain the rise of knowledge management (KM), what KM is, why it is important and why it is complex;
2   critically review major concepts in KM, such as knowledge sharing and learning organizations;
3   classify different approaches to KM;
4   appraise KM for obtaining competitive advantage;
5   critically evaluate a substantial case study using KM.

17.2 Background

Over the past two decades, the term 'knowledge management' has become a buzz phrase, yet the meaning of KM is still being widely debated. While many large and well-known private and public sector organizations have created KM departments, it is debatable as to what impact KM has had and how it should be measured. What is clear is that chief executives consider KM to be highly valuable in today's world.

In a global economy, business success and survival have become increasingly difficult to ensure, partly due to the emergence of a new era of organizational forms that embrace change. The emphasis is now on adaptability to the business environment and on addressing market and customer needs proactively. Organizations are evolving from traditional, permanently structured entities to more fluid businesses, across a wide range of sectors. These include manufacturing, health care, entertainment and education. Whatever the sector, there is a growing view that knowledge creation and retention are keys to gaining and retaining a competitive edge. KM is of major importance to all kinds of organizations, and this importance is growing. An Internet trawl will result in literally thousands of entries regarding this area. To emphasize the growth in this area, Sveiby (2001) gives the following as examples of organizations engaged in KM: Benetton, General Electric, National Bicycle, Netscape, Ritz Carlton, Agro Corp, Frito-Lay, Dow Chemical, Outokumppu, Skandia Switzerland, Steelcase, 3M, Analog Devices, Boeing, Buckman Labs, Chaparral Steel, Ford Motor Co., Hewlett-Packard, Oticon, WM-data, McKinsey, Bain & Co., Chevron, British Petroleum, PLS-Consult, Skandia AFS, Telia, Celemi, IBM, Pfizer, Affaersvaerlden, Honda, Xerox, National Technological University, Matsushita, IKEA.

There is little doubt that KM has grown quickly and is set to continue to grow. Knowledge is the prime resource, as without it, other resources are effectively unavailable and it is knowledge that is key to success. Organizations must now recognize that technology-based competitive advantages are transient and the only sustainable advantages are employees, and that the locus of success in the new economy is not in the technology, but in the human mind and organizational memory.

Organizations have seen huge changes to domestic and world economies, and services have become major business in most Western economies. During the last half of the twentieth century manufacturing declined in the Western world. The emphasis on providing services has put knowledge at a premium and physical goods are no longer the prime asset. Of course, physical goods (cars, televisions, etc.) are still produced and purchased, but the rate of increase in the purchase of services has been huge. In addition, many physical goods are now imported. Areas such as management consultancy, financial services, information systems, tourism and so on have grown enormously. All of these have knowledge as the key asset.

The Western world is now a set of knowledge economies – economies that have large proportions of their gross domestic product in the service sector, and where knowledge is at a premium. If organizations did not manage knowledge, they would be disregarding their prime asset. But what does managing knowledge mean? Lehaney *et al.* (2004) provide a comprehensive definition of KM, but it omits something important, and that is the contribution that KM makes to devising strategy. A revised, more accurate definition, based on that provided by Lehaney *et al.* (2004) is therefore:

Knowledge management refers to the systematic organization, planning, scheduling, monitoring and deployment of people, processes, technology and environment, with appropriate targets and feedback mechanisms, under the control of a public or private sector concern, and undertaken by such a concern, to facilitate explicitly and specifically the creation, retention, sharing, identification, acquisition, utilization and measurement of information and new ideas, in order to *inform* and achieve strategic aims, such as improved competitiveness or improved performance, subject to financial, legal, resource, political, technical, cultural and societal constraints.

KM is very strongly connected to systems thinking. In fact, the above definitions are what are known as root definitions, which are found within soft systems methodology. Those concepts are beyond the scope of this chapter, but there is an immense amount of material available on this area, and the interested reader should have no difficulty finding it. Systems thinking considers an organization as a whole. Within that whole (system) are other systems, and within those are even more systems. Each system interacts with others to create the firm's good or services. Communication is key to such interactions, and if communication is not managed, it may not be as effective and efficient as it could be. This may mean that valuable knowledge is not shared.

To compete effectively in the twenty-first century, organizations must generate, store, retrieve, retain and use knowledge. The type of knowledge we are considering is known as organizational knowledge, and KM is about managing this. Organizations need to interact with their environments, obtain information, turn it into knowledge and combine this with their experiences, values and internal rules in order to take effective action. Knowledge management is critically important in regard to organizational adaptation, survival and competence, especially when the environment is changing at a rapid pace. KM works at the interface of people, processes and technology, and it is about the creative capacity of human beings, the exchange of ideas and much more. Any design of a KM framework or system should ensure that adaptation and innovation of business performance take place in line with the changing dynamics of the business environment.

For many reasons, KM has become closely associated with technology. Yet discussion, focus groups, interviews, meetings and workshops do not require a computer. It would be difficult to deny these as means to create and exchange knowledge. Nowadays, technology has an enabling role in these activities and in the storage and retrieval of information, but it does not replace human communication. There is a danger that KM is being perceived as being so entwined with technology that its critical aspects and success factors will be lost. Vendors have relabelled document management software, databases and so forth as KM solutions, and this gives rise to the myth that KM is IT. It is not. ISs are about providing the right information to the right person at the right time, but KM goes far beyond that.

In the last two decades of the twentieth century, a resource-based theory of the firm became more widely accepted as an alternative to the traditional product-based or competitive advantage view. This resource-based view is linked to strategy and knowledge-based services. The term 'strategy' is usually associated with long-term perspectives about an organization and its environment. The resource-based approach tends to place more emphasis on an organization's capabilities or core competencies than do the competitive-based and product-based approaches. Thus KM is strongly linked to the concept of a learning organization, which again links to communication and change.

A knowledge-based strategy formulation should start with intangible resources, which are the people. Physical products and assets result from human actions, and depend on people for their continued existence. Organizations work on informal structures and dynamic relationships created by people. People can use their abilities to create value by creating and transferring knowledge externally or internally to their organization.

17.3 What is knowledge management?

The last section gave some background and a definition of KM. This section will discuss the meaning of KM in more detail.

KM, in an organizational sense, is about controlling, organizing and planning all or parts of processes to use information to help develop, share and retain new ideas. KM has various approaches and definitions according to the perspective and discipline of the individual or organization that engages with it. These include management, individual and organizational learning, communications, information systems and technology, artificial intelligence, intellectual assets and so on. Each discipline approaches KM with a different perception – for example, computer science focuses heavily on technology; human resources takes an individual and organizational approach emphasizing learning and reward factors; and intellectual assets focus on the explicit capture and registration of knowledge.

KM requires a mix of business awareness, creative attitudes and practices, systems, tools, policies and procedures, designed to release the power of information and ideas. KM is about supporting innovation, capturing insight, facilitating the finding and re-use of resources, fostering collaboration, improving the quality of decision-making and using intellectual assets wisely.

KM must focus an organization on improving its actions to exploit the power of knowledge. KM is concerned with the creation, generation, codification and transfer of information and ideas and with trying to make the best use of both tacit and explicit knowledge. The power of KM is in allowing organizations to enable and support explicitly these activities to leverage their value for the group and organization, as well as for the individual.

In a knowledge economy, the efficient and effective management of knowledge may help organizations gain and retain a competitive edge, but what exactly is it that is to be managed? Surely knowledge resides inside people's heads and cannot be managed? There are a number of ways in which these questions may be addressed, and this section begins by looking at the issues facing organizations in regard to knowledge and the management of the knowledge process.

Consider an organization that has key staff – that is almost any organization you could name. Let us imagine that this is a service organization, where knowledge is the key ingredient. Let us also imagine that the key members of staff do not return to work tomorrow, for whatever reason. In fact, they never return again. How will the organization fare? Well, if it has encouraged and facilitated knowledge sharing, if it has created contingencies and if it has engaged in succession planning, the impact, although not trivial, will be far less than if it had done none of those things. These are examples of KM, and are related to one of the major concerns of service organizations today, knowledge retention.

Suppose that some staff have left, and that the firm faces stiff competition in its markets. What can change its fortunes? The answer is the creation of new ideas, such as new ways to market existing products, new versions of old products and brand new products. In other words, they are based on knowledge creation, and knowledge creation is a key factor in competitiveness in a service economy. How is it that one firm creates new knowledge rather than another? It is not easy to force people to create knowledge, but firms can create the conditions under which staff may want to create knowledge, may feel empowered to create knowledge, and may feel rewarded for creating knowledge.

Such conditions may include incentive schemes, a good working environment, appropriate technology, a feeling of being listened to by the bosses and myriad other factors. These things may be seen purely as costs, or they may be seen as investments.

Knowledge creation is the reason that many large organizations have a research and development (R&D) department. If a purely short-term, bottom-line financial perspective were to be taken, such work would be unsupportable. However, firms see the benefits in the medium- to long-term, and they recognize their investment as just that. Investments cost money, and that is one of the reasons that knowledge retention is so important. It would be a severe blow to have someone in R&D leave to go to another firm before they reveal the results of a project on which they have been working for the last five years. How do firms guard against this? Knowledge sharing is one important way in which organizations may help reduce knowledge loss through staff leaving. The more people who are involved in a project, and who are familiar with it and understand it, the less of an impact on that project if one person leaves. Such sharing is often considered as a technical exercise. That is, if an organization obtains more hi-tech machines and a greater networking capability, it is seen as a knowledge-sharing solution.

This is far from the truth, and a number of things must be recognized about knowledge sharing. First, to share knowledge, by definition, communications must be open. Improving the quality of communications will help improve knowledge sharing. However, many organizations appear to measure quality in terms of quantity. If you ask how they have improved the quality of communications, they reply along the lines that they have spent thousands of dollars on computers and networks, and they have far more of them than they used to have. Whether or not communications have improved appears to be irrelevant as long as there are more of them. A further answer given would be something like: 'There are more people networked and on email than there used to be.' All of this misses the point. Technology may help facilitate communication between people, but it is people who decide whether to communicate and what they will or will not communicate. 'Rubbish in, rubbish out' is the old adage. In addition, people are impinged upon by the structures of an organization (i.e. its business processes). They also help to create such processes, and the structure may help or hinder knowledge sharing. Thus knowledge sharing depends upon staff, structures and technology, and these three are intertwined. These three elements are also intertwined when it comes to knowledge identification. Staff may be willing to share knowledge, but how do other staff know that knowledge is there and how do they identify it as being relevant to their needs?

Having identified knowledge, it is important also to examine knowledge acquisition. That is, in what ways is it possible for people to gain knowledge from inside or outside the organization? All of the rest is of no use whatsoever, unless that knowledge is used. Thus knowledge utilization must be considered. How is knowledge used, why is it used and in what ways? Could it be used to better effect? Finally, unless there are some knowledge targets and a knowledge feedback loop, we will not know if we are succeeding and if we can do better. The question of 'how do we know?' is key to knowledge management, and it is linked to the really difficult question of 'how do we know what we know?'. This, in turn, is linked to the question: 'What do we mean by the word *know*?'

Know-how may be used in the sense that we know how to do a particular task or activity, and the way we use the phrase in everyday terms, such as, 'he has a lot of know-how when it comes to cars'. This is concerned with the knowledge of how to get things done, and sometimes such knowledge is explicit in organizational policies and procedures, but it is very often tacit, within people's heads. You may even have experienced this in regard to car repairs. You can buy the manual, follow the instructions and it is straightforward – except that it often isn't. You become frustrated because the picture in the manual is slightly different to how your car is on the ground. The instruction to release the micro-adjuster bolt on the distributor is meaningless because there is no bolt. You take the car to the garage, and the guy fixes it – without even looking at a manual. Hey, guess what? You've just paid for his knowledge.

Know-who may be used to mean knowing who can help, knowing who won't help, knowing who will hinder, knowing who will laugh, knowing who will cry. This is very much about people and people skills. It relies to some extent on judgement, sensitivity and the ability to understand others' strengths and weaknesses. One of the most important abilities a manager can have is the judgement of people. This starts at recruitment, when the manager is faced with a stack of applications to short-list. After that, it may be a 15-minute interview with each candidate which decides who gets the job. How does the manager know which person to select? If we could distil that knowledge from good managers, and pass it around, we would all be much wiser. How many managers can say that they have never made a mistake in recruitment?

Know-when may be used in the standard everyday sense; it is about timing your words or actions. For example, skilled stockmarket operators seem to have the knack of buying when everyone else is selling. Some companies have made a virtue of their timing of take-overs and market entry strategies.

Know-where can mean knowing where knowledge may be obtained, and it can mean knowing where things are best carried out. Levers of change are often reinforced or reach critical mass in specific localities where people with specific skills congregate – places like Silicon Valley for high technology, or the City of London or New York for international finance.

Know-why refers to the wider context and the vision. This context knowledge allows individuals to go about unstructured tasks in the most appropriate ways. An example is doing what is right by a customer rather than slavishly following a procedure.

Know-that is the basic sense of knowing. It represents accepted 'facts', but also experience and access to learning. A skilled repairman, for example, instinctively knows that the cause of a problem is likely to be found in a particular component.

KM may be considered in a variety of ways. One typology is to classify KM by distinguishing between tacit and explicit. Pure data would be of little use to a typical manager, and structured data – as information – is useful to analyse and solve problems. Knowledge, however, is obtained from experts and is based on expert experience, as it requires a higher understanding than information alone. Explicit information comprises facts or data that is organized in a structured way, whereas knowledge incorporates values, beliefs, perspectives, judgements and know how.

Knowledge only becomes meaningful when it is seen in the larger context of culture, which evolves out of beliefs and philosophy. It is important to recognize context-dependent information as this distinguishes information and knowledge. For example, creating and reproducing conditional statements when exchanging and sharing knowledge presents problems for the codification of knowledge into information, and certain tacit knowledge cannot be reproduced anyway.

An alternative typology is by emphasis on technology or emphasis on people, but it is important that both aspects of KM are addressed, and that the available or developing technology is related to user requirements and is user-driven. Within the technical domain, researchers and practitioners are likely to have a computing or IT background, and will be involved in putting together the IT needed for management of ISs, artificial intelligence, reengineering, groupware, etc. In this sense, knowledge may be seen as objects that can be identified, monitored and controlled. If KM is considered this way, it is a relatively new discipline.

Within the people domain, researchers and practitioners are likely to have a background in business, organizational behaviour and management, or social science, and they will be involved in assessing, changing and improving skills or behaviour of individuals, or the examination and adjustment of the social systems that make up organizations. In this sense, knowledge may be seen as processes that comprise a range of experience and skills that are continually changing. They are traditionally involved in learning and in managing these competencies individually (like psychologists) or at an organizational level (like philosophers, sociologists or organizational theorists). If KM is considered this way, it may be seen as a discipline that stretches back for thousands of years. While the concepts of knowledge and management are old, only quite recently have they been put together in this way. This is probably because management has been seen to be principally about clearly definable objects and processes such as finances, project management, corporate strategy, etc. Those elements that did not appear on the financial returns often escaped specific attention.

Even the task of managing people (human resource management) has experienced difficulties in gaining recognition. Thus, despite its obvious importance for many industries, the roles of the various types of knowledge have seldom been specifically addressed in management theory and practice. Accountants normally cover it under terms such as intangibles and goodwill. Failure to consider concerns, which were not accounted for in traditional financial analysis, such as the feelings of communities and the social costs of a company's actions, could result in strategic weaknesses. Weaknesses may arise if firms ignore the acceptability of strategic options to key stakeholders. Stakeholders may seem relatively passive and even disinterested, but stakeholder groups tend to emerge and influence strategy as a result of specific events, such as the formulation and evaluation of potential new strategies. It is vitally important that the likely reactions of such groups, whether internal or external, are given appropriate consideration. Damaging situations may arise if their interest levels are underestimated. This is of particular concern if such groups act to thwart the implementation of a strategy that has involved time and cost to develop, and, even worse, if no sensible and acceptable alternative strategy has been formulated.

It should be clear from the previous paragraphs that these issues are raised because in the twenty-first century they may help determine the long-term success of an organization. Managers will typically try to reduce ambiguity by looking for that which is familiar. It is the abilities of managers to relate to their external environment, to their internal culture and to the people around them that will determine such success.

KM can help adaptability by enabling the sharing of knowledge more easily, more effectively, more efficiently and more systematically. The foregoing discussions are especially important in a post-industrial society and for service organizations within such a society. For both internal and external purposes, KM is important to success and competitive edge. If knowledge sharing is to occur, and if it is to be managed, it is self-evident that for the former communication is vital, and for the latter, policies, procedures and strategies will play a key role if anything other than ad hoc communications is to be achieved. Good communications are key to knowledge management and creation.

While communication is regarded as key to KM, it is also an essential ingredient in many management theories, from operational and strategic perspectives. For example, it would be difficult to deny the importance of corporate communications, the role and function of communication executives and the impact of corporate communications upon the formulation of corporate strategy. It would also be difficult to deny the importance of informal communications in excellent companies and the advantages in relation to action and progress, rather than formal bureaucratic communication, found in some organizations.

Communication is central to the success of KM, both from an information theory perspective in relation to the technical domain and a constructivist perspective in relation to the people domain. Organizations often experience difficulties achieving effective communication in both areas. This may be a common difficulty more often in traditional bureaucratic organizations and specifically in relation to tacit knowledge.

When thinking about classical management approaches and organization hierarchies, communication problems could be as a result of the environment and organizational structure, but may also be because the concept of communication is not fully recognized and often reflects a one-way process rather than an exchange or dialogue.

Formal and explicit knowledge can easily be processed by a computer, transmitted electronically or stored in databases. Explicit knowledge tends to be about hard facts, quantifiable information, policies and procedures, whereas tacit knowledge is the experience and wisdom developed as a result of using and applying hard information, while absorbing the internal and external environment and culture of the organization and its industry. While converting tacit knowledge into explicit knowledge is important, this could simply mean the systemization of people's thought processes and wisdom, rather than valuing the workforce's collective knowledge, as well as their individuality and the contribution they make to the organization. The process of converting tacit to explicit for purposes of communication and providing value to an organization, therefore, appears to be an idealistic concept.

It could be argued that formal organizational systems are limited in scope and cannot capture the culture of the organization. Alternatively, there may be methods that could provide means of translating tacit knowledge to an understandable language with aspects of knowledge converting to be explicit. However, only aspects of tacit knowledge will successfully convert, as much of tacit knowledge is built on a foundation of social conditioning, values and beliefs, which form individual perspectives of the world. Alternatively, perhaps there is no need to convert the tacit to the explicit; to manage tacit knowledge in a way that complements and implicitly contributes to the organization, managers create and access their own networks of informal communication.

While a communication process may incorporate a variety of techniques ranging from reports, visual identity, correspondence and electronic communications, there is no guarantee that the intended message has been received and understood. In the technical domain, often the information is more quantifiable so the same problems are less likely to arise. However, tacit and explicit knowledge are not entirely separable forms of knowledge, because all explicit knowledge has a tacit dimension. This is further highlighted when considering that communication is a broader concept than just exchanging information, but incorporating behaviour as well. Thus, communication addresses issues such as the interpretation of the intended message, intention of those delivering the information, relationship influences and the context in which the message is set, all of which clarify meaning, but still only to a certain extent. Social conditioning, cultural differences and other external influences will always impact to convert the message into a meaningful translation and context for the individual receiving, or not at all as the case may be.

It is clear from the foregoing that communication relates to KM generally, and learning is allied to this. The whole concept of learning involves sharing and acquiring knowledge, and from a sociological perspective, the interpersonal relationships that construct and convey meaning. Putting this in context, organizations consist of individuals and groups, which require management of complex relationships and processes that constitute or contribute to managing knowledge. To fully understand a message requires that the sender and receiver possess mutual mental models, and any prior knowledge individuals possess will influence the process. Teams, however, can eventually develop a common understanding and shared knowledge, but communicating the team knowledge to those outside the team can be difficult. This raises two issues. First, operational management processes in relation to individuals in a social context; it is a truism that knowledge sharing will only be successful if the facilities and systems are easily accessible and easy to use. Second, the concept of KM and complexity of communication appear to relate comfortably to the concept of systems and contingency strategic management. KM could be dependent on cross-organizational influences and interactions internally and externally, which set the context in which knowledge is shared.

The relationship between managing knowledge and people can be difficult and contentious, because knowledge is still regarded as a personal rather than organizational commodity and is still associated with power, money and organizational politics. Indeed, the status, incomes and power of professionals depend to a large extent on their expertise. The less able people are to understand this expertise, the greater the difference between the supply and demand for professional services.

The idea that organizations have knowledge is appropriate, assuming that individuals remain with the organization. However, when a member of staff leaves, they take with them tacit knowledge – and in some cases explicit knowledge, if it has not been codified effectively. Tacit knowledge is difficult if not impossible to replace, because the individual's contribution to the success of the organization could have been unique to that person. Furthermore, attempts to measure tacit knowledge require the organization to understand the concept of what the knowledge is that they are looking for in the first place.

The foregoing puts to question the view that no one is indispensable. For example, levels of dispensability may be different according to the amount of expertise and knowledge an individual has. If it is organizationally desirable for knowledge to be shared and transparent, then why would an individual volunteer that knowledge? Further, to what extent do managers truly know what knowledge resides in their organization and how this could be communicated effectively? If an organization does not have appropriate codification and communication of explicit knowledge, again, problems emerge if the member of staff responsible for a particular area leaves and has not shared that knowledge. One approach that could be considered to address this could be found by considering KM in the context of learning organizations.

Learning in an organization may be described as a process by which an organization gathers and uses new knowledge, with appropriate consideration for the tools, behaviours and values at all levels. Newly learned knowledge is translated into new goals, procedures, roles and performance measures. Learning organizations, however, can mean different things to different people. For example, one view refers to the organization as a whole. An alternative view makes reference to all of the individual systems and subsystems of learning throughout the organization. Learning is an issue in organizations that operate in fast-changing environments, and the role of learning, conceptualization of training and development, and maximization of learning becomes of greater importance as the pace of change increases.

From the discussion so far the question as to who owns organizational knowledge emerges. The concept of intangible assets has become more important as organizations increasingly become knowledge-driven. While, traditionally, strategic management viewed organizations as a compilation of physical and human resources and systems, the main objective related to profit maximization; however, with the increase in service organizations and focus on human resources, human assets are now considered as a key resource.

The ability to manage the intellect of human resources, including creativity and sharing of knowledge, has a direct impact on the maximization of the organization overall, not necessarily to be realized in the tangibles of the profit margin, but the overall market value of the organization. Intellectual capital includes organizational and individually accumulated knowledge, ability, skill and expertise. Individuals, however, do not necessarily possess the skills that incorporate everything; therefore the manager's challenge is to understand how their actions affect other elements of the organization.

From this discussion it may be concluded that managing knowledge should be on the strategic management agenda to achieve exceptional performance and sustainable competitive advantage, and to use knowledge efficiently and rapidly rather than rely on particular products or technologies, which, although tangible, can be easily imitated.

Intellectual capital is, however, extremely difficult to measure. Whereas physical assets are stable and consistent and can be accurately valued and depreciated, intellectual capital cannot be accurately financially valued and can appreciate as well as depreciate.

17.4 Summary

The foregoing discussions highlight that organizations have various resources and capabilities, based around the individual and collective human resources and learning, with internal and external influences. Key issues to emerge include cross-organizational working in people and service-based organizations. The concept of the learning organization can provide individual and collective contribution to improve performance, engendering the trust and interdependency among teams to achieve higher outputs. This involves knowledge sharing from, and influences on, the workforce at all levels and experiences within the organization, and management recognition of the intellectual capital therein.

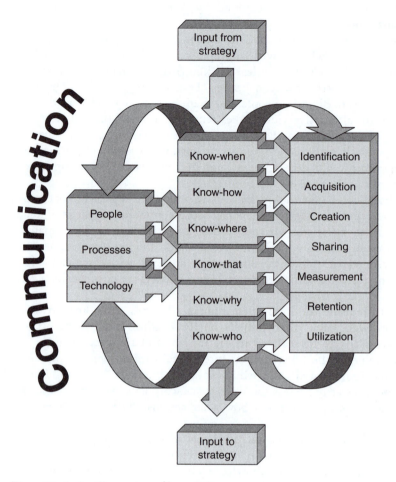

Figure 17. 1 An illustration of knowledge management.

The chapter may be summarized in the form of a diagram, as shown in Figure 17.1. People, processes and technology interact with the six basic forms of knowing and with knowledge processes. Communication is a key factor in KM working successfully. It is important that all of these areas are considered appropriately when organizations engage with KM.

Glossary

Competitive advantage   The relative (against rivals) beneficial differentiation in the market of an organization, by means of cost, market position, product or service.

Explicit knowledge   Knowledge that can be shared by way of discussion or by writing it down and putting it into documents, manuals or databases.

Holism   Holism is about the concept of a system whole being greater than the sum of its parts. It encompasses the notion of *emergent properties*. Holism is sometimes viewed as the antithesis of reductionism.

Information systems   The general term for computer systems in an organization that provide information about its business operations.

Intellectual capital   Knowledge (that can be converted into value or profit) and skills that lead to a competitive edge in the marketplace.

Knowledge assets   Knowledge regarding markets, products, technologies and organizations, owned by an entity allowing it to generate profits and add value.

Knowledge capture   The process of acquiring and storing information, ideas and relationship links in the people, processes and technology within an organization.

Knowledge creation   The creation of new ideas and thoughts.

Knowledge retention   Keeping ideas and thoughts at an organization.

Knowledge sharing   Mechanisms to communicate and disseminate knowledge throughout an organization.

Learning organization   An organization that views its success in the future as being based on continuous learning and adaptive behaviour.

Organizational learning   The ability of an organization to gain knowledge from experience through experimentation, observation, analysis and a willingness to examine both successes and failures, and to then use that knowledge to do things differently.

Procedural knowledge   Knowing rules, methods and documented organizational norms. Procedures: know-what, know-where, know-who, know-how.

Social network   A social structure comprised of nodes (individuals or organizations) that are tied together by one or more types of interdependency.

Soft systems thinking   Soft systems thinking is a holistic approach that aims at understanding problem situations and agreeing what problems exist, with a view to resolving the problem situation. Organizations are viewed as complex social systems in which resolution, as opposed to solution, is sought by debate.

Strategy   Strategy is about long-term planning to achieve competitive advantage.

System   A set of bounded activities, entities and their relationships that together comprise purposeful activity that has at least one emergent property not exhibited by the individual components within the set.

Systems thinking   The study and organization of parts and their dynamic relationships, which comprise a whole, rather than the study of static organizational parts.

Tacit knowledge   The knowledge or know-how that people carry in their heads. Compared with explicit knowledge, tacit knowledge is more difficult to articulate or write down and so tends to be shared between people through discussion, stories and personal interactions.

References

Bali, R., Wickramasinghe, N., and Lehaney, B. (2009) *Knowledge Management Primer*. New York: Routledge.

Brompton, A. (2002) Making Knowledge Management Work in Diverse and Autonomous Organisations, *Spectra Magazine*, Autumn.

Lehaney, B., Clarke, S., Coakes, E., and Jack, G. (2004) *Beyond Knowledge Management*. Hershey, PA: Idea Group Publishing.

Sveiby, K. (2001) *What is Knowledge Management?* Available online at www.sveiby.com/articles/ KnowledgeManagement.html (accessed 19 January 2010).

Suggested activities

1   Find four organizations that use knowledge management that are not listed in this chapter.
2   Discuss how the effectiveness of knowledge management might be evaluated.
3   The rise in services has played a role in the rise of knowledge management. Could knowledge management be used in the manufacturing sector? How?
4   'Knowledge management is not about technology but, other things being equal, firms with effective and efficient technology will be in the premier league and those that do not will be relegated.' Discuss this statement.

18 The project

Case study 18.1 Example of an abstract and Chapter 1 of a project report

This case study is provided to demonstrate the structure and nature of some typical project documentation. Some text has been omitted to reduce its length. Readers are recommended to read the rest of the chapter first, then return to the case study.

Project title

Using soft systems methodology to provide a system specification for outpatient clinic simulation modelling

Abstract

In recent years the United Kingdom's National Health Service (NHS) has received particular attention by various governments in regard to the efficient use of resources. Managing out-patient departments has been of particular interest, with 'league tables' providing published figures on the duration of patients queuing for clinical services. Simulation may be used to model complex problems that are difficult to address by analytical or numerical methods, and thus may be particularly appropriate for NHS applications.

While simulation is a powerful and popular modelling approach, it provides no methodology by which system boundaries and system activities may be identified. This proposal considers the use of soft systems methodology as an aid to drawing system boundaries and identifying system activities, for the purpose of simulating the out-patient department at a local hospital. The participative nature of soft systems methodology is intended to help increase the acceptability of the simulation model.

It is expected that a participatory approach will help improve the quality of model building and model inputs, but this quality is likely to be offset by increased development costs. The trade-off is proposed to be worthwhile, since many simulations have suffered from expectations' failures. In the longer term, 'cheap' development may lead to expensive failures.

1 Aim

This research aims to investigate the potential of soft systems methodology as an effective means to provide a system specification for simulation modelling within the NHS.

2 Objectives

The objectives are to:

a   assess the value of soft systems methodology as a system-specification methodology;

b   establish if a system specification based on a soft systems investigation is useful for simulation modelling;

c   evaluate the potential of such an approach for assisting the attainment of organizational improvements in the NHS.

3 Background

3.1 The NHS

Prior to the establishment of the NHS, health care was provided to some extent by the state, but much was also provided by charities, or on a private basis (Walker, 1995). The National Health Service Act of 1946 created a provision of clinical care for all, with six fundamental principles.

1   A distinction between primary and secondary care was made. General Practitioners (GPs) were to provide first-contact treatment and diagnosis, while hospitals and local health authorities were to provide a more comprehensive range of medical facilities.
2   All health care was to be provided free at point of service.
3   Financing of health care was to come from general taxes.
4   A full service was to be provided, from accident and surgery to geriatric and mental care.
5   Health care was to be available to all.
6   The government was to own the organization and to employ its staff.

[Text omitted here]

3.2 Simulation and soft systems methodology

Appendices 1 and 2 provide detailed discussions of what is meant here by simulation and soft systems methodology [not provided in this document, but this is to demonstrate that the flow would not be interrupted by details of methodologies or techniques].

Surveys, such as those by Hollocks (1992), Beasley and Whitchurch (1984) and Christy and Watson (1983), consistently demonstrate that simulation is one of the most popular techniques used by practitioners. This view is also expressed by many authors, such as Blightman (1987), Jasany (1989) and Kochhar (1989).

In summary, from the above surveys, and from Pidd (1992), and Paul and Balmer (1993), important reasons for using simulation are that:

•   simulation is widely used and is therefore familiar;

[text omitted here]

Simulation does not provide an approach to obtain agreement on system specifications, whereas this is a stated purpose of SSM (Wilson, 1984). SSM has no structure for assessing the feasibility of actions, nor can it demonstrate easily and quickly a number of options from which those that are desirable can be chosen. By using simulation to model a range of options, their desirability and feasibility may be assessed, and informed choices can be made. The combination of simulation with SSM may provide a methodology that is more powerful than either individual approach. It is only recently that SSM has been considered as a co-methodology for simulation (Lehaney and Paul, 1996), and many of the ways in which the linkages are made between the methodologies are left unclear, which leaves scope for further investigation.

4 Research design

4.1 Months 1–3

A substantial literature review of scheduling and planning health service applications of simulation, and of soft methods being used as co-methodologies with other management science approaches. CD-ROM is the main source of material. Write up: literature review (LR).

SSM will be assessed analytically as a system-specification tool. Write up: LR, analysis using SSM.

4.2 Months 4–6

The Information Systems Director of a local hospital has agreed to an investigation of one of the outpatient clinics. SSM will be assessed empirically as a system-specification tool. Write up: LR, empirical results, including interim reports at least every month.

4.3 Months 7–9

Interviews will be conducted with ten senior contacts within the NHS. The literature review will be updated. The case work will be written up.

Content analysis of the interviews will be undertaken. Material will be written up. Substantial chapters will be produced. All written work to date will be collated.

4.4 Rationale

The empirical investigation is intended to increase confidence in the results by means of different data-collection methods and different data sources (triangulation – the case and interviews). The case will provide an in-depth investigation of a single institution.
[text omitted here]

5 Results to date, conclusions and expected results

Some of the 'failures' of simulation in health service applications may be attributed to a lack of any formal process methodologies being applied. There is very little material on soft methods and simulation. The analytical review of SSM should reveal that it provides a good basis for undertaking a system specification for simulation modelling, and the case should support this view. The interviews will probably indicate a low awareness of simulation and SSM, but a high desire to address resource issues successfully. Whether SSM and simulation will be seen as acceptable approaches remains to be seen.

References

Anonymous (1994) Documents on the NHS Reforms. *Nursing Standard* 9(33), 33.
Blightman, B. (1987) Where Now With Simulation?. *Journal of the Operational Research Society* 38(2): 769–770.
Carter, L and Huzan, E. (1973) *A Practical Approach to Computer Simulation in Business.* George Allen & Unwin, London.
Checkland, P.B. (1981) *Systems Thinking, Systems Practice.* Wiley, Chichester.
Checkland, P.B. and Scholes, J. (1990) *Soft Systems Methodology in Action.* Wiley, Chichester.
Christy, D.P. and Watson, H.J. (1983) The Application of Simulation: A Survey of Industrial Practice. *Interfaces* 13(5): 47–52.

[text omitted here]

18.1 Intended learning outcomes

On completion of this chapter the reader should be able to:

1   explain the differences between doing project work and studying taught subjects;
2   devise a suitable topic for a project;
3   identify, use and reference appropriate academic information sources;
4   identify and apply appropriate research methods;
5   formulate a structure for a project report;
6   explain the nature of academic writing and plagiarism.

18.2 Introduction

Students in the final year of an undergraduate course, or undertaking a taught post-graduate course, are very often required to undertake a project to 'round off' their studies. Such a piece of work serves many useful purposes:

- It helps to integrate disparate topics (sometimes called 'islands of learning') studied in isolation from each other over previous years. This is an artificial situation. Real-world problems involve rich mixtures of disciplines and human activity systems, requiring an eclectic mix of technologies, tools, techniques, knowledge and abilities in order to address them.
- It gives students the opportunity to apply concepts, theories and techniques to problems or studies of realistic size and scope.
- It requires students to put together a substantial artefact (report, dissertation, thesis, etc.) which can serve as a 'showcase' to demonstrate their abilities to potential employers when they have completed their studies.
- It allows students to demonstrate their ability to take responsibility for managing their own time and workload.
- It develops students' investigative, organizational and communication skills.

It is sometimes the case that students who do well in more 'academic' subjects struggle with project work, and that those that have found their previous studies difficult are more successful when it comes to this way of working. Perhaps it is more to do with attitude than aptitude. Personal characteristics, such as the ability to exercise self-discipline, to cope with stressful situations, and to manage one's own time effectively, come to the fore when a student must assume responsibility for their own activities as well as the content of their study programme.

Potential employers often take a particular interest in students' project work. This is because employers would like to know that students can cope with the things they would really prefer to avoid (see Table 18.1).

18.3 Types of project

Not all projects are the same. Indeed, the very idea of what constitutes a project can vary greatly between countries, universities, departments and disciplines. We will try, on the one hand, not to be too restrictive or inflexible; on the other hand, we aim to reflect what the authors consider to be a 'good' project – i.e. one that, whether at first degree or masters level, will earn a high mark when assessed.

Table 18.1 Students' and employers' project requirements

What the student wants	What the student gets	What the employer is looking for
A clear schedule of what to do, and when	The lecturer's schedule	Time management skills
Study materials	Some, but most you must research yourself	The ability to carry out independent research
A template for the finished product	Generic advice of the type: 'It depends'	Originality; creativity
To choose your own supervisor	No choice (usually)	The ability to form working relationships
No problems	Problems	Problem-solving ability

Hopefully it will not be disputed that projects should be sizable – although size should be measured in the amount of effort expended rather than number of pages produced. The only other essential characteristic is that projects should be the result of independent work. However, independent certainly does not mean without supervision or guidance – the extent of which may vary considerably.

Most projects can be expected to fall into one or more of the categories discussed below. Those that do not may be so original that they will be spectacularly successful. On the other hand ...

18.3.1 Research

Projects of this type should pose and answer one or more questions. Furthermore, the question(s) should be difficult ones (or at least ones that are far from easy). While you will not be expected to discover the meaning of life, there is little point in setting yourself a problem to which the answer is obvious (or perhaps worse, one about which you have clearly made up your mind beforehand – you must be unbiased). You need to give yourself the opportunity to demonstrate your powers of fact-finding, logical reasoning, evaluation and analysis, etc. Research is *not* simply a matter of gathering and presenting information in a different form.

Try to find a topic about which information is not too readily available. It might be tempting to decide 'I'll do topic A – I can easily find material on that'. But this is likely to result in a project that is simply boring for you and your assessor, because it is based on common knowledge. Furthermore, because of the lack of challenge you are unlikely to earn many marks for it. A project at this level should not be a 'coffee table' product – a glossy offering that presents no challenge for the writer or reader.

18.3.2 Development

Assuming they are given the option, students may choose to undertake a project that entails building or creating something, rather than one that is essentially research-based. However, a significant element of research or its equivalent will still be expected. By 'equivalent' in this context is meant activities that require active investigation, rather than simply following procedures learned in earlier modules or subjects. Activities that might fall into this category include research into user requirements, an investigation into the state of the market for a particular product, or the exploration of alternative development methodologies.

Types of products that might result from a development-type project include:

- a website. However, the building of a website does not in itself pose a degree-level challenge. One might additionally expect one or more of: advanced functionality, originality, demonstration of a business idea; deeply researched content, etc.;
- a design for an information system (including requirements specification, feasibility study, risk analysis and recommendations for implementation);
- functioning software;
- an information system strategy for an organization;
- a network design.

As always, students should speak to their supervisor about what is acceptable or required by their institution.

18.3.3 *Investigation for a client*

If you are lucky, you might be able to find a client for whom you can carry out some work, on which you can base your project. This work may result in the production of an artefact (as in the previous project type), or in a report for your client.

It is important to realize that your aims and those of your client may be quite different, and that you will need to satisfy both. While your client's primary interest will be the benefits that his/her organization can gain from your collaboration, you must consider your academic objectives. Make sure that what is expected of you is agreed (and clearly documented) with the appropriate individuals from the outset. Notwithstanding these extra considerations, there are real advantages to be gained from working with a client, as discussed in the following section.

Some examples of the many possible types of IS and IT client-related project are:

- an investigation into the effectiveness of a recently adopted IS system or recently installed technology;
- an investigation into alternative software packages or solutions to meet a business need, accompanied by recommendations and reasons;
- an evaluation of a product under consideration for purchase and use by the client;
- a comparison of competitors' practices/business processes/information systems as compared to those of the client.

18.4 Finding and selecting a topic

Sometimes topics for student projects are provided by the educational establishment. This is often to match the interests of supervisors or to accommodate research groups seeking assistance or collaboration. If this is not the case, students must face the often daunting task of devising their own topic. Indeed, students' concerns about this can be justified – a good project topic can be a difficult thing to find, and a poor one can put a student at a significant disadvantage from the outset.

18.4.1 *Qualities of a good project*

The following guidelines may help in creating a good project:

- Projects need to provide an appropriate level of challenge. You want to impress your assessors, so your topic must be meaty enough to enable you to demonstrate your academic and organizational abilities. It should stretch you (but not to breaking point!).
- Aim for depth rather than breadth. Focus and drill down until information starts to become hard to find.
- For research topics in particular, pose and answer one or more questions.
- Your topic should be of interest to others – not just to yourself. This may be your client (if you have one) or a specialist target readership. But a project aimed at 'anyone who is interested' or 'the general public' is too unfocused to be of an academic standard.
- To help ensure your project is of the required academic standard you might decide to relate it closely to a previous item of academic work – e.g. 'applying X's theory of Y to (*your idea*)'. Of course, whatever your topic you will gain from a critical evaluation of relevant theories, frameworks, methods, techniques and concepts, etc.
- Be original. Assessors often have to mark many projects in a short space of time. This can be quite an ordeal, especially if the topics are very similar. Try to be a little bit different (while ensuring that your topic still relates to IS or IT). Hopefully your assessor will appreciate your thoughtfulness and this will be reflected in your marks.

The following is some advice on how to find a good project topic:

- Think about some of the theory you have studied over recent years. How could it be applied to organizations to provide competitive advantage? Who else could benefit from it?
- Think of bad experiences you have had with organizations in relation to their ISs. Could you recommend ways to prevent these from happening to other customers?
- Apply an existing idea to a new area. (For example, some companies are able to provide online quotations for their goods and services. Could this be extended to other types of product?).
- Think about your own hobbies and interests. Do they provide scope for, say, an IT application? Or a business opportunity?
- Investigate an existing topic in greater depth. Specialize, refine, dig deeper. Add focus.
- Approach friends/relations/contacts/complete strangers! Would they like to become clients? Do they have application areas or problems that you might tackle? Having a client is a big advantage.

18.4.2 *Candidate topics for projects, with comments*

Here are some topics that a student might consider, demonstrating the need for depth rather than breadth:

Topic: 'Knowledge management'

Comments: No good. MUCH too broad. Material could be obtained from textbooks.

Topic: 'Knowledge management in the foundry industry'

Comments: Better, but still lacks focus.

Topic: 'Can knowledge management solve the problems of the UK foundry industry?'

Comments: Good; calls for identification of the problems, an understanding of knowledge management and an analysis of its appropriateness and effectiveness for this purpose.

18.4.3 Advantages of having a client

The main advantage to your client of such a relationship is obvious – free labour. Clients rarely pay for this sort of work (although expenses might be covered). Additionally, members of the business community are often genuinely keen to make a contribution to the education of the younger generation, especially when it costs them nothing!

For the student, working on a concrete problem and dealing with real people tends to be a more satisfying experience than working with abstract theories or artificially engineered situations. A genuine requirements-gathering exercise can be carried out. The project deliverables can be delivered, systems can be tested and client feedback can be obtained. Client approval can be gained (assuming the client does approve of the work done), and this can be presented to the project assessors as part of the project report. Along the way, the student may gain access to experts in IS/IT and related fields (and even unrelated fields), and their knowledge and experience, and to the latest technology and ISs.

18.4.4 Things to avoid when thinking of projects

There are some areas that should be avoided when thinking of projects. These include:

- projects in which you provide advice (especially on heath matters), unless you are qualified;
- working with vulnerable adults or children – you may need authorization, which may delay your work;
- organizations that deal with confidential information or for whom security is especially important (such as banks). Can you expect them to trust an unknown student?
- local branches of large organizations (such as chain stores) – IS/IT matters tend to be centrally controlled;
- companies about to go out of business;
- highly emotive questions and topics – academic work should be based on evidence and reason.

18.5 The title

A project title should be informative rather than catchy. You are not writing a novel, and your potential readers will be attracted if they understand the title, and if it relates to their own interests – not because it is witty or funny. 'Choose-your-Shoes' might be a suitable name for a commercial product, but 'Development of an online system to allow customers to design their own footwear' is a much better project title.

If your project is research-based, then you might want to make the core research question the title of your project, e.g. 'Are rapid development methodologies suitable for safety critical systems?'

18.6 The proposal

It is usually the case that if a project is to be carried out, it will first need to be approved. If it is to be part of a student's programme of study, then the purpose of the proposal will be to ensure that it meets academic requirements (level of challenge, feasibility, ethical considerations, etc.), and the approver will be a supervisor or assessor. In most other circumstances, someone will need to meet the cost of the project (perhaps a research council or a commercial organization). The proposer will need to convince this body that the project will meet their needs. In either case, a proposal will be drawn up and submitted for approval. The format of the proposal may be stipulated, in which case this should be strictly adhered to.

A research proposal sets out the topic you want to research (the substance), what the research seeks to achieve (the aims and objectives), how you intend to go about researching it (the methodology), how you will undertake it within the time available (the project plan) and what the results might be (the potential outcomes). It also incorporates any practical and ethical issues which need to be addressed. The contents may vary depending on the type of project, but will be along the following lines:

- title
- aim
- objectives
- deliverables
- background (problem context, relevant concepts)
- methodology
- project plan.

The case study at the start of this chapter contains main elements of a project proposal.

18.7 The project report

The contents of a typical project report are:

- title page
- abstract
- contents
- list of figures
- list of tables
- acknowledgements
- declaration of originality
- main text
- references
- appendices (including project management documentation).

Most of these headings are self-explanatory. The content of the main text will vary from project to project, but the following is one possibility:

- introduction (including aim, objectives, background, research design, brief outline of chapters)
- the problem context
- critical review of the literature
- research methods
- presentation and analysis of results
- conclusions.

The sections that follow examine these in greater detail.

18.8 Aim and objectives

A project aim describes what is to be achieved in the project in a single sentence. For example:

> To produce a theoretically and practically sound framework to help assess the strategic and operational readiness of a group of SMEs to engage in both the organizational and technical aspects of knowledge management.

The title may then be a shortened version of the aim, such as:

> A framework for assessing the knowledge management readiness of SMEs.

Objectives break down the overall aim into smaller 'chunks' that can be clearly understood, and are of a manageable size. It is important that they should be written in such a way that it will be clear whether or not they have been achieved. Usually, some of the objectives will be met before the end of the project, and evidence of their completion will be produced in the form of 'deliverables'. These are project outputs (documents, software, artefacts, events, etc.) and, as the name suggests, they will be presented to the client, if one exists. The production of deliverables, on time according to the project plan, is an important measure of the success of the management of the project.

It is often said that objectives should be 'SMART'. This is an acronym meaning:

> Specific – clearly defined, not vague;
> Measurable – so that it is possible to tell whether they have been met;
> Achievable – realistic and not over-ambitious;
> Relevant – contributing towards the overall aim;
> Time-based – to avoid delay, postponement and procrastination.

If all of the objectives are met, this should automatically result in the achievement of your project aim.

18.9 Background

In a dissertation or project proposal, the reader will appreciate what it is you are trying to do from the title, the aims and the objectives. Chronologically, these will have emerged after you have done background reading and investigation into an organization and/or the specific problem situations you are addressing. But this does not have to be presented to the reader in the same order as your research. It makes for easier reading if the aim and objectives are stated first.

While the title, aim and objectives state what you are doing, they do not explain why you are doing it. The background will do that. It can be expected to cover both the project context and the academic concepts. The project context is an overview of the organization or situation that is the setting for the project, and the more specific area of concern you are to address. If necessary, there will also be a brief explanation of any relevant broader issues, such as a description of the industry sector or the current political, social or economic environment.

The concepts underpinning the work need to be explained. These will include a definition of terms, a discussion of previous work in the area and of current thinking, and any theories related to your work or upon which your work will be based. These will be heavily based on the literature. One of the things that helps distinguish a high-quality project is the synergy between the concepts and the empirical work. In other words, it is no use doing an applied project and just 'bolting on' a chapter headed 'Literature review'. The two must be linked sensibly.

18.10 The critical review

It is not necessary to have a section in your project report or dissertation entitled 'Literary review' or 'Critical review'. However, you do need to read widely, and you do need to demonstrate that you have done so by commenting intelligently on what you have read. You may choose to call this what you like – your heading may be related to the subject matter.

You need to review the relevant literature for a number of reasons. First, you need to demonstrate that you know the subject area – that you have studied what others have done – and that you will add to it rather than simply repeating or reporting on it. You need to identify the underpinning concepts, to distinguish between facts, inference and opinions and to refine and redefine the ideas. This will help you to show how your work maps onto the domain – in particular, whether there are any gaps in knowledge or understanding, what empirical work is needed, and what research strategies should be adopted. Reporting on the work of other researchers will also help to clarify just what you are claiming to be original, and will help to avoid any possible accusation of plagiarism.

It is important to appreciate that material relevant to your work may come from a wide range of sources, including academic journals, books (both research-based and text-books), conference proceedings, theses and dissertations, newspapers, trade magazines, professional periodicals, company reports, government publications and grey literature. Grey literature consists of papers, reports and technical notes, etc. produced by organizations such as governmental agencies and academic institutions that are not made publicly available by commercial publishers. Sometimes literature is categorized as 'primary' (the first occurrence of a piece of work, such as reports or theses), 'secondary' (subsequent publications of primary works, such as in journals or newspapers), or 'tertiary' (search tools or introductory coverage, such as in encyclopaedias and dictionaries).

Searching the literature for research purposes can be a daunting task – especially knowing how and where to begin. It tends to be a highly iterative process. One search at the beginning may help you to decide your broad topic area. As your research progresses and you drill down to your specialist area of interest you will need to do more searches.

18.11 Research methods

Your section on research methods will be about how you are to perform your investigation and why you have chosen to use these methods. You cannot select methods uncritically and simply state that you will use X or Y. Your assessors will be looking for explanation, justification, evidence and reasoning.

18.11.1 *Quantitative and qualitative research methods*

Quantitative methods may be useful when there is a lot of relevant numerical data available or you believe that it will be easily gathered. They are especially useful when things can be measured – e.g. the time it takes for a production process. Qualitative methods may be used when opinions are important, when there is not enough data for statistical significance, and to support statistically significant findings.

18.11.2 *Descriptive, exploratory and explanatory approaches*

The choice of approach to the way in which research is carried out will depend upon the types of information the researcher is trying to uncover. Descriptive approaches entail the accurate portrayal of situations, but go no further. Exploratory approaches 'dig deeper', attempting to find out what is really happening, rather than what appears on the surface. Explanatory approaches seek to find causal relationships.

18.11.3 *Data collection*

All research requires data or information as its raw material, and this may be obtained in many ways, some of which are described briefly below.

- Experiment. Suitable for situations in which the researcher can exercise a degree of control. For example, one variable might be changed while others are kept constant.
- Trial. This consists of one or more tests carried out on a limited group of subjects. For example, the effect of new packaging on product sales in one area.
- Survey. This allows for the economical collection of large amounts of data. However, the data collected often lacks real depth. Data is often collected by means of a questionnaire (which may be self-administered), structured observation or structured interview.

  Questionnaires need to be designed very carefully to avoid bias and to avoid poor wording of questions influencing the responses. They may be piloted in an attempt to eliminate these problems, then revised if necessary.
- Case study. This involves learning in detail about one or two example cases (either 'live' or historical). Various data-collection methods may be used within a case study (e.g. questionnaires, interviews, observation, focus groups and analysis of documents).

- Action research. This has many similarities to case study work. However, the researcher is not just a passive observer, but participates in the activities of the organization, and is part of the system. Action research embraces the idea of continuous reflection, not just on the case itself, but on the methods of undertaking the research.
- Cross-sectional study. This is concerned with the observation and measurement of particular characteristics, variables and so on, at a particular moment in time. For example, the effect on the heating costs of houses of various factors such as thermostat setting, types and thicknesses of loft insulation, double glazing and cavity wall insulation.
- Longitudinal study. This is the observation of events over time. For example, the qualifications of IT professionals or inflation.
- Multi-method studies. A number of approaches can be combined successfully in a single study. This can improve the credibility in the findings if different methods return the same, or similar, results.

18.12 Presentation of results

Project reports are serious documents, and consequently can be very dull documents to read. The presentation of results provides an opportunity to brighten them up a bit, using various forms of illustration. However, authors should be careful to make sure they are more than mere decoration. First and foremost, they should be accurate. They should also be relevant, complete, unambiguous and easy to follow. Keys should be shown where necessary.

Despite these reservations, succinct diagrams, charts and graphs are highly preferable to vast quantities of text and figures. The saying 'A picture tells a thousand words' is very true – it is much easier to make sense of a well-presented graph than to comprehend the raw data. If it is thought that the reader might want to see detailed data as evidence, then this can be provided in an appendix.

18.13 Analysis

Simply presenting a factual account of your findings (the descriptive approach to research) is not going to impress the reader of your project report. You need to explore and explain the results. What is their relevance and importance? What do they mean to various stakeholders within the organization? How should they affect the actions of your client in the future? If you keep asking these 'So what?' types of question, and if you can use the outputs of your research to answer them, then your work is likely to be of real value.

Let us assume that our research has revealed that:

Seventy per cent of people who sign up with 'Shifty Sid's Web Hosting Service' are still with the company two years later.

This might be true, but so what? In particular, can one assume from this that Sid is providing a good service? To do this we need to compare Sid's rate of customer retention with that of similar concerns. We need to know why 30 per cent of his customers leave. We need to know the terms of the customer agreement, especially whether there were any penalties for early termination. And then we need to answer the 'so what' question: 'Yes, this is a good rate of retention', perhaps, or 'Shifty Sid is pulling a fast one, because his clients pay for 24 months of service when they sign the contract'.

Another important point to consider is how your research results compare to the theoretical material, or the work of previous researchers, discussed in your literature review? Does it support them or contradict them? Your analysis of your results is as important as the results themselves.

A word of caution. Don't be tempted to engineer your results to produce the outcome you were expecting or hoping for (or that your client wanted). On the contrary, you should explain how you have analysed your results to make it clear that any interpretation is objectively justifiable. Similarly, you should avoid the practice, common among politicians, of presenting facts or (especially) statistics that although technically correct, are highly selective. This is deliberately misleading, and researchers engaging in this sort of behaviour can expect an early termination of their career.

18.14 Plagiarism

Plagiarism is a serious academic offence – generally regarded as being on a par with manipulating research results, as discussed in the previous section. It is, quite simply, the act of presenting another's work as your own. You can do this by:

- copying a section of text verbatim from a source without any acknowledgement;
- copying and pasting a section of text, using sentences of the original but omitting one or two and putting one or two in a different order;
- composing a paragraph by taking short phrases from a number of sources and putting them together, adding words of your own to make a coherent whole;
- copying diagrams, illustrations, charts, etc., without acknowledgement;
- Copying ANYTHING without acknowledging its source. This includes ideas, theories, etc., which are completely independent of the way in which they are worded.

Referring to the work of others in your field of study is perfectly acceptable – and indeed to be encouraged, for reasons discussed at the start of Section 18.10. This may be done by:

- paraphrasing a section of text with substantial changes in language and organization. The new version will also have changes in the amount of detail used and the examples cited. The original work should be acknowledged in the body of the text, e.g. '(Jones, 1999)' and included in reference list;
- quoting a phrase or sentence by placing it in quotation marks with the source cited in-text and in the list of references;
- quoting a section of text by placing it in block format with the source cited in-text and in the list of references.

18.15 Academic writing

A certain style is expected of academic works. That is not to say that they are 'stylish', i.e. that their style is to be admired, but that they are required to conform to certain norms and conventions. The result is often spectacularly dull, but readers are advised not to try to improve the situation by adopting a more creative or individual writing style – especially if their work is being assessed.

Textbooks may contain a joke or two, or at least the odd ironic comment. Perhaps you have noticed examples in this publication. No? Well, never mind. Academic reports on the other hand tend to be very formal. No jokes, no colloquialisms, no informal language. Correct English at all times, and certainly no slang or text-speak.

A particular peculiarity of academic English is the use of the 'passive mode'. In this, the author(s) never refer to themselves by name, or use the terms 'I', 'we', 'our', etc. It is as though they don't want to admit being responsible for what they have written. Instead of 'I carried out a survey in my home town', the acceptable form is: 'A survey was carried out in the author's home town'. The equivalent of 'We do not think we will be able to improve it' in passive mode is: 'It is not thought that it can be improved'. This is simply a convention we must follow. It is not known why.

18.16 Referencing

Referencing is a cornerstone of academic work, and being able to reference properly is part of an academic's credibility. It enables you to:

- acknowledge your sources;
- establish the credibility of your work;
- distinguish facts and inference from opinions;
- support your arguments;
- avoid accusations of plagiarism.

It enables readers to:

- find the sources you have used, so they can read further;
- verify that what you have written is consistent with the original and has been interpreted correctly.

References have at least two components. The first essential element is an indicator inserted in the body of the text. This shows that the author wants to acknowledge that he/she is referring to someone else's work. The indicator can take one of several forms – in this book the author name and date of publication are used, such as '(Donaldson, 2005)'. The other essential element is an entry in the list of references towards the back of the publication (or sometimes at the end of the chapter), describing the referenced publication in detail, and how the reader may find a copy. Additionally, it will probably be necessary to add to the text in some way, to make it completely clear what is being referenced. If text is copied word for word then indentation or quotation marks may be used. Otherwise, explanatory phrases may be added as in the following example:

> Reynolds (2008) argues that effective server virtualization can only be achieved via hardware. However, this is disputed by Wang and Saunders (2009), who propose a software framework based on 'virtual transferable parents'.

If you are to provide a full and detailed list of references when you write your report, it follows that you need to make a note of your sources as you do your research. You must remember to do this – otherwise you will find yourself making claims in your report for which you cannot provide supporting evidence because you cannot remember where you read it.

A bibliography is a list of publications the author has used, and in which the reader might be interested. It does not contain links to specific passages within the text, nor does it give details of how to find the publications. It might be a useful addition to, but is definitely *not* a substitute for, references, in any academic work.

18.17 Project conclusions

This section of your project report or dissertation may well be both the first and last section to be read by your examiners, so it is worth a little extra effort to leave a lasting impression on your reader. Briefly summarize your project here, especially your results, emphasizing any unusual or unexpected findings, but do not introduce any new material. You will probably want to discuss any problems or challenges encountered – and how you dealt with them. You should also discuss your objectives. Were they all met in full? If not, then why not? Is there anything you think you should have done differently, with the benefit of hindsight?

You may want to discuss possible future work. What have you discovered or created that could be built on further? If you have substantial proposals or ideas you may want to devote a separate section of your report to this topic.

Finally, remind the reader of your answers to the 'so what?' questions – these are the core and essence of your work.

18.18 Managing your project

Of course, much of what you have read on project management is relevant when it comes to managing your own project. The main difference is that we are now considering an individual venture, rather than one entered into by a team. Project management, and its documentation, are often considered by students to be somewhat of a chore. However, if carried out effectively, they will:

- result in a better quality product;
- help to ensure the product is delivered on time;
- minimize the risk of things going wrong;
- make life easier.

The essential elements of managing a student project are the planning, monitoring and control of time, quality and costs, and risk management and documentation. These are discussed in detail in Chapter 14, and some additional comments follow.

18.18.1 *Planning*

You should plan and document your project before you start work on it – not after it is finished. It may seem strange to suggest that anyone might do otherwise, but 'post-planning' of student projects, solely to gain some marks, is not an unusual occurrence.

18.18.2 *Monitoring*

You are advised to keep a log – a record of your day-to-day activities, such as meetings (with clients, stakeholders, your supervisor, domain experts, etc.), communications (such as important phone calls or emails), the results of experiments, observations, problems and how they were overcome, and so on. This will prove invaluable when you come to write up your work formally, and will mean you don't have to rely on your memory alone. You may want to include some sample pages from your log in your project management documentation, while some institutions will require you to submit your log in full.

18.18.3 *Control*

If you fall behind in your project work you may need to reschedule the remaining tasks, perhaps omitting some of them so you will finish on time. On rare occasions, students find that they are ahead of schedule, and are able to include some extra work. If either situation arises you should consult your supervisor for advice.

Your supervisor is a valuable resource, and it is important to form a working relationship with him/her, just as you will have to form working relationships with colleagues in the workplace. This does not mean that you have to like them! Your supervisor may be the person who marks your work, and will most probably be the person you ask to write a reference when making job applications, so it may be to your advantage if your supervisor likes you.

18.18.4 *Risks*

There are real risks to student projects. Software and hardware can fail. People can become ill. Clients can lose interest. Companies can go bust. The identification, evaluation and minimization of risks for a student project is not just an academic exercise. If your project is severely impaired by an event that could have been predicted as a risk, and if you have taken no action to prevent it from taking place, or at least to minimize its effects, then you cannot expect any dispensation from your assessors. As an example, if your laptop is stolen, and on it is stored the only recent copy of your work, then you are at fault for not countering this predictable risk by making a back-up, and you will lose your marks.

18.19 Ten ways to fail your project

1 Choose a topic with too little challenge.
2 Choose a topic that's too difficult or ambitious.
3 Lose touch with your supervisor, or ignore your supervisor's advice.
4 Plagiarize.
5 Under-estimate the time and/or effort needed to complete a project.
6 Fail to manage your time properly.
7 Decide to make a late change to your topic.
8 Be forced to make a late change to your topic (e.g. because you lose your client).
9 Stray from your objectives.
10 Fail to anticipate risks.

18.20 Ethical, legal and professional issues

Clearly, assessors will take a poor view of students who break the law in the course of their project. But it has happened – for example, students investigating online pornography have downloaded illegal material, and those investigating hacking have been tempted to break into systems without authorization. But it is also possible (and some would say easy) to commit an offence accidentally. Laws concerning data protection, copyright, confidentiality and intellectual property rights are complex and easily misunderstood.

Ethics and legality are not the same. It is quite possible to do things which are widely considered to be unethical or 'wrong' without breaking the law. But both illegal and unethical practices reflect badly on educational institutions, and many of them include a consideration of such issues in the project approval process.

18.21 Summary

A project is a major undertaking requiring skills and personal characteristics not fully tested by 'taught' subjects, but highly regarded by employers. These include the ability to manage one's own time and responsibilities, problem solving and the capacity to form working relationships. As such, it provides an excellent opportunity for students to demonstrate their 'employability'.

It follows that the wise student will devote extra effort to their project work, and will not ask the question: 'What must I do to succeed?', but rather 'What can I do to excel?' The wise student will not hope to avoid problems, but will welcome them, regarding them as opportunities to demonstrate the skills to deal with them.

Glossary

Deliverable   A project output corresponding to the accomplishment of an objective
Ethical issues   Issues concerning what is right and what is wrong.
Objective   A major task, the completion of which will contribute to the achievement of the project aim.
Plagiarism   Creating the impression that someone else's work is your own. This does not have to be the result of a deliberate action.
Project aim   The overall purpose of a project, expressed in a single sentence.

Further reading

Dawson, C.W. (2009) *Projects in Computing and Information Systems: A Student's Guide*. Reading, MA: Addison-Wesley.
Saunders, M., Thornhill, A., and Lewis, P. (2009) *Research Methods for Business Students*. New York: Prentice Hall.

Suggested activities

1   Think of a good idea for a project that is:

   a   research-based
   b   development-based
   c   client-based.

2   Discuss your ideas with fellow students, and decide whether they are:

    a   challenging enough
    b   over-ambitious
    c   focused
    d   original
    e   at risk of legal or ethical problems.

3   Think about unpleasant things that have happened to you in the past. How much were they a result of your own actions (or inaction)?

4   Explain the relevance of question 3 to projects.

19 Final thoughts

Comair is a subsidiary of Delta Air Lines, based in Ohio. Over the Christmas period in 2004 Comair cancelled 3,900 flights, which was reported to have affected around 200,000 passengers in 118 cities. This cost Comair and its parent company, Delta Air Lines, $20 million, damaged the airline's reputation and prompted an investigation by the Department of Transportation. Originally, due to weather and other problems, flights began to be cancelled as the backlog clogged the system. A company spokesman indicated that computer problems knocked out the system that manages flight assignments.

In 1997 Comair was an independent regional airline. The company was considering the replacement of its legacy system that was used to manage flight crews. The application, from SBS International, was one of the oldest in the company (11 years old at the time). It was written in the programming language Fortran (in which no one at Comair was fluent) and was the only system left that ran on the airline's old IBM AIX platform (all other applications ran on HP Unix). SBS made a pitch for its new Maestro crew management software, which was a first-generation Windows application. At the time this software was criticized by some as being clumsy. The existing crew management system was not elegant, but end users had grown adept at operating it, and a great number of Comair's existing business processes had sprung from it. The consensus at the meeting was that if Comair was going to shoulder the expense of replacing the old crew management system, it should wait for a more satisfactory substitute to come along.

A potential replacement was discussed again in 1998 and plans were made to select a vendor in 2000, but that did not happen. Comair's corporate leadership became distracted by a sequence of events: managing the approach of Y2K, the purchase of Comair by Delta in 2000, a pilot strike that grounded the airline in 2001, and 9/11 with the ensuing downturn in the airline industry.

A replacement system from Sabre Airline Solutions was finally approved, but the switch didn't happen soon enough to prevent the failure over the Christmas period. It appears that Comair senior executives did not consider a replacement system an urgent priority and that no risk analysis had been done. This was despite the fact that in 1998 Sabre had helped Comair to develop a long-term IT strategy to address the issue of legacy systems and architecture.

The consultants spent five months meeting with IT's various users in the business to find out what their needs were. They examined the airline's existing IT infrastructure and suggested a five-year strategic plan outlining (among other things) which systems needed to be retired, replaced or added, and a timeline for actions. The crew scheduling system was marked for retirement. It was clear that the existing SBS application was getting old, there was risk, new replacement technology was available, and that there were financial benefits to replacing the system in terms of crew productivity and expenses that could be controlled better in a new system.

By 1999 a significant amount of the work that had been laid out in the five-year plan had been completed or was under way. This included Y2K, implementing an e-ticketing system, upgrading the corporate network, replacing the maintenance and engineering system (another high-risk legacy system written in Cobol) and implementing a revenue management application.

The replacement of the crew scheduling system was among those next on the list, but after nearly 15 years in use, the business had grown accustomed to the SBS system, and much of Comair's crew management business processes had grown directly out of it.

To Delta, buying Comair in 2000 was not a difficult choice. Comair was a highly profitable regional airline. It was an industry leader in being on time, cancellation and missed baggage statistics, and it was valued well on the stockmarket. It appears that Delta took the approach of 'Why fix what isn't broken?' Partly because of end users' familiarity with the systems, Delta did not see anything wrong with Comair's IT provision. The only area that was affected directly by the take-over was marketing, and Delta replaced the entire marketing department at Comair within days of taking over. The five-year plan that had been developed with Sabre, and which was supposed to be revisited on a regular basis, languished.

In 2001 an 89-day strike by pilots from March to June shut down Comair and the Cincinnati/Northern Kentucky International Airport, where Delta and Comair operate 90 per cent of all flights. Comair closed its Cincinnati concourse, losing more than 800 daily flights and giving Delta a $200 million loss for the quarter. Once the strike was over, Comair's flight operations group, the primary users of the crew scheduling system, had their hands full getting aeroplanes back in the air.

During this period they gave little or no thought to replacing the crew scheduling system. Just a few months later the effects of 9/11 pushed some of the largest carriers into bankruptcy and Delta lost nearly $8.5 billion over the following four years, increasing the pressure to keep costs down.

Late in 2002 the Comair IT group turned its attention back to the crew management system and brought in several vendors, including Sabre and SBS, to perform demonstrations. Finally, Comair got approval from Delta to replace the legacy SBS system and agreed a deal with Sabre in June 2004 to implement its AirCrews Operations Manager. Implementation was set to begin in 2005.

On 16 December Comair reported an operating profit of $25.7 million in the third quarter of 2004. A week later, a severe winter storm hit the Ohio Valley. The snow came with sleet and freezing rain. De-icing the jets took much longer than expected and some jet tires froze to the ground. As a result of all this, over the period 22–24 December 2004 Comair had to cancel or delay 91 per cent of its flights.

The cancellations created a system backlog. Unknown to anyone at Comair, the crew management application could process no more than 32,000 changes per month. If there were any attempts to enter more the system would shut down. On Christmas Eve, all the rescheduling necessitated by the bad weather forced the system to crash. As a result, Comair had to cancel all 1,100 of its flights on Christmas Day, stranding tens of thousands of passengers heading home for the holidays.

It had to cancel nearly 90 per cent of its flights on Boxing Day, stranding even more passengers. There was no backup system and it took a full day for the vendor to fix the software. Comair was not able to operate a full schedule until 29 December. Within the USA, because of its vast physical size, the Christmas period is one of the busiest of the year as people often fly to visit families and friends.

Comair continued using the nearly 20-year-old crew management system from SBS, though with a lot more care. SBS implemented a bridge solution, dividing the legacy system into two modules, one for pilot scheduling and another for flight attendant scheduling, each with a 32,000 monthly limit of its own. Comair also began generating a daily report to monitor the volume of transactions going through the system.

IT staff had tried to tell Comair and Delta of the necessity for replacement over a period of years, but they had not done any risk analysis or cost–benefit analysis. Had they shown the potential cost of failure, the story may have been different. For IT to influence other corporate areas it is vital that organizational and market knowledge is used. Technical arguments rarely suffice.

19.1 Other topics

19.1.1 *Usability*

The material in this book covers major subjects in the domain, but of course it is not possible to cover everything. There are, however, some other topics of which you should have at least some basic understanding. Usability was discussed in the systems analysis chapter in the form of human–computer interface and information systems. Usability is also very important in website design. Nielsen (2001) watched users make 496 attempts at performing tasks on 20 e-commerce sites based in the USA. The research focused on large sites but included a few smaller ones as well. He concluded that e-commerce sites lose almost half of their potential sales because users cannot use the site, and that, with better usability, the average site could increase its current sales by 79 per cent. On average, the user was successful at completing a transaction only 56 per cent of the time. Nielson (2001) found that failures were often due to:

- navigation difficulties;
- obstructions before checkout (for example, credit cards that are or are not accepted, other forms to complete that seem unnecessary to the user);
- category errors;
- customers looking in the wrong place;
- terminology and language errors (for example, zip code and postcode);
- incomprehensible or difficult to use forms.

Failures were occasionally due to lack of browser plug-ins, such as Adobe Shockwave, Adobe Flash and Quick Time Virtual Reality. Failures were rarely due to problems with functionality, such as broken servers or slow networks, yet these are areas on which developers often focus.

A website may be used for many purposes, including marketing and sales. Providing an efficient online experience may not match the ways that people shop in the physical world. A focused product search strategy is different from browsing around a shop and buying items on impulse. Cross-selling can be used in both. In the physical world you may be asked 'Do you want fries with that?' In the virtual world you may be told 'People who bought this book also bought …' Upselling is about incremental add-ons, such as

'Supersize your meal for only 50 pence more', or 'Upgrade from widget-free to widget-professional for only ...'. Impulse items are things such as the mints by the checkout counter. In the virtual world, virtual mints may be on offer as you check out.

Web-shoppers tend to be price-sensitive and some sites are not good at conveying value (not just prices). Shipping costs may deter shoppers, and what at first may seem like a bargain can in fact be much more expensive once all costs have been included. Paying for returns costs time and money. Trust is vital and is the single biggest obstacle to making a sale on a website. A common consumer complaint that helps to erode trust is pricing inconsistency between an e-commerce site, off-line store and printed catalogue. Snyder (2001) notes that customers want:

- to apply in-store coupons online and vice versa;
- price matching (with other stores);
- clear and explicit return policies (for example, whether items can be returned to the local store, or at no cost);
- policies listed on site taken literally;
- returns, security, data protection and guarantees;
- what does not appear not to exist (vital for trust).

19.1.2 Development methodologies

Some development methodologies have been covered in the systems analysis chapter; this section provides some additional information.

The systems development lifecycle (SDLC) typically consists of seven phases:

1 project initiation
2 requirements definition
3 functional design
4 system building
5 verification
6 cut over, in which the new system is put in operation and links are established
7 maintenance and review.

Traditional SDLC methodologies are not always appropriate. Many systems projects fail to meet objectives because of the difficulty in estimating costs, especially as each project is unique and previous experience may not provide the necessary knowledge and skills. Objectives may reflect a scope that is too broad or two narrow so that the problem the system was designed to solve may still exist, or the opportunity that it was to capitalize upon may not be appropriately leveraged. If the business environment is very dynamic, there may not be enough time to adequately cover each SDLC phase. The SDLC may not work for all situations, requires a lot of planning and can be difficult to implement quickly.

Prototyping attempts to address some of the issues associated with the SDLC. Prototyping is a form of evolutionary development that helps to build a fast, high-level version of the system at the beginning of the project. End user involvement and comment early on and throughout the development process helps with successful buy-in. Users may not understand the realistic scope of the system, however, and documentation may be difficult to write.

Rapid application development (RAD) is similar to the SDLC, but it substantially reduces the time by having four phases instead of seven. Like prototyping, RAD uses iterative development tools to speed up development, and these include GUI, reusable code, code generation and programming, language testing and debugging. The aim is to build the system in a much shorter timeframe than normal. Joint application design (JAD) is a technique developed by IBM where users are more integrally involved throughout the development process. Computer-aided software engineering (CASE) tools often refer to software that is used for the automated development of systems software. CASE functions include analysis, design and programming, and CASE tools automate methods for designing, documenting and producing structured computer code. It also includes process activities such as requirement engineering, design, program development and testing. CASE tools therefore include design editors, data dictionaries, compilers, debuggers and system building tools.

Boehm (1988) described the *spiral model* as covering the traditional lifecycle, proto-typing and risk analysis. The model evolved to encompass the best features of the classic waterfall model, while at the same time adding risk analysis. It is most appropriate for large, industrial software projects and it has four major activities:

- planning, in which the objectives, alternatives and constraints are determined;
- risk analysis, in which potential problems are identified and alternative solutions are considered;
- engineering, in which the next release is developed;
- customer evaluation, in which software is assessed for features and usability.

The object-oriented (OO) approach combines data and processes (called methods) into single entities called objects. Objects tend to correspond to real things with which information is concerned, such as contracts, customers and suppliers. The model represents complex relationships, data and data processing, with a consistent notation that enables analysis and design within an evolutionary process. The approach aims to make system elements reusable, and that helps to improve system quality and the productivity of systems analysis. An object encapsulates both data and behaviour; specific objects in a system can inherit attributes from the global instance of an object, and objects can inherit attributes from more than one parent object. The system to be developed is observed and analysed and the requirements are defined as in any other method of system development. Following this, objects in the required system are identified. For example, in the case of a university system, a student is an object, an examination paper is an object and the student's record is an object. The basic steps of system designing using object modelling are:

- system analysis
- system design
- object design
- implementation.

OO methodology closely represents the problem domain, and it is therefore easier to produce designs and for them to be understood by developers and end users. The objects in a system are immune to requirement changes, which enables changes more easily. This approach encourages more re-use, and new applications can use existing modules, thereby reducing the development cost and cycle time.

The dynamic system development method (DSDM) is independent of tools, in that it can be used with the structured analysis and design approach or the OO approach. DSDM is dynamic as it is a RAD method that uses incremental prototyping. This method is particularly useful for the systems to be developed in a short timeframe and where the requirements cannot be frozen at the start of application building. Whatever requirements are known at the time, a design for them is prepared and that design is developed and incorporated into the system. In DSDM, analysis, design and development phases can overlap; DSDM has a five-phase lifecycle:

- feasibility study
- business study
- functional model iteration
- design and build iteration
- implementation.

Checkland (1981) developed soft systems methodology (SSM) to help consider areas of interest in human activity systems. SSM is therefore not a specific information systems methodology, though it has been used in information systems developments. It is an approach that may help stakeholders to agree on systemically desirable and culturally feasible possibilities. SSM has developed over time, though it is arguable as to whether the original format has been supplanted or replaced. The original basis of SSM was a seven-phase methodology, but it is important to note that the phases are not necessarily sequential, and that there are philosophical underpinnings to SSM that are just as important as the phases. The phases are:

- find out about the area of interest;
- capture the main factors and relationships (often in what is called a 'rich picture');
- use root definitions as phase one of modelling;
- use conceptual models in phase two;
- compare the conceptual models with reality;
- decide what is systemically desirable and culturally feasible;
- take action.

19.1.3 *Enterprise resource planning*

In the early days of enterprise resource planning (ERP) implementation, most management did not understand the magnitude of issues an organization has to consider before, during and after implementation. ERP systems are large and very different from conventional packaged software.

Many organizations have become more complex due to increased layers of management hierarchy and increased levels of coordination across departments, with each department having different information needs. No single information system can support all the business needs of an organization. In addition, each management level has different information requirements.

Over time, information systems have evolved as a jumble of independent non-integrated systems that create bottlenecks and reduce productivity, yet organizations need to be more agile and flexible than ever before. They therefore need their information systems to have integrated data, applications and resources from across the organization, as well as data from the external environment. To compete effectively, organizations must be customer focused, and this requires cross-functional integration among the accounting, marketing and other departments.

The potential business benefits of ERP are high, and they include increased agility of an organization, enabling quick response environments for growth and maintaining market share. The ability to integrate data and applications across functional areas, facilitating data being entered once only, but being available to all applications, can improve the accuracy and quality of the data. Consistency of the user interface across applications means less employee training, better productivity and cross-functional job flexibility. There are improvements in maintenance and support as IT staff is centralized. Security of data and applications is enhanced due to better controls and centralization of hardware. Sharing of information across functional areas helps collaboration between employees. Linking and exchanging information in real-time with supply-chain partners improves efficiency, leading to lower costs. Better customer service can arise due to quicker information flow across departments. Efficiency of business processes may be enhanced due to the re-engineering of business processes.

There are also limitations. Re-training of all employees with the new system can be costly and time consuming. Change of business roles and department boundaries can create upheaval and resistance to the new system. There can be complexity in installing, configuring and maintaining the system, requiring specialized IT staff, hardware and network facilities. ERP requires consolidation of IT hardware, software and human resources, which can be cumbersome and difficult to attain. Data conversion and transformation from an old system to a new one can be complex and time-consuming. Resistance to change can reduce productivity.

ERP systems are the first generation of enterprise systems meant to integrate data and support all the major functions of organizations, and there is an argument for ERPs to be considered as knowledge management in practice. ERP systems integrate various functional aspects of the organization, as well as systems within the organizations of its partners and suppliers. A major goal of an ERP system is to make the information flow dynamic and immediate, therefore increasing its usefulness and value. Another goal of ERP is to integrate departments and functions across an organization into a single infrastructure sharing a common database and serving the needs of each department. ERP systems are intended to replace an assortment of non-integrated systems that typically exist in organizations. ERP solves critical problems of integrating information from different sources and makes it available in real-time. Figure 19.1 shows a schematic of an ERP system.

Before implementing ERP, an organization has to plan and understand the lifecycle of their systems. The key to successful implementation is to use a proven methodology, take it one step at a time, and have a thorough understanding of the ERP lifecycle. ERP system implementations are very risky, and using a well-defined project plan with a proven methodology will assist in managing those risks. There must be a strong, well-communicated need to make the change from the existing information systems and applications to an ERP system.

For an ERP system to be implemented successfully, project management must provide strong leadership, a clear and understood implementation plan and close monitoring of the budget. It is often the case for organizations without much ERP implementation experience to use implementation partners such as consultants. Regardless of whether or not consultants are used, effective change management is essential. In

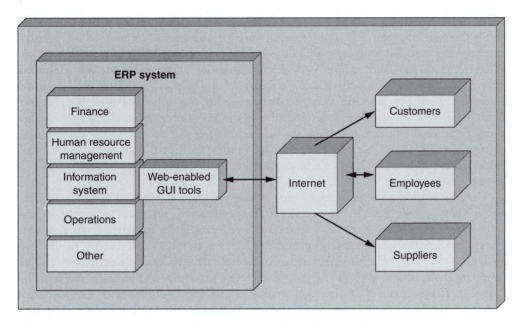

Figure 19.1 A schematic of an ERP system.

implementing new systems, communicating, preparing, setting expectations and explaining the business case are every bit as important as providing training, support and technical understanding. Business processes will need to be changed, adjusted or adapted to the new system to use the functionality of an ERP system fully. Outsourcing overseas, ethical issues, and problems with system security have also attracted a lot of attention in ERP implementation.

Going live is one of the most critical points in ERP success. It is vital to focus the efforts of all project teams to ensure that task and activities are completed before going live. Five areas are particularly important:

1   training for end users;
2   reactive support (help-desk, troubleshooting);
3   auditing support to make sure data quality is not compromised by the new system;
4   data fix to resolve data migration and errors revealed by audits;
5   new features and functionalities to support the evolving needs of the organization.

An organization that does not have experience in developing ERP systems might be sensible to purchase one. Factors influencing choice of vendor include business functions or modules supported, features and integration capabilities, financial viability of the vendor, length of time they have been in business, licensing and upgrade policies, customer service and help-desk support, total cost of ownership, IT infrastructure requirements, third-party software integration, legacy systems support and integration, consulting and training services and future goals and plans for the short- and long-term.

SAP is the recognized global leader among ERP vendors, with over 12 million users, providing solutions for all types of industries and for every major market. Oracle/Peoplesoft is the second largest ERP vendor, and Oracle provides solutions divided by industry category and promises long-term support for customers of PeopleSoft (acquired in 2004). Infor is the world's third largest provider of enterprise software. It delivers integrated enterprise solutions in supply chain, customer relationship and supplier management. Microsoft Dynamics (formerly Microsoft Business Solutions or Great Plains) is a comprehensive business management solution built on the Microsoft platform. Lawson provides industry-tailored software solutions that include enterprise performance management, distribution, financials, human resources, procurement and retail operations. SSA Global (which acquired Baan in 2004) claim to offer solutions that accomplish specific goals in shorter timeframes.

The functions of an organization (such as sales, manufacturing and HR) are important as they provide a structure by which an organization functions smoothly. A silo information system, however, is inefficient, inaccurate and expensive. Such a system creates bottlenecks for everyone and information is not available in real-time. Silos are basically compartmentalized operating units isolated from their environment. The problem of functional silos gave birth to business process re-engineering (BPR). The cross-functional business process can involve people and resources from various functional departments working together, sharing information at any level of the organization. The cross-functional organizational structure breaks the functional silos by opening up the informational flows from one department to another.

Systems integration is about developing information systems that allow organizations to share data with all of their stakeholders based on need and authorization. To develop such systems from the individual non-integrated information systems that may exist, management needs to change organizational structures, processes and employee roles and responsibilities. Business process re-engineering involves changing the mindset of the employees in the organization, encouraging and enabling them to do their tasks in a new way.

Before installing an ERP system, an organization may have to upgrade or install middleware, or get rid of their legacy system's hardware and software. Integration is also required at the data level, client level and application level. A good ERP implementation improves operational efficiency with better business processes that focuses on organizational goals rather than on individual departmental goals. It also leads to improved efficiency with a paperless flow and electronic data interchange (EDI) or a business-to-business (B2B) commerce environment with partners.

System integration has many challenges, however, including replacing old hardware and software, working with IT consultants, impacts on IT staff, department heads losing control of data, and rumours of layoffs. There are also ethical issues, such as the possibility of some employees exploiting information for personal advantage and illegal access of information. Remedies are time-consuming and costly, and may include developing policies on ethical usage of information, installing proper security software and hardware and allocating resources for training and education on accessing information.

A key role of an ERP system is to provide support for such business functions as accounting, sales, inventory control and production; ERP vendors provide modules that support the major functional areas of business. The ERP software embeds best business practices that implement the organization's policy and procedure via business rules.

A production module helps in the planning and optimization of manufacturing capacity, parts, components and material resources using historical production data and sales forecasting. A purchasing module streamlines the procurement process of required raw materials and other supplies. An inventory management module facilitates the processes of maintaining the appropriate level of stock in a warehouse. A sales and marketing module implements functions of order placement, order scheduling, shipping and invoicing. A finance module can gather financial data from various functional departments and generate valuable financial reports. A human resource module streamlines the management of human capital.

19.1.4 Operations management

Some aspects of operations management have been touched upon elsewhere in this book under other subject headings. There are, however, some major aspects of the domain that should be addressed before the book is concluded. These include stock control, just-in-time and materials requirements planning.

A manufacturing firm can be considered as a flow, with inputs, transformation and outputs. A sensible balance is needed between these activities. Demand for final goods is likely to fluctuate, and supply of materials may not be certain. It is easy to ensure that all demand is met by increasing stock. One major problem with this solution is that money tied up in stock is not liquid until the stock is sold. The more stock that is held the less liquidity an organization has. This means that a firm may not have the means to take advantage of new opportunities because of limited cash flow. Carrying too little stock may mean losing sales. Managing stock is therefore extremely important.

Stock can mean many things:

- raw materials, components and packaging
- work in progress
- finished items
- pipeline stocks (currently in transit, etc.)
- spare parts
- general stores.

Typically, in manufacturing, we are concerned mainly with materials coming in, work in progress and finished items. Issues for consideration include costs associated with purchase price, storage, handling, warehousing, service, pilferage, deterioration, damage and obsolescence. Holding costs and reorder costs are of particular interest. There are charges associated with ordering. Ordering just once per year instead of many times would keep those charges down. This would, however, mean holding materials for a whole year, with all the associated costs. Ordering frequently would reduce holding costs, but would increase reorder costs. Figure 19.2 shows how quantity varies over time with ordering.

Holding costs are associated with depreciation, labour, overheads, rent, storage, money tied up, obsolescence, deterioration, theft and insurance. Ordering costs are associated with ordering, receiving, clerical work, labour, inspection, returns, transport and handling. The *economic order quantity* (EOQ) is a simple model that balances holding and reorder costs. It results in high-value items being ordered often and low-value items being ordered infrequently. Figure 19.3 shows how costs are balanced using the EOQ.

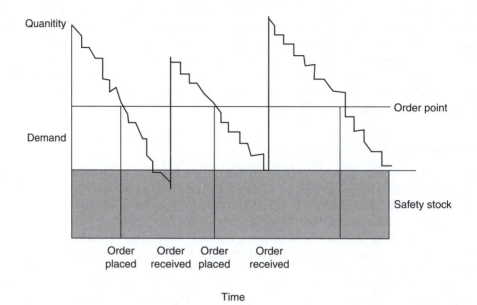

Figure 19.2 Demand and reorder.

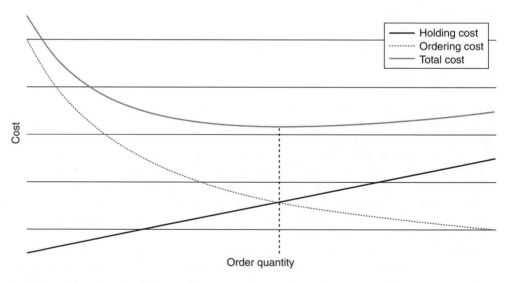

Figure 19.3 Economic order quantity.

$$EOQ = \sqrt{\frac{2rs}{ci}}$$

Where:
r = annual usage
s = cost per order
c = unit cost
i = holding cost per unit (percentage)

Example:

r = 10,000
s = £2
c = £4
i = 1 per cent

Using the formula, the EOQ is 1,000. Since annual demand is 10,000, stock should be ordered ten times per year.

Just-in-time (JIT) is a management philosophy that strives to eliminate sources of manufacturing waste by producing the right part in the right place at the right time. Waste can be classed as any activity that adds cost without adding value, such as moving and storing. It attempts to minimize holding space and reduce storage costs, and concomitantly enable quicker response time to customer orders. Items must be perfect, however, because there is no significant amount of inventory to cover mistakes and international shipments are often out of the company's control. JIT has been adopted by many organizations because it reduces costs, especially in the manufacturing industry.

JIT is a disciplined and systematic approach to improving overall productivity and eliminating waste. It provides for cost-effective production and delivery of only the necessary quantity of parts of the right quality, at the right time and place, while using a minimum amount of facilities, equipment, materials and human resources. It is dependent on a balance between supplier flexibility and user flexibility. It is accomplished through total employee involvement and teamwork. A key element of JIT is simplification.

JIT has three major philosophical underpinnings: the elimination of waste; the involvement of employees; and continual improvement. To be successful it has a number of requirements. Quality: avoid disruption, maintain throughput, maintain dependability of supply, avoid inventory build-up. Speed: fast throughput to meet customer demand from production, not inventory. Dependability: a prerequisite for fast throughput, needing reliable equipment and supply. Flexibility: achieve small batch sizes for fast throughput and short delivery times.

JIT may be considered as a 'pull' system, because it is pulled by customer demand. Materials requirement planning (MRP) is considered as a 'push' system. Activities are scheduled centrally and each work centre pushes out work, whether the next is ready or not. Work centres are coordinated by central operations but actual outcomes may differ from plans, possibly resulting in idle time, inventory build-up and queues. MRP requires demand forecasts, is linked to current inventory levels and uses aggregate planning to schedule production. An MRP system is intended to ensure materials and products are available for production and delivery to customers, to maintain the lowest possible level of inventory and to plan manufacturing activities, delivery schedules and purchasing.

In practice, there can be problems with any system. JIT suffers as a result of uneven demand and supply. A part solution is to take levelled scheduling further to cope with uneven cycle times. This means mixing JIT (pull) with MRP (push). Using demand forecasting and economic order quantities assists with managing production. Large organizations may incorporate operations management as a whole within their ERP system.

19.2 Conclusions

The previous section discusses just some of the areas not covered in this text. There are many more. The book provides you with the opportunity to learn the fundamentals in the area, and provides a sound basis on which you can build.

If you have read this book all the way through, and have understood the material, you should have a thorough grounding in the main subjects of the domain. The case studies provide practical contexts and should assist you in appreciating that the concepts in the chapters are relevant to practice. If you have engaged fully in the exercises you should have even greater understanding.

Remember that it is *your* programme of study and only you can do it. Participate, practice, prepare and reflect. If you move from study to the workplace, you will benefit substantially from the knowledge and skills you have gained in your study. If you move to higher-level programmes, such as a PhD or a DBA, the concepts in this book will be essential.

Keep in mind the following quotations.

> 'Diligence is the mother of good luck.'
> (Benjamin Franklin)

> 'The harder I work, the luckier I get.'
> (Samuel Goldwyn)

> 'The more I practice, the luckier I get.'
> (Variously attributed to Arnold Palmer,
> Gary Player and others)

Make your own luck. Enjoy your studies and your career.

References

Boehm, B. (1988) *A Spiral Model of Software Development Enhancement*. Los Alamitos, CA: IEEE Computer Society Press.

Checkland, P. (1981) *Systems Thinking, Systems Practice*. Chichester: Wiley.

Nielsen, J. (2001) *Did Poor Usability Kill E-Commerce?* Available online at www.useit.com/alertbox/20010819.html (accessed 7 April 2010).

Snyder, C. (2001) *Seven Tricks that Web Users Don't Know*. Available online at www-106.ibm.com/developerworks/usability/library/us-tricks/ (accessed 8 August 2010).

Further reading

Clarke, S.A. (2007) *Information Systems Strategic Management: An Integrated Approach*. London: Routledge.

Index

Page numbers in *italics* denote tables, those in **bold** denote figures.